Tonga

**Nancy Keller
Deanna Swaney**

✳✳✳✳✳✳✳✳✳✳✳✳

D0109623

✳✳✳✳✳✳✳✳✳✳✳✳✳✳✳✳✳✳✳✳✳✳✳✳✳✳✳✳✳

Tonga

3rd edition

Published by
Lonely Planet Publications
Head Office: PO Box 617, Hawthorn, Vic 3122, Australia
Branches: 150 Linden Street, Oakland, CA 94607, USA
               10a Spring Place, London NW5 3BH, UK
               71 bis rue du Cardinal Lemoine, 75005 Paris, France

Printed by
Colorcraft Ltd, Hong Kong

Photographs by

Fikco	Nancy Keller	Deanna Swaney
Patrick Horton	Holger Leve	Darryl Torckler

Front cover: Aerial shot of Tonga (Darryl Torckler)

First Published
March 1990

This Edition
September 1998

National Library of Australia Cataloguing in Publication Data

Keller, Nancy
    Tonga

    3rd ed.
    Includes index.
    ISBN 0 86442 568 6

    1.Tonga – Description and Travel. 2. Tonga – Guidebooks.
    I. Title.

919.30437

text & maps © Lonely Planet 1998
photos © photographers as indicated

Nancy Keller

Born and raised in northern California, Nancy worked in the alternative press for several years, doing every aspect of newspaper work from editorial and reporting to delivering the papers. She returned to university to earn a master's degree in journalism, graduating in 1986. She's been travelling and writing ever since. Nancy is author or co-author of several LP books including *Rarotonga & the Cook Islands, New Zealand, California & Nevada, Mexico, Guatemala, Belize & Yucatán – La Ruta Maya* and *Central America on a shoestring.*

Deanna Swaney

An incurable travel addict, Deanna Swaney escaped yuppiedom in mid-town Anchorage and fled to South America to write Lonely Planet's *Bolivia   a travel survival kit.* Subsequent wanderings resulted in the first and second editions of this book, as well as *Samoa* and *Iceland, Greenland & the Faroe Islands.* She has also written guides to *Zimbabwe, Botswana & Namibia* and *Madagascar & Comoros.* Deanna co-authored the 2nd editions of LP's *Brazil* and *Mauritius, Réunion & Seychelles* and contributed to shoestring guides to Africa, South America and Scandinavia.

From Nancy

On Tongatapu, thanks to Sione Finau Moala and Hon Luani of the Tonga Visitors' Bureau, with special thanks to Dr Michael G Horowitz ('Maikolo'), US Peace Corps volunteer working with TVB. Thanks to Jim Bradfield and James Fa'asolo of Royal Tongan Airlines; Larry Simon of Pacific Island Scaplanes; Viliami Mafi of the US Peace Corps in Nuku'alofa for help with the language section; Steve Burling of the Ha'atafu Beach Resort, Tongatapu, for the surfing section; and to Netatua Prescott, Senior Ecologist and Environmentalist, Ministry of Lands, Survey and Natural Resources.

Thanks to Waltraud and Sven Quick and Kalolina Fakaosi of the Heilala Holiday Lodge in Nuku'alofa for their hospitality, helpfulness and a clean, quiet 'home base'; to Tony Matthias of Toni's Guest House for pleasant trips around Tongatapu and good conversation; to David May of the Friendly Islands Bookshop for general helpfulness; and to 'I Futa Helu of 'Atenisi Institute for interesting observations about modern Tongan history.

Thanks to several US Peace Corps volunteers working in Tonga who generously shared their enthusiasm. Thanks to Mark & Kelly Lewis on Niuatoputapu, Amanda Rabinowitz on Niuafo'ou, Ann Routon on Ha'apai, and Melissa Forsberg on 'Eua. Thanks also to Mary Gutmann, director of the US Peace Corps in Tonga.

On 'Eua, thanks to Kalolina Fakaosi for

taking me over for a happy stay with her auntie and family; to Robin and Sia Shrubsole, their nieces 'Ofa and Soana, daughter Lowvain and son Michael, and to Grandma, for a happy stay on 'Eua and explorations around the island; to Melissa Forsberg for taking us to the Heke and Showers Cave, for talent with hand-drawn maps and for general good times; and to Peau Haukinima, director of the Ministry of Agriculture, for an enjoyable trip to southern 'Eua and for taking us to the ferry at 4.30 am.

On Ha'apai, thanks to Roland Schwara and 'Ofa Mahe Beazley of Watersports Ha'apai. Thanks to Virginia for her museum and research library; to Sela Falevai and family for providing a happy home base on Lifuka; and to Mick Hortle, Australian volunteer marine biologist in Pangai, for notes about a scientific expedition made to Tofua and Kao volcanoes. Special thanks to Mele of the Tonga Visitors' Bureau for help with transport, and to Hola Telefoni Vi for good conversation.

On Vava'u, greatest thanks to Bruno Toke of the Tonga Visitors' Bureau, who went above and beyond the call of duty to be helpful, and to his staff who took me around. Thanks to Franco Sabatini of the Hilltop Guest House; Carter Johnson of the Paradise International Hotel; Andy and Felipe of the *Melinda*; Rich Zubaty for interesting conversation; the Sunset Restaurant for the best cup of coffee I'd had in seven months of travelling; and to Vava'u itself, and the friendly people I met there.

Finally, thanks to Deanna, who suggested I come here to update her book. You were right, Deanna – I do love Tonga.

Dedication
Nancy dedicates this book to Evangelist Fredia M Holloway, church mother of the Greater Power House Church of God in Christ – a spiritual mother, a beautiful lady.

This Book
The first two editions of this book were researched and written by Deanna Swaney. This 3rd edition was updated by Nancy Keller.

From the Publisher
This book was edited by Liz Filleul and Wendy Owen and proofed by Liz, Wendy and Darren Elder. Jacqui Saunders was responsible for the maps, colourwraps and design, and she and Liz took the book through layout. Thanks to Margaret Jung for the cover, Quentin Frayne for laying out the language chapter, Andrew Tudor for help with Quark, and Katie Cody for assistance with layout.

Warning & Request
Things change – prices go up, schedules change, good places go bad and bad places go bankrupt – nothing stays the same. So, if you find things better or worse, recently opened or long since closed, please tell us and help make the next edition even more accurate and useful.

We value all of the feedback we receive from travellers. Julie Young coordinates a small team who read and acknowledge every letter, postcard and email, and ensure that every morsel of information finds its way to the appropriate authors, editors and publishers.

Everyone who writes to us will find their name in the next edition of the appropriate guide and will also receive a free subscription to our quarterly newsletter, *Planet Talk*. The very best contributions will be rewarded with a free Lonely Planet guide.

Excerpts from your correspondence may appear in new editions of this guide; in our newsletter, *Planet Talk*; or in updates on our Web site – so please let us know if you don't want your letter published or your name acknowledged.

Thanks
Many thanks to the following travellers who used the last edition and wrote to us with helpful hints, useful advice and interesting anecdotes:

John Bannister, Artur Correia, Doug Fischer, Tim Gourlay, Jill Hannah, Robin Hudson, Miynki Ishii, Paul Lufkin, Donna MacIntosh, Alfred MacRae, Linda Nagy, Jane Perkins, Tom Riddle, Connie Schmollinger, Dr James Terry, Kees Verloop, Peggy Weymouth, Helen Willis.

Contents

Boxed Asides

Cannibalism	13	Ferry Travel in Tonga	81
Mutiny on the HMS *Bounty*	15	Tu'i Malila	86
The King Sets a Good Example	17	How to Spend Sunday in Nuku'alofa	95
Sex & Coral	21	The Origin of Kava	120
What's in a Name?	22	Why is it Cooler on 'Eua?	121
Pandanus Weaving	27	The Flora & Fauna of 'Eua	123
Celebrating the Millennium	32	Blackbirders on 'Ata	130
Money in Tonga	37	Cook's 'Friendly Islands' – Perhaps a	
Medical Kit Check List	45	Misnomer?	134
Fakaleiti	55	William Mariner	136
Sunday in Tonga	56	The *Margarita*	146
'Singing Whales'	60	Climbing Tofua & Kao	148
Tuck into a Tongan Feast	64	Captain Cook's Fateful Turn	
Making & Using an 'Umu	64	Southward	153
DIY Tonga Feasts	64	Mariner's Cave	175
Traditional Tongan Recipes	65	Swiftlets in Swallows' Cave	176
Kava	67	'The Fo'ui Did It'	177
Air Travel Glossary	70	The Niuafo'ou Megapode	187
Yachting Regulations	78	Landing at Niuafo'ou	188

Map Index

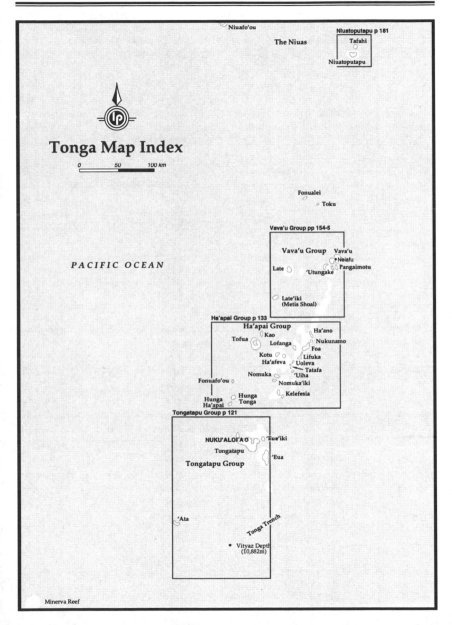

Niuafo'ou

The Niuas

Niuatoputapu p 181
Tafahi
Niuatoputapu

Tonga Map Index

0   50   100 km

Fonualei
Toku

Vava'u Group pp 154-5

Vava'u Group   Vava'u
Neiafu
Late   Pangaimotu
'Utungake

PACIFIC OCEAN

Late'iki
(Metis Shoal)

Ha'apai Group p 133

Ha'apai Group   Ha'ano
Kao   Nukunamo
Tofua   Lofanga   Foa
Kotu   Lifuka
Ha'afeva   Uoleva
Nomuka   Tatafa
'Uiha
Nomuka'iki
Fonuafo'ou   Kelefesia

Hunga   Hunga
Ha'apai   Tonga

Tongatapu Group p 121

NUKU'ALOFA   'Eue'iki
Tongatapu   'Eua
Tongatapu Group

'Ata

Tonga Trench

Vityaz Depth
(10,882m)

Minerva Reef

Map Legend

BOUNDARIES

.... International Boundary

.... Provincial Boundary

.... Disputed Boundary

ROUTES

A25 ..... Freeway, with Route Number

.... Major Road

.... Minor Road

.... Minor Road - Unsealed

.... City Road

.... City Street

.... City Lane

.... Train Route, with Station

.... Ferry Route

.... Walking Track

AREA FEATURES

.... Building

.... Cemetery

.... Market

❁ .... Park, Gardens

.... Pedestrian Mall

.... Reef

.... Urban Area

HYDROGRAPHIC FEATURES

.... Coastline

.... Creek, River

.... Lake, Intermittent Lake

.... Rapids, Waterfalls

.... Swamp

SYMBOLS

⊙ **CAPITAL** .... National Capital

◉ **CAPITAL** .... Provincial Capital

● **CITY** .... City

● **Town** .... Town

● Village .... Village

■ .... Place to Stay

⚑ .... Camping Ground

🚐 .... Caravan Park

⌂ .... Hut or Chalet

▼ .... Place to Eat

🍺 .... Pub or Bar

✈ .... Airport

... Ancient or City Wall

∴ .... Archaeological Site

🏖 .... Beach

♜ .... Castle or Fort

⌒ .... Cave

🏠 .... Church

.... Cliff or Escarpment

◥ .... Dive Site

◔ .... Embassy

⊕ .... Hospital

※ .... Lookout

▲ .... Mountain or Hill

← .... One Way Street

🅿 .... Parking

)(......................... Pass

🅟 .... Petrol Station

★ .... Police Station

✉ .... Post Office

❖ ...... Shopping Centre

🔲 .... Snorkelling

🏊 ....Swimming Pool

☎ .... Telephone

❶ .....Tourist Information

◕ .... Transport

Note: not all symbols displayed above appear in this book

Introduction

Spread across 362,000 sq km of the South Pacific Ocean, the Kingdom of Tonga consists of 171 remarkably diverse islands which, all told, occupy only 688 sq km of dry land. Despite the country's far-flung nature, the Tongan people, who inhabit only a few of their islands – less than 40 – are a homogeneous group and speak a uniform language with only minor local variations. In addition, nearly all Tongans speak some English as a second language and visitors will not need a working knowledge of Tongan in order to communicate with the islanders.

The country consists of four main island groups: Tongatapu, Ha'apai, Vava'u and the Niuas. Anyone who wants relative luxury and organised activities with a South Seas flavour will especially enjoy the main islands of Tongatapu and Vava'u. Divers and snorkellers will find the coral gardens of Vava'u and the countless reefs of Ha'apai irresistible. Bushwalkers will be surprised to find rugged and pristine wilderness on the islands of 'Eua and the Niuas and everyone will be completely enchanted by the clean turquoise water, the endless, deserted, white-sand beaches, the delicious and bountiful traditional food, the haunting dances and legends of the islands and the friendly and carefree attitude of their inhabitants.

Tonga is the only South Pacific country which was never colonised by a European power. One of the consequences of this is that it has pretty much been left alone by tourists, a fact which the Tonga Visitors'

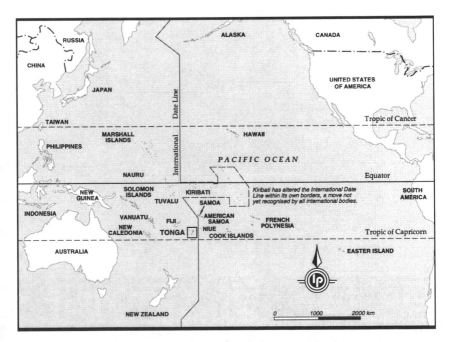

Bureau is desperately trying to change. Without super-luxury resort complexes or extensive advertising abroad, Tonga will be a long time waiting for the high-powered tourism it's courting – the kind that has drastically altered more traditional destinations such as Tahiti, Fiji and Hawaii. The bonus, of course, is that visitors arriving with a travel-poster dream of old Polynesia will certainly not be disappointed with Tonga.

In his journal, Captain James Cook, who visited Tonga three times in his voyages, wrote: 'This group I have named the Friendly Archipelago as a lasting friendship seems to subsist among the inhabitants and their courtesy to strangers entitles them to that name'. Those foreigners who do somehow 'wash up' on these islands will still find themselves on the receiving end of some of the most sincere and unconditional hospitality to be found on earth.

Since Cook's day, few visitors to the Friendly Islands have failed to respond to their relaxed atmosphere. Some call the syndrome 'Polynesian Paralysis', perhaps the one malady that should be welcomed in a world racked with stress. The best part is that it's contagious. Although there's plenty to see and do in Tonga, there's also plenty not to see and do. You'll find yourself an ocean away from deadlines, hassles, hurries and headaches. Add to all that one of the most pleasant climates around and you've got the elements of the gentle paradise that is Tonga.

Facts about the Country

HISTORY
Prehistory

One legend tells us that the Tonga Islands were fished out of the sea by the mighty Polynesian god Tangaloa, whose tortoise-shell and whalebone fish-hook had become entangled around an opening in the island of Nuapapu in the Vava'u Group. The islands emerged originally as a single land mass but, unfortunately, the fishing line broke at a most inopportune moment and bits of land sank back into the sea, leaving only those islands which break the surface today.

Another story has the demigod Maui, a temperamental hero well known throughout the Pacific islands, doing the fishing. Using a hook borrowed from an old man named Tonga, he yanked up the islands one by one and graciously named the largest one after the man who had made the successful hook.

Archaeologists and anthropologists have placed the date of the initial colonisation of the Tongan group at about 3000 BC, but the earliest date actually confirmed by radio-carbon dating is around 1100 BC.

The Tongan people are Polynesians. The area called Polynesia ('many islands') consists of a triangle with its corners at Hawaii, Easter Island (off the west coast of South America) and New Zealand, with outliers scattered through Fiji and the East Indies. It is presumed that the Polynesian peoples entered the Pacific from the west – the East Indies or the Philippine islands. Due to the fact that Lapita pottery similar to that found in the Bismarck Archipelago and New Caledonia has also been found in Tonga and Samoa, and that the use of pottery was not in evidence at the time of European contact in the 17th century, it seems likely that these were the first Polynesian areas settled. The discontinuation of the use of pottery is attributed to the lack of suitable clay in the islands and the availability of alternative materials like coconut shells and sea shells.

It is believed that the Lapita people, who arrived in Tonga between 3300 and 3500 years ago, had their first capital in Tonga at Toloa, near present-day Fua'amotu Airport on Tongatapu. The only evidence for this theory is the presence of several mounds which are believed to have supported significant buildings. Some time later, the capital was shifted to Heketa near the north-eastern tip of Tongatapu. It was here that King Tu'itatui constructed the famous Ha'amonga 'a Maui trilithon.

Due to their rugged coastlines, however, neither Toloa nor Heketa was really suitable as the capital of a maritime empire, as neither offered an adequate shelter or landing site for canoes. It is believed that the shifting of the capital to Mu'a by Tu'itatui's son, Talatama, was a pragmatic move designed to make the centre of government more accessible from the sea, especially when larger double-hulled canoes came into use. Similarly, it required better protection, hence the evidence that Mu'a was indeed a well-fortified settlement.

The theory put forth by an unconventional Norwegian scientist, Thor Heyerdahl, to the effect that the Polynesians migrated not from Asia but from the Americas, is based primarily on the presence of the *kumala* or *kumara*, the sweet potato, in the Pacific and South America but not in Asia. Interestingly enough, the Mormons, ubiquitous throughout the Pacific, also tell a tale of colonisation of the islands by South American mainlanders. The greater part of the scientific community, however, has never adopted this theory.

Early Royalty

Ironically, the legend explaining the origins of Tongan royalty is similar to that of the Incas; both groups profess that their first sovereign came to earth as the direct offspring of a solar deity. According to the Tongans, the first Tu'i Tonga (royal title

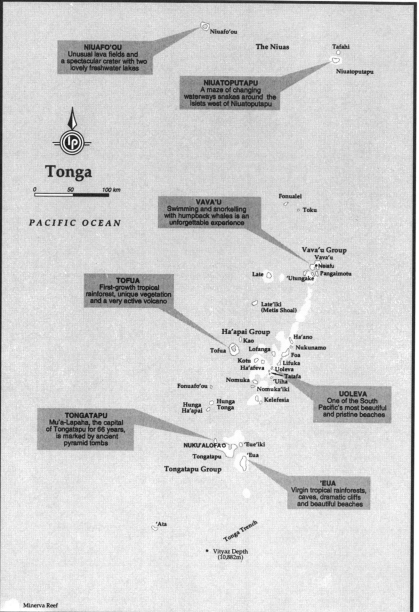

NIUAFO'OU
Unusual lava fields and a spectacular crater with two lovely freshwater lakes

The Niuas

NIUATOPUTAPU
A maze of changing waterways snakes around the islets west of Niuatoputapu

Niuafo'ou

Tafahi

Niuatoputapu

Tonga

0   50   100 km

PACIFIC OCEAN

VAVA'U
Swimming and snorkelling with humpback whales is an unforgettable experience

Fonualei

Toku

Vava'u Group
Vava'u
Neiafu
Pangaimotu
'Utungake

Late

Late'iki
(Metis Shoal)

TOFUA
First-growth tropical rainforest, unique vegetation and a very active volcano

Ha'apai Group
Kao
Lofanga
Tofua
Kotu
Ha'afeva
Nomuka
Nomuka'iki
Kelefesia

Ha'ano
Nukunamo
Foa
Lifuka
Uoleva
Tatafa
'Uiha

UOLEVA
One of the South Pacific's most beautiful and pristine beaches

Fonuafo'ou

Hunga
Ha'apai
Hunga
Tonga

TONGATAPU
Mu'a-Lapaha, the capital of Tongatapu for 66 years, is marked by ancient pyramid tombs

NUKU'ALOFA
Tongatapu

Tongatapu Group

'Eue'iki
'Eua

'EUA
Virgin tropical rainforests, caves, dramatic cliffs and beautiful beaches

'Ata

Tonga Trench

Vityaz Depth
(10,882m)

Minerva Reef

given to a Tongan ruler) was the product of a union between the sun god Tangaloa and a beautiful young earthling named 'Ilaheva. The girl was caught shellfishing one day by the amorous god on a small island near Tongatapu. Nine months later, she bore 'Aho'eitu, who was to become the first in a long line of Tu'is. Thanks to the wealth of oral history at the time of European contact, the date for this event has been placed at 950 AD.

The title of Tu'i Tonga commanded a great deal of respect from commoners. Distinctive ceremonies evolved which concerned the Tu'i Tonga's marriage, burial and mourning. He was addressed in a manner previously reserved for the gods and was not permitted to be either tattooed or circumcised. His responsibilities encompassed both governmental and religious matters and he was expected to preside over the festival of *'inasi*, an agricultural fair in which the biggest and best produce was presented to the gods in order to appease their wrath.

Over the following 400 years or so, the Tongans subscribed to the Fijian attitude that war and strife were activities pursued by noble and worthy men and that peace-loving fellows could only be considered cowardly and effeminate.

Accordingly, Tongan warriors in huge canoes called *kalia* wreaked all sorts of mischief in Fiji and throughout western Polynesia. In this manner they were able to extend the Tu'i Tonga's empire, so that it included territory from parts of Fiji and stretched eastward to Niue and northward as far as the Samoas and Tokelau.

The title of Tu'i Tonga was hereditary and was passed from father to son, or to the title-bearer's brother if there was no direct heir to accept it. The 24th Tu'i Tonga, however, created a new position which would take over the temporal responsibilities of his office. It carried the title Tu'i Ha'atakalaua and its first bearer was the Tu'i Tonga's brother.

Some time during the mid-17th century, yet another title emerged and the power as-

Cannibalism

Cannibalism was practised in Tonga until the missionaries came and explained that in polite society one doesn't roast and eat one's fellow humans, even if they are considered enemies. A few missionaries ended up in the 'umu while trying to get their point across but it has been well over 100 years since the last guest of honour became the main course. Cannibalism was associated with absorbing the power and cleverness of one's adversaries, and was not a necessary answer to a lack of protein!

sociated with it quickly surpassed the other two. At the time of European contact, the newly installed Tu'i Kanokupolu was the most powerful figure in Tonga.

European Contact

The first known contact between Europeans and Tongans occurred in 1616 when a couple of bumbling Dutchmen, an entrepreneur named Jacob Lemaire and his navigator, Willem Cornelius Schouten, visited the Niuas en route to the East Indies in their ships *Eendracht* and *Hoorn*. Although they never landed, they had a brief encounter with a Tongan sailing canoe, resulting in at least one Tongan being killed and several taken captive. However, the Europeans managed to trade a few trinkets for foodstuffs and, like all good explorers, saw fit to rename their 'discoveries': the islands of Niuatoputapu, Tafahi and Niuafo'ou became the Dutch equivalents of Traitor's Island, Coconut Island and Good Hope Island, respectively.

The next visitor happened to be another Dutchman, Abel Janszoon Tasman, who passed through the southernmost Tongan islands in 1643 with his ships *Heemskerck* and *Zeehan*. Tasman traded with the people of 'Ata, 'Eua and Tongatapu (which he named Pylstaart, Middleburgh and Amsterdam), and he took on board water from the freshwater springs on the island of Nomuka (this one he named Rotterdam!) in the Ha'apai Group.

Over a century later in 1767, the Englishman, Captain Samuel Wallis, who was credited with the discovery of Otaheite (Tahiti), arrived in his ship *Dolphin* in search of the fabled southern continent, Ptolemy's *terra australis incognita*. He spent several days trading in the Niuas and renamed Niuatoputapu and Tafahi (Traitors and Coconut) as Keppel and Boscawen, respectively.

Just seven years later the second Englishman to set foot on the Tongan islands landed at 'Eua. This was Captain James Cook (on his second Pacific expedition), the most peripatetic of all European explorers of the day; the man who said of himself, '...ambition leads me not only farther than any other man has been before me, but as far as I think it possible for man to go'. He had instructions from King George III to 'observe the genius, temper, disposition and number of the natives or inhabitants, if there be any, and endeavour by all proper means to cultivate a friendship and alliance with them ...'

During the course of his trip he stopped twice, both times briefly, in Tonga. In October 1773, he spent two days visiting 'Eua and five days on Tongatapu. Upon his arrival in the former, Tongans swarmed over his ship. Smiling, friendly and ready to trade (they undoubtedly had heard legends about Tasman's visit), they offered Cook and his men *tapa* (mulberry bark cloth) and women in exchange for iron. Cook's men performed musical numbers on the bagpipes, the Tongan women sang and danced for the visitors and food and *kava* (a drink made from the root of the pepper shrub) were served. The kava was prepared by chewing the root, spitting the pulp into a bowl and adding water. Among the Europeans, only Cook himself had the nerve to partake of it.

During his visit, Cook was particularly impressed with the friendly and verdant island of Tongatapu, which he compared to the most beautiful and fertile plains of Europe.

Eight months later, on his return voyage, he spent four days trading and taking on water at Nomuka. On his third voyage, however, he spent over two months (April to July 1777) in the Tongan islands. At Nomuka, his first landfall, chief Finau of Ha'apai told him of a wealthier island, Lifuka, where supplies would be available. Cook and his men had such a good time being feted on Lifuka that Cook bestowed the name 'Friendly Islands' on the Ha'apai Group (a monicker still treasured by Tonga), without ever knowing that the friendliness extended to him was part of a plot to kill him and his men, which went awry. See the Ha'apai chapter for more information on this fateful event.

Although Cook had been aware of the existence of the Vava'u Group, he'd never actually visited it and its European 'discovery' was left to the Spaniard Don Francisco Antonio Mourelle of the ship *Princesa*, who ran across it en route to Spanish America in 1781. Low on supplies and fair winds, Mourelle was overjoyed to see the island of Fonualei on the horizon, but as he approached he realised it was barren and uninhabited. Accordingly, he named it Amargura, or 'bitterness'. An unfavourable wind prevented his landing at the more promising island of Late. When he finally landed at Vava'u, he named its harbour Puerto de Refugio ('port of refuge'), and claimed the entire group for Spain. (The harbour still bears this name today.) After quickly taking on supplies, Mourelle set off southward in search of a fair wind to Mexico.

In 1787, en route from Siberia to the English colonies in Australia, the French explorer Jean de la Pérouse spent a short time passing through Tonga while recovering from the infamous attack his expedition had suffered on Tutuila, in Samoa. La Pérouse visited New South Wales, but after leaving the colony he was never seen again.

Mutiny on the HMS *Bounty*

In April 1789, Tonga experienced a historical event, the tale of which would be told and retold around the world for centuries to come. Off the volcanic island of Tofua in the Ha'apai Group, Captain William Bligh and 18 crewmen of the HMS *Bounty* were involuntarily relieved of their duties and set adrift in an open boat with a minimum of supplies.

They landed at Tofua briefly, hoping to secure some provisions, but local unrest forced them to cast off after loading only the most meagre of rations. Quartermaster John Norton was attacked and killed by islanders and the other English sailors only narrowly escaped. They reached Timor in the Dutch East Indies on 14 June, having survived the longest ever voyage in an open boat.

(Both his ships were subsequently discovered wrecked off Vanikolo island in the Solomons.) Antoine d'Entrecasteaux, who set out in search of La Pérouse, arrived in Tongatapu in 1793. His ship's botanist wrote an account of the visit, but little else came from the French connection in Tonga.

Meanwhile, Mourelle's raving accounts of the Vava'u Group and his claim to the islands created some excitement back in Spain. In 1793, Captain Alessandro Malaspina was sent chasing all over the Pacific – to Peru, Alaska, the Philippines, New Zealand and Vava'u – to make observations and surveys as well as investigate the feasibility of occupying Vava'u. He placed a decree of Spanish ownership in a bottle and buried it somewhere on the main island. It was never to be found again but that wasn't much of an issue – with numerous concerns in the Americas, Spain lost interest in the project.

The first permanent European settlers in Tonga were six deserters from the American ship *Otter*, who landed at 'Eua and Ha'apai

in 1796. The following year, 10 lay missionaries of the London Missionary Society arrived at Tongatapu on the ship *Duff*. Three were murdered in a local scuffle, six escaped to Australia and one, George Vason, renounced Christianity. He married a Tongan woman and remained among the islanders until 1804. During this time, the chief of Ha'apai, Finau 'Ulukalala, forcefully gained control of all the major island groups and the three royal titles began to fall into disuse.

William Mariner

On 29 November 1806, the *Port-au-Prince* privateer landed on Lifuka, in the Ha'apai group. The locals ransacked the ship and most of the crew were killed, but William Charles Mariner, a boy working on the ship, was spared and taken under the wing of chief Finau. Mariner ended up telling the story of his four-year adventure in Tonga in *An Account of the Natives of the Tonga Islands*, a masterpiece of Pacific literature. See the Ha'apai Group chapter for more information on Mariner.

Christian Influences

After the London Missionary Society fled Tonga in 1799, the kingdom was more or less free of salvationists, until 1822 brought a Wesleyan minister, Revd Walter Lawry, to Tongatapu. Resistance to his ideas sent him back to Australia after only a year. After he left, a Tongan chief became interested in Christianity and when the Wesleyans returned to the islands several years later, they enjoyed much more success. By the time the French Catholic missionaries arrived the Wesleyans had already succeeded in converting the nephew of the Tu'i Kanokupolu and the course of Tongan history was suddenly careening in a new direction.

This particular young man, Taufa'ahau, had become the ruler of his native Ha'apai in 1826, having forcefully attained the title of Tu'i Tonga from its heir apparent, Laufilitonga. Upon his baptism in 1831, he took the Christian name Siaosi, or George, after the king of England, and adopted the surname Tupou. His wife, who had previously been the wife of poor Laufilitonga, was baptised Salote, after Queen Charlotte.

Under George's influence, all of Ha'apai converted to Christianity and, shortly thereafter, thanks to the conversion of George's cousin, King 'Ulukalala III of Vava'u, that group followed suit. Upon the death of 'Ulukalala, George assumed his cousin's title as well.

In Tongatapu the Wesleyans were already having considerable success, including the conversion of George's great-uncle, the Tu'i Kanokupolu. Upon the death of that influential man in 1845, George Tupou assumed his title, thus becoming the most powerful man in a united Tonga under the name King George Tupou I.

The House of Tupou

After uniting Tonga and ascending to its throne, King George found that his troubles were only beginning. On one side, he had the Wesleyan missionaries battling the encroachment of the Catholics who had succeeded in converting several influential chiefs. On the other, he had the traditional chiefs and nobles who were accustomed to wielding the power of life and death over their subservient subjects.

As early as 1838, quite a while before his power over all Tonga became a foregone conclusion, King George saw the need for a uniform set of laws to govern the country. His first effort was the Vava'u Code, which forbade worship of the old gods and also prevented those in power from forcefully acquiring the means of the commoners. In 1853, the king made a visit to Australia and, upon learning that not all foreigners were as ignorant as the Wesleyan missionaries, he decided to seek help there in drafting a revision of the code.

The rift between the king and the Wesleyans grew until Reverend Shirley Baker appeared on the scene as a member of the Tongan Mission. George immediately took a liking to Baker and together they began working on government revisions. The main result was the perpetual prohibition of

serfdom in the kingdom. In addition, it was stipulated that no land in the kingdom could be sold to a foreigner (and this, many years before the king could have imagined what was to happen to his fellow Polynesian kingdom of Hawaii!). Lastly, the revised code mandated the distribution of land to male subjects over 16 years of age. Every man was to receive a village lot and an *'api* (plantation of 3.34 hectares) for an annual fee of T$3.20.

The missionaries, jealous of Baker's preferential treatment, launched an unsuccessful effort to have him expelled from the church and Tonga on charges of adultery. Undaunted, Baker continued on his course of statesmanship. Together, he and the king came up with a national flag, a state seal and a national anthem, then embarked on the drafting of a constitution. It included a bill of rights, a format for legislative and judicial procedures and a section on land tenure. It also contained laws of succession to the throne. The new constitution was passed on 4 November 1875.

In 1879 the church disassociated Shirley Baker from its mission. The king responded by cancelling Wesleyan leases and appointing Shirley Baker prime minister of Tonga, much to the dismay of nearly everyone else. In 1885, Baker created the Free Church of Tonga and the king urged all his subjects to abandon the Wesleyans and join the new church. A small-scale 'holy war' ensued. An attempted assassination of the prime minister resulted in the execution of six Wesleyans and exile for four others. Most of the remaining Wesleyans in Tonga emigrated to Fiji.

The strife caught the attention of Britain, which saw Tonga's moment of weakness as an opportunity to gain influence in the country. Assuming that the 89-year-old king had gone a bit senile and that Baker had turned the situation to his own advantage, the British sent an investigatory committee to Tonga to ascertain the stability of the political situation. While they learned that the king's mental health was sound, they forcefully convinced him that religious freedom was necessary in Tonga and eventually had Baker deported.

In 1893, upon King George's death at the age of 96, his great-grandson assumed the throne and took the name George Tupou II. He was by no means a statesman and lacked the flair and character of his great-grandfather and predecessor. The British, fearing loss of control under such an administration, coerced him into signing a treaty which placed Tonga under British protection in the field of foreign affairs. King George Tupou II died at the age of 45 in 1918, and his 18-year-old daughter Salote became queen.

Queen Salote's primary concerns for her country were not squabbling churches and greedy chiefs but medicine and education. With intelligence, compassion and a naturally regal stature and attitude, she made friends for Tonga throughout the world and was greatly loved by her subjects and by foreigners alike. The tale of her attendance at Queen Elizabeth II's coronation in 1953 has been told and retold. Tongan tradition does not allow imitation of those whom one holds in great respect, so while Elizabeth rode in a covered carriage through pouring rain to Westminster Abbey, the Tongan queen refused to allow her own carriage to be covered. When she died in 1965, she was mourned by the world and Tonga regarded itself as a child that had lost its mother.

King Taufa'ahau Tupou IV

Queen Salote's son, King Taufa'ahau Tupou IV, is the current ruler of Tonga. Although he is known worldwide primarily for his ample girth – and now for having lost a great deal of weight through a diet that created great interest in Tonga (see the boxed text) – he has brought about a number of notable accomplishments, including the re-establishment of full sovereignty for Tonga on 4 June 1970 and admission to the Commonwealth of Nations shortly thereafter. In 1976, realising that his nation was being largely ignored by the western powers, the king attracted their attention by establishing diplomatic relations

---

The King Sets a Good Example

King Taufa'ahau Tupou IV was once the world's heaviest monarch – in the 1976 *Guinness Book of Records*, he weighed in at 201kg (444lb). He was by no means the only person in Tonga to be on the hefty side – estimates have been made that as much as 60% of Tonga's population could be classified as clinically obese. Traditionally, the people in Tonga's royal and noble families are much larger than the commoners.

In recent years, however, the king decided to set a good example for his subjects. He went on a diet and fitness programme, lost around 75kg and still does regular exercise, working out with weights at the gym even at 80 years of age. He continues to urge his subjects to take care of their health, not only by telling them to do so but by being a good example himself.

---

with the Soviet Union. As a result, New Zealand, the USA and Australia immediately began taking notice of his awakening kingdom in the South Pacific.

King Taufa'ahau's reign has emphasised economic development for Tonga. (See Economy, later in this chapter.) It hasn't been an easy task to bring this small island nation into the modern world. It seems Tonga would like to plunge wholeheartedly into the modern economic world – with new cars, television, videos, international travel and other trappings of materialistic western society – while at the same time preserving the traditional customs and values which came from a different time and economic situation. It's a very fine tightrope to walk, and one wonders if such a thing is even possible.

The Pro-Democracy Movement

Tonga's new pumpkin-based prosperity (see Agriculture in the Economy section later in this chapter), combined with paradoxical economic discontent – as well as government corruption and increasing foreign influence – brought about a measure of dissatisfaction with the old traditional ways in the early 1990s.

In February 1990, a parliamentary election resulted in an unexpected victory for the dissident Tongan Pro-Democracy Movement (TPDM); two of the nine parliamentary seats reserved for commoners were filled by TPDM's 'Akilisi Pohiva and his ally, Laki Niu. Pohiva's platform included popular demands for the power of the aristocracy to be curbed, and a constitutional monarchy based on the British model rather than one in which government ministers must also be nobles and enjoy lifetime appointments. The king outwardly decried the movement, claiming in an interview on New Zealand TV that it was only the monarchy and the nobles who were keeping Tonga free from communism.

In the election of February 1992, 'Akilisi Pohiva was re-elected as were other TPDM leaders. In the end, the body of nine elected commoners in Parliament contained six members who espoused pro-democracy ideals. In late August, Pohiva set out a motion calling for all the country's legislators to be democratically elected, but this was defeated by the nobility's automatic majority.

In late November 1992, the TPDM, headed by Pohiva and Catholic Bishop Patelisio Finau, organised a four-day conference in the Basilica in Nuku'alofa to discuss the matter and perhaps reach some sort of consensus about the future of their ideas. The movement enjoyed the backing of the Wesleyan and Roman Catholic churches, two of Tonga's largest religious bodies. The government refused an invitation to attend and as far as it was concerned, the conference amounted to sedition with aims to overthrow the monarchy. It banned public broadcasts of news or information concerning the conference.

The privileged (and threatened) nobility responded with anger. The Prime Minister,

Baron Vaea, the king's cousin, reacted more calmly and suggested that some authorities might be persuaded to consider changes.

At the February 1993 election, six of the nine People's Representative seats in the Legislative Assembly were won by members of the TPDM. A month later, 2500 demonstrators, again led by Bishop Finau and opposition MPs, gathered in Nuku'alofa to protest at the government sale of Tongan passports and granting of citizenship to 426 foreigners, including Imelda Marcos and her children.

In 1995 the king, in response to the TPDM's continued urging for democracy, stated that although the monarchy would probably cede more power to representatives of the common people at some future point, the country's elected representatives did not have enough experience or integrity to govern the country.

Six of the nine People's Representative seats in the Legislative Assembly were retained by the TPDM at the next election, held in January 1996; Pohiva, leader of the movement, won 64% of the vote in his constituency.

Two months later, three journalists, including the editor of the *Taimi Tonga* (*Tonga Times*), were arrested and imprisoned for a newspaper article criticising Clive Edwards, the newly appointed Minister of Police, Fire Services and Prisons, for making unfavourable remarks about the TPDM. In April the three were convicted under a law which makes it a criminal offence to anger a civil servant, sparking protest by journalists' and civil rights groups around the world.

The Current Situation

The question of Tonga's form of government continues to be an issue. Most Tongans do not openly favour democracy or change in their political system. To do so would seem to be disrespectful of those in royal or noble positions. However, at the ballot box, when they repeatedly elect pro-democracy representatives.

TPDM asserts that the common people

would like to have a fair share of resources and to have more say in who governs them. The government, meanwhile, is pushing for economic development for Tonga, but development often means that the rich get richer while the poor stay the same.

Although most people don't talk about it much, there's a widespread feeling that in government, the royally-appointed cabinet ministers and the nobles' representatives, who together form an unbeatable majority in the Legislative Assembly, work together to promote the interests of their privileged class. The commoners' elected representatives, six out of nine of whom openly favour a more democratic system, are working to promote the interests of their class. In the Legislative Assembly they are always outnumbered.

There seems to be no hope for change. Meanwhile, the TPDM leaders continue to be harassed and imprisoned.

The TPDM hopes that pressure from the international community will break the stalemate. The TPDM is planning another large convention for mid-1998.

GEOGRAPHY

The Kingdom of Tonga is composed of four major island groups which are, from south to north: Tongatapu, Ha'apai, Vava'u and the Niuas. Altogether the four groups include some 171 individual islands and a total land area of 688 sq km.

The Tongatapu Group is the largest in both area and population. It includes the main island of Tongatapu as well as 'Eua, 'Ata, 'Eue'iki, Kalau and numerous small islands within the barrier reef north of the main island. Minerva Reef, 350km southwest of Tongatapu, is Tonga's southernmost extreme (although its ownership is currently disputed with New Zealand).

The Ha'apai Group, 100km north of Tongatapu, is a cluster of 36 major islands and numerous submerged reefs. The main inhabited islands include Lifuka, Ha'ano, Foa, 'Uiha, Ha'afeva and Nomuka. Tonga's highest point is the summit of Kao, whose perfect volcanic cone rises sharply to 1109m above sea level. Kao's sister island, Tofua, is an active, spewing volcano. The 'up and down' island of Fonuafo'ou, which builds up and erodes away with some frequency, occupies the westernmost extreme of the Ha'apai Group.

Another 100km to the north are the 34 major islands of the Vava'u Group, the largest of which is Vava'u. The smaller islands are merely peaks rising out of drowned valleys of the same landmass – Hunga, Nuapapu, 'Ovaka, Pangaimotu, 'Utungake, Koloa, Kapa, 'Ofu and Vakaeitu. Volcanic outliers include Toku, Fonualei, Late and Late'iki.

The three islands of the Niuas Group, nearly 400km north of Vava'u, comprise the farthest reaches of the kingdom. Niuatoputapu is a reef-encircled, eroded volcano, while its near neighbour Tafahi is a perfect cone rising 656m above sea level. The doughnut-shaped island of Niuafo'ou is the remnant of an enormous cone which collapsed violently and has been destructively active as recently as 1946.

GEOLOGY

At the Tonga Trench, which reaches a depth of 10,882m at Vityaz Deep, the Pacific plate is being subducted underneath the Indo-Australian plate. The four island groups of Tonga lie in two parallel lines which trend north-south on the Tonga Ridge, on the Indo-Australian plate just west of the trench. To the west side of this ridge is the Lau Basin, where the sea floor is opening and spreading.

At the subduction zone, where the Pacific plate is submerging underneath the Indo-Australian plate, the materials which constitute the Pacific plate are being melted and recombined deep in the earth's mantle. This process is accompanied by a great deal of seismic activity; earthquakes and vulcanism are the results apparent on the surface. According to geologists, Niue is approaching Vava'u at about 20cm per year. The maximum subduction rate occurs near

Niuatoputapu, where the Pacific plate enters the trench at a rate of about 24cm annually.

Most of Tonga's high islands were created by geologically recent activity. As mentioned previously, Tafahi, Late and Kao form nearly perfect cones, and Niuafo'ou and Tofua remain active. Fonualei and 'Ata are well eroded but their fiery origins remain obvious. The two very recently formed islands of Fonuafo'ou (also known as Falcon Island) and Late'iki (Metis Shoal) evidence a most bizarre geological phenomenon. In the words of one Tongan, 'Yes, they come and they go'. (These oddities are explained in more detail in the respective sections on the two islands.)

The eastern line of islands is the result of the sagging weight of the new crust along the zone of vulcanism to the west, centred on Kao and Tofua. This line of islands has been pushed up mainly by displacement. The islands of 'Eua, Tongatapu and Vava'u are the best examples of tilted blocks of crust – all are leaning towards the great weight of Ha'apai's Kao and Tofua volcanoes on the earth's crust. Their respective east, south and north coasts consist of abrupt cliffs, while their respective west, north and south coastlines are submerging. In the case of Vava'u and Tongatapu, this is evidenced by mazes of islets, reefs and mangrove-choked lagoons on the Ha'apai side.

The main body of the Ha'apai Group consists of two large and eroding coral atolls, the Nomuka and Lulunga groups, and a raised barrier reef (the Lifuka Group). The Ha'apai Group contains several *motu* (coral islets) and countless shoals and barrier reefs, all sustained by coral polyps.

CLIMATE

Despite its great latitudinal variation, Tonga does not experience drastically diverse climatic conditions, although Vava'u and the Niuas are noticeably warmer than Tongatapu, and 'Eua is noticeably cooler (for different reasons). The Vava'u and Niua groups receive both more precipitation and

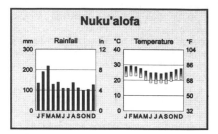

higher average temperatures than the more southerly islands.

Tonga is far enough from the equator, as far as Hawaii or the southern Cooks, to enjoy a milder and more comfortable climate than the Samoas or the Solomons. Winter (July to September) temperatures are pleasantly cool – 17°C to 22°C or so – but certain weather patterns such as southerly winds and strong south-east trades can create less-than-idyllic conditions, with rainstorms and extremely chilly weather.

Summer (December to April) temperatures vary from 25°C to 33°C, but even then cooler nights are not unusual. Extreme humidity is normally tempered by a light breeze. During early summer, Tonga experiences one of the world's most ideal climates. Later in the season, however, the islands receive most of their annual rainfall.

Tonga lies squarely within the South Pacific's notorious cyclone/typhoon belt and has experienced quite a few devastating blows over the years. Hurricane season is from 1 November to 30 April, with the period from January to March having greatest likelihood of cyclones. Yachties should try to clear out and head for New Zealand or the Solomons by at least the end of November. The only marginal hurricane shelter for yachts in the islands is Vava'u's Port of Refuge, but winds over 50 knots render it potentially hazardous. Other travellers can be assured that there will be sufficient warning to enable them to move inland before the situation grows too threatening. A severe cyclone may occur about

Sex & Coral

Sex may be infrequent for coral (it only happens once a year) but, when the time comes, it's certainly spectacular. Some colonies of coral polyps are all male or all female while polyps of other colonies are hermaphrodite (both male and female). In a few types of coral, hermaphrodite polyps can produce their own young which are released at various times over the year. In most cases, however, sperm of these polyps cannot fertilise their own eggs or other eggs from the same colony.

Although the mass spawning which creates new coral only takes place once a year, the build-up to the big night lasts for six months or more. During that time the polyps ripen their eggs which are initially white but later turn pink, red, orange and other bright colours. At the same time, male coral develops testes and produces sperm.

The big event comes in late spring or early summer, beginning a night or two after a full moon and building to a crescendo on the fourth, fifth and sixth nights. At this time water temperatures are ideal and there's a minimum of tidal variation. Within the coral, the eggs and sperm from the hermaphrodite coral are bundled together and half an hour prior to spawning time, the bundles are 'set'; ie they are held ready at the mouth of the polyp, clearly visible through the thin tissue. Suddenly, all across the reef these tiny bundles are released and are allowed to float upward towards the surface.

Remarkably, this spawning takes place simultaneously all over the reef. Different colonies release their egg and sperm bundles; single sex polyps eject their sperm or their eggs; and everything floats upward. The egg and sperm bundles, large enough to be seen with the naked eye, appear spectacular. The release has been described as a fireworks display or an inverted snowstorm. Since the event can be so accurately predicted divers are often able to witness it.

Once at the surface the bundles break up and the sperm swim off in search of eggs of the same coral species. Obviously corals of the same species must spawn at the same time in order to unite sperm and eggs of different colonies. Amid the swarm, it's obviously not easy for an individual sperm to find the right egg but biologists believe that by spawning all at once they reduce the risk of being consumed by the numerous marine creatures which would prey on them. By spawning soon after the full moon the reduced tidal activity means there is more time for fertilisation to take place before waves and currents sweep them away.

Once fertilisation has occurred, the egg cells begin to divide and within a day have become swimming coral larvae known as *planulae*. These are swept along by the current but after several days the planulae sink to the bottom and, if the right spot is found, the tiny larvae become coral polyps and a new coral colony is begun.

every 20 years, while milder ones occur on average every three or four years.

About 60% of the time the prevailing winds are south-easterly, north-easterly and southerly winds occur about 10% of the time. Westerly and north-westerly winds bring the worst weather, but it rarely lasts for more than 24 hours.

The average annual precipitation at Nuku'alofa is 1700mm and measurable rainfall occurs on 35% of the days. Vava'u is the wettest of all the island groups with around 2200mm of rain falling annually.

ECOLOGY & ENVIRONMENT

Although most of the land in Tonga has been converted into either 'api (plantations) or town tracts, large areas of natural rainforest and bushland occur on the Niuas and 'Eua as well as on the volcanic islands. The upland areas of 'Eua contain a relatively large forest reserve; along with the crater forest of Tofua island, it represents the last significant stand of first-growth rainforest in the country. For more information on environmental issues in Tonga, see Protected Areas under Flora & Fauna.

FLORA & FAUNA

Tonga's national flower is the *heilala*, a small, sweet-smelling, reddish flower that blooms in winter. Tongatapu's Heilala Festival in early July corresponds with its blooming. Many other flowers are seen in Tonga, including several varieties of hibiscus. The most common plant you will see in Tonga is the coconut palm, which represents the 'tree of life' for all South Pacific peoples. Its nuts are used for food and water all year round and its leaves are used to make houses.

Over 100 species of colourful tropical fish, including the tiny but brilliant blue damselfish, brightly coloured clownfish and parrotfish, and a host of others, are readily observed by snorkellers and divers. The reefs themselves form beautiful gardens of shapes and colours of hard and soft corals. Black coral, common around Tonga, is carved into jewellery and artistic pieces. The beaches and reefs are also home to numerous species of crabs, shellfish, starfish and crustaceans.

If you're flying around the islands at certain calmer periods of the year, you'll observe vast fields of coloured streaks on the surface of the ocean, some stretching for many kilometres. These are caused by a species of orange or brown algae measuring just 2mm in length. It collects in masses until it's broken up by rough wave action.

Porpoises and migrating humpback whales may also be seen in the waters around Tonga. The humpbacks are here from June to November and can often be seen offshore from the major islands. Whale watching trips are made during this time.

The only land mammal native to Tonga is the flying fox, an extremely large fruit bat with a wingspan of up to 1m. Kolovai in

What's in a Name?

After a while, you may begin to notice that Tongans have a rather ethnocentric way of referring to their flora and fauna. For example, fleas and body crabs are called *kuto fisi* (or Fijian bugs) and *kuto ha'amoa* (Samoan bugs) respectively. Likewise, poisonous kava plants are called *kava fisi* while good drinking kava is *kava tonga*. Large tuna are called *valu tonga* while the smaller variety are *valu ha'amoa*.

western Tongatapu has a reserve dedicated to its protection. Hundreds of bats may be seen snoozing upside down in casuarina trees there, an impressive sight. Flying foxes are found on other places around Tongatapu, too, in small colonies which may shift from place to place – a big tree behind the PATCO building on Taufa'ahau Rd in central Nuku'alofa was full of bats on our last visit – and on other islands as well. Although the flying foxes are technically protected, the royal family is allowed to hunt them for sport, and people (illegally) eat them.

Reptiles, in the form of several species of small lizards, are also found in abundance. The banded iguana (*fokai*) lives throughout Tonga but is extremely difficult to spot in the bush. It is believed that iguanas arrived in the Pacific, probably from Central America, on floating rafts of mangrove and other drifting woods some one million years ago. Two species of iguana can be found in Tonga.

Tonga has surprisingly few birds, but of interest are the blue-crowned lorikeet (*henga*) found on some islands of the Vava'u and Ha'apai groups, the red shining parrot (*koki*) of 'Eua, the tropic birds that nest on cliffs throughout the islands, and the incubator bird or Niuafo'ou megapode (*malau*) found only on the island of Niuafo'ou. The red shining parrot and the megapode occur only here. You'll probably also encounter mynah birds, which are an introduced species, not native to Tonga, but are now established on the islands.

Protected Areas

Tonga has seven officially protected areas, including five national marine parks and reserves, one national historic park (the 23-hectare Ha'amonga Trilithon reserve) and the 449-hectare 'Eua national park on 'Eua. Recently, both the land and water of Ha'apai have been designated the Ha'apai Conservation Area. The national marine reserves and coastal reserves have been established to protect particularly vulnerable coral reefs and beaches and their rich underwater ecosystems. In addition, there's a forest farm on 'Eua which is a bit like a US national forest in that it combines timber extraction with recreation.

Unfortunately, funds are short and conservation doesn't take a particularly high priority in Tonga. As a result, regulations are generally not enforced and, according to one cynical conservationist, quite a few locals take the words 'marine reserve' to mean 'fishing reserve' and permanent moorings which have been set to protect sensitive coral from haphazard anchoring are stolen as soon as they are set.

Visitors should note that collecting of plants, shells, coral or fish is prohibited within any of these reserves. Collecting live shells is officially discouraged and disturbing giant clams *(Tridacna derasa* or *tokonoa* in Tongan) and Triton's trumpet shells is prohibited throughout the kingdom.

The following is a list of reserves. Their area in hectares is given in brackets. (See the conversion table at the back of this book for the imperial equivalent).

- Ha'amonga Trilithon National Historic Park (23ha) – north-eastern Tongatapu
- Ha'atafu Beach Reserve (8.4ha) – 20km west of Nuku'alofa, on the western tip of Tongatapu

- Hakaumama'o Reef Reserve (126ha)– 14km north of Nuku'alofa
- Malinoa Island & Reef Reserve (73ha) – 7km north of Nuku'alofa
- Monu'afe Island & Reef Reserve (33ha) – 6.5km north-east of Nuku'alofa
- Pangaimotu Reef Reserve (49ha)– north-east of Queen Salote Wharf in Nuku'alofa
- 'Eua National Park (449ha) – on 'Eua's east coast

GOVERNMENT & POLITICS

Technically, Tonga is a constitutional monarchy based on the British parliamentary system. However, the current king, Taufa'ahau Tupou IV, is one of the world's most powerful reigning monarchs. Since its original draft in the 1870s, the constitution has undergone relatively little amendment.

The system provides for a sovereign and a privy council. The king or queen is the head of both the nation and its government. The monarch's cabinet consists of the prime minister (a post currently occupied by the king's cousin, Baron Vaea) and ministers of the crown. All these positions are appointed by the monarch and the occupants remain in office until voluntary retirement or death. The governors of Ha'apai and Vava'u are also members of the cabinet. When presided over by the monarch, the cabinet is called the privy council.

The legislature is unicameral and is composed of an appointed speaker, the cabinet, nine nobles elected by Tonga's 33 hereditary nobles and nine representatives elected by literate taxpayers over 21. Elections are held every three years.

Tonga's highest judicial assembly is the court of appeal, composed of the privy council and the chief justice. Below it is the supreme court, the land court (also presided over by the chief justice) and the magistrates' court. In criminal law, the accused may opt for trial by jury or by a judge alone.

Local governments consist of town and district officers, who respectively preside over villages and groups of villages. The Tongan Defence Forces are composed of three branches: an infantry, royal guards and maritime forces.

ECONOMY

Although increasing employment in the Nuku'alofa area is drawing people from the countryside into the cash economy, the majority of Tongans are still involved in a subsistence lifestyle.

Agriculture

Staple subsistence-level agricultural products include pineapples, papayas, kava, taro, watermelons, bananas, manioc, yams, sweet potatoes and, of course, coconuts. As a soil-saving measure, subsistence crops are normally rotated, though land shortages have meant that decreasing amounts of land are left fallow at any given time. In addition, most households have breadfruit and mango trees and keep horses, pigs and chickens. Many supplement their diet with seafood.

Leading agricultural exports are pumpkins, coconut products and vanilla. Tonga also produces export quantities of peppers, tomatoes, watermelons, limes and kava.

A recent addition to the local diet is pumpkins; Tongans happily consume those less-than-perfect specimens which have been rejected by the Japanese. The mad rush to plant pumpkins for the profitable Japanese export market has increased pressure on the land and drawn attention away from subsistence production. These lucrative exports have allowed many Tongans to purchase vehicles, businesses and other items that were once considered luxuries.

Fishing & Forestry

With the help of Japanese aid, the fishing industry provides minimal income for small, privately owned fishing boats. On a larger scale, the government owns and operates a 34m tuna-fishing boat, the *Lofa*, which trawls all over the Pacific.

A new export industry, which appears to be doing well, is the sale of live tropical fish. Every Tuesday afternoon, 1500 live fish are packed in seawater and plastic and flown out of Nuku'alofa, bound for the exotic pet market in the USA. The American owners of the business claim that fish

mortality is low and that their practices are 100% environmentally sound.

A sawmill at Ha'atu'a on 'Eua island prepares forestry products for local use and export. However, 'Eua's small area of remaining rainforest cannot sustain large-scale exploitation and there are already signs of erosion and other ecological problems. Fortunately, current forestry activities focus on non-native species such as pine and eucalyptus, planted especially for that purpose, but any expansion of the industry will necessarily mean incursion into natural forest and bushland, as well as subsistence agricultural areas.

Industry

In order to encourage overseas investments and new business, the Tongan government has developed a water, electricity and telecommunications infrastructure and offers five-year tax holidays and other tax breaks. A number of small industries have taken advantage of the opportunities provided as well as Tonga's relatively low rents and inexpensive labour market (trade unions are banned in Tonga). Businesses in Tonga, however, may not be more than 49% foreign controlled. Furthermore, land may not be purchased by foreigners and leasing of land requires parliamentary approval.

A Small Industries Centre in the Maufanga suburb of Nuku'alofa has been successful in producing knitwear, paper products, paint, furniture and sporting goods. A coconut oil processing plant in the same vicinity has been extremely profitable, exporting up to 15,000 tonnes annually.

Tongan exports receive duty-free access to Australasian markets and favoured trading status in North America and the European Union.

Tourism

Currently, the star on Tonga's economic horizon is tourism. With increasing tourism in the South Pacific, Tonga is hoping to cash in on its share of Australian, North American and European tourists. Prior to the great pumpkin blitz, tourism provided double the income of all other exports combined.

Emigration

It's interesting to note that many Tongans who have migrated abroad in search of greener pastures discover that they cannot cope with the hectic pace of life there and ultimately return to Tonga. Their native country may well be the easiest place in the world to live with a minimum of effort, and Tongans invariably notice that thriving abroad requires a rigid schedule dominated by work (except for a very privileged few).

The 'brain drain' created by those skilled or well educated Tongans who do remain outside the country does not present as significant a problem to the Tongan economy as it would initially seem. In Tongan tradition, food, clothing, homes, money and all material goods are communally owned by the extended family and, therefore, any member in need is considered welcome to and deserving of the means of any other member, including those of relatives living overseas. A great deal of money earned by Tongans living and working around the world eventually finds its way back to Tonga and, to a great extent, the nation depends on this income as a vital economic asset.

This system allows Tongan life to continue at a suitably Polynesian pace, while much of the cash economy and its associated headaches are contained elsewhere. Justifiably, families in Tonga are concerned that the second overseas generation, reared in a foreign culture, won't be so generous toward the folks back in the 'old country', relatives they may never have met.

POPULATION & PEOPLE

Tongans are a fairly homogeneous Polynesian group.

The 1996 census counted a total population of 97,446. Tongatapu, with 66,577 people, had 68.3% of Tonga's total population. Vava'u was next, with 15,779 (16.2%), followed by Ha'apai with 8148 (8.4%),

'Eua with 4924 (5.0%) and finally the Niuas with 2018 (2.1%).

This 1996 population figure represents an average annual growth rate of 0.3% during the previous decade, up from a population of 94,649 counted in the 1986 census. Population growth was by no means even, however: Tongatapu's population grew by 4.4%, Vava'u's by 4.0% and 'Eua by 12.1%, while Ha'apai showed a population decline of 8.6% and the Niuas' population declined by 14.8%.

The population density of the country as a whole is about 150 per sq km, but density varies widely throughout the kingdom.

Widespread emigration relieves a bit of the pressure on the limited territory and resources of the archipelago. You'd be hard-pressed to find a Tongan without relatives in New Zealand, Australia or the USA. Estimates state there are 50% to 100% more Tongans living abroad than there are in Tonga.

EDUCATION

Education is compulsory for children between the ages of five and 14. It's free in state schools, but the vast majority of Tongans receive their primary and secondary education at one of the numerous Christian institutions.

Tonga has 10 technical and vocational colleges and one teacher training college. Tertiary education is available at the University of the South Pacific extension and the private 'Atenisi Institute, both on Tongatapu. The government and other commonwealth countries also offer scholarship programmes enabling students to go overseas for higher education.

ARTS
Dance

Unlike the vibrant *tamure* of Tahiti and the Cook Islands or the erotic *hula* of Hawaii, Tongan dances for females are subtle, artistic and require the dancer to convey meaning with an economy of motion.

The most frequently performed traditional dance in Tonga is called the *lakalaka*.

The dancers, most often women but occasionally including men, stand in rows, dressed in similar costumes decorated with leaves, shells, flowers and pandanus. They sway, sing, smile broadly and tell stories with their hand movements. One person of high rank, called the *vahenga*, performs apart from the other dancers and is dressed differently. A female vahenga will perform the female part of the dance and a male will follow the male dancers.

The *ma'ulu'ulu* is a dance performed at feasts, on holidays and at special state functions. Its movements, known as *haka*, are choreographed by an artist, the *punake*, who is always a man of high rank. He also writes the song the dance is meant to illustrate. The dancers are always women; they seat themselves in rows and use only hand movements to convey the story.

The female solo dance, the most beautiful and graceful of all Tongan dances, is called the *tau'olunga*. The qualifications for a dancer are rather strict. The ideal candidate would be fair with long black hair, shapely but not thin (big is beautiful in Tonga), with an attractive face and legs and a flawless complexion. The dancer performs wearing a flowing knee-length dress with bare shoulders and with flowers in her hair and on her wrists and ankles. Her body is covered with coconut oil in order to draw attention to her skin. The dancer must always smile genuinely and keep her knees together. The tau'olunga is performed at government and village functions, on the birthdays of influential people and for visits by dignitaries. A girl will also perform it at her own wedding, a suitable occasion to display her charms.

While the female dances are gentle and accompanied by music, the male dances are meant to convey the fierce warrior spirit of Tongan tradition. The most popular is the *kailao*, the war dance, which is meant to be reminiscent of the days when canoes full of Tongan men set out on raiding missions to neighbouring islands. The rapid movements re-enact violent attacks and are accompanied by loud, ominous drumming, fierce cries, beating feet and the pounding of *pate*, or spear-like pales, which represent war clubs.

The fire dance, perhaps the most dramatic Tongan dance, is also the favourite of most visitors. One or two dancers gyrate, leap and spin while juggling flaming knives to the time of a rapid, primeval drumbeat.

The *fakapale* is a curious custom associated with Tongan dancing. The word means literally 'to award a prize'. Originally, the prizes consisted of fine mats and tapa heaped before a dancer in recognition of ability. Nowadays, handicrafts have been replaced with money: notes are plastered onto the oiled bodies of the dancers during the performance by admiring spectators. Tongan performances are excellent for fundraising.

Tapa

From the cool early hours of the morning until the hour of the evening meal, rural Tonga is filled with the sound of pounding tapa mallets. Along with pandanus weavings, tapa is considered part of the *koloa*, or wealth, of Tongan families. On an important occasion such as a wedding, funeral, graduation or royal event, large amounts of tapa in lengths of 25m to 150m are made and exchanged.

In Tongan, this product is only referred to as tapa in its early undecorated stage. The Tongan name for the elaborately decorated finished product is *ngatu*. It is made from *hiapo*, the underbark of the paper mulberry tree *(Broussonetia papyrifera)*, which grows primarily on 'Eua and Tongatapu.

The mature trees are cut near their base, which normally measures only 3cm or so in diameter, and the bark is removed. After a day or two of drying, the rough outer bark is peeled away leaving the soft and fibrous inner bark. It is then beaten with an ironwood *(toa)* mallet called an *'ike* on a long wooden anvil, or *tutua*, to separate and spread the fibres. When it is about 45cm in width, it is folded with another piece and pounded further. A single length of cloth is known as a *feta'aki*; once it has been pasted

✳✳✳✳✳✳✳✳✳✳✳✳✳✳✳✳✳✳✳✳✳✳✳✳✳✳✳✳✳✳✳ ✳

Pandanus Weaving

The preparation of the pandanus leaf is quite involved. First, it is cut and then stripped of thorns and rough spots. Once this initial process is completed, different methods are used to bring out the unique qualities and colours of each type.

Four types of pandanus are used in Tonga, each with its own texture and colour. They are *tofua*, which is nearly white, *pa'ongo*, which is brown, *tapahina*, off-white or light brown, and *kie*, the finest of all, which is creamy white.

Tofua requires the simplest of the four processes. The leaves are bundled, boiled in water for an hour or two and laid in the sun to dry. Pa'ongo and tapahina are derived from leaves which are covered with a mat (pandanus, of course) and turned daily to prevent rot. After a few days they turn a chocolate brown colour and are gathered, braided into plaits called *fakate'ete'epuaka*, bundled up and hung in a dark place to dry.

The soft fibres of the kie leaves are peeled away from the coarser undersides, tied into bunches and blanched by placing them in the sea for up to a fortnight. After being brought ashore they are carefully washed to remove the salt, and dried in the sun. Each leaf is then curled and made softer by pulling it between the fingers and the lip of a clam shell. It is then cut to the desired width, ready to be woven.

The kie fibres, when cut into threadlike strips, become extremely valuable, silk-like fine mats called *fihu*, unmatched anywhere in the world. A good *fala fihu* will require thousands of hours of weaving time, and mothers often begin work on one at the birth of a daughter in the hope of finishing in time to present it as part of her dowry.

Other types of mats include the *fala tu'i, fala pa'ongo*, and *fala tofua*. The first is the most complex – a mat of double thickness, one layer woven of coarse tofua and the other of finer pa'ongo. The fala pa'ongo on its own is dark in colour and is normally presented to those of high status in the society. The fala tofua is of a lighter colour.

The black seen in many pandanus baskets is derived by dyeing the leaves with the juice of *loa 'ano* or *manaui* before weaving. Baskets are stiffened by weaving around ribs of coconut frond. Fibres of *fau* or hibiscus bark are often used along with the pandanus when making baskets or dancing costumes.

✳✳✳✳✳✳✳✳✳✳✳✳✳✳✳✳✳✳✳✳✳✳✳✳✳✳✳✳✳✳✳ ✳

into long strips it is known as *langanga*. These strips placed side by side are also pasted together using sticky, half-cooked tubers of manioke.

First a *kupesi*, or relief of the pattern, is made. A kupesi has a woven pandanus base, called the *papa*. A design made with coconut fronds *(tui'aniu)* is sewn to the base with coconut sennit. The strips of tapa are placed over the kupesi tablet and rubbed with feta'aki and coconut husk dipped in a ruddy vegetable dye in order to bring out the design.

After the tapa has dried, the stencilled designs are handpainted in black and rich earthy reds and browns, usually derived from candlenuts and mangrove bark.

Weaving

Like tapa, woven pandanus mats are traditionally considered a form of wealth by Tongan families and are therefore exchanged as tokens of esteem on special occasions. Tongan weaving, however, is not limited to mats – hats, clothing, toys, baskets, belts and trays are also woven of pandanus and put to everyday use. Historically, even the long-distance sailing canoes carried sails of woven pandanus.

Literature

Tales of the Tikongs and *Kisses in the Nederends* by 'Epeli Hau'ofa are books not to be missed by anyone travelling to Tonga. They are tales of the coming of age of a small Pacific island kingdom called Tiko (a thinly disguised Tonga), by Tonga's most renowned and respected author. Humorous and thought-provoking reading.

Po Fananga: Folk Tales of Tonga by Tupou Posesi Fanua is a highly enjoyable book of traditional Tongan tales, told in Tongan and English. *Tales from the Friendly Islands* by Vaka Pole'o is another book of Tongan tales, written in English.

Tales and Poems of Tonga by EEV Collocott, the classic 1928 study, is now being reprinted.

Konai Helu Thaman, a Tongan woman with an illustrious personal history, has published several excellent books of poetry including *YOU, The Choice of my Parents; Langakali; Hingano; Kakala* (all in English) and *Inselfeuer* (in German).

Malo Tupou: An Oral History by Tupou Posesi Fanua with Lois Wimberg Webster tells the story of the author's first 21 years, 1913 to 1934, recounted when she was 81 years old. An oral history of early 20th-century Tonga told from a woman's perspective, it's a very good read.

SOCIETY & CONDUCT

Although on the whole Tongans are an open and extremely hospitable people, western travellers throughout the Pacific are frequently bewildered by local behaviour and sense that they are not being let in on some vital details about the Tongan way.

A few examples: Christianity is professed loudly but some old Polynesian ways and superstitions quietly remain. Warm and generous adults invite foreigners into their homes and lavish gifts and food on them yet seem to regard their own children coldly and without affection. Honest and upstanding individuals will quite openly rummage through the pockets of an unconscious drunk and help themselves to money.

It would be quite safe to say that few outsiders, if any, will ever come to understand all the underlying nuances of any Polynesian culture. Ritual and custom may be easily observed and recounted, but to grasp the meaning of it all is another issue,

indeed. I wish it were possible to describe the significance of such things − an innocently raised eyebrow, a formal kava ceremony, the gestures and expressions of a *matapule* (talking chief) ritually accepting a gift for royalty − but any explanation I, a non-Tongan, can offer will be quite superficial and probably not entirely correct. Tonga, like other little-known places on earth, challenges visitors to observe and discover, and it greatly rewards those who do.

Social Hierarchy

With the advent of Christianity as the state religion, all Tongans became theoretically equal 'under God' and social ranking lost a great deal of its importance. The constitution of 1875 abolished the traditional feudal system of subservience and serfdom for commoners, and chiefs and nobles were denied the privilege of indiscriminate pillage to which they'd been previously accustomed. Old habits die hard, however, and remnants of the traditional system may still be seen today.

Although caste is not as rigid and elaborate as it was before European contact, there remains a two-tier system which determines privilege among individuals and in which no upward mobility is possible. The royal family and the 33 hereditary nobles and their families enjoy the highest rank in Tongan society. All other Tongans are commoners. Nobles may not marry commoners without risk of losing their titles. A commoner who marries a noble can never attain noble status.

In a sense, a third class does exist: it is composed of expatriates of European descent who, by virtue of their relative wealth (in most cases) and education, receive deferential treatment.

The Family

In Tonga, the basic social unit is the extended family which, in a sense serves as a mini social welfare system. Within families, all wealth, belongings, work, problems and even shame are shared by all and the excessive accumulation of wealth and personal belongings is considered to be out of line. (Understandably, this sometimes creates conflicts for Tongans returning from working in western countries or for non-Tongan spouses.)

So fundamental is the concept of the communal extended family that in Tongan there are no separate words for 'brother/sister' and 'cousin'. Aunts and uncles may also be referred to as 'parents' and all older people may be considered 'grandparents' by the younger generations. The notions of childless families and orphaned children are unknown.

Parents have no real sense of 'possession' of their children and children are frequently shifted from one household to another. In the end, they are effectively reared by the entire family and may have several places to call home.

Social Protocol

In most cases, visitors will not be expected to participate in or even be aware of Tongan codes of behaviour, but those who do are likely to be more accepted by the people.

Respect for those considered superior to oneself, whether they really are or not, is a principal motivation in Tongan behaviour. In the presence of royalty, nobles, high commissioners, politicians or religious leaders, Tongans become more guarded and deliberate. As a foreigner, you are likely to be regarded in a similar fashion, hence the 'arm's length' feeling many people get when dealing with hospitable locals.

In extreme cases, such as when dealing with royalty and nobles, 'respect' translates into veneration. In the presence of such people Tongan commoners wear *ta'ovala*, woven mats tied around the waist with coconut sennit, as a sign of respect. Tongan commoners physically lower themselves before a royal who is standing up, in order to demonstrate willing subservience, and in no way imitate their actions. At any gathering at which royalty is to be present, everyone else must be seated before the guests of honour arrive. Once royalty is seated, no other commoners may be admitted or seated (in this one case, western-style punctuality is absolutely necessary). For those who are privileged enough to address royalty, there is a special level of the Tongan language which must be used. The death of a monarch sets off a six-month period of mourning during which, in effect, the entire country shuts down.

As a corollary, anyone entering a room or other place in which people are seated lower than they are, or where people are sitting while they are standing, should utter *tulou* or 'excuse me'. This is intended to emphasise that everyone is standing on equal ground, regardless of their physical position relative to the others.

One practice, which is in no way unique to Tonga but is ubiquitous here, is gift giving. Gifts are given as a matter of course to new friends, especially if they are foreigners. Gifts are presented to kings and nobles by a family in which there has been a birth, death, marriage or university or high school graduation, in honour or memory of the family member. Tongans leaving on a visit abroad are laden with gifts to be presented to their family members and to the family members of any friends and acquaintances living at their destination. They are also likely to return laden with reciprocal gifts.

Among commoners, gifts will most often come in the form of agricultural produce. Foreigners are often presented with food and handicrafts. Family members abroad get tinned corned beef and kava. New parents, newly married couples and royalty receive the finest agricultural produce, pigs, intricately designed fine mats and immense rolls of tapa.

Gifts are given ceremoniously and accepted graciously. A gift will most often be prefaced by verbal self-abasement, such as 'We are a poor family and our gift is therefore very humble and insufficient to convey the honour you deserve but please be so kind as to accept it as it represents the best that we are capable of producing'. This speech will often refer to a fine mat which represents hundreds or thousands (yes, thousands!) of hours of work. Although the giver of the gift downplays its worth, the recipient praises the gift and shows how delighted they are to receive it.

Shame and loss of face are not taken lightly in Tonga. An individual who has been seriously shamed or caught (or even suspected of) doing something considered socially unacceptable endures untold measures of self-imposed personal agony. In extreme cases people are driven to suicide. In their dealings with Tongans, foreigners should be especially sensitive to this. If a travel agent botches a reservation, a waiter delivers the wrong plate, or a person on the street admits he or she doesn't know where a particular point of interest is (it requires fortitude to do this), a foreigner who becomes outwardly upset in most cases inspires feelings of shame that go deeper than is immediately visible. A *laissez-faire* attitude will go a long way towards preserving a traveller's mental health as well.

Visiting Smaller Islands

It seems that the smaller the island, the more warmly visitors are welcomed. Just try asking permission to camp on the more remote islands and you'll quickly learn that the locals will be offended that you'd consider staying somewhere other than in their homes! Having said that, life on the outer islands is almost strictly subsistence style and hospitality must not be abused. Prospective visitors will be least disruptive if they have a contact on the islands and announce their intention to visit in advance. They should also bring enough supplies for themselves as well as gifts for their hosts (tinned corned beef will be heartily welcomed).

Dress

Although their attire is growing increasingly western, Tongans are by law required to dress modestly in keeping with strict fundamentalist Christian ideals.

Men experience fewer restrictions than women but they are required to wear a shirt at all times when in public. Failure to do so brings a fine of T\$20; this applies to foreigners too. This rule doesn't apply to the beaches, where men are permitted to go shirtless.

Women, however, may not go topless at any time and usually cover their shoulders and chests completely and cover their legs at least to the knees. A Tongan woman who doesn't comply with this guideline risks being regarded as disreputable. Very few Tongans have bathing costumes – they just hop into the sea in whatever they happen to be wearing at the time.

You'll often see Tongans wearing distinctive pandanus mats called *ta'ovala*, secured around the waist with a cord of coconut sennit called a *kafa*. Ta'ovala are worn frequently by older people and by everyone when they go to work, to church, to town, on formal occasions or whenever they might encounter someone of noble status. Worn in this context, the ta'ovala serves roughly the same social purpose as a tie (for men) or a special dress (for women) in western culture: it signifies that the wearer is 'dressed up'. Ta'ovala are handed down through several generations as valued heirlooms and the older and tattier they appear, the more they are prized.

In place of a ta'ovala, women often wear a *kiekie*, a decorative waist band from which dangle woven strips of pandanus, strands of seeds, bits of cloth or fibre cords. Men often wear a wraparound skirt known as a *tupenu* extending below the knees and women an ankle-length *vala*, or skirt, and *kofu*, or tunic.

When mourning a relative or friend, Tongans dress in black and wear particularly prominent ta'ovala. During the six months of mourning for a member of the royal family, all Tongans are required to don ta'ovala and wear black.

Dos & Don'ts

Dress is important not only for Tongans, but for foreigners visiting Tonga as well. Requirements are slightly different for women and men, but one thing definitely applies to both: be clean and presentable in your appearance. To Tongans, being clean and presentable signifies respect for yourself and others; conversely, being dirty and/or raggedy in your appearance when you're around other people is taken to mean that you don't respect them. Respect is extremely important in Tongan culture.

Short shorts should not be worn in public by either women or men. They will cause offence. Women should see the Women Travellers section in Facts for the Visitor for more tips on dress.

Also be sure to dress neatly and respectably when you go to church. This is easy to do. Men should wear a shirt (preferably with a collar) and long pants; women should wear a loose dress or skirt with a hemline below the knee and keep their chests and upper arms covered. That's all there is to it.

RELIGION

Tongans take their religion seriously, or at least that's what they'd have you believe. Since the constitution of the nation was outlined by a missionary, Shirley Baker, it's not surprising that national adherence to Christian principles was written into it.

Although Tonga technically permits religious freedom, anyone practising anything other than Christianity should probably keep it to themselves. In late 1988, Tonga began refusing tourist visas to Fijian Indians. Ostensibly, it was feared that illegal immigration by these people would take away jobs from Tongans; one suspects, however, that the encroachment of Hinduism was also an issue.

The Free Wesleyan Church claims the largest number of adherents, followed by the (Methodist) Free Church of Tonga, the Church of England, the Roman Catholics,

Seventh Day Adventists and the Mormons. The Mormon church seems to be growing rapidly in Tonga, if you can judge by the high number of Mormon churches that seem to be popping up everywhere, especially on Tongatapu. All of these sects operate educational facilities. Royal watchers should head for the Free Wesleyan Church's Centenary Chapel in Nuku'alofa, where the Royal Family worships.

No discussion of religion in Tonga would be complete without relating the tired old anecdote about the Seventh Day Adventists. Normally, they celebrate their Sabbath on Saturday, of course, but in Tonga they accept Sunday as their holy day. Why? Because the International Date Line bends out of its path in order to include Tonga. Were it not for that fact, Sunday in Tonga would actually be Saturday!

Tongan cemeteries provide the ultimate examples of post-mortem kitsch. Non-Catholic burials (Catholics use monuments) consist of sandy mounds topped with artificial flowers beneath inverted goldfish bowls, plastic images or photos of Jesus Christ, teddy bears, ribbons, banners, shells and beer bottles and cans, often backed up with a hanging quilt.

With all the hoopla over Christianity, one would assume that the pre-European religious beliefs had been totally abandoned. But many Tongans still believe in the spirits, taboos, superstitions, medical charms and Polynesian gods that characterised the well-defined religious traditions before the arrival of the missionaries. For anyone interested in the details of ancient Tongan religious rites and traditions, William Mariner & John Martin's book, *Tonga Islands: William Mariner's Account* contains a fascinating in-depth discussion of pre-missionary beliefs.

Facts for the Visitor

PLANNING
When to Go

May to October is the best time to visit Tonga. Summer, from November to April, is hot, humid and wet, and is also hurricane season. Though serious hurricanes are rare, yachties will want to avoid summer. See Climate in the Facts about the Country chapter for more information.

Most people visit Tonga from May to October and during the December-January summer holidays. If you're planning to come during December-January, when huge numbers of Tongans living abroad (mostly in New Zealand, Australia and the USA) return home for the holidays, it's wise to make air reservations well in advance.

Tonga's special annual events are another attraction; see Public Holidays & Special Events later in this chapter. The busiest time to come to Tonga will be at the end of 1999, as Tonga will be one of the first places in the world to greet the dawn of the new millennium. The celebration plans are already underway.

What Kind of Trip?

Tonga can be visited alone, as part of an island-hopping jaunt through the South Pacific, or as a stopover when crossing the Pacific between the USA and Australia or New Zealand. Most travellers arrive by plane, but some come by yacht – Vava'u's Port of Refuge is a major stopover on the yachting route across the Pacific.

You might want to visit all of Tonga's major southern islands (Tongatapu, 'Eua, Ha'apai and Vava'u). They are all very different to each other and are all well worth visiting. Royal Tongan Airlines offers convenient flights. Inter-island ferries are not for the faint-hearted; only the two-hour hop between Tongatapu and 'Eua is easy (see the Getting Around chapter for further information).

The Niuas are more remote and receive

Celebrating the Millennium

Tonga, in the first time zone to greet any new day (13 hours ahead of Greenwich Mean Time) has long advertised itself in tourist brochures as 'The Place Where Time Begins'. Now, quite naturally, it is promoting itself as the place that will be first to usher in the new millennium.

It's hoped that the millennium celebrations will bring heaps of tourists – and their money – to Tonga. In 1998 Tonga's plans for celebrating the millennium include cultural events, sports competitions, parades on land and sea and, of course, plenty of feasting. At the time of writing, the International Dateline Hotel in Nuku'alofa was already booked out for 31 December 1999, even though prices for that date had yet to be announced! If you do plan to be in Tonga at that time make reservations well ahead. You can count on prices for everything being several times higher than normal.

Although most of the celebrations will centre on Nuku'alofa, the first place in Tonga to actually see the dawn of the new millennium will be the highest point on the island of 'Eua – being the island farthest south.

One popular way of celebrating the new millennium will be to welcome it in Tonga, then take a plane or boat to Samoa (in the last time zone) and celebrate it all over again next day. A number of people are already making plans to do this.

DARRYL TORCKLER

DARRYL TORCKLER

DARRYL TORCKLER

FIKCO

DARRYL TORCKLER

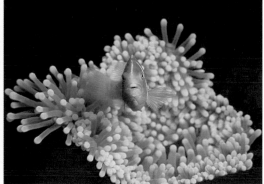

DARRYL TORCKLER

A	B
C	D
E	F

A: Lion fish
B: Anemone fish
C: Christmas tube worms on coral

D: Hermit crab
E: Soft corals
F: Anemone fish

PATRICK HORTON

FIKCO

HOLGER LEUE

PATRICK HORTON

PATRICK HORTON

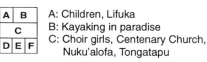
HOLGER LEUE

A	B
	C
D	E	F

A: Children, Lifuka
B: Kayaking in paradise
C: Choir girls, Centenary Church,
    Nuku'alofa, Tongatapu

D: Man in palm leaf woven hat, Lifuka
E: Woman, Lifuka
F: Methodist woman, Neiafu, Vava'u

fewer visitors, making a trip there all the more adventurous. Even Tonga's most remote uninhabited islands can be visited – Pacific Island Seaplanes provides seaplane transport everywhere in Tonga, or you can charter a yacht.

You can have a great time focusing your trip around favourite activities such as scuba diving, snorkelling, sailing, sea kayaking, fishing, tramping, caving, rock climbing etc. See the Activities section in this chapter for suggestions.

But just as there's plenty to do in Tonga, there's also plenty not to do. You may find Tonga ideal for slowing down, relaxing and taking life easy.

Maps
The tourist office hands out a free map containing a collection of simple hand-drawn maps of Tonga's major islands and island groups, plus separate street maps of Nuku'alofa, Neiafu and Lifuka. A similarly sketchy map of the island groups is available at the Friendly Islands Bookshop.

Tonga's Ministry of Lands, Survey & Natural Resources (☎ 23-611; fax 23-216), PO Box 5, Vuna Rd, Nuku'alofa, sells topographical maps in varying degrees of detail for all Tonga's islands, for T$5 each. The Friendly Islands Bookshop in Nuku'alofa also carries some of these maps.

What to Bring
Given Tonga's comfortable and relatively consistent climate, clothing can be kept to a minimum. It can sometimes get chilly in winter, so take a light jacket. Also keep Tonga's dress codes in mind (see Society & Conduct in the Facts about the Country chapter, and the Women Travellers section later in this chapter). Bring rain gear at any time of year.

Items like sunblock, tampons, contraceptives, mosquito repellent and contact lens solution should probably be brought from home, since availability and price are unpredictable in Tonga. Film and camera equipment is also best brought from home. A few paperbacks to read on the beach, a torch (flashlight) for exploring caves, a Swiss army knife, a universal-type drain plug and your own snorkelling gear are also worth bringing.

If you'll be bushwalking or travelling by overnight ferry, a sleeping bag and ground cover will be essential. A tent will allow you the freedom to stay overnight on a particularly appealing beach, forest or mountain.

SUGGESTED ITINERARIES
If you have only a few days or a week in Tonga, you might do best to choose one of the southern islands (Tongatapu, 'Eua, Ha'apai or Vava'u) and concentrate your holiday there, getting to know that island. Even if your international flight arrives in Tongatapu, you can easily move on to other islands – short, convenient domestic flights connect Tongatapu to all the others most days of the week (except Sunday). Vava'u, Ha'apai, 'Eua and Tongatapu all have their aficionados.

If you have more time, you can visit more islands.

HIGHLIGHTS
Every visitor to Tonga will have a different list of favourite things to see and do, but the following get our vote for Tonga's top attractions.

- Snorkelling and scuba diving – these are world-class in Tonga, especially in Ha'apai and Vava'u. See the Activities section to understand why.
- Humpback whales – the 'singing whales' visit Tonga annually from around June to November to mate and bear their young. Whale watching trips in which you can snorkel with these huge creatures are an unforgettable experience.
- Tongan feast – At least once, take the opportunity to pig out Tongan-style, and enjoy Tonga's beautiful traditional music and dance.
- Mapu'a 'a Vaca Blowholes, Tongatapu – Mapu'a 'a Vaca is a long coastline with dozens of blowholes which spout dramatically, especially during periods of high seas.
- Ha'amonga 'a Maui Trilithon, Tongatapu – One of Polynesia's most impressive ancient monuments, the Ha'amonga 'a Maui trilithon

is believed to have been used for astronomical observations.

- Lapaha tombs, Mu'a, Tongatapu – This concentration of ancient tombs and other constructions marks the site of Lapaha, which served as the capital of Tongatapu for 600 years.
- Bushwalking on 'Eua, Tongatapu Group – The quiet rural island of 'Eua offers forests, caves, savannas, sea cliffs, beaches and a large network of bush roads, walking tracks and camping possibilities.
- Tofua island, Ha'apai – The mutiny on the Bounty took place near here but there's also a beautiful blue crater lake, stands of first-growth rainforest, unique vegetation and a very active volcano.
- Vava'u Group – The Vava'u Group is heaven on earth for sailing, and several yacht charter and day tour operators enable you to do it. Sea kayaking is excellent here, too.
- Hiking around Niuafo'ou, Niuas – The island of Niuafo'ou offers unusual lava fields and a spectacular crater containing two lovely freshwater lakes.
- Waterways of Western Niuatoputapu, Niuas – The maze separating the islets west of Niuatoputapu is an enjoyable place to wade and soak up the pervading sense of mystery.

TOURIST OFFICES
Local Tourist Offices
Nuku'alofa, Ha'apai and Vava'u all have tourist information offices. The head office address is Tonga Visitors' Bureau, Vuna Rd, PO Box 37, Nuku'alofa, Kingdom of Tonga (☎ (676) 25-334; fax 23-507; tvb@candw.to; www.vacations.tvb.gov.to).

Tourist Offices Abroad
For advance information, contact the Tonga Visitors' Bureau in Nuku'alofa or one of the following offices:

Australia
    Tonga Visitors' Bureau, 642 King St, Newtown, Sydney, NSW (☎ (02) 9519-9700; fax 9519-9419)
New Zealand
    Tonga Visitors' Bureau, PO Box 24-054, Royal Oak, Auckland (☎ (09) 634-1519; fax 636-8973)
UK
    Tonga High Commission, 36 Molyneux St,

London W1H 6AB (☎ (0171) 724-5828; fax 723-9074)
USA
    Tonga Consulate, 360 Post St, Suite 604, San Francisco, CA 94108 (☎ (415) 781-0365; fax 781-3964)

VISAS & DOCUMENTS
Visas are not required for visits to Tonga. Upon arrival you must present a valid passport and an onward ticket to be granted a stay of 30 days (sometimes only three weeks). The only exceptions are Fijian passport holders of Indian descent, who are not admitted to Tonga at all.

Your stay can be extended for up to six months at any immigration office; each island group has one. You'll need to give them your passport, pay T$26, show that you still have your vital onward ticket and prove that you have sufficient funds to support yourself for the time you want to stay in Tonga.

For information on arriving by yacht, see the Getting There & Away chapter.

International and home country driving licences are not valid in Tonga. Those intending to drive or hire a vehicle must obtain a Tongan driving licence at the police station in Nuku'alofa or Neiafu. There are no written or practical tests; just produce your home driving licence, your passport and T$10, and off you go.

If you're entering from an infected area, which is usually interpreted as sub-Saharan Africa or Latin America, you'll need proof of vaccination against yellow fever.

Make photocopies of all your important documents, especially your passport, airline tickets and credit cards. This will help speed up replacement if they are lost or stolen. Keep these, and a list of travellers cheque numbers, separate from your other valuables, and also leave a copy with someone back home.

Long-Term Residency
Unless you marry a Tongan citizen, non-business immigration is extremely difficult. Business immigrants are normally permit-

ted to remain, but only as long as they retain their jobs. Those intent upon setting up a business will normally be required to place controlling interest in the hands of a Tongan partner.

For more information on business investments in Tonga, contact the Ministry of Labour, Commerce & Industries (☎ 23-688; fax 23-887), PO Box 110, Nuku'alofa, Kingdom of Tonga. The immigration office at the police station in Nuku'alofa (☎ 24-763; fax 23-226), PO Box 8, Nuku'alofa, Kingdom of Tonga, can fill you in on all the current immigration requirements.

Those who aren't interested in business may be able to volunteer their services as an English teacher in a village. (Classes are in Tongan until sixth year, when the students learn English; after sixth year, all classes are conducted in English). People with exceptional skills like medical professionals or secondary school teachers willing to work voluntarily will also normally have a chance of immigration. The US Peace Corps, Australian Volunteers Abroad and Japanese Overseas Cooperation Volunteers get two-year stints.

Travel Insurance

It's always worth taking out travel insurance. Work out what you need. You should be covered for the worst possible case: an accident, for example, that will require hospital treatment and a flight home. It's a good idea to make a copy of your policy, in case the original is lost. If you are planning to travel for a long time, the insurance may seem very expensive – but if you can't afford it, you certainly won't be able to afford to deal with a serious medical emergency overseas.

EMBASSIES & CONSULATES
Tongan Representatives Abroad

Tonga has diplomatic representatives in the following countries:

Australia
Tongan Consulate-General, 158 Pacific Highway, North Sydney, NSW 2060 (☎ (02) 9929-8794, fax 9929-6778)

New Zealand
Tonga Visitors' Bureau, PO Box 24-054, Royal Oak, Auckland (☎ (09) 634-1519; fax 636-8973)
UK
Tonga High Commission, 36 Molyneux St, London W1H 6AB (☎ (0171) 724-5828; fax 723-9074)
USA
Tonga Consulate, 360 Post St, Suite 604, San Francisco, CA 94108 (☎ (415) 781-0365; fax 781-3964).
Tonga Consular Agent, 220 South King St, Suite 1230, Honolulu, Hawaii (☎ (808) 521-5149, fax 521-5264)

Foreign Representatives in Tonga

The following foreign diplomatic representatives can all be found in Nuku'alofa, except for one Italian consular correspondent in Neiafu.

Australia
High Commission, Salote Rd (☎ 23-244; fax 23-243)
Canada
Limited consular services available at the Australian High Commission
European Union
European Commission office, Taufa'ahau Rd (☎ 23-820; fax 23-869)
Germany
Consulate, Otto G Sanft Store, Taufa'ahau Rd (☎ 23-477; fax 23-154)
Italy
Italy has no consulate in Tonga, but it has two consular correspondents attached to the Italian embassy in New Zealand. The correspondent in Nuku'alofa is Umberto Mottini at the Fasi Moe 'Afi Italian Garden Restaurant on Vuna Rd (☎ 22-289; fax 23-313). In Neiafu, Vava'u it's Dr Alfredo Carafa at the Italian Clinic (☎ 70-607)
Korea
Consulate, Salote Rd (☎ 23-874; fax 24-043)
New Zealand
High Commission, Taufa'ahau Rd (☎ 23-122; fax 23-487)
Sweden
Consulate, Ministry of Labour building, Salote Rd (☎ 22-855, 21-260; fax 22-882)
Taiwan
Embassy, Vuna Rd (☎ 21-766; fax 23-726)
UK
British High Commission, Vuna Rd (☎ 24-285, 24-395; fax 24-109)

CUSTOMS

Travellers aged 18 or older may import up sto 200 cigarettes, 1L of spirits and 1L of wine duty-free. Animals, fruit and other plant products require a quarantine certificate. Firearms, ammunition, drugs and pornographic material may not be imported under any circumstances.

MONEY

Costs

For imported goods such as electronic equipment, film and packaged foods, prices in Tonga are considerably higher than in the USA or Europe, and a bit higher than in Australia or New Zealand. Thanks to extortionate duties, prices for motor cars and their components are beyond the bounds of reason. (So are Nuku'alofa's traffic levels, thanks to a recent pumpkin export boom which ignited a fury of car purchases among Tongans.)

Basic food and accommodation are generally more reasonably priced than they are in other South Pacific countries – slightly higher than in Samoa and Fiji but considerably lower than in French Polynesia. You can get by quite comfortably in Tonga on T$50 per day and can live austerely for half that.

Duty-free shopping is available at the International Dateline Hotel in Nuku'alofa, at the Leiola duty-free shop beside the tourist office in Neiafu, and in the international lounge at Fua'amotu International Airport, Tongatapu.

Carrying Money

Theft from the person is very rare in Tonga. On the other hand, things left lying around are considered ripe for the picking. Always keep this in mind. Don't take all your money to the beach, for example, and then leave it lying on the sand while you go snorkelling. See Security under Dangers & Annoyances later in this chapter

Credit Cards

Visa and MasterCard are the most frequently accepted cards. Credit cards are accepted at major tourist facilities such as the International Dateline and Pacific Royale hotels in Nuku'alofa or the Paradise International Hotel on Vava'u. Royal Tongan Airlines, some handicraft shops, the Friendly Islands Bookshop in Nuku'alofa, and several other beach resorts also accept credit cards.

Cash advances on Visa and MasterCard can be made at the Bank of Tonga, which has offices in Nuku'alofa, 'Eua, Pangai (Ha'apai) and Neiafu (Vava'u). In Nuku'alofa and Neiafu you can also get cash advances at the ANZ (Visa & MasterCard) and MBF (MasterCard only) banks. The International Dateline Hotel in Nuku'alofa changes money and gives cash advances on credit cards 24 hours a day (since it charges a hefty 10% commission on credit card advances, you're better off going to one of the banks).

There are no ATMs in Tonga.

Currency

Notes come in denominations of one, two, five, 10, 20 and 50 pa'anga (written T$1, T$2 etc). Coins come in denominations of one, two, five, 10, 20 and 50 seniti. Older T$1 and T$2 coins will sometimes turn up in change. The T$2 coin is huge, and one old T$1 coin is rectangular in shape. If you get one of the latter, hold onto it – collectors have been known to pay quite a lot for one of these coins in good condition. For further information on numismatics in Tonga, contact the National Reserve Bank of Tonga (☎ 24-057; fax 24-201) on Salote Rd, Nuku'alofa.

Currency Exchange

Currency exchange is fairly straightforward. US, New Zealand and Australian dollars and British sterling seem to be the currencies most easily exchanged, but Deutschmarks, yen and francs are also acceptable, as are Fijian dollars.

A currency exchange window at the airport on Tongatapu is open for all arriving and departing international flights. In Nuku'alofa and Neiafu (Vava'u) you can change money at the Bank of Tonga, ANZ

✳✳✳✳✳✳✳✳✳✳✳✳✳✳✳✳ ✳✳✳✳✳✳✳✳✳✳✳✳✳✳ ✳

Money in Tonga

In the early 1800s, when young William Mariner explained the monetary system used by Europeans to the Tongan chief Finau, the latter understood it perfectly and immediately grasped the advantages it had over the Tongan Islands' traditional bartering system. In his innocent intelligence, however, he also realised the potential drawback of such a system and determined it unsuitable for use in his country. From Mariner's book:

If money were made of iron and could be converted into knives, axes and chisels there would be some sense in placing a value on it; but as it is, I see none. If a man has more yams than he wants, let him exchange some of them away for pork ... Certainly money is much handier and more convenient but then, as it will not spoil by being kept, people will store it up instead of sharing it out as a chief ought to do, and thus become selfish ... I understand now very well what it is that makes the *papalangis* so selfish – it is this money!

During the initial raid of the *Port-au-Prince*, Finau had been disappointed to find very little of value to him. Unlike Captain Cook's ships, which had carried all sorts of valuable trade baubles, Mariner's ship contained only whale oil, bits of iron and, for some inexplicable reason, 10,000 pieces of metal reminiscent of the beanlike *pa'anga* – playing pieces the Tongans used in a game called *lafo*. Finau had taken them for worthless objects and assumed that the ship had belonged to a very poor man indeed – perhaps to King George's cook (a cook being the lowest rank in Tongan society at the time). It was with regret that, later, he realised he had burned the ship of an extremely rich man without first securing all his 'pa'anga'. Not surprisingly, the Tongan unit of currency is now called the pa'anga.

✳✳✳✳✳✳✳✳✳✳✳✳✳✳✳✳✳ ✳✳✳✳✳✳✳✳✳✳✳✳✳✳ ✳

or MBF banks. The Bank of Tonga also has offices in 'Ohonua ('Eua) and Pangai (Ha'apai).

Banks are open from 9 am to 4 pm weekdays; in Nuku'alofa and Neiafu they're open on Saturday mornings as well. Money can be changed at the Treasury offices on the more remote islands of Niuatoputapu and Niuafo'ou.

Several middle and upper range hotels, such as the International Dateline Hotel in Nuku'alofa and the Paradise International Hotel in Vava'u, will exchange currency, but at a lower rate than the banks. It's a convenient service, though, when the banks are closed. Visitors must produce their passport when they want to change currency at a bank or hotel.

All brands of travellers cheques are acceptable and fetch 4% to 5% more than cash. If you need to purchase travellers cheques in Tonga, bear in mind that any

transaction with foreign currency will first be converted into pa'anga, then converted into the desired currency. You lose twice.

In mid-1998, exchange rates were:

Australia	A$1	=	T$0.86
New Zealand	NZ$1	=	T$0.77
United States	US$1	=	T$1.28
Canada	C$1	=	T$0.90
United Kingdom	UK£1	=	T$2.14
Germany	DM1	=	T$0.72
France	FFr1	=	T$0.21
Japan	¥100	=	T$0.99
Fiji	F$1	=	T$0.84

Tipping & Bargaining

Tipping and bargaining are not practised in Tonga.

Consumer Taxes

All prices in Tonga include 5% VAT. Hotel prices are subject to an additional 2.5%

room tax. No refunds are available to foreigners.

POST & COMMUNICATIONS
Post
Postage stamps in Tonga are unusual and
very collectible. They often come in odd
fruity shapes, vibrant colours and envelope-
swallowing sizes, and depict colourful
shells, birds and Tongan scenes or commemorate events such as royal birthdays,
exhibitions and visits by foreign heads of
state. The island of Niuafo'ou uses its own
stamps which colourfully represent that
island's uniqueness. Old and unusual
stamps may be purchased at the Philatelic
Bureau upstairs at the post office in
Nuku'alofa.

Tongan postal services are slow but generally reliable; service to Europe, North
America and Australasia is quite good.
There's a post office on every major island.
Post offices are generally open weekdays
from 8.30 or 9 am to 4 pm, except holidays,
with special opening hours and abbreviated
services around Christmas and New Year.

If possible, avoid posting anything from
the Niuas, particularly Niuafo'ou, since
communications there are limited and
weeks can go by without mail service.

Postage rates for letters sent from Tonga
are 60 seniti to the South Pacific region (including Australia and New Zealand), 80
seniti to the rest of the world. Postcards cost
45 seniti to send anywhere in the world.

Telephone & Fax
Cable & Wireless has offices in Nuku'alofa, 'Ohonua ('Eua), Pangai (Ha'apai),
Neiafu (Vava'u), Hihifo (Niuatoputapu) and
Niuafo'ou. International telephone calls,
telegrams, telex and fax services are available.

Reverse charge (collect) telephone calls
can be made only to Australia, New
Zealand, the USA, the UK and to other
South Pacific island nations.

Telephone calling cards from some international systems are accepted, including
AT&T, BTI, OTC, NZ Telecom, FINTEL

(Fiji), HTC (Hawaii) and ITU FORMAT.
Visa and MasterCard are accepted at the
Cable & Wireless office in Nuku'alofa.

Tonga's emergency phone number is
☎ 911. The international operator is ☎ 913.
Directory assistance is ☎ 910.

Tonga's country code is ☎ 676. It has no
local area codes.

Email & Internet
Tonga is on the Internet and an increasing
number of businesses have email and web
pages.

In Nuku'alofa you can send and receive
email messages on the computers at Moore
Electronics, upstairs in the Tungi Arcade on
Taufa'ahau Rd for $5 per day. If you'll be
staying a while, ask them about getting your
own email account, for T$20 per month.
Two Internet cafes will soon be opening in
Nuku'alofa.

In Vava'u, talk to the people at The
Moorings – they may be setting up a site
providing email access for travellers.

If you have your own computer (or
access to one), you can get an email/Inter-
net account from Cable & Wireless. A
temporary account (one month) will cost
you T$30.

Coconut Wireless
You may notice another means of communication in use throughout the islands: the
'coconut wireless'. Through an amazing
system unknown to western technology,
people all over the islands, especially in
Tongatapu, know what's going on in government, what foreigners are up to (they're
watching you), who is sleeping with whom,
what the king is doing at the moment and so
on, while it's happening or immediately
thereafter.

BOOKS
Given the brief history of its written language and relatively obscure geographical
position, a surprising number of books have
been written about Tonga. If you'd like to
do a bit of background reading before you
go, the following list includes many titles

which should be available in bookshops or libraries abroad.

Many of these books, though, are available only in Tonga. If you can't find them through your local bookshop or library, they can be ordered from the Friendly Islands Bookshop in Nuku'alofa (see Bookshops & Libraries at the end of this section).

Lonely Planet
If you're travelling farther afield in the Pacific, check out Lonely Planet books about other Pacific nations. See the back of this book for a complete list of Lonely Planet publications.

Guidebooks
If you're travelling by yacht in Tonga or elsewhere in the Pacific, a highly recommended guide is the hard-to-find *Landfalls of Paradise: The Guide to the Pacific Islands* by Earl R Hinz. The author, who has been a Pacific yachtie for much of his life, provides all the nitty-gritty on anchorages, navigation, marinas, fees and officialdom throughout the South and Central Pacific region. If you can't find it at marine supply stores, write to the publisher: Western Marine Enterprises, 3611 Motor Ave, Los Angeles, CA 90034 USA.

The Cruising Yachtsman's Guide to the Kingdom of Tonga by Colin Bailey, a more recent yachting book, and *A Yachtsman's Guide to Ha'apai* by Phil Cregeen, are available at the Friendly Islands Bookshop in Nuku'alofa.

Travel
An entertaining account of travel through the South Seas is *Slow Boats Home* by Gavin Young , the sequel to his earlier book *Slow Boats to China*. Combined, they recount the author's 1979 around-the-world voyage aboard a wide range of maritime transport. Although there are only a few pages dealing with Tonga, a good part of his journey is aboard a Tongan boat. It's a worthwhile read for any South Pacific traveller.

The Pacific by Simon Winchester is an entertaining but rather hastily assembled account of his journalistic journeys around the great ocean. *Transit of Venus: Travels in the Pacific* by Julian Evans chronicles the author's shoestring travels around the Pacific by boat and ship. It includes a very entertaining chapter on Tonga and is probably the best modern travelogue about the Pacific.

Then there's the book travellers love to hate, *The Happy Isles of Oceania: Paddling the Pacific* by Paul Theroux. This time, the perpetually miserable Theroux finds himself kayaking around in the South Pacific islands. Cynics will love the amusingly downbeat prose; his observations all seem to have been made through grey-coloured glasses and he is particularly hard on Tonga in general and Nuku'alofa in particular.

History
Tonga Islands: William Mariner's Account by Dr John Martin was originally published as *An Account of the Natives of the Tonga Islands* in 1817, and is the best work available on the nature of pre-Christian Tonga. It tells the story of the capture of the *Port-au-Prince* and Mariner's enforced stay on Tonga from 1805 to 1809, and discusses the religion, language, customs and lifestyle of the Tongan people. It makes very interesting and entertaining reading. *The Tonga Book* by Paul W Dale is a contemporary reworking of Mariner's story.

Island Kingdom: Tonga Ancient and Modern by IC Campbell is a comprehensive, up-to-date, very readable history of Tonga.

Nomads of the Wind follows the 1993-94 BBC series of the same name. It deals with the Polynesian migrations around the Pacific and how they relate to the divergence and development of present Polynesian cultures.

Pathways to the Tongan Past by Dick Spennemann is an introduction to the ancient history and archaeology of Tonga, with interesting maps. *Archaeology of Tonga* by WE McKern, an academic book telling of a detailed archaeological study made here in 1920-21, is now in reprint.

The Journals of Captain Cook, edited by JC Beaglehole, is a straight-from-the-horse's-mouth account of early exploration in the Pacific and elsewhere. *The Mutiny on Board the HMS Bounty* by William Bligh is taken from his journals during and after his command of the *Bounty*.

Slavers in Paradise by HE Maude is a tragic and enlightening account of the kidnapping of Pacific Islanders by the Peruvian slave traders in the early 1860s.

A Dream of Islands by Gavan Dawes deals with the lives and perspectives of island-inspired authors and artists such as Gauguin, Melville and Stevenson.

Shirley Baker and the King of Tonga by Noel Rutherford tells the story of Revd Shirley Baker and King Tupou I.

The Fire Has Jumped, edited by Garth Rogers, is a rather disorganised but interesting account of the volcanic eruptions on Niuafo'ou in the mid-1940s and the subsequent resettlement of the people who lived there.

The King of Tonga: King Taufa'ahau Tupou IV by Nelson Eustis is a biography not only of Tonga's current king but also of the royal lineage that preceded him. It concentrates particularly on his mother, the beloved Queen Salote.

Missionaries & Churches

Church & State in Tonga by the Tongan historian Sione Lalukefu is an essential guide to the church's background and Tonga's religious origins.

In Some Sense the Work of an Individual: Alfred Willis and the Tongan Anglican Mission, 1902-1920 by Stephen L Donald tells the story of the introduction and development of the Anglican church in the kingdom of Tonga.

Story of My Life by Semisi Nau is the autobiography of an early Tongan Methodist missionary to Ontong Java in the Solomon Islands. *Joel Pulu – Autobiography of a Tongan Minister* is the autobiography of the first Tongan missionary to Fiji.

Residents' Accounts

The most famous account by a resident of Tonga is of course the account of William Mariner's sojourn in pre-Christian times; see the History section.

Friendly Isles: A Tale of Tonga and *'Utulei, My Tongan Home* by Patricia Ledyard both relate anecdotes of Tongan life by an American woman who came to Vava'u as a teacher in the 1950s. She married the doctor there and never left. Both books are quite entertaining.

South Sea Reminiscences: Mrs Emma Schober in the Kingdom of Tonga 1902-1921 is the autobiography of the postal bride of a German trader who lived in Tonga.

Tales of the South Pacific, *Rascals in Paradise* and *Return to Paradise*, by James Michener, are collections of short stories dealing with life in, and observations of, the South Pacific from WWII onward.

Sociology & Anthropology

Tongan Society by Edward Windlow Gifford, the definitive 1929 study, was reprinted in New York in 1985 and is now being reprinted again.

The New Friendly Islanders by Kenneth Bain deals with the recent social changes and how they relate to Tongan tradition and world trends. Recommended.

Becoming Tongan: An Ethnography of Childhood by Helen Morton is an ethnographic study of factors influencing the bringing up of children in Tonga.

Kinship to Kingship: Gender Hierarchy and State Formation in the Tongan Islands by Christine Ward Gailey is an ethnohistorical anthropology book presenting a feminist view of women's loss of power over a 300-year period as the state of Tonga evolved.

Our Crowded Islands by 'Epeli Hau'ofa is an enlightening essay about population growth and outside influences on the island of Tongatapu. Recommended.

Art, Music & Dance

The Art of Tonga by Keith St Cartmail is a

high-quality coffee-table book on Tongan art and artefacts.

Sounds of Change in Tonga: Dance, Music and Cultural Dynamics in a Polynesian Kingdom by Ad Linkels is a study of changes taking place in traditional music and dance in Tonga.

Otuhaka by Kik Velt is a detailed diagrammatic explanation of movements in this ancient sitting-down dance. *Poetry in Motion* by Adrienne Kaeppler is a detailed description and explanation of Tongan dancing, for the specialist.

Tapa in Tonga by Wendy Arbcit presents photos and text showing and explaining the manufacture, uses and significance of tapa in Tonga. *Making Mats and Barkcloth in the Kingdom of Tonga* by KE James is about the manufacture and uses of mats and tapa in Tonga. *Patterns of Polynesia: Tonga* by Ailsa Robertson shows the patterns used to decorate tapa.

Photography

Tonga the Friendly Islands by Fred J Eckert is a fine, glossy book of photographs of people and places.

Pathways to the Tongan Present by Kurt Düring is a book of historical photos.

Nature

Birds of Fiji, Tonga & Samoa by Dick Watling is the definitive book on the birds of the South Pacific region. It includes lovely colour illustrations of all the region's endemic and migratory birds.

Field Guide to Landbirds of Tonga by Claudia Matavalea of the Tongan Wildlife Centre Bird Park on Tongatapu is available at the Bird Park and at the Friendly Islands Bookshop in Nuku'alofa.

Tongan Herbal Medicine by W Arthur Whistler is a good book relating how Tongans use the vegetation around them to heal illnesses and wounds.

Language

Introduction to the Tongan Language by Edgar Tu'inukuafe is a simple introduction to Tongan grammar, phrases and vocabu-lary. *Tongan Grammar* by CM Churchward is a complete study of the Tongan language, but you must be familiar with the principles of linguistics in order to get much out of it.

For serious students, Eric Shumway of Brigham Young University has put together *An Intensive Course in Tongan*, with 200 lessons accompanied by 23 cassette tapes. It costs around US$100. Contact the Institute for Polynesian Studies, BYU, Laie, HI 96762, USA. The book alone, or limited numbers of the book with tapes, are available through the Friendly Islands Bookshop in Nuku'alofa.

The Student's English-Tongan and Tongan-English Dictionary by Rev Richard & 'Ofa Thompson and *A Simplified Dictionary of Modern Tongan* by Edgar Tu'inukuafe are good, simple paperback Tongan-English dictionaries. C Maxwell Churchward's *Tongan-English Dictionary* is a more complete (though somewhat dated) English-Tongan and Tongan-English tome.

Cookbooks

The Niu Idea Cookbook (The Peace Corps), available only at the Friendly Islands Bookshop in Nuku'alofa, is a good collection of recipes for delicious Tongan dishes.

The Tastes of Tonga by the Vaiola Hospital Board of Visitors is another fine book containing Tongan and international recipes.

Miscellaneous

Pacific Tourism as Islanders See It has essays by islanders regarding the increase of tourism and, consequently, outside influences on their cultures and lifestyles – a pertinent moral dilemma.

Tongan Place Names by Edward Winslow Gifford gives 4776 place names, their meanings and explanations.

A fun book for tourists, especially yachties and mariners, is *Stars Over Tonga* by Kik Velt. It has lots of information about Tongan tradition and language, in addition to the astronomical descriptions and 'star charts' for Tonga. The separate *Stars Over*

Tonga – Star Locator enables you to construct your own mobile star locator.

Bookshops & Libraries

Although reading material is available in Tonga, it's a good idea to bring along most of the books you'll be needing. Once you've exhausted your supply, you can trade books at most hotels or guesthouses, or at Tapacraft in Nuku'alofa (or buy used books for T$1). Other travellers are another good source of exchange material.

The only bookshop of any consequence in Tonga is the Friendly Islands Bookshop, with its main store on Taufa'ahau Rd in Nuku'alofa, plus branch stores in Vava'u, Ha'apai and 'Eua. The branch stores have a much more limited selection of books than the main store (the paperbacks are kept in a box under the counter, you must ask for them), but you can order any book from the main store, which sends a weekly delivery to each of the branch stores.

Friendly Islands offers a good selection of books about Tonga as well as paperback novels, biographies, travel guides (including Lonely Planet books), travelogues, newspapers, magazines and plenty more.

The Friendly Islands Bookshop address is PO Box 124, Nuku'alofa, Kingdom of Tonga (☎ (676) 23-787; fax 23-631; fibs@candw.to).

If you'll be in Tonga for a while you can get a library card for T$2 annually (T$1 for students) and borrow books from the library downstairs in the basilica in Nuku'alofa.

NEWSPAPERS & MAGAZINES

The Tonga Chronicle, the official newspaper published by the Tongan government, comes out weekly in two editions: one in Tongan, the other in English. The English version is smaller, and it tells only what the government wants foreigners in Tonga to know about – crime and other news considered unpleasant by the government goes unreported. Most news is local, with little information about the outside world. It comes out on Thursday and costs 40 seniti.

Taimi Tonga (Tonga Times), published weekly in Tongan, is an independent newspaper representing the views of the middle class both inside Tonga and abroad. It's a very middle-of-the-road paper, but since it is independently published and doesn't only give the official government line, it's considered pretty racy for Tonga. It comes out every Wednesday.

The most radical newspaper in Tonga is the *Ko e Kele'a* (The Conch Shell), published in Tongan by the parliamentary opposition leader 'Akilisi Pohiva and supported by his Tongan Pro-Democracy Movement. Suffice to say that you'll read things here that don't appear in the *Chronicle*! This paper comes out as the need arises, usually monthly or bi-monthly.

A variety of religious newspapers (published in Tongan by the Catholics, the Wesleyans etc) are published monthly.

The bi-monthly news magazine, *Matangi Tonga* (Wind of Tonga), published in English, deals with Tongan issues at home and abroad.

The Friendly Islands Bookshop in Nuku'alofa carries all the Tongan newspapers, plus international newspapers and magazines. The *New Zealand Herald* and the *Fiji Times*, both daily newspapers published in English, arrive in Tonga on a weekly basis. *The Guardian* (a daily paper from England), *The Economist* (a weekly international business magazine) and the international edition of *Time* magazine are all available· here, along with various other international magazines.

RADIO & TV

The government-owned Radio Tonga, A3Z, broadcasts a mix of traditional Tongan music, international rock music and worldwide news. New Zealand news is broadcast at 9 am Monday to Saturday, and is repeated in the evening. There are no news broadcasts on Sunday. The Voice of America is broadcast at 1.15 pm daily except Sunday; the BBC World Service is broadcast at 7 am, 1 pm and 8 pm Monday to Saturday and at 4 pm on Sunday.

Tonga has one TV station, channel 7,

which is a private Christian broadcasting station. CNN news is broadcast from 7.30 to 8 pm, Monday to Saturday evenings. Only Tongatapu has television – it has yet to reach the other islands, although video is popular everywhere. In the Niuas, you can pick up American Samoan broadcasting on very clear days.

PHOTOGRAPHY & VIDEO
Film & Equipment
Film is more expensive in Tonga than in Europe, North America and Australasia, so stock up before you leave home. In Nuku'alofa, film costs around T$7/8 for a roll of 24/36 colour print film, or T$7/14 for a roll of 24/36 colour slide film. This is for 100ASA film; 200ASA and 400ASA film is available, but it costs more. You can buy film at a few shops in Nuku'alofa and Neiafu.

Colour print processing can be done in Nuku'alofa; the one-hour photo processing at the Fung Shing Fast Photo shop on Railway Rd is often recommended. There's nowhere in Tonga to process black-and-white prints or slides.

If you're shooting slides, you'll probably get the best results with Fujichrome 100, Velvia 50 or Kodachrome 64. Slide film is sold in Nuku'alofa.

Camera equipment is expensive in Tonga so bring everything from home, especially spare batteries for cameras and flash units. Useful accessories include a small flash, a cable release, a polarising filter, a lens cleaning kit and silica-gel packs to protect against Tonga's high humidity.

Photography
Points worth remembering about photography in Tonga include the heat, humidity, very fine sand, tropical sunlight, equatorial shadows and the wonderful opportunities for underwater photography. Don't leave your camera for long in direct sunlight and don't store used film for long in the humid conditions, as it will fade.

The best times to take photographs on sunny days are the first two hours after sunrise and the last two before sunset. This brings out the best colours and takes advantage of the colour-enhancing, long, red rays cast by a low sun. At other times, colours will be washed out by harsh sunlight and glare, although it's possible to counter this by using a polarising (UV) filter. If you're shooting on beaches, it's important to adjust for glare from water or sand; and keep your photographic equipment well away from sand and salt water.

When photographing outdoors, take light readings on the subject and not the brilliant background or your shots will all turn out underexposed. Likewise for people shots: dark faces will appear featureless if you set the exposure for background light.

Video
Make sure you keep batteries charged, and have the necessary charger, plugs and transformer for the country you're visiting. In most countries, including Tonga, you can buy video cartridges easily in large towns and cities, but make sure you buy the correct format. It's usually worth buying at least a few cartridges duty free to start off your trip.

The rules regarding people's sensitivities are the same as for still photography. A video camera shoved in their face is probably even more annoying and offensive for locals than a still camera.

Photographing People
If you think the quest for the perfect 'people shot' is a photographer's greatest challenge, go to Tonga. It would be safe to say that nowhere else in the world will you find so many willing and photogenic subjects for your camera as in Tonga. In fact, if you're not quick about it, your perfect 'people shot' could easily turn into a crowd scene!

Having said that, some Tongans may be suspicious of your motives or simply interested in whatever economic advantage they can gain from your desire to photograph them. Others may simply be self-conscious about their appearance; many people will feel they must change into their Sunday clothing before they can pose for a photo. So although most people will be falling over each other to get into your photographs, respect the wishes of anyone who doesn't wish to be photographed. Always ask permission to photograph if a candid shot can't be made, and don't insist or snap a picture anyway if permission is denied.

Often people will want a copy of your photos. Take their address and send the photo by post once it's processed. Since most Tongans don't have cameras, photos make excellent gifts.

TIME

Tonga promotes itself as the 'land where time begins'; along with the Chukotka peninsula in far eastern Russia, Tonga is the first place to see a new day. It is also the place where the local way of doing things is 'tomorrow', 'maybe some day', 'come back later' or 'never'.

Due to an odd kink in the International Date Line, Tonga is actually 20 minutes east of the 180th meridian, placing it 13 hours ahead of Greenwich Mean Time. Noon in Tonga is 11 pm the previous day in London, 3 pm the previous day in Los Angeles and 9 am the same day in Sydney. When New Zealand is on summer daylight saving time, Tonga and New Zealand share the same time; the rest of the year there's a one-hour difference. In the Samoas, which are directly north of Tonga, the time would be noon the previous day!

ELECTRICITY

Power in Tonga is 240V, 50HZ AC. Three-pronged plugs used in New Zealand and Australia are OK here. European appliances require a plug adaptor. US appliances require a plug adaptor plus a voltage converter.

WEIGHTS & MEASURES

Tonga uses the standard metric system for everything except land area, which is measured in acres. For help converting between metric and imperial units, see the table inside the back cover of this book.

LAUNDRY

All places to stay in Tonga make some provision for guests' laundry needs, offering a laundry service, a place to wash your own clothes, or both. Nuku'alofa and Neiafu (Vava'u) have commercial laundries.

TOILETS

Tonga has flush toilets. You may not spot any public toilets, but you can usually duck into a restaurant in an emergency. In remote areas or islands, pit toilets are used.

HEALTH

There are few serious health risks in Tonga. You probably won't get anything worse than 'Polynesian paralysis' (laziness).

Overall, Tonga has a fairly healthy population and environment. However, there is a chance of contracting hepatitis or possibly a bacterial infection. Food poisoning is also a possibility (as it is at home) but, if you do become ill and symptoms persist, or if you come up against a serious health problem, you should seek trained medical assistance. It's also a good idea to see your doctor before travelling to another country, especially in the tropics.

Travel health depends on your predeparture preparations, your daily health care while travelling and how you handle any medical problem that does develop. While the potential dangers can seem quite frightening, in reality few travellers experience anything more than upset stomachs.

Predeparture planning

Immunisations Vaccinations provide protection against diseases you may encounter along the way. A yellow fever vaccination and related documentation is only necessary if you arrive in Tonga directly from an infected area such as Africa or South America. You usually have to go to a special yellow fever vaccination centre for immunisation. Otherwise, the only recommended jabs for travel to Tonga are tetanus, polio and gamma globulin or a hepatitis vaccine.

Plan ahead for getting your vaccinations: some require more than one injection, while

✳✳✳✳✳✳✳✳✳✳✳✳✳✳✳✳✳✳✳✳✳✳✳✳✳✳✳✳✳✳✳✳✳✳

Medical Kit Check List

- Aspirin or paracetamol (acetaminophen in the US) – for pain or fever
- Antihistamine (such as Benadryl) – useful as a decongestant for colds and allergies, to ease the itch from insect bites or stings, and to help prevent motion sickness. Antihistamines may cause sedation and interact with alcohol so care should be taken when using them; take one you know and have used before, if possible
- Antibiotics – useful if you're travelling well off the beaten track, but they must be prescribed; carry the prescription with you
- Loperamide (eg Imodium) or Lomotil for diarrhoea; prochlorperazine (eg Stemetil) or metaclopramide (eg Maxalon) for nausea and vomiting
- Rehydration mixture – for treatment of severe diarrhoea; particularly important for travelling with children
- Antiseptic such as povidone-iodine (eg Betadine) – for cuts and grazes
- Multivitamins – especially for long trips when dietary vitamin intake may be inadequate
- Calamine lotion or aluminium sulphate spray (eg Stingose) – to ease irritation from bites or stings
- Bandages and Band-aids
- Scissors, tweezers and a thermometer (note that mercury thermometers are prohibited by airlines)
- Cold and flu tablets and throat lozenges. Pseudoephedrine hydrochloride (Sudafed) may be useful if you are flying with a cold, to avoid ear damage
- Insect repellent, sunscreen, chap stick and water purification tablets
- A couple of syringes

✳✳✳✳✳✳✳✳✳✳✳✳✳✳✳✳✳✳✳✳✳✳✳✳✳✳✳✳✳✳✳✳✳✳

some vaccinations should not be given together. It's recommended you seek medical advice at least six weeks before your travel date.

Record all vaccinations on an International Health Certificate, which is available from your doctor or government health department.

Discuss your requirements with your doctor. Vaccinations you should consider for this trip include:

Hepatitis A – the most common travel-acquired illness after diarrhoea which can put you out of action for weeks. Havrix 1440 is a vaccination which provides long term immunity (possibly more than 10 years) after an initial injection and a booster at six to 12 months. The long term protection offered by this vaccine should prove particularly useful for frequent or long-term travellers. Gamma globulin is not a vaccination but is a ready-made antibody collected from blood donations. It should be given close to departure because, depending on the dose, it only protects for two to six months.

Diphtheria & Tetanus – diphtheria can be a fatal throat infection and tetanus can be a fatal wound infection. Everyone should have these vaccinations. After an initial course of three injections, boosters should be given every 10 years.

Hepatitis B – this is spread by blood or by sexual activity. Travellers who should consider a hepatitis B vaccination include those visiting countries where there are known to be many carriers, where blood transfusions may not be adequately screened or where sexual contact is a possibility. It involves three injections, the quickest course being over three weeks with a booster at 12 months.

Polio – polio is a serious, easily transmitted disease, still prevalent in many developing countries. Everyone should keep up to date with this vaccination. A booster every 10 years maintains immunity.

Health Insurance It is vital that you make sure you have adequate health insurance.

See Travel Insurance under Documents in this chapter for details.

Travel Health Guides If you are planning to be away or travelling in remote areas for a long period of time, you may like to consider taking a more detailed health guide.

Staying Healthy in Asia, Africa & Latin America, Dirk Schroeder, Moon Publications, 1994. Probably the best all-round guide to carry; it's detailed and well organised.
Travellers' Health, Dr Richard Dawood, Oxford University Press, 1995. Comprehensive, easy to read, authoritative and highly recommended, although it's rather large to lug around.
Travel with Children, Maureen Wheeler, Lonely Planet Publications, 1995. Includes advice on travel health for younger children.

Travel Health Information In the US you can request a health and safety information bulletin on the South Pacific countries by writing to the Overseas Citizens Emergency Center, Bureau of Consular Affairs Office, State Department, Washington, DC 20520. This office also has a special telephone number for emergencies while abroad (☎ (202) 632-5525).

The International Association for Medical Assistance to Travellers (IAMAT) at 417 Center St, Lewiston, New York, NY 14092, USA can provide you with a list of English-speaking physicians in the Pacific countries.

In the UK, contact the Medical Advisory Services for Travellers Abroad (MASTA) (☎ (0171) 631-4408), Keppel Street, London WC1E 7HT. MASTA provides a wide range of services including a choice of concise or comprehensive 'Health Briefs' and a range of medical supplies. Another source of medical information and supplies is the British Airways Travel Clinic (☎ (0171) 831-5333). The Department of Health publishes leaflets SA40/41 on travellers' health requirements, and operates a phone service (☎ (0800) 555-777).

In Australia, contact a Travellers' Medical and Vaccination Centre in Sydney (☎ (02) 9221-7133) or Melbourne (☎ (03) 9602-5788) for general health information pertaining to Pacific countries.

There are also a number of excellent travel health sites on the Internet. From the Lonely Planet home page there are links at www.lonelyplanet.com.au/weblinks/wlprep .htm#heal to the World Health Organisation, the US Center for Disease Control & Prevention and Stanford University Travel Medicine Service.

Other Preparations Make sure you're healthy before you go away. If you're going on a long trip make sure your teeth are OK. If you wear glasses or contact lenses, take a spare pair and your prescription.

If you require a particular medication take an adequate supply, as it may not be available locally. Take part of the packaging showing the generic name, rather than the brand, which will make getting replacements easier. It's a good idea to have a legible prescription or letter from your doctor to show that you legally use the medication to avoid any problems.

Basic Rules
Food Care in what you eat and drink is the most important health rule; stomach upsets are the most common travel health problem in Tonga but most of these will be minor. The most common complaint of visitors is called 'Tonga Tummy'. Don't be paranoid about sampling local foods, though – it's all part of the travel experience and shouldn't be missed.

There is an old colonial adage which says: 'If you can cook it, boil it or peel it you can eat it, otherwise forget it'. Vegetables and fruit should be washed with purified water or rainwater, or peeled where possible. Beware of ice cream which is sold in the street or anywhere it might have been melted and refrozen; if there's any doubt (eg a power cut in the last day or two) steer well clear. Shellfish such as mussels, oysters and clams should be avoided as well as undercooked meat, particularly in the form of mince. Steaming does not make shellfish safe for eating.

If a place looks clean and well run and the vendor also looks clean and healthy, then the food is probably safe. In general, places that are packed with travellers or locals will be fine, while empty restaurants are questionable. The food in busy restaurants is cooked and eaten quite quickly with little standing around and is probably not reheated.

Water The water that emerges from Tongan taps can taste foul and briny but it's safe to drink in the major towns. It's more suspect in the villages, or out in the bush. Nuku'alofa's tap water is safe to drink, but it doesn't taste good – it has such a high natural mineral (limestone) content that you can see a white film floating on top of the water after you boil it.

Most people in Tonga drink rainwater, which is collected in concrete rainwater tanks (*vaisima*). Rainwater is available almost everywhere in Tonga; bottled purified water is available in Nuku'alofa and larger towns. Remember that rainwater is only as clean as whatever it's kept in – while most rainwater is fine to drink, there's the possibility of contamination if it's not properly stored.

If you don't know for certain that the water is safe, assume the worst. Special care should be taken immediately following a cyclone or other bad storm. Reputable brands of bottled water or soft drinks are generally fine, although in some places bottles may be refilled with tap water. Only use water from containers with a serrated seal – not tops or corks.

Take care with fruit juice, particularly if water may have been added. Milk should be treated with suspicion as it is often unpasteurised, though boiled milk is fine if it is kept hygienically. Tea or coffee should be OK, since the water should have been boiled. Don't forget ice is just as suspect.

Water Purification The simplest way of purifying water is to boil it thoroughly. Vigorously boiling for eight to 10 minutes should be satisfactory.

Consider purchasing a water filter for a long trip. There are two main kinds of filter. Total filters take out all parasites, bacteria and viruses and make water safe to drink. They are often expensive, but they can be more cost effective than buying bottled water. Simple filters (which can even be a nylon mesh bag) take out dirt and larger foreign bodies from the water so that chemical solutions work much more effectively; if water is dirty, chemical solutions may not work at all. It's very important when buying a filter to read the specifications, so that you know exactly what it removes from the water and what it doesn't. Simple filtering will not remove all dangerous organisms, so if you cannot boil water it should be treated chemically.

Chlorine tablets (Puritabs, Steritabs or other brand names) will kill many pathogens, but not some parasites like giardia and amoebic cysts. Iodine is more effective in purifying water and is available in tablet form (such as Potable Aqua). Follow the directions carefully, but remember that too much iodine can be harmful.

Medical Care in Tonga

Not surprisingly, medical care is limited in Tonga. There are hospitals in Vaiola (Tongatapu), Hihifo (Ha'apai) and Neiafu (Vava'u) which are competent with minor ailments and will dispense medicines, but serious medical problems should be taken to Hawaii (expensive!), Australia or New Zealand. An entire day should be set aside for a visit to hospital clinics. Consultations cost T$2; medicines are free for Tongans and foreigners pay only a token fee.

Tonga has several private physicians. In Nuku'alofa you may want to visit Kiwi Dr Glennis Mafi at the Ha'ateiho Village Mission Clinic (☎ 29-052) in Ha'ateiho, 5km south of Nuku'alofa, or German Dr Heinz Betz at the German Clinic (☎ 22-736, home 29-978) on Wellington Rd, in town. In Vava'u, try Dr Alfredo Carafa at the Italian Clinic & Pharmacy (☎ 70-607) in Neiafu. In Ha'apai, your only choice is the hospital in Hihifo, on the south end of

Pangai, Lifuka, but the care there is not the best (to put it politely). If you develop a serious health problem in Ha'apai, try your luck with the hospital but if the problem persists, go somewhere else for treatment.

Pharmacies & Medicines If you come down with a potentially dangerous bacterial infection requiring antibiotic treatment, you may be faced with a problem. Those travelling in Tonga away from Tongatapu or Vava'u may want to carry a cycle each of a range of antibiotics – talk to your doctor before you leave home and ask to be prescribed treatments for all the ailments described later in this section.

Medical Problems & Treatment
Self-diagnosis and treatment can be risky, so you should always seek medical help. Although we do give drug dosages in this section, they are for emergency use only. Correct diagnosis is vital.

Your hotel or guesthouse, an embassy, consulate or major hotel can usually recommend a good place to go for medical care and advice. In some places standards of medical attention are so low that for some ailments the best advice is to get on a plane and go somewhere else.

Environmental Hazards
Fungal Infections Fungal infections occur more commonly in hot weather and are usually found on the scalp, between the toes or fingers, in the groin and on the body (ringworm). You get ringworm (which is a fungal infection, not a worm) from infected animals or other people. Moisture encourages these infections.

To prevent fungal infections wear loose, comfortable clothes, avoid artificial fibres, wash frequently and dry carefully. If you do get an infection, wash the infected area at least daily with a disinfectant or medicated soap and water and rinse and dry well. Apply an antifungal cream or powder like tolnaftate (Tinaderm). Try to expose the infected area to air or sunlight as much as possible and wash all towels and underwear

in hot water, change them often and let them dry in the sun.

Heat Exhaustion Dehydration and salt deficiency can cause heat exhaustion. Take time to acclimatise to high temperatures, drink sufficient liquids and do not do anything too physically demanding.

Salt deficiency is characterised by fatigue, lethargy, headaches, giddiness and muscle cramps; salt tablets may help, but adding extra salt to your food is better.

Heat Stroke This serious, occasionally fatal, condition can occur if the body's heat-regulating mechanism breaks down and the body temperature rises to dangerous levels. Long, continuous periods of exposure to high temperatures and insufficient fluids can leave you extremely svulnerable to heat stroke.

The symptoms are feeling unwell, not sweating very much (or at all) and a high body temperature (39°C to 41°C or 102°F to 106°F). Where sweating has ceased the skin becomes flushed and red. Severe, throbbing headaches and lack of coordination will also occur, and the sufferer may be confused or aggressive. Eventually the victim will become delirious or convulse. Hospitalisation is essential, but in the interim get victims out of the sun, remove their clothing, cover them with a wet sheet or towel and then fan continually. Give fluids if they are conscious.

Jet Lag Jet lag is experienced when a person travels by air across more than three time zones (each time zone usually represents a one-hour time difference). It occurs because many of the functions of the human body (such as temperature, pulse rate and emptying of the bladder and bowels) are regulated by internal 24-hour cycles. When we travel long distances rapidly, our bodies take time to adjust to the 'new time' of our destination, and we may experience fatigue, disorientation, insomnia, anxiety, impaired concentration and loss of appetite. These effects will usually be gone within three

HOLGER LEUE

PATRICK HORTON

HOLGER LEUE

PATRICK HORTON

HOLGER LEUE

Top: Store, Nuku'alofa, Tongatapu
Middle Left: Red taro, Vava'u
Middle Right: Fish, Atata Island

Bottom Left: Fish catch, Nuku'alofa
Bottom Right: Roast pig, Neiafu, Vava'u

NANCY KELLER

DEANNA SWANEY

Top: Blowholes, Tongatapu
Bottom: Looking down from the cliffs at 'Anokula, 'Eua

days of arrival, but to minimise the impact of jet lag:

Rest for a couple of days prior to departure.
Try to select flight schedules that minimise sleep deprivation; arriving late in the day means you can go to sleep soon after you arrive. For very long flights, try to organise a stopover.
Avoid excessive eating (which bloats the stomach) and alcohol (which causes dehydration) during the flight. Instead, drink plenty of non-carbonated, non-alcoholic drinks such as fruit juice or water.
Avoid smoking.
Make yourself comfortable by wearing loose-fitting clothes and perhaps bringing an eye mask and ear plugs to help you sleep.
Try to sleep at the appropriate time for the time zone you are travelling to.

Motion Sickness Eating lightly before and during a trip will reduce the chances of motion sickness. If you are prone to motion sickness try to find a place that minimises movement – near the wing on aircraft, close to midships on boats, near the centre on buses. Fresh air and looking at the horizon usually help; reading and cigarette smoke make it worse. Commercial motion-sickness preparations, which can cause drowsiness, have to be taken before the trip commences – if you wait until you feel sick to take it, it's too late. Ginger (available in capsule form) and peppermint (including mint-flavoured sweets) are natural preventatives.

Prickly Heat Prickly heat is an itchy rash caused by excessive perspiration trapped under the skin. It usually strikes people who have just arrived in a hot climate. Keeping cool, bathing often, drying the skin and using a mild talcum or prickly heat powder or resorting to air-conditioning may help.

Sunburn In the tropics you can get sunburnt surprisingly quickly, even through cloud. Use a sunscreen, hat, and barrier cream for your nose and lips. Calamine lotion, Stingose or aloe vera are good for mild sunburn. Protect your eyes with good quality sunglasses, particularly if you will be near water or sand.

Infectious Diseases
Diarrhoea Simple things like a change of water, food or climate can all cause a mild bout of diarrhoea, but a few rushed toilet trips with no other symptoms is not indicative of a major problem.

Dehydration is the main danger with any diarrhoea, particularly in children or the elderly as dehydration can occur quite quickly. Under all circumstances *fluid replacement* (at least equal to the volume being lost) is the most important thing to remember. Weak black tea with a little sugar, soda water, or soft drinks allowed to go flat and diluted 50% with clean water are all good. With severe diarrhoea a rehydrating solution is preferable to replace minerals and salts lost. Commercially available oral rehydration salts (ORS) are very useful; add them to boiled or bottled water. In an emergency you can make up a solution of six teaspoons of sugar and a half teaspoon of salt to a litre of boiled or bottled water. You need to drink at least the same volume of fluid that you are losing in bowel movements and vomiting. Urine is the best guide to the adequacy of replacement – if you have small amounts of concentrated urine, you need to drink more. Keep drinking small amounts often. Stick to a bland diet as you recover.

Lomotil or Imodium can be used to bring relief from the symptoms, although they do not actually cure the problem. Only use these drugs if you do not have access to toilets, eg if you *must* travel. For children under 12 years Lomotil and Imodium are not recommended. Do not use these drugs if the person has a high fever or is severely dehydrated.

In certain situations antibiotics may be required: diarrhoea with blood or mucous (dysentery), any fever, watery diarrhoea with fever and lethargy, persistent diarrhoea not improving after 48 hours and severe diarrhoea. In these situations avoid gut paralysing drugs like Imodium or Lomotil.

Giardiasis This is another type of diarrhoea. The parasite causing this intestinal disorder is present in contaminated water. The symptoms are stomach cramps, nausea, a bloated stomach, watery, foul-smelling diarrhoea and frequent gas. Giardiasis can appear several weeks after you have been exposed to the parasite. The symptoms may disappear for a few days and then return; this can go on for several weeks. Tinidazole, known as Fasigyn, or metronidazole (Flagyl) are the recommended drugs. Treatment is a 2gm single dose of Fasigyn or 250mg of Flagyl three times daily for five to 10 days.

Hepatitis Hepatitis is a general term for inflammation of the liver. It's a common disease worldwide. The symptoms are fever, chills, headache, fatigue, feelings of weakness and aches and pains, followed by loss of appetite, nausea, vomiting, abdominal pain, dark urine, light-coloured faeces, jaundiced (yellow) skin and the whites of the eyes may turn yellow.

Hepatitis A is transmitted by contaminated food and drinking water. The disease poses a real threat to the western traveller. You should seek medical advice, but there is not much you can do apart from rest, drink lots of fluids, eat lightly and avoid fatty foods. You should avoid alcohol for some time after the illness, as the liver needs time to recover.

There are almost 300 million chronic carriers of Hepatitis B in the world. It is spread through contact with infected blood, blood products or body fluids, for example through sexual contact, unsterilised needles and blood transfusions, or contact with blood via small breaks in the skin. Other risk situations include having a shave, tattoo, or having your body pierced with contaminated equipment. The symptoms of type B may be more severe and may lead to long term problems.

HIV & AIDS HIV, the Human Immunodeficiency Virus, develops into AIDS, Acquired Immune Deficiency Syndrome, which is a fatal disease. HIV is a major problem in many countries. Any exposure to blood, blood products or body fluids may put the individual at risk. The disease is often transmitted through sexual contact or dirty needles – vaccinations, acupuncture, tattooing and body piercing can be potentially as dangerous as intravenous drug use. HIV/AIDS can also be spread through infected blood transfusions; some developing countries cannot afford to screen blood used for transfusions.

If you do need an injection, ask to see the syringe unwrapped in front of you, or take a needle and syringe pack with you. Fear of HIV infection should never preclude treatment for serious medical conditions.

Intestinal Worms These parasites are most common in rural, tropical areas. The different worms have different ways of infecting people. Some may be ingested on food, including undercooked meat, and some enter through your skin. Infestations may not show up for some time and, although they are generally not serious, if left untreated some can cause severe health problems later. Consider having a stool test when you return home.

Sexually Transmitted Diseases Gonorrhoea, herpes and syphilis are among these diseases; sores, blisters or rashes around the genitals, discharges or pain when urinating are common symptoms. In some STDs, such as wart virus or chlamydia, symptoms may be less marked or not observed at all, especially in women (women often show no symptoms of gonorrhoea, though men will have a painful discharge). Syphilis symptoms eventually disappear completely but the disease continues and can cause severe problems in later years.

While abstinence from sexual contact is the only 100% effective prevention, using condoms is also effective. The treatment of gonorrhoea and syphilis is with antibiotics. The different sexually transmitted diseases each require specific antibiotics. There is no cure for herpes or AIDS.

Insect-borne diseases

Dengue Fever There is no preventative drug available for this mosquito-spread disease which can be fatal in children. A sudden onset of fever, headaches and severe joint and muscle pains are the first signs before a rash develops. Recovery may be prolonged. Travellers are advised to prevent mosquito bites at all times to avoid this disease. See the following section on Insect Bites & Stings. With any type of dengue, aspirin-based drugs should be avoided.

Cuts, Bites & Stings

Insect Bites & Stings Ants, gnats, mosquitoes, bees, wasps and flies are annoying in Tonga. Cover yourself well with clothing and use insect repellent on exposed skin. Burning incense or mosquito coils and sleeping in screened rooms, under mosquito nets, in air-conditioned rooms or under fans also lowers the risk of being bitten. Mosquito coils are widely available in Tonga and the pyrethrin-based smoke kills mosquitoes – lighting a mosquito coil will make your room mosquito-free for several hours, or you can use insect spray. If you're going walking in humid or densely foliated areas, wear light cotton trousers and shoes, not shorts and sandals or thongs. Regardless of temperature, never wear shorts or thongs in the forest and remember to carry an effective insect repellent.

Bee, wasp, centipede and other insect stings are usually painful rather than dangerous. The large centipedes which live in Tonga (but are rarely seen) can give a painful or irritating bite but it's no more dangerous to your health than a bee or wasp sting. Calamine lotion or Stingose spray will give relief; ice packs and antihistamine cream will reduce the pain and swelling. Or you can reduce the itch by using a local remedy: pick a frangipani leaf and rub the white liquid oozing from the stem onto the bite. Aloe vera, which is often seen growing in Tonga, is also helpful. If you are allergic to bee or wasp stings, be sure to carry your medication with you.

The good news is that Tonga is free of both malaria and rabies at present. Buzzing mosquitoes may drive you to insanity at night and the fierce barking dogs may appear threatening, but they won't give you malaria or rabies. Mosquito repellent and nets will usually protect you from the insects, while a few well-aimed stones should keep aggressive dogs at bay. If you are bitten by a dog, you should have a tetanus vaccination within a few hours if you haven't had one during the past three years.

Bedbugs & Lice Bedbugs live in various places, but particularly in dirty mattresses and bedding, evidenced by spots of blood on bedclothes or on the wall. Bedbugs leave itchy bites in neat rows. Calamine lotion or Stingose spray may help.

All lice cause itching and discomfort. They make themselves at home in your hair (head lice), your clothing (body lice) or in your pubic hair (crabs). You catch lice through direct contact with infected people or by sharing combs, clothing and the like. Powder or shampoo treatment will kill the lice and infected clothing should then be washed in very hot, soapy water and left in the sun to dry.

Sea Creatures Certain cone shells found in Tonga (and other places in the Pacific) can sting dangerously or even fatally. *Do not touch any cone-shaped shell.*

Various fish and other sea creatures can sting or bite dangerously, or are dangerous to eat. Listen to local advice to avoid them.

Several species of jellyfish deliver an excruciating sting. Local advice is also the best way of avoiding contact with these sea creatures. If you do get stung, carefully pull the tentacles off your skin and rinse with cold water. Dousing in vinegar will neutralise the venom, get rid of the sting and de-activate any stingers that have not fired; this is also useful if you touch fire coral, which causes a stinging skin reaction. Stingose is a good treatment; calamine lotion, antihistamines and analgesics may also reduce the reaction and relieve the pain. The most effective folk remedy for jellyfish stings, used all over the world, is to apply fresh urine to the stings as soon as possible – something in the urine neutralises the jellyfish venom.

On very rare occasions someone will see a poisonous stonefish or stingray. Stonefish look exactly like stones, hence their name; when they are hanging around coral or stony areas, as they usually do, their natural camouflage makes it practically impossible to see them. The poison of the stonefish is legendary and, although they are not common, utmost care should be taken to avoid accidentally treading on one. Don't touch anything unfamiliar while snorkelling. If you do get stung by a stonefish, go to the hospital where they will give you an injection.

More commonly encountered is stinging coral – it's the bright, sulphur yellow-coloured coral with a smooth surface. Don't touch this coral. If you do, however, the sting is only bothersome, not dangerous. Applying vinegar or fresh urine will neutralise the sting.

There are no sharks in the lagoons but they do live in the open sea. The sharks here are not the human-eating variety so they pose no danger to divers.

Tonga has one species of sea snake, the banded sea snake, which is poisonous but rarely seen. It's small, up to 1.5m in length, and easily recognised by its black and white bands. If you gently push it aside, it will usually swim away. It's extremely rare for anyone to be bitten.

Cuts & Scratches Wash well and treat any cut with an antiseptic such as povidone-iodine. Where possible, avoid using bandages and Band-aids, which keep wounds moist and encourage the growth of bacteria.

Coral cuts are notoriously slow to heal and if they are not adequately cleaned small pieces of coral can become embedded in the wound. Clean any cut thoroughly with an antiseptic. Severe pain, throbbing, redness, fever or generally feeling unwell

suggest infection and the need for antibiotics promptly as coral cuts may result in serious infections.

Since the waters around populated areas of Tonga can harbour staphylococcus bacteria, it is best not to swim in these areas with an open wound. Staph infections are miserable and are very difficult to treat. Sadly, Tongan villagers occasionally die of such infections that have ulcerated and spread to vital organs.

Women's Health

Gynaecological Problems Sexually transmitted diseases are a major cause of vaginal problems. Symptoms can include a smelly discharge, painful intercourse and sometimes a burning sensation when urinating. Male sexual partners must also be treated. Medical attention should be sought and, remember, in addition to these diseases HIV or hepatitis B are also transmitted sexually. While abstinence from sexual contact is the only 100% effective prevention, using condoms is also effective.

Use of antibiotics, synthetic underwear, sweating and contraceptive pills can lead to fungal vaginal infections when travelling in hot climates. Maintaining good personal hygiene, and wearing loose-fitting clothes and cotton underwear will help to prevent these infections.

Yeast and fungal infections, characterised by a rash, itch and discharge, can be treated with a vinegar or lemon-juice douche, or with yoghurt. Nystatin, miconazole or clotrimazole pessaries or vaginal cream are the usual treatment. Trichomoniasis is a more serious infection; symptoms are a discharge and a burning sensation when urinating. Male sexual partners must also be treated and, if a vinegar-water douche is not effective, medical attention should be sought. Metronidazole (Flagyl) is the prescribed drug.

Pregnancy Most miscarriages occur during the first three months of pregnancy. Miscarriage is not uncommon and can occasionally lead to severe bleeding. The last three months should also be spent within reasonable distance of good medical care. A baby born as early as 24 weeks stands a chance of survival, but only in a good modern hospital. Pregnant women should avoid all unnecessary medication; vaccinations and malarial prophylactics should still be taken where needed. Additional care should be taken to prevent illness and particular attention should be paid to diet and nutrition. Alcohol and nicotine should be avoided.

WOMEN TRAVELLERS
Most of the time women travellers have no special problems in Tonga. However, your travels will go more smoothly if you keep a few things in mind. Dress is important. Another big issue is whether you are accompanied or alone.

If you're staying at a tourist resort or an international hotel, these issues won't apply. In general, the closer you are to Tongan culture and people, the more these things will apply to you.

Respect the local culture, use common sense, and you shouldn't have any problems. The female authors of this book travelled alone while researching and both enjoyed Tonga immensely.

What to Wear
The way you dress will have a lot to do with how other people perceive and treat you in Tonga.

Tongans want women to dress modestly. Women will be most accepted if they wear loose skirts or dresses, with hemlines below the knee. Sleeves are probably best, but sleeveless shirts or dresses are all right in casual situations, as long as they are modest. Modesty is the operative concept – don't walk around in a halter top or with a low-cut neckline, and don't wear sheer, see-through clothing. Long, baggy shorts are acceptable for casual wear – ie for hiking or going to the beach – but tight or short shorts are not acceptable at any time.

The only place that western-style swimwear is worn is at tourist facilities. Tongan women usually swim in shorts and a T-shirt (at the very least) or in their normal clothes. If you go swimming with Tongan people, watch what they do and do likewise. Tonga is not the place for nude or topless sunbathing.

See Dos & Don'ts under Society & Conduct in the previous chapter for more about dress. (It's an issue for all visitors to Tonga – men, too.)

Women Alone
In traditional Tongan culture, it is not customary for a woman to be alone at any time. When women go outside their homes they are normally accompanied. If you are in the company of someone, anyone, even a child, you will usually not have any problems in Tonga.

If you are alone, Tongan people will notice it, and it doesn't look good to them – it makes you look unprotected. If you combine this with putting yourself in a vulnerable situation where you couldn't get help if you needed to – for example, walking on a deserted bush track or back road – you're putting yourself in a very risky situation.

This can seem tricky if you are a solo woman traveller. Many times it's easy to go places with other people – other travellers at the place you're staying, a child of the family you're staying with etc. If this is not possible, stick to places where there are other people. Tell people you're connected to someone in Tonga – by saying, 'I'm staying at X's place' or 'I'm here visiting X', you are considered to be under X's protection.

Male/Female Relations
In Tonga, as elsewhere, there can be an impression that an unaccompanied foreign woman is fair game. You may get attention from men whether you want it or not. If they make comments as you walk past, just walk on by as if you never heard it. In all situations, keep in mind that the threat of rape does exist in Tonga.

Some women travellers have started

seemingly innocent friendships with Tongan men and later regretted it. Keep in mind that in traditional Tongan culture, women are not permitted to freely associate with men on their own – they must be chaperoned. If you do something like go to an isolated place alone with a man you've met, or go for a drink with him, you are giving him the signal that you are available for sex.

This difference of cultural assumptions applies not only to foreign women relating to Tongan men, it also applies to foreign men relating to Tongan women. For example, a foreign man might not understand a local woman's refusal to go somewhere alone with him, even for a simple thing like lunch or a coffee, not understanding that, in her culture, she cannot do this.

There's no need to be paranoid about relating to people of the opposite sex – certainly there are many happy friendships (and marriages) between foreigners and Tongans. Just be aware that Tonga has a strong culture, and it's very different from yours.

Women & Alcohol

Alcohol is another important issue. A respectable Tongan woman does not drink with men. If you drink with Tongan men, you are putting yourself at risk. This was bluntly explained to us as follows: 'If a woman drinks with men, she deserves whatever she gets.'

Alcohol changes the dynamics of everything. Any time alcohol is involved in a situation in Tonga, you cannot count on being safe. Often there's no middle ground – even a couple of drinks can result in drunkenness, with resulting problems.

Obviously, Tongans have no problem with a woman traveller going out for a drink with her male partner or with other foreign men.

GAY & LESBIAN TRAVELLERS

Homosexuality is an accepted fact of life in Tonga, as in most of Polynesia, and you'll see plenty of gay men around. There are

fakaleiti (like a lady), men who dress and behave as women (see the boxed text), and there are other gay men around too. Lesbians keep themselves much more under cover; Tonga must have lesbians, but they aren't vocal about it.

There's no need for gay or lesbian travellers to hide their sexuality in Tonga. Public displays of sexual affection are frowned upon, though, whether gay or straight.

DISABLED TRAVELLERS

Special facilities for the disabled are practically nonexistent in Tonga. The only wheelchair-accessible accommodation we found on our last visit was the luxurious Sandy Beach Resort in Ha'apai – a beautiful spot.

It's extremely rare to see anyone in a wheelchair in Tonga and access ramps are almost never seen either.

SENIOR TRAVELLERS

Tonga is a good destination for senior travellers. The warm climate, the relaxed pace of life and the easy-going friendliness of the Tongan people are all ideal for the elderly traveller. Older people are respected and venerated in Tonga; seniors are treated well here.

TRAVEL WITH CHILDREN

Children are loved in Tonga, and travelling with them presents no special problems. Tonga is full of children. One Tongan author put it this way: ' ... the people of these islands feel children are the greatest of life's gifts.'

Tonga offers plenty to keep children happy. Swimming, snorkelling, beachcombing, bicycling or kayaking (for older children), short boat trips, visits to interesting places, cultural events (especially the Tongan feasts), etc are all possibilities.

Sun is strong in the tropics, so protect your child from sunburn. Make sure your health and travel insurance also covers your child.

Bring along a baby carrier if you'll need

Fakaleiti

Fakaleiti, men who dress and behave as women, are Tonga's most obvious example of creative sexuality.

While most fakaleiti are probably gay, not all of them are; while many consider themselves ladies and wouldn't think of relating sexually to anyone but a masculine man, this is not true of all fakaleiti – some are married to women! Fakaleiti get away with promiscuity with men on a scale forbidden to biological females, however.

Seeing fakaleitis' open flaunting of sexuality and transvestitism, and their acceptance as part of Tongan society, it might seem there is no social stigma attached to being a fakaleiti. This is partly true, partly not. Although adult fakaleiti are accepted, growing up as a fakaleiti is not easy. Many are tormented by other children and teenagers and to most Tongan fathers it's not a great source of pride if their sons turn out to be effeminate.

On Tongatapu, the Tonga Leitis' Association is an active group – note that members prefer to call themselves simply leiti (ladies). The association sponsors several popular, well attended annual events, including the international Miss Galaxy competition each June which attracts fakaleiti and transvestites from several countries. The association can be contacted via the president, Papiloa, at Papiloa's Friendly Islander Hotel in Nuku'alofa, or the vice-president, Joey, at the unisex hair salon in the Kinikinilau Shopping Centre, Nuku'alofa.

one. Nappies (diapers) are expensive, so you might want to bring some aong too.

Some hotels in Tonga allow children to stay free of charge, others have a reduced children's rate, and a few do not accept children at all. Be sure to ask the policy when you make your bookings. Babysitting can sometimes be arranged.

Travel With Children by Maureen Wheeler, co-founder of Lonely Planet, is a helpful book for travelling with children anywhere in the world.

DANGERS & ANNOYANCES
Security
Theft from the person is not a problem in Tonga, whether by robbery or pickpocketing, so you don't need to be paranoid about carrying belongings around with you.

'Borrowing', however, is rife. By Tongan reckoning, all property is effectively communal. If one person has something another needs, the latter either asks for it or surreptitiously 'borrows' it. Of course it can be 'borrowed' back if needed, but it will otherwise never again see its rightful owner.

Unattended items are considered ripe for 'borrowing', so if you're concerned about your material possessions, keep an eye on them. Careless travellers could be quickly separated from their belongings.

The threat of rape does exist, but you can easily protect yourself by using common sense. Women should read the section on Women Travellers earlier in this chapter.

The police and government officials in Tonga seem friendly and straightforward. I've never heard of a tourist having problems with officials unless they've overstayed or been caught carrying illegal substances.

Marine & Health Hazards
Reefs and the sea harbour some health hazards which you should be aware of – eg coral is sharp and can cause nasty cuts which may become infected. See the Health section earlier in this chapter.

Feuds & Rivalries
Tonga is a small country with a growing number of expats, many of whom have set

up tourist-oriented businesses and are competing among themselves for trade. As a visitor, you may be exposed to some strong criticism of competition, which may or may not actually have anything to do with the quality of services provided.

When faced with negative assessments of Tongans, tourists, other expats or their businesses, try to take it with a grain of salt and make your own observations or hunt up another opinion or two before accepting anything as absolute truth.

BUSINESS HOURS

Business hours are flexible. Banks are usually open weekdays from 9 am to 4 pm; in Nuku'alofa and Neiafu (Vava'u) they also open for a few hours on Saturday morning. Government offices are open weekdays from 8.30 am to 12.30 pm and 1.30 to 4 pm. Post offices are open weekdays from around 9 am to 4 pm.

Shops are usually open weekdays from 8.30 am to 4 pm, with an hour off for lunch, and Saturday from around 9 am to noon. Restaurants usually operate from around 7 to 10 am for breakfast, noon to 2 pm for lunch, and 6 to 10 pm if they serve the evening meal. (Many restaurants serve only one or two meals, not all three.) Produce markets normally get under way by about 6 am and close around 4 pm.

On Sunday everything is closed until the afternoon, when bakeries are allowed to open and sell bread and cakes. They open at noon, or around 5 pm, depending on location

PUBLIC HOLIDAYS & SPECIAL EVENTS

Primary and secondary school holidays include two weeks beginning the second week of May, two weeks beginning the third week of August and six weeks begin-

---

Sunday in Tonga

Sunday in Tonga is for eating, sleeping, and going to church – but since Tongans normally attend at least two worship services (in addition to choir practice), they have little time left over for eating and sleeping.

Tongan law states that the Sabbath Day is forever sacred. A Sunday stroll in Tonga will give a visitor the eerie feeling that someone has dropped the bomb. Buses and taxis don't operate, businesses are closed, sports events are prohibited and planes may not land. Contracts signed on Sunday are considered null and void and any Tongan caught fishing or guilty of any other breach of the Sabbath is subject to a T$10 fine or three months' hard labour. Even swimming at the beach is a no-no on Sunday, except at beach resorts or on very remote beaches, away from public contact. Some yachting acquaintances ran up on a reef one Sunday and the Tongan harbour personnel refused to respond to their Mayday call on the grounds that it was Sunday!

Foreign tourists are exempt from the swimming and beach restrictions and relaxations of the law now permit the Sunday opening of tourist hotel restaurants and beach resorts. Driving on Sunday is also now allowed, though you won't see many people doing it.

Bakeries are permitted to open on Sunday afternoon thanks to an emergency law which was enacted after a devastating cyclone in the 1980s. It permitted bakeries to provide Sunday bread to replace traditional crops, which had been decimated. The law was never repealed.

Many travellers take the 'if you can't beat 'em, join 'em' attitude and attend church on Sunday, only to find that Tongans have astonishing musical ability and that their rendition of traditional hymns is consistently magnificent.

ning the first week of December. Public holidays include:

1 January
  New Year's Day
March/April
  Good Friday, Easter Sunday & Easter Monday
25 April
  Anzac Day
4 May
  HRH Crown Prince Tupouto'a's Birthday
4 June
  Emancipation Day
4 July
  King Taufa'ahau Tupou IV's Birthday
4 November
  Constitution Day
4 December
  King George I's Birthday
25 December
  Christmas Day
26 December
  Boxing Day

You may get the feeling that '4' is the royal lucky number!

The king's birthday is celebrated on Tongatapu with the Heilala Festival, named after the country's national flower, a week-long bash featuring parades and processions, music festivals and competitions, cultural events and dance, art, craft, beauty and sports competitions. Coinciding with this festival is the torch-lighting ceremony, Tupakapakanava, in which people line the northern coastline of Tongatapu carrying flaming torches of dry reeds. The origins of this ceremony are hazy; Tongans seem content simply to liken it to the USA's July 4 fireworks or Britain's Guy Fawkes Day.

The most prominent annual event in the Ha'apai group is the three-day Ha'apai Festival, which coincides with Emancipation Day festivities in early June. In Vava'u, the Crown Prince's birthday in early May sets the stage for the Vava'u Festival, a popular week of partying.

The week-long Easter Festival features youth choirs, passion plays, band concerts and cultural performances. Another major event is the week-long Red Cross Festival, which is capped off with the Red Cross Grand Ball. It takes place every year in May.

Agricultural fairs, which are derived from the ancient 'inasi festivals, take place in all the major island groups from late August to October and are presided over by the king. The first is normally on Vava'u, followed by fairs on Ha'apai, Tongatapu and 'Eua.

In late September the Tonga International Billfish Tournament attracts both local and international anglers to Vava'u. Another international competition, the Miss Galaxy pageant, is held in Nuku'alofa in late June – for men! Actually they are transvestites, or fakaleiti. Contestants from several countries participate. It's great fun, a very popular event.

Tongan families need little excuse for a feast: a birthday, a visitor, an academic accomplishment, a birth, a marriage or just a sunny Sunday are all good reasons. Coronations, university graduations, religious holidays, children's' first birthdays and royal birthdays invite celebration on an even larger scale, often with several days of feasting, dancing, organised entertainment and general lightheartedness. Instead of fireworks, children and youths detonate home-made bamboo and kerosene bazookas that explode with the same impact as heavy artillery.

ACTIVITIES
Bushwalking

Tonga – especially 'Eua – offers some fine bushwalking. Other good hiking venues include the Niuas and many of the Ha'apai islands. Plantation tracks, sandy beaches, reefs, rainforests and volcanoes all invite exploration on foot.

Walkers are advised to carry plenty of liquid or a bush knife which can be used to open coconuts. Be sensitive when collecting coconuts – most of the trees belong to a plantation owner and visitors should ask permission before collecting nuts indiscriminately.

Caving

Tongatapu has one cave, 'Anahulu Cave, with a freshwater pool good for swimming. Vava'u also has several fine caves, notably Swallows' Cave and Mariner's Cave, both of which can only be entered from the sea. Tonga's king of caves, though, is undoubtedly 'Eua, with dozens of limestone caves. Avid spelunkers with a bent for bush exploring would be in heaven.

If underwater caves are your thing, talk to Roland Schwara at Watersports Ha'apai on Lifuka, Ha'apai. He knows some great underwater caves, including a deep one full of flashlight fish! Underwater caves are also found in Tonga's other island groups.

Rock Climbing

Rock climbers and abseilers (rapellers) will quiver at the sight of the high, sheer limestone cliffs on 'Eua's east coast. You'll have to bring all your own gear, and climbing these cliffs would not be for the fainthearted – in addition to the impressive height of the cliffs there's also the easterly wind to consider, which comes across the ocean and blasts straight into these cliffs.

Cycling

Cycling is enjoyable on any island in Tonga, allowing you to see the islands up close, at an island pace. Vava'u is hilly, and 'Eua has mountains on its east side, though its west side is flat. Tongatapu and Lifuka (Ha'apai) are both as flat as a pancake. Bicycles can be rented on Tongatapu, 'Eua, Ha'apai and Vava'u.

Snorkelling & Diving

Each of Tonga's three main island groups offers a different sort of underwater experience. The range of colours and variety of healthy, living hard and soft corals is truly amazing, as are the colourful and abundant tropical fish. The outstanding visibility averages 30 to 50m on the barrier reefs around Tongatapu; in Ha'apai it's greater, 25 to 30m in summer, up to 70m in winter. This, combined with the comfortable water temperatures (23°C to 30°C) and sheltered waters, creates magnificent conditions for diving. Canyons, walls, caverns, caves, overhangs, tunnels, channels, drifts, coral gardens, shipwrecks and volcanoes make for a great variety of diving possibilities.

The presence of humpback whales mating and bearing their young in Tonga's waters from June to November each year is a special treat – the singing of the males can often be heard in the water during their mating season. Dolphins and sea turtles are present all year. See the regional chapters for more information.

Surfing

Tonga enjoys world-class surf year-round, with two distinct surfing seasons. Winter south swell season runs from April to October and is reliant on storm activity in the Tasman Sea, around Australia and New Zealand, to produce rideable waves. Summer north swell season runs from November to March, with prevailing swells originating both in the north Pacific (the same swells that hit Hawaii) and from local south Pacific tropical cyclones.

There are no beach breaks in Tonga. All surfing is over shallow coral reefs, which demands intermediate to advanced skill levels. Visiting surfers are advised to carry basic first-aid kits to deal with the inevitable cuts and grazes.

Great surf can be found throughout Tonga's three main island groups. Ha'apai and Vava'u have excellent waves, but yachts are necessary for easy access.

On Tongatapu, the best surfing can be found at Ha'atafu Beach, 21km from Nuku'alofa on the Hihifo Peninsula. A number of surf spots here require only a short paddle (100m) across the lagoon to access.

For more detailed information about surfing in Tonga, contact Steve Burling, President, Tonga Surfriders Association, PO Box 490, Nuku'alofa (☎ 41-088; fax 22-970). Steve has over 20 years' experience surfing in Tonga and also runs Ha'atafu Beach Resort, Tonga's only resort specialising in surfing holidays.

Sailing
If you aren't on a strict budget and are looking for the freedom to wander at will from one uninhabited tropical island or anchorage to another, you couldn't do better than Tonga. Most of Tonga's yacht charters are based in Vava'u, which is heaven on earth for sailing, but there's also one based at Tongatapu's Royal Sunset Island Resort which offers charters around Tongatapu, Ha'apai and Vava'u.

For more information on sailing, see the regional chapters.

Kayaking
With its myriad islands, lagoons and beaches, Tonga offers wide scope for sea kayakers. The clear, calm, sheltered waters of the Vava'u Group couldn't be better for kayaking. Kayaking in Ha'apai involves a bit more open sea, depending on where you decide to go, but it too has plenty of sheltered waters. On Tongatapu, kayaking is good in the lagoon, the ocean and for trips to the islands offshore from Nuku'alofa. See the regional chapters for further information.

Whale Watching
Humpback whales mate, bear young and care for their baby calves each year in Tonga. Whale watching season is from June to November in Tongatapu and Ha'apai, July to November in Vava'u. On whale watching trips you will be given underwater microphones so you can hear the whales singing, and snorkelling gear so you can jump in and swim with the whales. It is possible that Tonga is the only place in the world where you can do this, as most other countries have regulations about how close you can come to the whales.

For details about individual operators, see the regional chapters.

Fishing
An increasing number of game-fishing charters are springing up in Tonga. The main game fish available are yellowfin tuna, bluefin tuna, skipjack, albacore, wahoo, barracuda, sailfish, mahimahi and blue, black and striped marlin. In September the Tonga International Billfish Tournament, which is sponsored by the Tonga International Game Fishing Association (TIGFA), attracts local and international anglers to Vava'u. See the regional chapters for further information on opportunities for fishing.

COURSES
Certification and advanced courses in scuba diving are offered on Tongatapu, Vava'u and Ha'apai; see the Activities section, above. Visitors spending some time on Tongatapu might want to check out the courses at the 'Atenisi Institute in Nuku'alofa or the University of the South Pacific (USP) on Tongatapu.

WORK
Being in Tonga on a tourist permit means you're specifically prohibited from working. Like everywhere else in the world, the idea is to save jobs for Tongans, who need the work.

Nevertheless, you'll see plenty of foreigners working in Tonga. Many have set up small businesses considered beneficial for Tonga. Foreigners also work here on various aid programmes (US Peace Corps, Australian Volunteers Abroad, Japanese Overseas Cooperation Volunteers etc).

Officially, you must get a work permit from the immigration office in order to be employed in Tonga. You must have a specific offer of employment, file an application with the immigration office, pay a fee of T$76 and perhaps wait quite a while for the processing. The immigration office at the police station in Nuku'alofa (☎ 24-763; fax 23-226), PO Box 8, Nuku'alofa, can fill you in on all the current requirements.

ACCOMMODATION
Unless you're on a package holiday, don't trust accommodation bookings made by airlines or travel agents, since there are often weak or missing links in the system. Make

✳✳✳✳✳✳✳✳✳✳✳✳✳✳✳✳✳✳✳✳✳✳✳✳✳✳✳✳✳✳

'Singing Whales'

Tonga is an important breeding ground for humpback whales, and one of the best places in the world to see them.

The whales can be seen in Tongatapu and Ha'apai from June to November and in Vava'u from July to November, bearing young, caring for new calves, and engaging in elaborate mating rituals. It is thought that they come to bear their young in warm waters because the newborn calves cannot stand the freezing polar waters; the calmness of the reef protected ocean is important too. Each year, calves are born in Tonga that were conceived there the year before; their gestation period is 11 months.

Humpbacks are dubbed 'singing whales' – the males sing during courtship routines. The low notes of their 'songs', which can reach a shattering 185 decibels, can carry 100km through the open ocean. It has been assumed that the songs are sung to attract the female, but it could be for other reasons too – perhaps to warn other males away from their breeding territories.

Humpbacks are also known for their dramatic antics in the water. They breach (throw themselves completely up out of the water, landing with a terrific splash), spyhop (stand vertically upright in the sea, gazing around at the world above water), barrel roll (splashing the water with their long pectoral fins as they do so), slap the water repeatedly with their tail flukes or pectoral fins, and perform other remarkable acrobatic feats.

A mature male adult is about 16m (52 feet) long and weighs around 40 to 45 tonnes. The whale's pectoral fins (flippers) are the longest in the animal kingdom, at about 4m to 6m (13 to 20 feet) long measuring almost 30% of its overall body length. The calves are around 4m (13 feet) long at birth and weigh up to 2.5 tonnes. They gain approximately 25 kilos (55 pounds) each day – about a kilo per hour – feeding on their mothers' milk, which contains twice as much protein and 10 times as much fat as cows' milk. When the calves have put on around 10cm (four inches) of blubber, the whales return to their Antarctic summer feeding grounds.

These baleen whales feed by straining small fish and crustaceans through hundreds of keratin plates – keratin being the stuff that hair and fingernails are made of. The whales feed only in their summer Antarctic feeding grounds. During their long reproductive pilgrimage, which lasts about half the year, they do not eat at all, but live on the blubber stored during the summer. Once back in Antarctica, they eat with a vengeance.

Interestingly, though humpbacks live in several parts of the world their populations do not mix; not only do the Tongan whales not mix with the populations which breed in New Caledonia, eastern or western Australia, but northern and southern hemisphere hump-

✳✳✳✳✳✳✳✳✳✳✳✳✳✳✳✳✳✳✳✳✳✳✳✳✳✳✳✳✳✳

bookings yourself by post or telephone if you want to be assured of a room upon arrival. There's a 7.5% government tax on all accommodation (5% VAT plus 2.5% room tax), which must be added to the room prices given in this book unless otherwise noted. (Room rates are normally quoted without the tax in Tonga, but it's added when you pay your bill.) Many middle and top-end places charge 10% to 15% agency commission for accommodation booked through overseas tour operators or travel agencies.

Camping

Camping is generally discouraged in Tonga. It seems that quite a few people in Tonga's tourist industry view campers not as recreationalists or outdoors enthusiasts but merely as cheapskates hoping to dodge the cost of overnight accommodation. Understandably, few Tongans share westerners' backs never see each other either. Southern hemisphere humpbacks are distinguished from those in the northern hemisphere by their undersides: southern hemisphere whales have white undersides, while the undersides of those in the northern hemisphere are dark.

Humpback populations around the world have declined rapidly in the 20th century, due to the commercial whaling industry that got its start in the early 1900s. In 1963 the International Whaling Commission established full protection for humpback whales in the southern hemisphere, banning commercial whaling operations, but illegal poaching of humpbacks by Soviet whalers continued into the 1990s. Subsistence whaling in Tonga, where maybe 10 whales were taken per year by primitive methods, continued until 1979 when the king banned all whaling.

Nowadays, whale watching is becoming a viable industry in Tonga and everywhere else that humpbacks breed. The same predictable migration habits that once made the giants easy prey to whalers now make them easy for whale watchers to find and their aerial displays make them a most impressive sight.

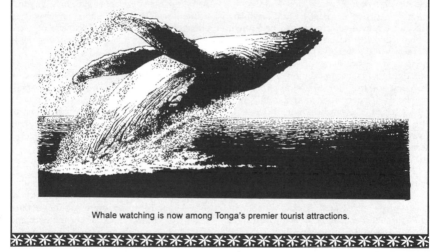

Whale watching is now among Tonga's premier tourist attractions.

appreciation of activities that they would consider drudgery, and the government is concerned that those who prefer to camp on deserted islands and travel around under their own steam aren't contributing their fair share to Tonga's economy.

On our last visit to Tonga we were told that camping has been made illegal in both the Ha'apai and Vava'u Groups unless it's part of a guided trip (ie sea kayaking).A few accommodation places on Tongatapu, 'Eua, Ha'apai and Vava'u are now offering camping in designated areas as an option for their guests. They are mentioned in the relevant island chapters.

Be sure to practise minimum impact camping – leave no trace of your visit, carry out everything you carry in, etc.

Guesthouses
Budget accommodation is found throughout the islands and prices are quite low

compared to those in neighbouring countries, with the possible exception of Samoa and Fiji. In every island group you'll find comfortable and homey guesthouses where travellers can settle in and spend some time savouring local culture without going broke in the process.

Most guesthouses are clean and several have cooking facilities. The average price per night will be around T$10 to T$25 per person for a bed, more if meals are included. Ordinarily, bath and toilet facilities are communal and often only cold showers are available.

Hotels & Resorts

Hotels and beach resorts are slightly upmarket, but don't expect to find anything like what's available in Hawaii or French Polynesia. Most beach resorts are pleasant, but some of the 'luxury' hotels are quite expensive while not living up to international standards of accommodation or service. Anyone looking for Sheraton or Hilton standards of accommodation should forget about Tonga. The plushest hotel in Tonga is the Paradise International Hotel in Neiafu (Vava'u), followed pathetically by the International Dateline and the Pacific Royale in Nuku'alofa.

Tonga's best upmarket beach resorts include the Royal Sunset Island Resort and Fafá Island Resort, both offshore from Nuku'alofa, the Sandy Beach Resort in Ha'apai, and the Tongan Beach Resort and Mounu Island Resort in Vava'u.

Tonga also has a number of more economical beach resorts – and even backpackers beach resorts. See the Tongatapu, Ha'apai Group and Vava'u Group chapters.

Homestays

Frequently, foreigners will be invited by friendly Tongans to stay in their homes. There could be no better way to learn about the culture and lifestyle of the country, and the hospitality of the Tongan people is abundant and genuine. Keep in mind, however, that their means are limited and

although most Tongan families would proudly and happily give you their last cent and refuse any compensation it's best not to let things come to that. This is more easily said than done, however.

Simple gifts such as kava or alcohol will normally be accepted where cash will not. Gifts for the children will also be welcomed. Most families are also short of tinned corned beef, which is a staple in the Tongan diet; since it cannot be grown on the family plantation, a gift of this commodity will be greatly appreciated.

One word of warning: there have been occasional reports of local 'hospitality' resulting in robbery of gullible foreigners. Although many cases seem to involve prostitutes and their drunken or unwitting clients, a couple of travellers have reported that valuable items have gone missing while they were staying in local homes.

Bear in mind that Tonga is not a western nation and that westerners' concepts of ownership apply more in law than in tradition or practice. Keep your valuables in a safe place and don't leave anything of obvious value lying around within view. (See Security in the Dangers & Annoyances section, earlier in this chapter.)

FOOD

Visitors will find most Tongan food a delight. The people's diet consists mostly of root vegetables, coconut products, taro, fresh fruit, pork, chicken, corned beef and fish, but the delicious and imaginative recipes derived from these items make good Tongan cuisine a favourite of anyone fortunate enough to try it.

Unfortunately, however, the situation in Tonga is getting fairly grim food-wise. The health of the people is suffering as junk foods and expensive supermarket items invade and replace the healthy diet to which Tongans have long been accustomed. The ultimate blasphemy is the availability and status of products such as tinned vegetables, fish and fruit. White bleached bread, greasy fried *sipi* (mutton) and artificial snack foods are also popular, while traditional items lie rotting on the ground throughout the kingdom.

Outdoor markets sell a variety of local produce and can be found in Nuku'alofa, Neiafu (Vava'u) and Pangai (Ha'apai). Private supermarkets and the Tonga Cooperative Federation also exist in those places.

Restaurants

Most Tongans are too poor to eat out, so the more expensive restaurants feature foreign cuisines – Chinese, North American, Italian and so on – aimed at tourists. Most cheaper eating establishments serve only greasy and gristly American or Australian fast food. With a few notable exceptions, these places could prove hazardous to your health. Normally, good Tongan cuisine is available at feasts, island nights, some guesthouses and a couple of restaurants.

Feasts

No section on food in Tonga can be complete without a mention of Tongan feasts, an important part of the culture. See 'Tuck into a Tongan Feast' on page 64.

DRINKS
Nonalcoholic Drinks

The most refreshing drink available is the juice of the immature coconut, which is slightly carbonated and quite delicious. Tongans are normally happy to scramble up a tree in order to secure green drinking nuts for visitors. If you hope to drink coconuts instead of carrying water while bushwalking, you must always ask permission from landowners before collecting nuts and carry a bush knife to hack away the tough green husk. More mature nuts can be opened (with some difficulty) with a pointed stick and a bit of elbow grease. The meat of the green coconut is soft and pliable and many people prefer it to the crunchy meat of the brown nut.

Fruit juices are available everywhere to those willing to extract them. A particularly nice combination is the speciality of Keleti Beach Resort on Tongatapu – the juice of watermelon, pineapple and coconut over ice. Unfortunately, most restaurants, inexplicably, serve tinned juice.

Sweet and syrupy foreign soft drinks are available almost everywhere. In addition to the ubiquitous Coca-Cola, Fanta, 7-Up, Lift and the like, you can buy GLO, exported from New Zealand. The local soft drink is called Slake.

For coffee, the locally grown Royal Coffee can't be beat. It's sold in packages at the larger supermarkets, FIMCO shops and duty-free shops and is served at all the top-end hotels and restaurants.

Kava, of course, is Tonga's most famous drink of all – see the boxed text.

Alcoholic Drinks

Alcohol is very popular in Tonga, particularly on Tongatapu and Vava'u, where you're never far from a cold beer (except on Sunday, of course). The beer you'll find everywhere is Royal, produced locally, which is quite good. It comes in three varieties (Premium, Draught and Ikale) and is made in Tonga in cooperation with Pripps brewery of Stockholm, Sweden.

However, thanks to the relatively high price of alcoholic beverages, many Tongans resort to a yeasty but bearable home brew (also called bush beer) made from things found around the house. This is illegal, of course, and can also be dangerous. Get a complete rundown of the ingredients and preparation method before you drink!

Wines from New Zealand, Australia, France, California and other places are available in shops in Nuku'alofa.

ENTERTAINMENT

Don't miss attending a traditional feast while you're in Tonga. Feasts usually include welcoming kava ceremonies, string band music and performances of traditional Tongan singing and dancing. These events are put on for tourists, but they're not for tourists alone – go to a feast at the Tongan Cultural Centre or the Good Samaritan Inn on Tongatapu and it's likely you'll see just as many locals out for a good time as tourists. Bring along plenty of T$1

‍✳‍✳‍✳‍✳‍✳‍✳‍✳‍✳‍✳‍✳‍✳‍✳‍✳‍✳‍✳‍✳ ✳‍✳‍✳‍✳‍✳‍✳‍✳‍✳‍✳‍✳‍✳‍✳‍✳ ✳

Tuck into a Tongan Feast

A Tongan feast is an event not to be missed. Feasts are staged to commemorate notable events like a royal visit, a school graduation, an agricultural fair, a state holiday or the arrival of a friend or relative from overseas. For events like coronations or royal birthdays, whole villages spend days preparing enough food to feed entire islands! A pig is slaughtered and roasted for each invited guest and, after the VIPs have eaten their fill, the villagers feast on the ample remains.

A feast normally requires an *'umu*, an underground oven used to bake the food. Dishes traditionally served include roasted suckling pig, chicken, *'ika* (fish), *fingota* (shellfish), *'ota 'ika* (raw fish dish similar to Mexican or Chilean ceviche), *lu pulu* (corned beef and boiled taro in coconut cream), *feke* (octopus), *manioke* (cassava), *kumala* (sweet potato), *lu* and *talo* (taro leaves and roots), *'ufi* (yams), curries and delicious *faikakai* (breadfruit pudding). An array of fresh fruits and juices will also be served. Women spend hours preparing food, weaving *polas* (stretchers of coconut frond on which food is carried and served) and building palm-leaf pavilions to shelter the invited guests.

Visitors who are not fortunate enough to attend a local feast can still participate in one staged to give tourists an idea of what the Tongan tradition is all about.

Making & Using an 'Umu

An 'umu is a very effective underground oven used throughout Polynesia and Melanesia. Those who attend a Tongan feast are likely to see smoke one wafting from a small sandy mound.

The Tongan 'umu is quite easy to make. First, dig a hole in the ground 25cm or so deep and a metre in diameter. Collect enough coral or volcanic rocks (each 7cm or so in diameter) to fill the bottom of the pit. Then, collect wood, coconut husks and other flammable natural materials and start a bonfire in the pit. Throw the rocks on top and, when they're glowing hot, remove the remnants of wood and cover the rocks with split banana tree trunks, banana leaves or bark.

Now for the food. The root vegetables (talo, 'ufi, manioke and kumala) together with the breadfruit should be spread out evenly on top of the rocks. Cover them with a layer of sticks for ventilation and then place the meat on the sticks. If you're baking an entire animal, prepare a larger 'umu. It would help, also, to place several of the heated rocks inside the animal in order to cook it throughout. Over the meat place more sticks, banana leaves and burlap (hessian) or flour sacks. Fill in with earth and pack tightly.

The less steam that escapes, the more effective the oven. Baking time will depend on the nature of the meat. Whole pigs should bake for up to six hours, while small slices will be ready in two. Once everything's been dug out, you're ready to eat.

DIY Tonga Feasts

Try cooking Tonga-style by using the recipes on the opposite page.

✳‍✳ ✳

notes so you can stick them onto the oiled skin of the dancers to show your appreciation should you feel so inclined – that's what the Tongans will be doing.

Tongan feasts are held regularly on Tongatapu and Vava'u; see those chapters for details. In Ha'apai, the Niu'akalo Hotel used to do them and may start again; check when you're there.

Friday is the big night for dancing in Tonga. Tongatapu has several nightclubs to choose from, Neiafu (Vava'u) has two, 'Eua

Traditional Tongan Recipes

Lu Pulu

1 chopped onion
1 cup coconut cream
340gm corned beef
20 young taro leaves (lu)
1 tsp salt

Lu Pulu is one of the few ways to turn tinned corned beef into a delightful ingredient. To make coconut cream, grate the meat of three to four mature coconuts. Add one cup of hot water for each two cups of coconut meat, let it stand for a quarter of an hour or so, then pass through cheesecloth or coconut sennit to extract the cream. Next, cut the taro leaves into small pieces and boil with corned beef, coconut cream, onion and salt for 10 to 15 minutes. For a more traditional version, wrap the mixture in a banana leaf, tie with a banana leaf rib and bake in an 'umu for an hour or so.

'Ota 'Ika

1 onion
1 carrot
1 cucumber
1 tomato
1 tsp salt
5 lemons
cream from six mature coconuts (see lu pulu recipe)
½ tsp pepper
1 kg raw fish (snapper, tuna, etc)

Clean and de-bone fish, and cut it into 2cm chunks. Extract juice from four lemons, stir in the salt and allow fish to marinate in it for 1½ hours. Chop vegetables into fine pieces. Drain fish mixture and add coconut cream and unsalted juice from the remaining lemon. When ready to serve, add vegetables and pepper.

Faikakai Topai

2 cups coconut cream (see lu pulu recipe)
2 cups sugar
1 roasted breadfruit

Bake roasted breadfruit (in skin) for one hour. Pound flesh into a paste and cut into small squares. Melt sugar until brown. Add coconut cream and boil for about 10 minutes or until mixture thickens into a gooey mass. Pour over breadfruit chunks. At this point it may be served, or you can wrap the whole mixture in a banana leaf, tie it with a banana leaf rib and bake in an 'umu for up to an hour. It is also possible to use yam or taro in place of the breadfruit, or to add papaya to the sugar mixture. Be creative with this one – it's delicious!

has one. In Ha'apai, dances are sometimes held in church halls.

On Tongatapu there are also several places where you can hear live music. In Vava'u, don't miss the string band at the Mermaid Restaurant. They welcome stray musicians sitting in; this has been called 'the musicians' hangout of the South Pacific' by enthusiastic yachties. Even the dance hall in 'Eua has a live band. Tongatapu, Vava'u and 'Eua all have bars.

Nuku'alofa has one cinema, Loni's. In

Vava'u, video movies are shown nightly at the Paradise International Hotel. Several guesthouses and hotels have videos. Tongatapu is the only island with television.

SPECTATOR SPORTS

Tongans love sport. Rugby is the national favourite. Rugby union and rugby league are played with all-out passion during rugby season, roughly from March to August, when important matches can be seen at Teufaiva Stadium on Tongatapu. The game is also played for fun all year round throughout the country, just about anywhere there's a field or vacant lot. Tonga's national rugby union team, 'Ikale Tahi, represents Tonga in international competitions.

Other sports played at Teufaiva include basketball and squash. The gym at Taufaiva is where the king and crown prince come to work out (at their own private times) and you can work out here too.

The cricket season is roughly from March to July. This is a popular game and just about every village has a green. Soccer, which is played by both men's and women's teams, is also popular. Cricket and soccer matches are held on the lawn beside the Royal Palace in Nuku'alofa.

Tennis is another popular sport played by both men and women. An international tennis tournament is held at the 'Atele Indoor Stadium on Tongatapu during the Heilala Week festivities in early July each year. Other sports played at 'Atele include volleyball, badminton, table tennis, boxing, basketball and netball.

Netball is probably the most popular women's sport. Nine-a-side netball is played from November to January.

Golf is played on the golf course opposite the 'Atele Indoor Stadium.

THINGS TO BUY

Tongan handicrafts are beautiful and, despite the skill, care and time required to create the expert carvings, weavings, basketry, jewellery and tapa, they are quite reasonably priced.

If you watch a woodcarver at work, or women singing and laughing together while weaving or making tapa, it becomes obvious that they are caught up in the joy of creation for its own sake, not only for the benefit of tourists (and, hence, their own bank accounts). With the exception of the carvings, Tongans themselves use the products they design and make.

The methods used in producing handicrafts are the same today as they were in ancient times and only natural materials are used, including bone, sandalwood, shells, mulberry bark, pandanus fronds and coral.

Items which are popular with tourists include carvings. Although most Tongan carvings are skilfully made and quite beautiful, they are not traditional. In this case, Tonga has given in to the tourist market. Tourists expect to find *tikis* (wooden statues representing an old Polynesian god) in Polynesia and Tonga happily provides them; never mind that such items did not figure in the pre-tourism scheme of things. Woodcarving provides not only income but also relaxing creativity for Tongan men.

The most common subjects are of course those that appeal to tourists, such as turtles, tikis, fish, weapons and masks. Some kitschy items like salad bowls, floor lamps, ashtrays and soap dishes are also available. The woods that are most often used include the mahogany-like *milo* and the similar but heavier *pua-pua*. Sandalwood, from 'Eua, with its distinctly beautiful fragrance, is also very popular but is becoming increasingly rare due to over-harvesting and illicit export to the Chinese and other Asian markets. Please take this into consideration before purchasing such items.

Black coral is becoming a popular medium. At the time of writing it was not considered endangered in Tonga but an increased market could well cause problems and, in any case, most western countries prohibit its importation. The same goes for materials for which concern is immediately warranted, such as whalebone and tortoiseshell. It is claimed that whalebone carved in Tonga is collected by divers who take it from whales that have died naturally.

✳✳✳✳✳✳✳✳✳✳✳✳✳✳✳✳ ✳✳✳✳✳✳✳✳✳✳✳✳✳✳✳

Kava

Kava is a drink derived from the ground root of the pepper plant *(Piper methysticum)* and it is ubiquitous in Tonga. You'll often hear that it tastes like dishwater – it certainly looks like it! – but dishwater may actually contain a residue of foodstuffs while kava is just murky and almost tasteless. The description, however, belies its popularity and Tongans can drink bucketfuls of it in one sitting. Kava circles are basic social units and on Friday nights, Tongan men gather and drink kava from late afternoon to the wee hours of the morning.

The active ingredients in kava include 12 or 14 chemicals of an alkaloid nature. Kava is both anaesthetic and analgesic, high in fibre content, low in calories and serves as a mild tranquilliser, an antibacterial and antifungal agent, a diuretic, an appetite suppressant and a soporific. Kava is legal in North America, Europe and Australia, and Tongans habitually send packages of it to family members overseas who can't seem to do without it.

Kava is found in a number of Pacific nations, and some of the best kava in Tonga is grown on the island of Tafahi, up in the Niuas.

The ground-up root of the kava plant is mixed with water in a carved four-legged bowl. The men (and, on rare occasions, women) seat themselves in a circle with the bowl at the head. Each man in turn claps and receives a coconut shell full of kava. He'll down it, re-serving a bit to sprinkle over his shoulder. Then he'll hurl the shell across the floor back to the server. This procedure continues for hours on end until the men begin to feel very vague and hazy. Kava is not a narcotic, but it does make one feel lethargic or even nauseous when consumed in large quantities (which it usually is).

Friday night kava clubs may be found all over the islands. Some are simply social events and others are used as fund-raisers and include entertainment and music. Visitors are always welcome and any taxi driver will be able to tell you the location of the nearest one

Kava also has a more serious side; it's an essential part of traditional Tongan culture. Marriages are not considered sealed until the bride has consumed a coconut half-shell of kava, offered to her by the groom. When conferring a title of nobility, a kava ceremony is held and the new titleholder's drinking of a half-shell of kava confirms the acceptance and investiture of the new title. Contracts and agreements of all kinds are traditionally sealed not with a handshake, but a kava ceremony. Kava ceremonies are also held to commemorate important occasions – including the arrival of visitors. Don't be surprised if you're invited to a kava ceremony while you're in Tonga.

✳✳✳✳✳✳✳✳✳✳✳✳✳✳✳✳✳ ✳✳✳✳✳✳✳✳✳✳✳✳✳✳✳✳

All Tongan jewellery is made from natural products but many of these products are protected or restricted overseas and concern for the environment as well as import laws should be considered before purchasing any, particularly tortoiseshell.

Other materials used in the production of every imaginable type of ornament include sharks' teeth, whalebone, coral, coconut shell, *pueki* shells, *tuitui* (candlenut) and *taku misi* or sea urchin spines. Taku misi are small salmon, peach or orange-coloured shafts which make lovely necklaces when polished. Even more commonly they are used to make wind chimes.

For information on Tongan weaving and tapa-making, refer to the Arts section of the Facts about the Country chapter.

Another item which will prove useful and inexpensive in Tonga is a sarong. These large rectangles of normally colourful cloth are worn all over the Pacific. They take up little space, wash and dry easily and can be tied and worn in several ways.

Getting There & Away

The South Pacific is a relatively expensive place transport-wise, so if you don't have unlimited funds to allow you the luxury of whim-to-whim travel, some careful route-planning is in order. Remember that all passengers arriving in Tonga need either an air ticket out, an onward ticket on a cruise ship, or a guarantee by a yacht owner that they'll be departing on the same boat on which they arrived.

AIR

The majority of Tonga's visitors arrive on scheduled flights at Fua'amotu International Airport on Tongatapu. A smaller number enter the country at Lupepau'u International Airport on Vava'u. While Tonga isn't as remote or obscure a destination as Tuvalu or Kiribati, neither is it as popular as Fiji or Tahiti and airfares often reflect that.

From New Zealand, Australia, Fiji, Samoa, Hawaii and Los Angeles, access to Tonga is fairly straightforward. From anywhere else, travelling to Tonga will entail first reaching one of those connecting points. Auckland (New Zealand) and Nadi/Suva (Fiji) seem to be the most convenient and best served places; the weekly direct Honolulu flight is convenient for connections to the USA and Canada. The four major carriers are Royal Tongan Airlines, Air New Zealand, Air Pacific (code-sharing with Qantas) and Polynesian Airlines. Samoa Air has direct flights between Vava'u and Pago Pago (American Samoa).

Buying Tickets

The plane ticket will probably be the single most expensive item in your budget and buying it can be an intimidating business. There's likely to be a multitude of airlines and travel agents hoping to separate you from your money and it is always worth putting aside a few hours to research the current market. Start early: some of the cheapest tickets have to be bought months in advance and some popular flights sell out early. Talk to other recent travellers, look at ads in newspapers and magazines (not forgetting the press of the ethnic group whose country you plan to visit), consult reference books and watch for special offers. Then phone round travel agents for bargains. (Airlines can supply information on routes and timetables; however, except at times of inter-airline price wars they do not supply the cheapest tickets.) Find out the fare, the route, the duration of the journey and any restrictions on the ticket. (See restrictions in the Air Travel Glossary.)

You may discover that those impossibly cheap flights are 'fully booked, but we have another one that costs a bit more ...' Or the flight is on an airline notorious for its poor safety standards and leaves you in the world's least favourite airport in mid-journey for 14 hours. Or they claim only to have the last two seats available for that country for the whole of July, which they will hold for you for a maximum of two hours. Don't panic – keep ringing around.

Use the fares quoted in this book as a guide only. They are approximate and based on the rates advertised by travel agents at the time of going to press. Quoted airfares do not necessarily constitute a recommendation for the carrier. If you are travelling from the UK or the USA, you will probably find that the cheapest flights are being advertised by obscure bucket shops whose names haven't yet reached the telephone directory. Many such firms are honest and solvent, but there are a few rogues who will take your money and disappear, to reopen elsewhere a month or two later under a new name.

If you feel suspicious about a firm, don't give them all the money at once – leave a deposit of 20% or so and pay the balance when you get the ticket. If they insist on cash in advance, go elsewhere. And once you have the ticket, ring the airline to confirm that you are actually booked onto the flight.

You may decide to pay more than the rockbottom fare by opting for the safety of a better-known travel agent. Firms such as STA, which has offices worldwide, Council Travel in the USA or Travel CUTS in Canada are not going to disappear overnight, leaving you clutching a receipt for a non-existent ticket, but they do offer good prices to most destinations.

Worldwide, there are a number of student travel organisations which offer bargain-basement airfares to out-of-the-way destinations the world over, including the Pacific. These agencies also offer normal travel agency services to non-students, so it's worth checking with them even if you aren't a student, especially if you are under 26 years old.

Once you have your ticket, write down its number, together with the flight number and other details, and keep the information separate. If the ticket is lost or stolen, this will help you get a replacement.

Travellers with Special Needs

If you have special needs of any sort – you've broken a leg, you're vegetarian, travelling in a wheelchair, taking the baby, terrified of flying – you should let the airline know as soon as possible. You should remind them when you reconfirm your booking (at least 72 hours before departure) and again when you check in at the airport. It may also be worth ringing round the airlines before you make your booking to find out how they can handle your particular needs.

Airports and airlines can be surprisingly helpful, but they do need advance warning. Most international airports will provide escorts from check-in desk to plane where needed, and there should be ramps, lifts, accessible toilets and reachable phones. Aircraft toilets, on the other hand, are likely to present a problem; travellers should discuss this with the airline at an early stage and, if necessary, with their doctor.

Guide dogs for the blind will often have to travel in a specially pressurised baggage compartment. Guide dogs are subject to the same quarantine laws (six months in isolation etc) as any other animal when entering or returning to countries currently free of rabies such as Britain or Australia.

Deaf travellers can ask for airport and in-flight announcements to be written down for them.

Children under two travel for 10% of the standard fare (or free, on some airlines), as long as they don't occupy a seat. They don't get a baggage allowance either. 'Skycots' should be provided by the airline if requested in advance; these will take a child weighing up to about 10kg. Children between two and 12 can usually occupy a seat for half to two-thirds of the full fare and do get a baggage allowance. Pushchairs can often be taken as hand luggage.

International Air Passes

International air passes can be great if you want to do some island-hopping around the Pacific. Polynesian Airlines' Polypass is good for 45 days and includes Tonga, Samoa, American Samoa, Fiji, Australia (Sydney, Melbourne or Brisbane) and New Zealand (Auckland, Wellington or Christchurch).

The basic cost is US$999 (children US$500, infants US$100). There's also an option to include Honolulu (US$1149), or Honolulu and Los Angeles (US$1399). Travel can be started at any point. The USA/Australia/New Zealand sectors are limited to one round-trip each, but you are allowed unlimited travel between Tonga, Samoa, American Samoa and Fiji.

Fiji's national flag carrier, Air Pacific, offers several international air passes. One South Pacific Triangle 60-day pass lets you visit Tonga, Apia (Samoa) and Nadi (Fiji) for T$609. Another 60-day pass visits Tonga, Fiji and Auckland for T$967 (or NZ$1248 or FJ$1140).

Any Air Pacific office should be able to provide information about these and other Air Pacific passes.

The Visit South Pacific Pass does have a

❋❋❋❋❋❋❋❋❋❋❋❋❋❋❋❋❋❋❋❋❋❋❋❋❋❋❋❋❋❋

Air Travel Glossary

Apex Apex, or 'advance purchase excursion' is a discounted ticket which must be paid for in advance. There are penalties if you wish to change it.

Baggage Allowance This will be written on your ticket: usually one 20kg item to go in the hold, plus one item of hand luggage.

Bucket Shop An unbonded travel agency specialising in discounted airline tickets.

Bumped Just because you have a confirmed seat doesn't mean you'll get on the plane – see Overbooking.

Cancellation Penalties If you have to cancel or change an Apex ticket there are often heavy penalties involved, insurance can sometimes be taken out against them. Some airlines impose penalties on regular tickets as well, particularly against 'no show' passengers.

Check In Airlines ask you to check in a certain time ahead of the flight departure (usually 1½ hours on international flights). If you don't check in on time and the flight is overbooked the airline can cancel your booking and give your seat to somebody else.

Confirmation Having a ticket written out with the flight and date you want doesn't mean you have a seat until the agent has checked with the airline that your status is 'OK' or confirmed. Meanwhile you could just be 'on request'.

Discounted Tickets There are two types of discounted fares – officially discounted (see Promotional Fares) and unofficially discounted. The lowest prices often impose drawbacks like flying with unpopular airlines, inconvenient schedules, or unpleasant routes and connections. A discounted ticket can save you other things than money – you may be able to pay Apex prices without the associated Apex advance booking and other requirements. Discounted tickets only exist where there is fierce competition.

Full Fares Airlines traditionally offer first class (coded F), business class (coded J) and economy class (coded Y) tickets. These days there are so many promotional and discounted fares available from the regular economy class that few passengers pay full economy fare.

Lost Tickets If you lose your airline ticket an airline will usually treat it like a travellers' cheque and, after inquiries, issue you with another one. Legally, however, an airline is entitled to treat it like cash and if you lose it then it's gone forever. Take good care of your tickets.

❋❋❋❋❋❋❋❋❋❋❋❋❋❋❋❋❋❋❋❋❋❋❋❋❋❋❋❋❋❋

number of restrictions but, if you can meet all the requirements, this is probably one of the most economical ways to travel in the South Pacific region, offering savings of up to 50% off the prices of normal fares. The pass can be bought through participating airlines and also through any IATA travel agent.

It offers discounted airfares on a wide variety of South Pacific routes. The options are many and varied – altogether the pass covers 45 possible routes. Ask a travel agent for route details. The cost is US$175 per sector for 'Group A' flights, US$220 per sector for 'Group B' flights and US$320 per sector for 'Group C' flights. Tonga-Nadi, Tonga-Apia and Tonga-Niue all cost US$175, Tonga-Auckland US$220, and Tonga-Sydney US$320 (all prices one-way, double for return).

Airlines which participate in this scheme include Air Caledonie, Air Nauru, Air Niugini (Air New Guinea), Air Pacific, Air Vanuatu, Polynesian Airlines, Qantas, Royal Tongan Airlines and Solomon Airlines.

The requirements are as follows: fares must be purchased in conjunction with international air or sea travel to/from points in the south-west Pacific region *before* you

❋❋*❋*❋*❋*❋*❋*❋*❋*❋*❋*❋*❋*❋* *❋*❋*❋*❋*❋*❋*❋*❋*❋*❋*❋*

No-Shows No shows are passengers who fail to show up for their flight. Full fare passengers who fail to turn up are sometimes entitled to travel on a later flight. The rest of us are penalised (see Cancellation Penalties).

On Request An unconfirmed booking for a flight, see Confirmation.

Open Jaws A return ticket where you fly out to one place but return from another. If available this can save you backtracking to your arrival point.

Overbooking Airlines hate to fly empty seats and since every flight has some passengers who fail to show up (see No Shows) airlines often book more passengers than they have seats. Usually the excess passengers balance those who fail to show up but occasionally somebody gets bumped. If this happens guess who it is most likely to be? The passengers who check in late.

Promotional Fares Officially discounted fares like Apex fares which are available from travel agents or direct from the airline.

Reconfirmation At least 72 hours prior to departure time of an onward or return flight you must contact the airline and 'reconfirm' that you intend to be on the flight. If you don't do this the airline can delete your name from the passenger list and you could lose your seat.

Restrictions Discounted tickets often have various restrictions on them – advance purchase is the most usual one (see Apex). Others are restrictions on the minimum and maximum period you must be away, such as a minimum of 14 days or a maximum of one year. See Cancellation Penalties.

Standby A discounted ticket where you only fly if there is a seat free at the last moment. Standby fares are usually only available on domestic routes.

Tickets Out An entry requirement for many countries is that you have an onward or return ticket, in other words, a ticket out of the country. If you're not sure what you intend to do next, the easiest solution is to buy the cheapest onward ticket to a neighbouring country or, alternatively, buy a return ticket from a reliable airline which can later be refunded if you do not use it.

Transferred Tickets Airline tickets cannot be transferred from one person to another. Travellers sometimes try to sell the return half of their ticket, but officials can ask you to prove that you are the person named on the ticket. This is unlikely to happen on domestic flights; on an international flight tickets may be compared with passports.

❋❋*❋*❋*❋*❋*❋*❋*❋*❋*❋*❋*❋*❋*❋* *❋*❋*❋*❋*❋*❋*❋*❋*❋*❋*❋*

travel to the region. The fares may only be sold to residents of a country outside the south-west Pacific region (proof of residency must be provided).

You must purchase a minimum of two flights before you arrive in the south-west Pacific region. Once you are there, you can purchase additional flights from participating airline offices or alternatively from travel agents for the same prices, up to a maximum of eight flights (or you can buy up to eight from the beginning). The maximum stay on the pass is six months from the date of commencement of travel on the first sector of the pass.

Round-the-World Tickets & Circle Pacific Fares

Round-the-world (RTW) tickets have become very popular in the last few years. Since Tonga is pretty much on the opposite side of the world from Europe and the North American east coast, it can work out no more expensive or even cheaper to keep going in the same direction right around the world rather than backtrack on your return. Prices start at about UK£850, A$1800 or US$1300.

The official airline RTW tickets are generally put together by a combination of airlines and permit you to fly anywhere you want on their route systems so long as you do not backtrack. Other restrictions are that you (usually) must book the first sector in advance and cancellation penalties then apply. There may be restrictions on how many stops you are permitted and usually the tickets are valid for 90 days for up to one year. An alternative type of RTW ticket is one put together by a travel agent using a combination of discounted tickets.

Circle Pacific tickets use a combination of airlines to circle the Pacific – combining Australia, New Zealand, North America and Asia, with the option of stops at a number of South Pacific islands. As with RTW tickets there are advance purchase restrictions and limits to how many stopovers you can make. These fares are likely to be around 15% cheaper than Round-the-World tickets.

The USA

Los Angeles and Honolulu are the two major gateway cities for travel between the USA (and Canada) and the South Pacific.

From the USA mainland, Los Angeles is the major gateway city. However, there are also direct flights to Honolulu from nearly every major city in the country. In Honolulu you can connect with a direct flight to Tonga on either Air New Zealand or Royal Tongan Airlines – they code-share portions of a weekly flight which goes Los Angeles-Honolulu-Tonga-Auckland-Sydney (and return). See the section on Air New Zealand's Pacifica fares if you plan to visit a number of South Pacific islands.

The fastest way into the south-west Pacific, coming from the USA, is to take the Air Pacific/Qantas flight direct from Los Angeles to Nadi (Fiji). It flies three times a week. From Nadi, you can catch a direct flight to Tongatapu with either Air Pacific or Royal Tongan Airlines. Royal Tongan also has a flight routed Nadi-Vava'u-Tongatapu, enabling you to enter or exit Tonga at either Tongatapu or Vava'u. From Nadi it's a 1-1/4-hour flight to Tongatapu or a two-hour flight to Vava'u.

In general, December and January are the most expensive and congested months to travel, while the northern summer, corresponding to the Tongan winter, is the cheapest and easiest time to get a booking, and is fortunately also the driest and most comfortable season to visit Tonga.

Two of the most reputable discount travel agencies in the USA are STA Travel and CIEE/Council Travel Services. Contact STA Travel, National Head Office, 6560 North Scottsdale Rd, Suite F100, Scottsdale, AZ 85253 (toll-free ☎ (800) 777-0112; fax (602) 922-0793) or CIEE/Council Travel Services, National Head Office, 205 East 42nd St, New York, NY 10017 (☎ (212) 822-2600; toll-free (800) 226-8624; fax (212) 822-2699) to ask about prices, find an office near you, purchase tickets by mail or buy an ISIC card. STA has offices in Los Angeles, Santa Monica, San Francisco, Berkeley, Seattle, Chicago, Boston, Cambridge, Philadelphia, New York, Washington DC, Miami, Gainesville and Tampa. Council Travel has 52 offices throughout the USA.

Two other reputable agencies specialise in travel in the South Pacific region; both do a lot of nationwide business and they can mail tickets to you, wherever you are. Island Adventures, 574 Mills Way, Goleta CA 93117 (☎ (805) 685-9230, toll-free (800) 289-4957; fax (805) 685-0960; email motuman@aol.com) specialises in personal service; owner Rob Jenneve is very helpful and knowledgeable about all kinds of options for travel in the South Pacific region, a great resource for trip planning. Discover Wholesale Travel, 2192 Dupont Drive, Suite 116, Irvine, CA 92612-1322 (toll-free (800) 576-7770 in California, (800) 759-7330 elsewhere; fax (714) 833-1176; email disc_tvl@ix.netcom.com) specialises in discounted fares – it's worth checking with them.

The Sunday travel sections of papers like the *Los Angeles Times*, the *San Francisco Examiner*, the *Chicago Tribune* and the *New York Times* always have plenty of ads for cheap airline tickets and there are often good deals on flights across the Pacific, especially in the west coast papers. Even if you don't live in these areas, you can have the tickets sent to you by mail. The magazine *Travel Unlimited* (PO Box 1058, Allston, Mass 02134) publishes details of the cheapest airfares and courier possibilities for destinations all over the world from the USA.

Air New Zealand's 'Pacifica' Fares Air New Zealand's flights between Los Angeles and New Zealand have some excellent stopover options, especially handy if you'd like to visit several Pacific islands. Stopover options include Honolulu, Tahiti, Rarotonga, Samoa, Tonga and Fiji. You can also continue on from Auckland to Australia for an extra US$103 as another stopover option. You can ask for as many or as few stopovers as you like, with a few restrictions on how you can organise your routing (there's no direct flight between Honolulu and Tahiti, for example). There's no limitation on how long you can stay at any stopover point, as long as you finish your entire trip by the specified time.

One-month, three-month, six-month and one-year return tickets are available. No stopovers are allowed on one-month tickets, but three-month and six-month tickets allow one free stopover, with the option of additional stopovers for US$135 each. Six free stopovers are allowed on one-year tickets.

The basic one-month return (round-trip) Los Angeles-Auckland-Los Angeles flight costs US$925. A three-month Los Angeles-Auckland-Los Angeles ticket with one stopover is US$1048 to US$1108, with additional stopovers for US$135 each. Six-month tickets are US$1198 with the same stopover options; one-year tickets, allowing six free stopovers, cost US$1758.

All these prices are low season; add US$200 for shoulder season, or US$400 for high season travel. Low season prices apply from mid-April to the end of August. High season prices apply from December to February. Shoulder season prices apply during the rest of the year.

Air New Zealand also has arrangements with other airlines whereby you can add the Solomon Islands, Vanuatu, New Guinea and New Caledonia as further stopover options. Check with Air New Zealand for details on these, as these fares are outside their basic Pacifica fare structure. Or see the above section on international air passes, which can be a good option for travel once you are in the south-west Pacific.

Canada

Canadians will probably find the best deals travelling to the South Pacific via Honolulu. Air Pacific, Fiji's national airline, has direct flights to Honolulu from Vancouver and Toronto; from Honolulu you fly first to Nadi (Fiji), from where you can catch direct flights to Tonga and various other places around the South Pacific including Australia and New Zealand.

Air New Zealand's weekly Vancouver-Honolulu-Tonga-Auckland flight is convenient. See the USA section for more details on Air New Zealand's options for travel in the Pacific region. See also the section on international air passes earlier in this chapter.

In Canada, the student and discount agency is Travel CUTS/Voyages Campus, which has 46 offices around Canada. You don't have to be a student to use its services. Its national head office is at 187 College Street, Toronto, ON M5T 1P7 (☎ (416) 979-2406 or (416) 798-CUTS; fax (416) 979-8167; mail@travelcuts.com; www.travelcuts.com).

The *Toronto Globe & Mail* and the *Vancouver Sun* carry travel agents' ads. The magazine *Great Expeditions* (PO Box 8000-411, Abbotsford BC V2S 6H1) is useful. Travellers interested in booking flights with Canadian courier companies should obtain a copy of the *Travel Unlimited* newsletter mentioned in the USA section.

South America

Lan Chile airline has three flights a week between Papeete (Tahiti) and Santiago

(Chile), with a stop at Easter Island on the way. In Papeete you can connect with Air New Zealand's flights coming across the Pacific. See the USA section for more on Air New Zealand's services in the South Pacific.

The UK & Europe

Europeans usually fly to the South Pacific via Los Angeles, Sydney or Auckland. Considering the location of the South Pacific relative to Europe, a Round-the-World ticket may be the most economical way to go (see earlier in this chapter).

Currently, the best fares from Europe to the South Pacific are with Air New Zealand from London or Frankfurt to Los Angeles, with connections from Los Angeles to the rest of the South Pacific (see the USA section). If you'd like to visit a few places, these fares work out cheaper overall if you fly with Australia or New Zealand as your final destination. Stopover possibilities between Europe and Australia include Los Angeles, Honolulu (Hawaii), Papeete (Tahiti), Rarotonga (Cook Islands), Nadi (Fiji), Apia (Samoa), Tonga and Auckland (New Zealand). It's also possible to break your journey in Los Angeles, overland to Vancouver, and fly from there for no extra charge. These tickets may be used in combination with another carrier as part of a Round-the-World routing.

Air New Zealand's fares are the same whether you start from London or Frankfurt. Its flights to Tonga stop first in Los Angeles; then you have the option of a stopover in either Honolulu or Apia, for an extra £55 per stopover. There are six price brackets: January to February £1176, February to mid-April £996, mid-April to June £656, July to October £1142, November £1081, December £1148 to £1580.

Fares to Australia and New Zealand cost a bit more, but they include unlimited stopovers in the Pacific. Again there are six price brackets: January £1198; February to April £1176-£1024, April to June £874, July to October £1171, November £1109, December £1176-£1608.

If you want to stop over in Asia at any of the destinations covered by Air New Zealand you are looking at a Round the World fare, which in high season (December to February) is £1564 and in low season (the rest of the year) is £1440.

There are bucket shops by the dozen in London, Amsterdam, Brussels, Frankfurt, Paris and a few other places. In London, several magazines with lots of bucket-shop ads can put you on to the current deals. In these magazines, you'll often find discounted fares to the US west coast, Honolulu, New Zealand or Australia, some of which allow stopovers or inexpensive connections to the Pacific islands.

Most British travel agents are registered with ABTA (Association of British Travel Agents). If you have paid for your flight to an ABTA-registered agent who then goes out of business, ABTA will guarantee a refund or an alternative. Unregistered bucket shops are riskier but cheaper. Other sources of information for budget travellers include *Trailfinder* magazine, *Time Out*, *TNT* magazine and *Globe*, the Globetrotters' Club newsletter. Look for travel agents' ads in the *Saturday Telegraph*, *Exchange & Mart* and the Sunday papers.

To initiate your price comparisons in the UK, try contacting travel agents such as Trailfinders (☎ (0171) 938-3939/3366) and Bridge the World (0171) 911-0900), both in London; or the helpful and highly recommended Travel Bug (☎ (0161) 721-4000) in Manchester. STA also has branches in the UK. For courier flight details, contact Polo Express (☎ (0181) 759-5383) or Courier Travel Service (☎ (0171) 351-0300).

On the Continent, the newsletter *Farang* (La Rue 8 à 4261, Braives, Belgium) deals with exotic destinations, as does the magazine *Aventure au Bout du Monde* (116 rue de Javel, 75015 Paris). In Amsterdam, NBBS is a popular travel agent.

Australia & New Zealand

Travelling to Tonga from Australia or New Zealand is straightforward, but not necessarily inexpensive.

Air New Zealand, Royal Tongan Airlines and Polynesian Airlines all operate direct flights between Auckland and Tonga, a 2½ to three-hour flight. They also offer flights between Sydney or Melbourne and Tonga, routed through Auckland. Basic return fare from Auckland to Tonga is around NZ$980 for a 90-day ticket, NZ$1600 for a one-year ticket. From Sydney or Melbourne a six-month ticket costs around A$1100.

Air New Zealand's routing, code-shared with Royal Tongan, flies weekly Sydney-Auckland-Tonga-Honolulu-Los Angeles and return. Polynesian Airlines has a weekly Auckland-Tonga-Apia (Samoa) return flight.

Air Pacific, Fiji's international airline, operates direct flights connecting Fiji with Auckland, Wellington and Christchurch (New Zealand), and with Brisbane, Sydney and Melbourne (Australia). They have direct flights between Nadi (Fiji) and Tongatapu three times a week, a short 1¼-hour hop, code-shared with Royal Tongan Airlines. Royal Tongan also offers a separate flight routed Nadi-Vava'u-Tongatapu, enabling you to enter or exit Tonga at either Tongatapu or Vava'u. From Nadi it's a two-hour flight to Vava'u, or a 1¼-hour flight to Tongatapu.

The December-January holiday season is the busiest time to fly between Australia, New Zealand and Tonga, as large numbers of Tongans living in these countries travel home to Tonga for the holidays. Keep this in mind if you want to travel at this time, and make your bookings as far in advance as possible. Special discounted fares are often on offer during this season, costing about 25% less than the normal fares.

STA and Flight Centres International are major dealers in cheap air fares in both Australia and New Zealand. In addition to the student travel agencies listed earlier in this chapter, you may want to check with the Pacific Island Travel Centre (☎ (02) 9262-6011 in Sydney; (03) 9663-3649 in Melbourne; fax (02) 9262-6318), which specialises in Pacific travel. Another possibility is Pacific Unlimited Holidays in Sydney (☎ (02) 9390-2266; fax 9290-2419) or in Melbourne (☎ (03) 9650-2387; fax 9654-6994).

Asia & Japan

Several convenient air routes exist between Tonga, Asia and Japan. Air Pacific operates direct flights connecting Tokyo and Osaka with Nadi (Fiji); Air New Zealand operates direct flights between Nagoya and Nadi. In Nadi you can connect to a direct flight to Tonga with Air Pacific (going to Tongatapu) or Royal Tongan Airlines (going to Tongatapu or Vava'u).

Coming from other parts of Asia, your flight will probably be routed through Auckland (New Zealand). Innumerable flights connect Auckland with many parts of Asia, some via Australia. From Auckland it's a direct 2½ to three-hour flight to Tonga.

Ticket discounting is widespread in Asia, particularly in Hong Kong, Singapore and Bangkok; Hong Kong is probably the discount air-ticket capital of the region. There are a lot of fly-by-nights in the Asian ticketing scene so a little care is required. STA, which is reliable, has branches in Hong Kong, Tokyo, Singapore, Bangkok and Kuala Lumpur.

Other Pacific Islands

There's plenty of scope for island-hopping within the South Pacific region. Consider one of the international air passes (see the International Air Passes section) or Air New Zealand's Pacifica fare schedule (see the USA section), which offer big savings.

Nadi (Fiji) and Auckland (New Zealand) are the region's two major air transport hubs. Nadi is just a quick 1¼-hour hop from Tonga; Auckland is a 2½ to three-hour flight.

Direct Royal Tongan Airlines/Air Pacific flights between Tongatapu and Nadi operate three times weekly. The cost is T$379 return for a 28-day ticket, more for a one-year ticket.

Royal Tongan operates a weekly flight Tongatapu-Vava'u-Nadi and return, enabling you to enter or exit Tonga at either

Tongatapu or Vava'u. Fares are T$380 return for a Vava'u-Nadi 30-day ticket, T$480 for a 30-day ticket Vava'u-Nadi-Tongatapu-Vava'u, more for a one-year ticket. From Nadi it's a two-hour flight to Vava'u, or a 1¼-hour flight to Tongatapu.

Direct flights between Tongatapu and Apia (Samoa) are offered weekly by both Polynesian Airlines and Royal Tongan Airlines. Cost is T$305 return for a 28-day ticket, more for a one-year ticket.

Direct flights between Vava'u and Pago Pago (American Samoa), a 1½-hour flight, are offered by Samoa Air twice each week, for T$235/424 one-way/return.

Direct flights between Tongatapu and Niue, a two-hour flight, operate once or twice each week. Cost is T$340 return for a 28-day ticket, more for a one-year ticket. Royal Tongan is the only international airline serving Niue.

Once a week there's a direct flight between Tonga and Honolulu (Hawaii), which continues on to Los Angeles. See the USA section.

SEA
Cargo Ship
Many travellers arrive in the South Pacific with grand dreams of island-hopping aboard cargo ships, but few actually manage it. All sorts of insurance and freight company restrictions have made such travel difficult now; the days of working or tramping your way around the world on cargo ships are just about over. Coming by yacht, however, is a real possibility.

Yachts
Between May and October the harbours of the South Pacific swarm with cruising yachts from around the world. Almost invariably, they'll be following the favourable winds west from the Americas.

Routes from the US west coast take in Hawaii and Palmyra before following the traditional path through the Samoas, Tonga, Fiji and New Zealand. From the Atlantic and Caribbean, yachties will access this area via Venezuela, Panama, the Galápagos

Islands, the Marquesas, the Society Islands and Tuamotus, possibly making stops at Suwarrow in the northern Cook Islands, Rarotonga or Niue en route. Because of the cyclone season, which begins in November, most yachties will want to clear Fiji or Tonga and be on their way to New Zealand by the early part of that month.

Access to Tonga is almost always from Samoa or American Samoa. Often, yachts anchor for a few days in Niuatoputapu where they check into Tonga before crowding into Vava'u's Port of Refuge, anchoring in front of the Paradise International Hotel and proceeding to set up the annual yachting social colony that is really going strong by the beginning of October. Most yachties take day trips around the Vava'u Group before proceeding on to Nuku'alofa, with a possible intermediate visit to the Ha'apai Group.

The yachting community is quite friendly, especially toward those who display an interest in yachts and other things nautical. Often they are looking for crew, and for those who'd like a bit of low-key adventure, this is the way to go. Most of the time, crew members will only be asked to take a turn on watch – that is, scan the horizon for cargo ships, stray containers and the odd reef – and possibly to cook or clean up the ship. In port, they may be required to dive and scrape the bottom, paint or make repairs. In most cases, sailing experience is not necessary and crew members have the option to learn as they go. Most yachties will charge crew US$10 to US$15 per day for food and supplies.

The best places to secure a passage on a cruising yacht are, naturally, east or northeast of Tonga. The west coast of the USA is a prime hunting ground – San Francisco, Newport Beach, San Diego and Honolulu are all good. Likewise, it shouldn't be too difficult to crew on in Papeete, Pago Pago or Apia.

The best way to make known your availability is to post a notice on the bulletin board of the yacht club in the port. It would also be helpful to visit the docks and ask people if they know anyone setting off on a cruise around the time you'd like to go who might be looking for crew members. It may be a matter of interest that the most successful passage-seekers tend to be young women who are willing to crew on with male 'single-handers' (that is, who sail alone). Naturally, the bounds of the relationship should be fairly well defined before setting out!

For sanity's sake, bear in mind that not everyone is compatible with everyone else and that under the conditions of a long ocean voyage, rivalries and petty distress are magnified many times. Only set out on a long passage with someone with whom you can feel relatively comfortable and remember that, once aboard, the skipper's judgement is law.

If you'd like to enjoy some relative freedom of movement on a yacht, it's a good idea to try to find one that has windvane steering. Nobody likes to spend all day and all night at the wheel staring at a compass, and more often than not such a job is likely to go to the crew members of the lowest status. Comfort is also greatly increased on yachts which have a furling jib, a dodger to keep out the weather, a toilet and shower.

Yachts rigged for racing are generally more manageable than simple live-aboards. As a general rule, about 3m of length for each person aboard affords relatively uncrowded conditions.

For those who aren't interested in cruising, yachties still have a mind-boggling store of knowledge about world weather patterns, navigation and maritime geography and can be considered a good source of information regarding such things.

While they seem to give off an aura of wealth, most yachties are as impecunious as the average backpacking traveller and are always looking for ways to pick up a bit of money. If you're looking for a babysitter or a day charter, just ask around the harbours, particularly in Neiafu and Nuku'alofa. Quite a few skippers are of necessity certified divers also, and those with credentials to teach and certify others will normally be happy to do so. Many yachties will also teach celestial navigation and sailing for a reasonable fee.

Arriving by Yacht If you're arriving by yacht, ports of entry for cruising yachts are Nuku'alofa (Tongatapu), Neiafu (Vava'u), Pangai, Lifuka (Ha'apai), Falehau (Niuatoputapu) and Futu (Niuafo'ou).

In Nuku'alofa, in order to check in and clear immigration, raise your yellow quarantine flag and anchor in the restricted anchorage area, or pull up alongside Queen Salote wharf or the yacht harbour (2.6m deep at the entrance and dredged to 3m inside) and summon customs and immigration officials by radioing VHF channel 16 or 68. Instruction will be given on VHF channel 12.

Customs and immigration officials will board, ask the usual questions about food and health, and request passports and a passenger list. Officers are on duty weekdays from 8.30 am to 12.30 pm and 1.30 to 4.30 pm. Currently, there is no check-in on weekends.

At Niuafo'ou, it will be impossible to pull up alongside so you'll have to anchor offshore and wait for a calm moment to battle your way through the waves to the shore. For this daring feat, you'll need a motorised dinghy.

Passengers and crew will initially be granted 30-day tourist visas, which may be extended for up to six months at the police stations in Nuku'alofa and Neiafu. Firearms and ammunition must be deposited with customs officers, to be returned when you depart the country. There's a monthly charge, based on the length of the yacht, for anchoring anywhere in Tongan waters. The average charge is about T$20 to T$40 per month or portion thereof.

Day cruising within island groups is not restricted, but if you'll be cruising between island groups (Tongatapu, Ha'apai, Vava'u and the Niuas), you'll have to pay all harbour dues and pick up a Coastal Clearance Permit from a customs officer. A

Yachting Regulations

Never anchor in coral beds or allow your anchor to drag through live coral. Always anchor in sand or deeper water.

Loud parties, noise, making repairs and working with power tools are prohibited on Sunday.

Nude (or, for women, topless) sunbathing on deck is not permitted in the harbours or when anchored within view of the shore.

Export by yacht of any marine product, such as shells, carved black coral or commercial quantities of fish or shellfish, requires a permit from customs (this will also prevent headaches in subsequent ports of call). Uncarved black coral may not be exported under any circumstances.

Commercial activities are officially discouraged.

permit to cruise between Nuku'alofa and Vava'u may be amended to include Ha'apai, allowing you to stop in Ha'apai without picking up a separate permit. You must always check in with customs when visiting a port, even if you've already been admitted to the country.

DEPARTURE TAXES

Departure tax is T$20, payable at the airport.

WARNING

The information in this chapter is particularly vulnerable to change: prices for international travel are volatile, routes are introduced and cancelled, schedules change, special deals come and go, and rules and visa requirements are amended. Airlines and governments seem to take a perverse pleasure in making price structures and regulations as complicated as possible. Check directly with the airline or a travel agent to make sure you understand how a fare (and ticket you may buy) works. The travel industry is highly competitive and there are many lurks and perks.

The upshot of this is that you should get opinions, quotes and advice from as many airlines and travel agents as possible before you part with your hard-earned cash. The details given in this chapter should be regarded as pointers and are certainly not a substitute for your own up-to-date research.

Getting Around

AIR

Flying is by far the easiest and fastest way to get around Tonga.

Domestic air travellers in Tonga have only two choices: Royal Tongan Airlines, the national flag carrier, and the tiny Pacific Island Air. Royal Tongan is the only one with regularly scheduled flights; Pacific Island Air's small eight-seater seaplane operates only by charter or arrangement and it is hoping to have an eight-passenger Beech 18 aeroplane in Tonga before this book comes out.

Royal Tongan operates three planes: a 19-seat Twin Otter and a 40-seat HS748 for domestic flights and a 126-seat Boeing 737, jointly leased with Air Pacific, for overseas routes.

The busiest time of year for both domestic and international flights is summer holiday season in December and January. Mid-June to mid-July is another busy time, and there may be others, depending on special events in Tonga.

Schedules & Fares

Royal Tongan operates a convenient schedule of flights around Tonga every day except Sunday. Flights make the short 10-minute hop between Tongatapu and 'Eua five days a week. Direct return flights between Tongatapu and Vava'u operate five days a week, with extra flights on Friday. Direct return flights between Tongatapu and Ha'apai operate three days a week. And there is a Tongatapu-Ha'apai-Vava'u-Tongatapu flight three times weekly, along with a Tongatapu-Vava'u-Ha'apai-Tongatapu flight twice a week.

Flights between Tongatapu and the Niuas, flying via Vava'u, operate once a week, with the plane going to Niuatoputapu for two weeks and to Niuafo'ou on the third week. There are no direct flights between Niuatoputapu and Niuafo'ou.

There's a 10kg baggage allowance on do-mestic flights unless you're connecting with Royal Tongan from an overseas flight, in which case you're allowed 20kg of checked baggage per person. Fares and flying time are as follows:

Flight	One-Way	Return
Tongatapu/'Eua	T$19	T$36
Tongatapu/Ha'apai	T$67	T$129
Tongatapu/Vava'u	T$129	T$248
Tongatapu/Niuatoputapu	T$227	T$433
Tongatapu/Niuafo'ou	T$279	T$536
Ha'apai/Vava'u	T$67	T$124
Vava'u/Niuatoputapu	T$114	T$217
Vava'u/Niuafo'ou	T$170	T$330

Air Passes

Royal Tongan Airlines' Kingdom Pass allows you to travel between Tongatapu, Ha'apai, Vava'u and 'Eua, all for T$250 (children between two and 12 pay 67% of adult fare; children under two, 10%). The pass is sold only in combination with international travel commencing in the northern hemisphere (ie Europe, UK, USA, Japan etc), so you must buy it *before* you arrive in Tonga, at the same time as you buy your international flight tickets. Domestic reservations may be made after you have arrived in Tonga.

The pass is good for a minimum/maximum of seven/30 days. There's no charge to change your dates once reservations have been made, but there's a T$10 charge per coupon if you want to change your route.

CAR & MOTORCYCLE

Rental cars are available on Tongatapu, Ha'apai and Vava'u; see those sections for details. Hiring a car or van with a driver is another option; this can be done on all of these islands, and on 'Eua.

Drinking and driving is strictly forbidden in Tonga, even though it's apparent that some people don't take much notice of this law. If there's an accident and you have alcohol on your breath, you're sent to prison whether or not you were at fault.

Drivers should be careful to keep their speed down to 40km/hr in villages and towns and 55km/hr elsewhere, especially now that the government has purchased radar guns. If you're caught speeding, you'll have to pay a fine.

On Tongatapu, if you see a blue-and-grey Chevrolet Silverado with the number plate HM1 led by police escort, pull off the road and wait for it to pass. If it's accompanied by a siren, the king is aboard (or the senior royal present in the country at the time). If there's only a flashing blue light, it could be the queen, the princess or one of the princes.

BICYCLE

Cycling is a cheap, convenient, healthy, environmentally sound and above all fun way of travelling. Cycling allows you to see the islands at island pace. Distances aren't great in Tonga and the low traffic density is conducive to travel by bike. Tongatapu and the Lifuka Group in Ha'apai are pancake-flat; Vava'u and 'Eua can be negotiated with a bit of effort.

Rental bicycles are available on all of these islands; see the individual island chapters for details. Rental costs around T$5 to T$10 per day, with discounts possible by the week.

Bicycles can travel by air, so if you want to bring your own bike, that is an option. You *can* take it to pieces and put it in a bike bag or box, but it's much easier simply to wheel your bike to the check-in desk, where it should be treated as a piece of baggage. You may have to remove the pedals and turn the handlebars sideways so that it takes up less space in the aircraft's hold; check all this with the airline well in advance, preferably before you pay for your ticket.

One note of caution: before you leave home, go over your bike with a fine-tooth comb and fill your repair kit with every imaginable spare. You probably won't be able to buy that crucial gizmo for your machine if it breaks down in Tonga.

HITCHING

Hitching is never entirely safe in any country in the world and we don't recommend it. Travellers who decide to hitch should understand that they are taking a small but potentially serious risk.

Hitchhiking is not the custom in Tonga and it's quite likely you'll never see anyone do it. If you do, it will be a foreigner, not a local. Hitching is not illegal, however, and if you do hitchhike you'll probably get a ride in short order. You may have better luck if you flag down a vehicle rather than sticking your thumb out.

BOAT
Inter-Island Ferry

Several passenger freighters travel between the main island groups.

A trip by ferry in Tonga is a cultural experience on a major scale. Cabin space is limited but the price of a cabin will set you back more than the cost of an airfare anyway, so you'll probably end up being a deck passenger. Indoor spaces are stuffy, cramped and claustrophobic, while outdoor spaces are likely to be wet and/or cold.

The information published here about schedules, fares, etc was correct at the time of writing, but you should double-check before making plans as these details can change at any time.

The MV *'Olovaha* (known as the 'Orange Vomit' by those who know her well) was built in Bremen, Germany, in 1981 and is now owned by the Shipping Corporation of Polynesia (☎ 21-699, fax 21-617 in Nuku'alofa), which has an office on Queen Salote Wharf in Nuku'alofa and others near the wharves in Vava'u and Ha'apai. The *'Olovaha* does weekly runs between Tongatapu (Nuku'alofa), Ha'apai (Lifuka and Ha'afeva) and Vava'u (Neiafu). About every couple of months or so it continues to the Niuas, but it is rarely able to land at Niuafo'ou.

The *'Olovaha* has three classes of tickets: deck, business class (you get a table and chairs indoors, but no bed or place to lie down) and cabin (two-bed cabins). The

Ferry Travel in Tonga

Tongans are normally not very good sailors (neither are many travellers), and the sight of people vomiting everywhere as well as the smell, filth, cockroaches and rubbish all over the ships which go to the northern islands are bound to have some effect even on those not normally prone to seasickness. You'd be wise to take precautions. The toilets on board the ferries surpass the unspeakable; a pair of hip waders and a gas mask may come in handy as the filth from the overflowing toilets will be sloshing everywhere.

The ships are often severely overcrowded, not only to the point of discomfort but probably also to the point of being dangerous – if two or three times the recommended number of people are crammed onto a ship, do you suppose it has enough lifeboats to save all of them should an accident arise? Combine all of the foregoing with the long hours and distances involved, the often very rough open seas around Tonga, etc, and come to your own conclusion. If you have an idea of romantic South Seas boat travel, this is not it. Unless you're a glutton for punishment, do yourself a favour and don't take these boats. In Tonga, if you want to visit the outer islands, it's better to fly.

If you do decide to go by boat, you might want to pay in sections – we've heard of plenty of travellers who thought they could withstand any gruelling form of travel, who jumped ship at the first opportunity and preferred to lose their money and fly the rest of the way, rather than to continue on these boats.

However, David May, former manager of the Friendly Islands Bookshop in Nuku'alofa,

NANCY KELLER

The SS 'Olovaha is better known to seasick travellers as the 'Orange Vomit'.

said he doesn't think the 'Olovaha is all that bad, as long as you stay out on deck, avoid eating or drinking anything for 12 hours before the trip so you won't have to use the toilet, and manage to stake out and guard your 45cm of deck space, so that you have a place to sit down!

On the other hand, boat trips between Nuku'alofa and 'Eua are not bad, especially if you take the Alaimoana, a fine little boat. The journey takes only two hours, about half of which is spent on the open sea. It's quite pleasant, especially if you perch yourself on the bough of the boat, where you may see flying fish or dolphins accompanying you across the channel, and even humpback whales in season (June to November).

fares for business class and cabin passengers include all meals; deck passengers must bring their own food. On particularly crowded runs, the business class section is often full of deck-class passengers because there simply isn't any space elsewhere. Videos are shown and food is available in business class, but few people actually feel like eating it.

On the 'Olovaha, deck/business/cabin class prices from Tongatapu to Ha'apai are T$28/51/120. From Tongatapu to Vava'u they are T$42/74/170, and from Ha'apai to Vava'u they are T$21/41/120. Between Vava'u and the Niuas, prices are T$45/70/200; between Niuatoputapu and Niuafo'ou they are T$31/50/120. To go all the way from Tongatapu to the Niuas costs T$86/

126/360. All of these are one-way prices (double for return).

The *'Olovaha* schedule is:

Dep	Nuku'alofa	5.30 pm	Tues
Arr	Ha'afeva	2 am	Wed
Dep	Ha'afeva	4 am	Wed
Arr	Pangai	7 am	Wed
Dep	Pangai	8 am	Wed
Arr	Vava'u	2 pm	Wed
Dep	Vava'u	3 pm	Thurs
Arr	Pangai	11 pm	Thurs
Dep	Pangai	1 am	Fri
Arr	Ha'afeva	4 am	Fri
Dep	Ha'afeva	5 am	Fri
Arr	Nuku'alofa	11 am	Fri

When the *'Olovaha* goes to the Niuas, it takes about 24 hours between Vava'u and either of the Niua islands and about 12 to 15 hours between Niuatoputapu and Niuafo'ou.

Alternatively, there's the Walter Line (☎ 23-855, 23-847, fax 23-860), whose Tongan name is *'Uliti 'Uata*. Their office in Nuku'alofa is upstairs on the 1st floor of the office building at the corner of Taufa'ahau and Wellington Rds. Walter Line operates two boats: the MV *Tautahi* and the decrepit MV *Lotoha'angana*, which is even less comfortable than the *'Olovaha*. Each carries around 380 passengers, plus cargo. Either boat may be pressed into service for the weekly inter-island run connecting Tongatapu (Nuku'alofa), Ha'apai (Lifuka) and Vava'u (Neiafu).

Their schedule is:

Dep	Nuku'alofa	5 pm	Mon
Arr	Pangai	3 am	Tues
Dep	Pangai	4 am	Tues
Arr	Vava'u	1 pm	Tues
Dep	Vava'u	2 pm	Tues
Arr	Pangai	9 pm	Wed
Dep	Pangai	10 pm	Wed
Arr	Nuku'alofa	8 am	Thurs

The fare from Tongatapu to Ha'apai is T$25, from Ha'apai to Vava'u it's T$20, and between Tongatapu and Vava'u it's T$40. Only deck class is available.

The MV *Alaimoana* sails between Nuku'alofa and 'Eua every day except Sunday. It leaves Nuku'alofa at 1 pm, and departs from Nafanua wharf on 'Eua for the return trip at 5.30 am the next morning. The trip takes two hours each way in fine weather; in rough seas it can be a fairly hair-raising trip, and take longer. One-way fare is T$6 (double for return). The boat is operated by Tofa Shipping (☎ 21-326, fax 25-970), whose office is on Unga Rd in Nuku'alofa, in the white two-storey building opposite Tonga Telecom. The *Alaimoana* is much smaller than the boats going to the northern groups, and it's in much better condition – this is a fine way to travel.

Another boat, the MV *Pulupaki*, sails between Nuku'alofa and 'Eua at about the same times as the *Alaimoana*. It gets started a little earlier, because it is much slower – the *Alaimoana* often passes it on the way. Its centre of gravity is higher, making it a rougher trip. If possible, it's better to go on the *Alaimoana*.

Yacht

The yachtie route through Tonga begins in Niuatoputapu and runs southward to and through Vava'u, to Ha'apai and thence to Nuku'alofa. Many yachts heading for New Zealand stop at Minerva Reef en route. October and November are the best months for yacht hitchhiking in Tonga. Details about yachting and crewing onto a yacht are covered in the Getting There & Away chapter.

Yacht and sailing charters are available in Tongatapu and Vava'u. See those chapters for details.

Other Vessels

Smaller islands off the main ferry routes can be reached by smaller boats. The Tongatapu, Vava'u and Ha'apai Groups all have boats providing transport to islands within their groups; see the respective island group chapters for details.

Or you can try your luck hitchhiking on private yachts, fishing boats and launches. Just ask around port and landing areas for one going your way.

HORSE

Horses can be rented on all inhabited islands: just ask anyone who owns a horse and you're likely to be able to strike up an informal deal. Expect to pay around T$5 to T$10 per day. Horses are usually only available without saddle, reins and other amenities, so unless you're a good bareback rider, you could have some problems. Tongan horses also seem to be adept at shedding unwanted objects that might have climbed onto their backs – this could also be a matter for concern if your horse decides it doesn't like you!

LOCAL TRANSPORT

To/From the Airport

Taxis provide airport transport on every island with an airport. Buses meet incoming flights on Tongatapu and Vava'u. Some hotels and guesthouses provide airport transfers for their guests, sometimes for free, sometimes not. Details are covered in the individual island chapters.

Most international travellers arrive in Tonga at the international airport on Tongatapu. A taxi ride between Fua'amoto airport and Nuku'alofa is limited to T$12 by the government and most drivers charge only T$10.

If your airport taxi driver insists that your selected hotel is closed, fully booked or no good, don't take it too seriously. Chances are that you've chosen an establishment that doesn't pay as much commission as the driver would like to collect for dropping you there.

Bus

Local buses run on the islands of Tongatapu, 'Eua, Vava'u, and on Lifuka and Foa in the Ha'apai Group. Fares range from 20 seniti to T$1 depending upon the island and the distance travelled. On most buses, passengers pay the fare when they leave the bus.

Tongatapu is fairly well covered by bus routes but on other islands transport is limited. In the urban areas of Tongatapu, bus stops are marked with a sign reading 'Pasi'. Elsewhere, flag down buses by waving your outstretched arm.

The biggest problem with bus travel on the outer islands is that the buses operate infrequently or only if enough passengers accumulate for a trip. Buses may quit running early in the day, even when they are scheduled to run later, and remaining passengers counting on bus service may be left stranded. Don't rely on catching a bus after about 3 pm.

Another difficulty on the outer islands is that buses in the outlying districts often exist only to take students and villagers into town in the morning and home again in the afternoon.

Taxi

Taxis throughout Tonga can be recognised by a 'T' in front of the numbers on the vehicle's license plate.

There are plenty of taxis on Tongatapu and Vava'u, as well as a few on Lifuka and 'Eua. Although taxis are not metered, the government has set maximum rates. This doesn't prevent some scampsters trying to charge more, however – unwary foreigners have been taken for T$60 rides! Always agree on the fare you will pay before you climb into a taxi. If you are still overcharged, take down the number plate and report the driver to the Tonga Visitors' Bureau.

ORGANISED TOURS

Organised tours can be a good introduction to an island and a quick, easy way to visit major sights. Commercial island tours operate on Tongatapu and Vava'u; less formal arrangements can be made on 'Eua and Ha'apai, which are smaller. Diving companies (and some of the tour companies) run tours to reefs and outlying islands. See the individual island chapters for details.

Air tours around Tonga are another possibility. Pacific Island Air Tours (☎ 25-177; fax 25-165; pacisair@candw.to; PO Box 1675, Nuku'alofa) offers charter flights to any island in Tonga, whether or not the island has an airstrip. It also offers day trips from Nuku'alofa to Tofua (see Tofua in the Ha'apai chapter) and flightseeing and transfers anywhere in Tonga. The service is extremely expensive, but very convenient.

Another option is Pacific Island Air's attractive tourist packages which offer travellers the chance to visit both the easy-of-access as well as the more remote reaches of Tonga.

Tongatapu

• *area 260 sq km* • *population 66,212*
Tongatapu (sacred south), along with its capital, Nuku'alofa (abode of love), is the hub of all activity within the kingdom of Tonga. With a land area of 260 sq km, Tongatapu constitutes one third of the country's territory. The majority of the island's population lives in Nuku'alofa and its adjoining villages.

The island of Tongatapu is pancake-flat, tilting slightly toward the sagging weight of the Ha'apai volcanoes. Cliffs on the southern shore rise to 30m while the northern coast is a drowned maze of islands and reefs.

Because the island has been Tonga's capital for at least 600 years, the Lapaha area of eastern Tongatapu contains most of the country's archaeological sites, and one of the densest concentrations of ancient structures in the Pacific. The area is riddled with *langi* (tiered tombs), and criscrossed with networks of moats. Those which have been cleared and excavated are easily visited.

Tongatapu also offers a myriad beaches, caves and quiet villages, all of which invite exploration. On the south coast you can visit the famous blowholes near the village of Houma, as well as Hufangalupe, a dramatic natural limestone arch. Reefs and motu (coral islets) are abundant in the seas north of the main island. Four of these islets have small resorts, great either for staying over or for day trips from the capital. Others are protected as national marine parks and reserves.

Old and new Tonga collide and sometimes successfully coexist on Tongatapu. For most visitors Tongatapu is their first port of call, and so provides their introduction to the kingdom. Even if you're planning exploration around the more remote areas of the country, Tongatapu is well worth a stay of at least a couple of days.

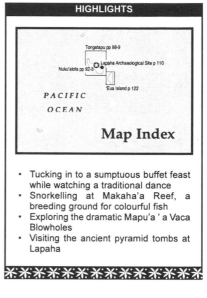

Tongatapu pp 88-9
Lapaha Archaeological Site p 110
Nuku'alofa pp 92-3
'Eua Island p 122

PACIFIC
OCEAN

Map Index

• Tucking in to a sumptuous buffet feast while watching a traditional dance
• Snorkelling at Makaha'a Reef, a breeding ground for colourful fish
• Exploring the dramatic Mapu'a 'a Vaca Blowholes
• Visiting the ancient pyramid tombs at Lapaha

History

Thanks to oral tradition, the known history of Tongatapu reads like a long series of Old Testament 'begats' with a bit of editorialising thrown in when one Tu'i Tonga or another did something notable. The first Tu'i, as you may remember, was the son of the sun god Tangaloa and a lovely Tongan maiden. He came to power sometime in the middle of the 10th century. Between that time and the ascent of King George Tupou I, the title was held by 38 men.

Around the year 1200, the Tu'i Tonga Tu'itatui set about building the only trilithic gate in Oceania. The Ha'amonga 'a Maui (Maui's burden), near the village of Niutoua, has been compared to Stonehenge, to which it bears a superficial resemblance. The present king noticed the similarity and suggested that a design on the lintel may represent some astronomical phenomenon.

NANCY KELLER

The church still has great impact on contemporary life in Tongatapu.

Experiments have confirmed that the diagram represents the directions of the rising and setting sun on the solstices.

The legend was, however, that the Tu'i Tonga constructed it originally to remind two quarrelling sons that unity was better than division. After creating a wonderful future tourist attraction for Tonga and Niutoua, he moved his capital to Lapaha, on the calm lagoon near present-day Mu'a.

During the following 100 years or so, war canoes full of Tongan raiding parties set off for neighbouring islands. They created an empire ranging from the Lau Group in Fiji to the west, across to Niue in the east and northward to Futuna and Samoa, all of it ruled by the Tu'i Tonga from his capital on Tongatapu.

Sometime in the 1400s, the Tu'i Tonga Kau'ulufonua delegated some of his power and authority to his brother, creating the title Tu'i Ha'atakalaua. About 200 years later, the title of Tu'i Kanokupolu was created by the reigning Tu'i Ha'atakalaua, Mo'ungatonga.

All these title-holders struggled for power. The Tu'i Tonga gradually lost influence, and with the death of the last one, Laufilitonga, in 1865, the Tu'i Kanokupolu became the supreme power in the islands, and it still is today.

Tongatapu's first European visitor was

Tu'i Malila

While visiting Tongatapu on his third Pacific voyage in 1777, Captain James Cook befriended Fatafehi Paulaho, the 30th Tu'i Tonga. Cook was amazed at the reverence and ceremony which surrounded this person: 'I was quite charmed at the decorum ... had nowhere seen the like ... not even amongst more civilised nations.'

Out of respect and affection, Cook presented the Tu'i Tonga with a fully grown tortoise. Later given the noble title Tu'i Malila, the creature lived nearly another 200 years. At the time of its death in 1966, bearing the scars of many traumatic experiences (among them encounters with a truck and a bushfire), Tu'i Malila enjoyed a seat at the royal *kava* circle and the run of the palace gardens.

When the beloved tortoise died – no one knows at what age – the king sent its remains to the Auckland Museum to be studied and possibly preserved. It was determined that the noble tortoise was of a species originally found in the Seychelles, an island group in the Indian Ocean.

Tu'i Malila was so sorely missed at the palace that the king had another tortoise brought over from Madagascar. He named it Tu'i Malila II.

Today the remains of Tu'i Malila I can be seen in the exhibition hall at the Tongan National Centre near Nuku'alofa.

Dutchman Abel Janszoon Tasman, who spent a few days trading with islanders and named the island Amsterdam. The next European contact came with Captain James Cook, who became close friends with the 30th Tu'i Tonga, Fatafehi Paulaho, and presented him with Tu'i Malila, the tortoise that was treated as a chief and given the run of the palace for nearly 200 years. See the boxed text on Tu'i Malila.

Information
A good source of information on Tongatapu is the booklet *Tongatapu Island Tour Guide* by Tevita 'Ofa Helu (Tonga Government Printer, 1990). It's usually available at the Friendly Islands Bookshop in Nuku'alofa. Otherwise, contact the author directly: Tevita 'Ofa Helu (☎ 23-276), PO Box 957, Nuku'alofa.

Nuku'alofa

Nuku'alofa is Tonga's big smoke. Although it's a drowsy place by international standards, a traveller returning to Nuku'alofa from 'Eua, Ha'apai or the Niuas may feel like a country child arriving in New York. Nuku'alofa has shops, restaurants, hotels, discos, travel agents ... all the trappings of a small-scale big city.

Besides being the seat of government and home of the royal family, Nuku'alofa is also Tonga's industrial centre, transport hub and distribution point for imported goods entering the country. As a result, prices and availability of imported goods are more favourable in Nuku'alofa than on the outer islands. Although locally produced items such as agricultural goods and handicrafts tend to be a bit higher, the selection is greater than in the rest of the country.

These days, the city is expanding and swallowing up surrounding agricultural land and wetlands, and shantytowns are springing up around the outskirts (the one at the east end of Vuna Rd is known disparagingly as Garbage Town). As long as the population of Tonga continues to grow, migration from outer islands puts pressure on the capital to absorb the population, and some Tongans are growing concerned that their tranquil lifestyle is slipping away. Their once beautiful, mangrove-edged lagoon is now suffering from contamination and overfishing, leaving it almost devoid of marine life, and in many areas the mangroves have been removed.

Although Nuku'alofa doesn't have any earth-shaking 'must sees', there are still a lot of interesting things around town, all accessible on foot.

History
Nuku'alofa began life as a fortress for the western district of Tongatapu. Will Mariner recounts in depth the sacking of the fort of 'Nioocalofa' by Finau, the chief of Ha'apai. It seems that attacks on this fort had become a sort of annual event with the Ha'apai raiders, having been faithfully executed for at least 11 years, but this particular visit (in about 1807) was the sacking to end all sackings. Finau and his men fired on the fort with cannons they took from the *Port-au-Prince* (the British privateer which had brought Mariner to Tonga and had been subsequently destroyed), set fire to it and burned it to the ground.

After the fun their priests, who claimed to be speaking for the gods, advised them that it would be necessary to reconstruct the fort, which they did. At least it provided the opportunity to embark upon their annual holiday of destruction the following year! Unfortunately, a rival chief set it on fire shortly afterwards; Finau was watching from Pangaimotu, which prevented him from doing anything to stop the devastation. He later learned that the other chief, Tarki, had destroyed Finau's building just for the fun of irritating him while he was watching and powerless to prevent it.

Today the city is far less stormy and the inhabitants are more concerned about living in the 20th century than playing feudal war games. But would anyone expect the 'abode of love' to be anything but pleasant?

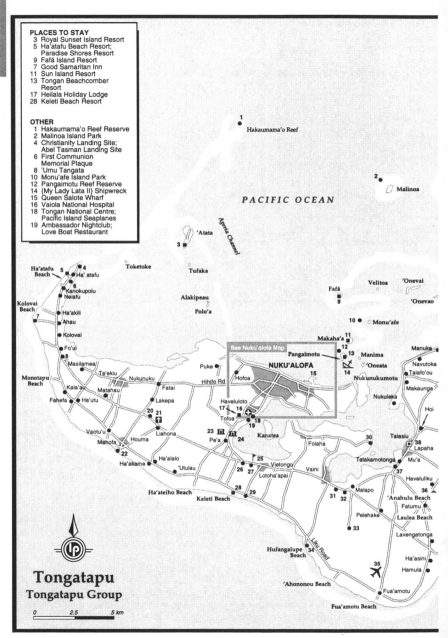

PLACES TO STAY
3 Royal Sunset Island Resort
5 Ha'atafu Beach Resort;
   Paradise Shores Resort
9 Fafá Island Resort
7 Good Samaritan Inn
11 Sun Island Resort
13 Tongan Beachcomber
   Resort
17 Heilala Holiday Lodge
28 Keleti Beach Resort

OTHER
1 Hakaumama'o Reef Reserve
2 Malinoa Island Park
4 Christianity Landing Site;
   Abel Tasman Landing Site
6 First Communion
   Memorial Plaque
8 'Umu Tangata
10 Monu'afe Island Park
12 Pangaimotu Reef Reserve
14 {My Lady Lata II} Shipwreck
15 Queen Salote Wharf
16 Vaiola National Hospital
18 Tongan National Centre;
   Pacific Island Seaplanes
19 Ambassador Nightclub;
   Love Boat Restaurant

PACIFIC OCEAN

Hakaumama'o Reef

Malinoa

'Atata

Toketoke

Tufaka

Fafá

Velitoa   'Onevai

'Onevao

Ha'atafu
Beach   Ha'atafu

Kanokupolu
Neiafu

Kolovai
Beach   Ha'akili

'Ahau

Kolovai

Fo'ul

Alakipeau

Polo'a

Monu'afe

Makaha'a

Pangaimotu

Manima

'Oneata

NUKU'ALOFA

Manuka

Navutoka

Talafo'ou

Nukunukumotu

Makaunga

Nukuleka

Hoi

See Nuku'alofa Map

Masilamea

Monotapu
Beach   Te'ekiu   Nukunuku

Kala'au   Matahau   Fatai

Fahefa   Ha'utu

Puke

Hofoa

Hihifo Rd

Haveluloto

Tofoa

Lakepa

Vaotu'u

Mahofa   Houma   Liahona

Ha'akame

Ha'alalo

'Utulau

Pe'a

Kanatea

Folaha

Vietongo

Lotoha'apai

Vaini

Talasiu

Lapaha

Tatakamotonga   Mu'a

Haveluliku

Malapo

Pelehake

'Anahulu Beach

Fatumu

Laulea Beach

Lavengatonga

Ha'asini

Hamula

Ha'ateiho Beach

Keleti Beach

Hufangalupe
Beach

Liku Road

'Ahononou Beach

Fua'amotu

Fua'amotu Beach

Tongatapu
Tongatapu Group

0   2.5   5 km

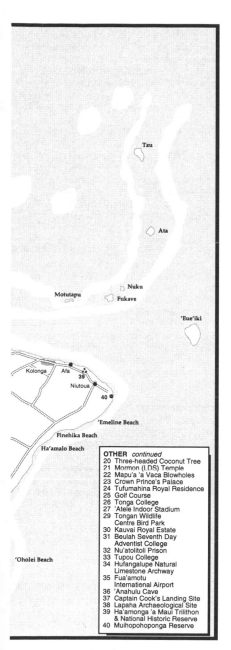

Tau

Ata

Nuku

Motutapu   Fukave

'Eue'iki

Kolonga   Afa
                39
       Niutoua
              40

'Emeline Beach

Finehika Beach

Ha'amalo Beach

'Oholei Beach

OTHER *continued*
20 Three-headed Coconut Tree
21 Mormon (LDS) Temple
22 Mapu'a 'a Vaca Blowholes
23 Crown Prince's Palace
24 Tufumahina Royal Residence
25 Golf Course
26 Tonga College
27 'Atele Indoor Stadium
29 Tongan Wildlife
     Centre Bird Park
30 Kauvai Royal Estate
31 Beulah Seventh Day
     Adventist College
32 Nu'atolitoli Prison
33 Tupou College
34 Hufangalupe Natural
     Limestone Archway
35 Fua'amotu
     International Airport
36 'Anahulu Cave
37 Captain Cook's Landing Site
38 Lapaha Archaeological Site
39 Ha'amonga 'a Maui Trilithon
     & National Historic Reserve
40 Muihopohoponga Reserve

Orientation

Maps The Visitors' Bureau hands out a free collection of simple hand-drawn maps of Tonga's major islands and island groups, plus separate street maps of Nuku'alofa, Neiafu and Lifuka. A similarly sketchy map of the island groups is available at the Friendly Islands Bookshop.

The Ministry of Lands, Survey & Natural Resources (☎ 23-611) on Vuna Rd sells topographical maps in varying degrees of detail for all Tonga's islands, for T$5 each. The Friendly Islands Bookshop also carries some of these maps.

Information

Tourist Office The Tonga Visitors' Bureau (☎ 25-334; fax 23-507; tvb@candw.to; www.vacations.tvb.gov.to; PO Box 37, Nuku'alofa) is on Vuna Rd, just west of the International Dateline Hotel. It's open weekdays from 8.30 am to 4.30 pm, Saturday and holidays 9 am to 12.30 pm.

The office provides the usual tourist information, plus a series of informative handouts describing various aspects of Tongan life, maps of Nuku'alofa and of the country's major islands, and a bulletin board with useful information including current tide tables. The airline and ferry schedules posted here should be verified elsewhere since they may be out of date. Even if you're not after information, the staff are a friendly lot and the architecture of the building is worth a look.

Further information is available on the Internet (www.candw.to/tonga.htm).

Money Nuku'alofa has three banks – the Bank of Tonga, ANZ and MBF – all of which change money (cash and travellers cheques) and give cash advances on Visa and MasterCard. They're open weekdays from 9 am to 4 pm, and on Saturday mornings.

The International Dateline Hotel also changes money (cash or travellers cheques) and gives cash advances on Visa and MasterCard. Its front desk is open 24 hours every day, so it's a convenient service when the banks are closed. When the banks are open the hotel changes money for the same rates as the banks, but when they are closed, it offers a lower rate. Unlike the banks it charges a hefty 10% commission for cash advances.

Currency exchange counters are open at the airport for all international flights.

Western Union (☎ 24-345) has an office upstairs in the Tungi Arcade, which is on Taufa'ahau Rd.

Post The GPO, on the corner of Taufa'ahau and Salote Rds, is open weekdays from 8.30 am to 4 pm. Poste restante is at the window just outside the main entrance. The address is Poste Restante, GPO, Nuku'alofa, Kingdom of Tonga. Letters are filed alphabetically by surname (or by the name of the yacht). You must ask specifically for any larger parcels you might be expecting. The Philatelic Bureau is upstairs.

Telephone, Telegraph, Telex & Fax The Cable & Wireless Office on Salote Rd offers international telephone, telegraph, telex and fax services. The office is open weekdays from 6 am to midnight, Saturday 7 am to 4 pm, Sunday 4 pm to midnight. You can buy a telephone card during these hours and use it in the international card phones in the lobby 24 hours a day, every day.

For T$1, reverse charge calls can be connected to Australia, New Zealand, the USA, the UK and to Pacific Island nations. Visa and MasterCard can be used here, along with several international calling cards (see Post & Communications in the Facts for the Visitor chapter for a list of which ones).

Telephone cards can also be bought at the Philatelic Bureau office upstairs in the post office, and at the Pacific Royale Hotel; its front desk is open 24 hours every day. Card phones are outside the post office, and in the Pacific Royale Hotel lobby, but they can only be used for international phone calls.

A domestic telephone and fax service is available at the Tonga Telecom office on 'Unga Rd, behind the Bank of Tonga which is on One-Way Rd. It's open 24 hours, every day.

Mini Mart USA (☎/fax 25-042), the small shop on the corner of One-Way and Laifone Rds, offers both domestic and international fax services.

Email & Internet Email and Internet services are available at Moore Electronics (☎ 23-758) upstairs in the Tungi Arcade on Taufa'ahau Rd. You can use the email for T$5 per day, or get an email account for T$20 per month.

If you have your own computer, you can get a temporary email/Internet account from Cable & Wireless for T$30; contact Cable & Wireless (☎ 23-499, 23-807; fax 22-746; info@candw.to; www.candw.to).

Plans are afoot for two email cafes to open in Nuku'alofa by late 1998. The *Kalia Cafe* (www.invited.to/kaliacafe), affiliated with Cable & Wireless, will be upstairs in the Tonga Co-Operative Federation (TCF) supermarket building on Taufa'ahau Rd, opposite the Pacific Royale Hotel. Another, affiliated with Moore Electronics, will be opening in a new building on Taufa'ahau Rd between the post office and the Bank of Tonga.

Visa Extensions Visa extensions are available from Nuku'alofa's immigration office (☎ 24-763) in the police station. It's open weekdays from 9 am to noon, with additional afternoon hours from 2 to 4 pm on Monday, Tuesday and Thursday.

Airline Offices The airline offices in Nuku'alofa include:

Air New Zealand
    Tungi Arcade, Taufa'ahau Rd (☎ 23-192; fax 21-645)
Air Pacific
    Jones Travel, corner Taufa'ahau & Wellington Rds (☎ 23-422/3; airport ☎ 32-244; fax 23-418)
Polynesian Airlines
    corner Salote & Fatafehi Rds (☎ 24-566; fax 24-225)

Royal Tongan Airlines
Royco Building, Fatafehi Rd (☎ 23-414; fax 23-554; rtamktng@candw.to; kalianet.candw.to/rta)
Samoa Air
contact Teta Tours (☎ 23-690; fax 23-238)
Pacific Island Air
(☎ 25-177; fax 25-165; pacisair@candw.to), PO Box 1675

Weather The Tonga Meteorological Service (☎ 23-401) on Tuopulahi Rd is a good source of weather information; each day a satellite weather map is posted outside the door. Another weather office (☎ 32-123) is at the airport. Current weather information is also available on the Internet (www.candw.to/weather/index.html).

Bookshops & Libraries The only bookshop of any consequence in Tonga is the Friendly Islands Bookshop on Taufa'ahau Rd, with a good selection of paperback books, travel-oriented titles (including Lonely Planet guidebooks), books about Tonga and related island topics which are difficult if not impossible to find elsewhere.

Nuku'alofa has a couple of other bookshops too, including Rowena's opposite the Talamahu Market and the Dateline Bookshop opposite Loni's Cinema, but their selection is more limited.

The Tapacraft handicrafts shop on Lavinia Rd has a book exchange, or you can buy used paperbacks for T$1 each. Several guesthouses have book exchanges for their guests.

With a library card (T$2 annually), you can borrow books from the library downstairs in the basilica.

The libraries at the New Zealand and Australian high commissions have selection of newspapers, magazines and books on Kiwi and Aussie topics.

Photography Fung Shing Fast Photo on Railway Rd offers one-hour colour print processing and sells Fuji film. This is most people's preferred place for processing; they do a fine job. Foto-Fix on Taufa'ahau Rd also does processing, and sells Kodak film. A shop in the Tungi Arcade on Taufa'ahau Rd does basic camera repairs, and sends film to New Zealand for processing. Slide film processing is not available in Tonga.

Laundry Virtually every hotel and guesthouse makes some arrangement for its guests' laundry needs.

The Savoy Dry Cleaner on Fatafehi Rd is Nuku'alofa's only commercial laundry. We've heard of (and personally know) travellers who've had items go missing here. A sign on the wall warns: 'All customers are bringing their laundry on their own risk.' If you want to risk it, write out a list of every item and check it over with the staff both when you drop off your laundry and when you retrieve it. Wash and dry is T$1 or T$1.20 per kilogram, depending on weight.

Medical Services Nuku'alofa has two pharmacies, one in the Nuku'alofa Clinic behind the post office and the other in the Ministry of Labour building under the Swedish Consulate on Salote Rd. A doctor is available for consultation at the former from 9.30 am to 4 pm weekdays and 9.30 am to noon on Saturday. No appointments are necessary.

If you prefer a private doctor, New Zealander Dr Glennis Mafi at the Ha'ateiho Village Mission Clinic (☎ 29-052) in the village of Ha'ateiho, 5km south of Nuku'alofa, is highly recommended. The consultation fee of T$15 often includes medicine. Make an appointment before you come.

The German Clinic (☎ 22-736, home 29-978) on Wellington Rd is operated by a German doctor, Dr Heinz Betz.

The National Hospital is in Vaiola, 3km south of Nuku'alofa, a 10-minute bus ride from the centre. No appointments are accepted and queues can be horrendous. At the hospital dispensary, medicines are free to Tongans and foreigners pay only a token fee – 15% or so of the market price.

Yet another alternative is the Catholic Clinic in Pe'a. Take the Vaini bus from the

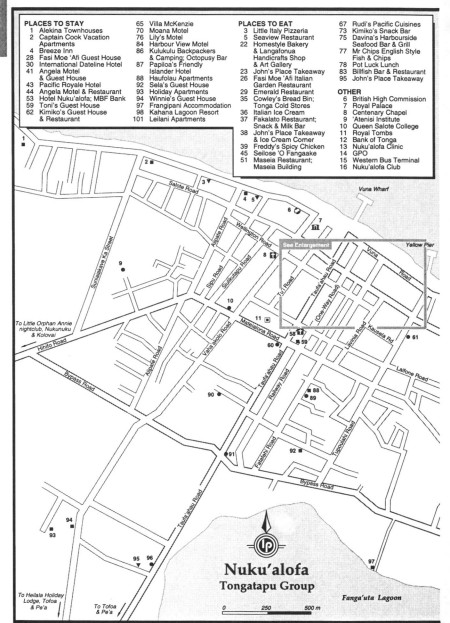

PLACES TO STAY
1 Alekina Townhouses
2 Captain Cook Vacation Apartments
4 Breeze Inn
28 Fasi Moe 'Afi Guest House
30 International Dateline Hotel
41 Angela Motel & Guest House
43 Pacific Royale Hotel
44 Angela Motel & Restaurant
53 Hotel Nuku'alofa; MBF Bank
59 Toni's Guest House
62 Kimiko's Guest House & Restaurant
65 Villa McKenzie
70 Moana Motel
76 Lily's Motel
84 Harbour View Motel
86 Kulukulu Backpackers & Camping; Octopusy Bar
87 Papiloa's Friendly Islander Hotel
88 Haufolau Apartments
92 Sela's Guest House
93 Holiday Apartments
94 Winnie's Guest House
97 Frangipani Accommodation
98 Kahana Lagoon Resort
101 Leilani Apartments

PLACES TO EAT
3 Little Italy Pizzeria
5 Seaview Restaurant
22 Homestyle Bakery & Langafonua Handicrafts Shop & Art Gallery
23 John's Place Takeaway
26 Fasi Moe 'Afi Italian Garden Restaurant
29 Emerald Restaurant
35 Cowley's Bread Bin; Tonga Cold Stores
36 Italian Ice Cream
37 Fakalato Restaurant; Snack & Milk Bar
38 John's Place Takeaway & Ice Cream Corner
39 Freddy's Spicy Chicken
45 Seilose 'O Fangaake
51 Maseia Restaurant; Maseia Building
67 Rudi's Pacific Cuisines
73 Kimiko's Snack Bar
75 Davina's Harbourside Seafood Bar & Grill
77 Mr Chips English Style Fish & Chips
78 Pot Luck Lunch
83 Billfish Bar & Restaurant
95 John's Place Takeaway

OTHER
6 British High Commission
7 Royal Palace
8 Centenary Chapel
9 'Atenisi Institute
10 Queen Salote College
11 Royal Tombs
12 Bank of Tonga
13 Nuku'alofa Clinic
14 GPO
15 Western Bus Terminal
16 Nuku'alofa Club

Vuna Wharf

See Enlargement

Yellow Pier

To Little Orphan Annie nightclub, Nukunuku & Kolovai

To Heilala Holiday Lodge, Tofoa & Pe'a

To Tofoa & Pe'a

Nuku'alofa
Tongatapu Group

Fanga'uta Lagoon

0   250   500 m

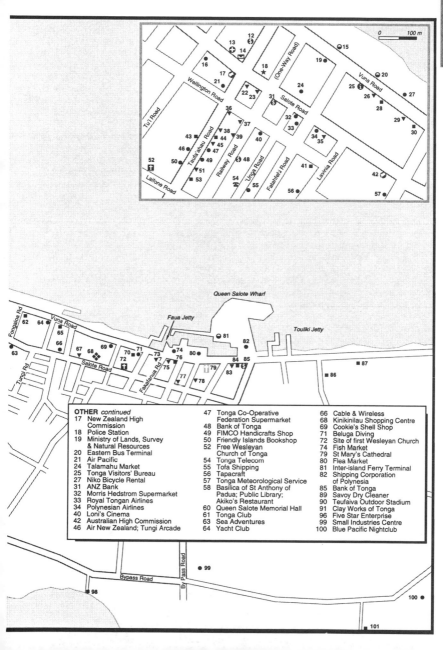

OTHER *continued*
17 New Zealand High
   Commission
18 Police Station
19 Ministry of Lands, Survey
   & Natural Resources
20 Eastern Bus Terminal
21 Air Pacific
24 Talamahu Market
25 Tonga Visitors' Bureau
27 Niko Bicycle Rental
31 ANZ Bank
32 Morris Hedstrom Supermarket
33 Royal Tongan Airlines
34 Polynesian Airlines
40 Loni's Cinema
42 Australian High Commission
46 Air New Zealand; Tungi Arcade

47 Tonga Co-Operative
   Federation Supermarket
48 Bank of Tonga
49 FIMCO Handicrafts Shop
50 Friendly Islands Bookshop
52 Free Wesleyan
   Church of Tonga
54 Tonga Telecom
55 Tofa Shipping
56 Tapacraft
57 Tonga Meteorological Service
58 Basilica of St Anthony of
   Padua; Public Library;
   Akiko's Restaurant
60 Queen Salote Memorial Hall
61 Tonga Club
63 Sea Adventures
64 Yacht Club

66 Cable & Wireless
68 Kinikinilau Shopping Centre
69 Cookie's Shell Shop
71 Beluga Diving
72 Site of first Wesleyan Church
74 Fish Market
79 St Mary's Cathedral
80 Flea Market
81 Inter-island Ferry Terminal
82 Shipping Corporation
   of Polynesia
85 Bank of Tonga
89 Savoy Dry Cleaner
90 Teufaiva Outdoor Stadium
91 Clay Works of Tonga
96 Five Star Enterprise
99 Small Industries Centre
100 Blue Pacific Nightclub

eastern bus terminal and ask to be dropped at the clinic.

Chinese medicine and acupuncture treatments are available at the Chinese Clinic & Emergency Centre on Wellington Rd, which offers 24-hour service. Horst Berger, an Austrian, offers Shiatsu massage at his home office just off Bypass Rd; walk back between the houses of Paula Helu and Mele Patiola, where you'll see the sign.

Royal Palace

The Royal Palace on the waterfront, a white, Victorian timber structure surrounded by large lawns and Norfolk Island pines, has come to be a symbol of Tonga to the world.

The palace was prefabricated in New Zealand in 1867 and was transported to Tonga exclusively as a royal residence. In 1882, the upstairs verandah was added and the Royal Chapel was constructed behind the palace. Sunday services used to take place in the chapel before it was damaged in a hurricane. The coronations of King George II, Queen Salote and King Taufa'ahau Tupou IV took place there in 1893, 1918 and 1967, respectively. The coronation chair in the chapel is partially constructed from the *koka* tree on Lifuka (Ha'apai) under which King George I was invested with the title Tu'i Kanokupolu. The small octagonal gazebo in the gardens is called the Palesi and was used as a rest house for visiting chiefs.

The palace grounds are not open to visitors but you can get a good view of the palace from the waterfront area on the west side. Just beyond it, on the slopes of Mt Zion, is the Sia Ko Veiongo, the 'royal estate'. It was here that the fortress of Nuku'alofa once stood and its ludicrous history of attacks and conflagrations took place. Now the site is occupied by a radio tower and the grave of Captain Croker of the HMS *Favourite*, who was killed attacking the fortress on 24 June 1840.

Tonga Visitors' Bureau

The Tonga Visitors' Bureau on Vuna Rd, just west of the International Dateline Hotel, is worth a visit. It was commissioned by the king to promote the traditional Tongan construction methods and to encourage tourism as a source of revenue after Tongatapu was damaged by a serious earthquake on 23 June 1977. The building costs of T$45,000 were donated by the Australian government as part of an earthquake recovery programme.

The building was constructed mainly from Tongan materials. The posts are made of *tangato* and *tamanu* wood from the island of 'Eua and the framing is of bamboo. The walls are covered with pa'ongo pandanus mats woven in Niuafo'ou. The ceiling and roof are of finely designed, plaited coconut fibre, while the bindings on the ceiling beams depict the Norfolk Island pines, which are relatively abundant around Nuku'alofa. In addition, there are about 89 sq metres of tapa depicting the royal crest, which was designed in 1862 by the grandson of King George Tupou I.

The wooden poles in front of the office are a gift from the people of New Zealand. They represent both ancient and modern patterns used in the designs painted on tapa. Below these are depictions of vines and shells native to Tonga. One pole is considered 'male' and the other 'female'. The male pole portrays a *motoku* (heron), whale, pig, octopus and rat. The heron is of a type found in New Zealand and represents the common Polynesian ancestry of the two island groups. On the 'female' pole are a sea turtle, a bat and a dog, the design of which was taken from an ancient Tongan war club.

Vuna Wharf

Vuna Wharf, at the end of Taufa'ahau Rd, was constructed in 1906 and once served as Tonga's main disembarkation point. It was replaced in 1966 by Queen Salote Wharf several kilometres to the east and then nearly destroyed in the earthquake of 1977. If you walk to the end of the wharf at low tide, you'll see two large anchors which have sunk into the muck.

❋❋❋❋❋❋❋❋❋❋❋❋❋❋❋❋❋ ❋❋❋❋❋❋❋❋❋❋❋❋ ❋

How to spend Sunday in Nuku'alofa

- Go to church. The magnificent singing lifts the roof. A particular favourite with visitors is attending Centenary Chapel to worship with the king and royal family. The main service begins at 10 am at all churches, with other services at dawn and late afternoon.
- Visit Tongatapu's many natural attractions, such as the Blowholes, the Ha'amonga Trilithon, the Mu'a archaeological site, or one of the beaches.
- Cycle round the island.
- Take a round-the-island tour with Toni's Guest House Tours, Paea Tours or Quick Tours.
- All four of the offshore island beach resorts are great on Sunday. Their white-sand beaches are beautiful, and all have restaurants. Pangaimotu is the most popular and least expensive (round-trip boat transfers T$10). Sun Island is cheap, too, and isn't crowded. Fafá is beautiful, and a day trip ($30) includes lunch. Most special of all is Royal Sunset, which offers a fabulous all-you-can-eat buffet, snorkelling trips to the reef nearby, plus the 45-minute boat transfers there and back, all for T$30.
- The Good Samaritan Inn in Kolovai has an all-you-can-eat family-style 'umu (traditional Tongan underground oven feast) every Sunday.
- The Paradise Shores Resort on Ha'atafu Beach is a pleasant place to relax on Sunday, with a mixed crowd of locals and foreigners.
- You can use the swimming pool at the International Dateline Hotel all day long for T$2. Lounging around the pool, and eating at the poolside Splash Cafe & Bar, is a relaxing way to while away a Sunday.

❋❋❋❋❋❋❋❋❋❋❋❋❋❋❋❋ ❋❋❋❋❋❋❋❋❋❋❋❋❋ ❋

Railway (One-Way) Rd

There was once a railway along Railway Rd – it was used to transport copra to Vuna Wharf, where it was loaded onto steamers for export. Railway Rd is the only one-way road in Nuku'alofa and it is often called One-Way Rd.

Yellow Pier

For a convenient snorkelling site, try Yellow Pier at the end of Tupoulahi Rd. It's not as spectacular as the reefs further out, but you will see lots of small fish and even rays. It's also a popular swimming area for local children.

Royal Tombs

The Mala'ekula, the large park-like area opposite the basilica, was named after the Katoanga Kula festival, which was held here in the days of King George Tupou I (the *mala'e* part of the name refers to a sacred area). Since 1893 it has contained the royal tombs: the graves of all the Tongan sovereigns as well as their husbands, wives

and other close relatives. The large green was once used as a golf course. It's off-limits to the public but you still have a fairly good view from the perimeter fence.

'Atenisi Institute

The only private university in Tonga, the 'Atenisi Institute is a unique institution that operates without subsidy from either church or state and therefore without obligation to further the views of either. It was founded in 1967 by an extraordinary individual, 'I Futa Helu, to operate under a classic western format in the tradition of Oxford. He writes in the university syllabus:

... concern with the classical tradition means the keeping of a traditional core of studies. This is the academic equivalent of the English attitude that a university which does not teach philosophy as a discipline is a 'Mickey Mouse' university ... all South Sea island communities have created beautiful cultures, but it must be pointed out that in all these cultures criticism as an institution is discouraged, and criticism is the very heart of education.

Classes in Tongan language and culture are offered as well as philosophy, sciences and other disciplines. Associate, bachelor's and postgraduate degree programmes are offered, in conjunction with Auckland University. Tuition is T$270 per annum, per course. Visitors who'll be spending some time in Tonga may want to check out their classes. Contact PO Box 90 or PO Box 200, Nuku'alofa, Kingdom of Tonga (☎/fax 24-819)

If you're visiting in November, try not to miss 'Atenisi's graduation ceremony, which is unlike any you'll have seen before. There's dancing, entertainment, royal gifting and feasting, as well as a unique tradition called 'presentation of the *vala*'. During this ceremony, the villages of 'Atenisi graduates present the university with gifts of elaborate fine mats and immense pieces of tapa, all of which end up in a heap on the common. Rarely will you ever see so many hours of work and so much artistic expertise treated so casually.

Nuku'alofa Club

The Nuku'alofa Club is the exclusive pub/billiards hall just behind the palace grounds. It was founded as a private club in 1914 and now serves as a meeting place of the 'upper crust' in Tongan business, society and government. It is open to only male members and male guests, although male tourists are sometimes admitted.

British High Commissioner's Office & Residence

This is on the waterfront, west of the palace. It was presented to the government by its original owner in 1901 in exchange for another waterfront lot and was in turn leased to the British government. On the front lawn are four cannons from the British privateer *Port-au-Prince*, which was ransacked at Lifuka (Ha'apai) in 1806.

Queen Salote College & Tupou High School

Although the Queen Salote College was planned by King George Tupou I in 1876 as

a tribute to 50 years of Christianity in Tonga – and he personally donated £1000 to build a Wesleyan ladies college to be named after his wife – the project wasn't actually chartered until 1923. It was finally positioned beside Tupou College on Mateialona Rd, ostensibly a boys school (although it had accepted female students as early as 1869). In 1948, the boys college moved to the south-eastern corner of Tongatapu.

Beside Queen Salote College is the Tupou High School. The land for the school was donated by King George Tupou I in 1882. Although the first school was relocated in 1941, construction on a new high school was begun by Queen Salote in 1962. Today, the English language school (Tonga Side School) and the government kindergarten are also housed here.

Free Wesleyan Church President's Residence

This building is on the corner of Siulikutapu and Wellington Rds. Built in 1871 for Revd Shirley Baker (who would later become Tonga's first prime minister), it's a rather opulent structure.

Prince Tu'ipelehake's Residence

On Vuna Rd near the Visitors' Bureau is the residence of Prince Tu'ipelehake, Tonga's former Prime Minister. Built in 1953, it previously housed an agricultural store and a drinking establishment, the Tonga Club.

Langafonua Building

This gingerbread-style structure on Taufa'ahau Rd was built by a British expat for his five daughters who lived in New Zealand and spent winters in Tonga. It now houses the women's handicraft cooperative founded by Queen Salote in 1953.

New Zealand High Commission

The Ovalau Building on Salote Rd, now used as a New Zealand High Commission residence, was built at Levuka on the island of Ovalau, Fiji. This attractive old weatherboard structure was shipped to Tonga and reconstructed in the early 1950s. It's oppo-

DEANNA SWANEY

HOLGER LEUE

DARRYL TORCKLER

Top: 'Uoleva, Ha'apai Group
Middle Left: Fisherman, Atata Island
Middle Right: Enjoying warm clear waters from charter yacht
Bottom: Volcanic landscape, Tofua, Ha'apai Group

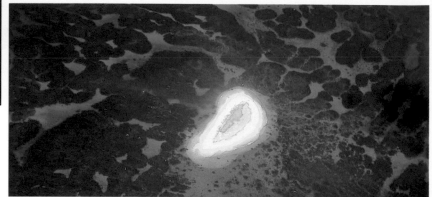

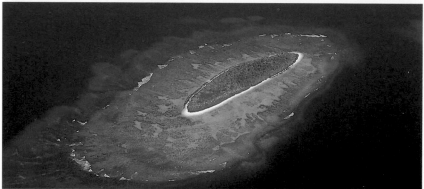

Top & Middle: Tiny islands in the Vava'u Group
Bottom: Tongan Beach Resort, Vava'u

site the GPO and is probably Nuku'alofa's finest piece of architecture.

Prime Minister's Office
The Prime Minister's Office, on Taufa'ahau Rd opposite the GPO, contains numerous government offices and is the source of much of the hot air blowing around Tonga. The tower was damaged in the 1977 earthquake but was rebuilt shortly thereafter.

Churches
Nuku'alofa's most distinctive structure is the **Basilica of St Anthony of Padua,** on Taufa'ahau Rd opposite the Royal Tombs. Much of it was built by volunteer labour between May 1977 and January 1980. It resembles something that belongs on the head of a Chinese peasant in an old film. The interior, however, is quite lovely and represents a great deal of artistic accomplishment on the part of those who produced it.

The large ceiling beams are made of wood imported from New Zealand and the smaller cross-beams came from the Royal Estate on 'Eua. Beam joints are covered with coconut sennit mats woven locally. The altar, lectern, baptistry, pews and tables were handcrafted and the Stations of the Cross are made of coconut wood inlaid with mother-of-pearl. At Station XI, a tiny gold coconut tree that belonged to Queen Salote Tupou III is fitted into the hair of Christ. The library on the ground floor is decorated with intricate shellwork designed by local women; the shells come from all over Tonga.

The other Catholic church in town is **St Mary's Cathedral**, near Faua Jetty on Vuna Rd. Although it's a more conventional structure, it's worth visiting for its beautiful rose gardens, stained glass and vaulted ceiling.

The **Centenary Chapel**, on Wellington Rd behind Mt Zion, was completed in 1952 and accommodates more than 2000 people. Like the basilica, it was constructed mostly by volunteer labour. Visitors to Tonga, even non-Christians, often attend church here in order to catch a glimpse of the royal family (who attend services here) and hear the magnificent, booming singing of the congregation.

The old **Free Wesleyan church** was built in 1888 on the present site of the Centenary Chapel, but it was moved in 1949 to its current location on the north side of the Royal Tombs. What made this monumental task (you'll realise how monumental when you see the building) so extraordinary was that it was transported the 274m to its new position in just one day!

The **first Wesleyan church** built in Nuku'alofa was once a ramshackle building. It was loaded with character and resembled a *fale* (a traditional thatched house). It has been rebuilt in recent years and is now just another church.

Parks
The **Pangao Si'i** area of the waterfront, beside the royal palace, is a public ground used for royal kava ceremonies, feasts and Saturday football and cricket matches. On one corner is the dolphin fountain (which rarely seems to spout water) which was presented by the British government to commemorate the HMS *Dolphin*, the first British warship to land in Tonga. On the waterfront is a line-up of big guns and a flagpole used on ceremonial occasions.

The **town common** is a large lawn area behind the Treasury (on the corner of Vuna and Taufa'ahau Rds). It contains a small bandstand and the Tongan War Memorial, honouring Tongans who served in the world wars. Across the street to the east is the quaint little Parliament building, that was pre-fabricated in New Zealand, transported to Tonga and reconstructed in 1894. The huge green area is used for sports and picnics.

Markets
Nuku'alofa's **Talamahu Market**, where all sorts of agricultural produce is sold, is the best in the country and will serve as a sort of crash course in tropical fruits and vegetables. Upstairs (go up the inside ramp on

the east end of the building) are a number of stalls selling new and used clothing, household items and some excellent Tongan art, including carvings, tapa and pandanus mats.

Tapa and pandanus mats are sold both upstairs and downstairs in the market. If you're hoping to purchase a tapa or high quality fine mat, bear in mind that the traditional value of these items is justifiably high, especially given the amount of work required to produce them.

There's a Saturday morning **flea market** on the waterfront, opposite St Mary's Cathedral. Get there early for the best selection.

Tongan National Centre

The Tongan National Centre (☎ 23-022), beside the lagoon in Vaiola, about 2km south of Nuku'alofa, was constructed in 1988. It serves as a cultural centre, where visitors can see displays about Tongan history, paintings of its monarchs and a museum of historical artefacts as well as demonstrations of Tongan arts such as mat and basket weaving, tapa making, wood, bone and black coral carving, painting, kava preparation and serving and 'umu construction. Naturally, visitors may purchase any of these articles, which are on sale at the centre's handicrafts shop.

The large exhibition hall, with its magnificent high roof, is worth seeing for its splendid architecture alone. It's open weekdays from 9 am to 4 pm; admission T$2 (children T$1). Guided cultural tours including cooking, basketry, tapa making, mat weaving, carving, dancing, a kava ceremony and *lafo* playing demonstrations, are conducted daily at 2 pm; cost is T$8 (children T$4).

At lunchtime there's a traditional lunch and fashion show of Tongan ceremonial dress for T$12 (children T$6); you must reserve a seat before 10 am on the day you wish to attend.

On Tuesday and Thursday evenings at 7 pm there's a traditional Tongan feast, with a kava ceremony, a Tongan string band and

an excellent show of traditional Tongan dances. Cost is T$20 (children T$10), with transport provided for an extra T$1. Bookings must be made before 4.30 pm on the day of your visit. The exhibition hall opens for guests at 6.30 pm, so it's worth coming early. Many people say this is the best traditional dance show presented in Tonga; this is a favourite evening out not only for tourists, but for locals as well.

To come here by bus, take the Vaiola bus from town and get off at Vaiola Hospital, opposite the centre.

Activities

Many activities are available on Tongatapu, including snorkelling, scuba diving, surfing and whale watching.

Diving & Snorkelling Beluga Diving, PO Box 2660, Nuku'alofa (☎/fax 23-576), on the corner of Vuna and Kinikinilau Rds, opposite Faua Jetty, offers two-tank dives for T$80/95 with your own/hired gear, or T$95 for a one-tank night dive. PADI open water diving certification courses cost T$300 (two students or more) or T$350 (one student), with advanced courses also available. Halfday 'discover scuba' courses are T$95 (no certification or experience required). Scuba diving equipment can be rented for T$8.50 per item, per day, if you're already certified; snorkelling gear is rented for T$7 per day.

Royal Sunset Scuba Diving, PO Box 960, Nuku'alofa (☎/fax 21-254; royalsun@candw.to) is based at the Royal Sunset Island Resort and offers one/two-tank dives for T$60/80 (one to three divers) or T$50/70 (four divers or more), equipment included.

Deep Blue Diving Centre, PO Box 913, Nuku'alofa (☎/fax 25-392), offers two dives for T$120, including lunch, morning and afternoon snack, and all gear. A five-dive package is T$540, 10 dives $1060. Discounts are offered for long-stayers, or if you use your own equipment. Open water diving courses are T$400, with advanced courses available; instruction is in English or German. The centre is affiliated with

PADI, SSI and other international organisations. Cruises, charters and transport to other islands are also available.

Coralhead Diving, PO Box 211, Nuku'alofa (☎ 22-176; fax 22-970) offers dives only for groups of five or more. However, you can be certified through Coralhead after seven to 10 days of instruction. PADI open water diving certification classes cost T$400 (one to four students) or T$350 (five students or more) per student. They also rent equipment.

Sailing Royal Sunset Island Cruising's *Impetuous*, a 51-foot (15m) Benetau luxury sailing yacht, has sailing charters throughout all the Tongan island groups. Daily rates are T$189 to T$457 per person, including all meals, depending on how many people are sharing the cost; the *Impetuous* sleeps up to six guests. Scuba diving equipment is available on board, at extra cost. Day charters around the Nuku'alofa area are T$300 per day, with a maximum of eight passengers; it also does whale watching trips (June to October).

Sea Adventures, Salote Rd, PO Box 1774, Nuku'alofa (☎/fax 24-823; kiwitonga@candw.to), rents kayaks for T$20/30 per day for a single/double kayak with no guide, or T$30 per person with a guide. The friendly Kiwi owners provide plenty of orientation and will transport you to a variety of good spots to get you started.

Whale Watching Royal Sunset Island Cruising, PO Box 960, Nuku'alofa (☎/fax 21-254; royalsun@candw.to), runs whale watching boat trips around the Tongatapu area for a cost of T$60 per hour for the whole boat, divided among the number of passengers (up to six passengers).

Atiu Charters, PO Box 1872, Nuku'alofa (☎ 22-489 (Darren), 26-019 (Alfred); fax 24-365), runs whale watching trips. Costs are T$450 for a full 12-hour day (6 am to 6 pm), T$300 for a half-day trip of six hours (maximum five people). If you don't catch them at home, contact them at the Billfish Bar in Nuku'alofa (☎ 24-084; fax 23-729).

Fishing Royal Sunset Sport Fishing, PO Box 960, Nuku'alofa (☎/fax 21-254; royalsun@candw.to), is based at the Royal Sunset Island Resort. Its 24-foot (7m) *Atata Clipper* sportfishing boat costs T$240/480 for half/full day trips including all gear (maximum four anglers), or T$60 per hour (minimum four hours).

Atiu Charters, PO Box 1872, Nuku'alofa (☎ 22-489 (Darren), 26-019 (Alfred); fax 24-365), runs fishing trips on the *Striker*, a 28-foot (8.4m) Kevlar Cat Sportfisher Deluxe. They cost the same as the company's whale watching trips (see Whale Watching earlier).

Hakula Charters, based at Faua Jetty, Nuku'alofa (☎ 11-236; fax 23-759), has a 40-foot (12m) motor catamaran *Hakula* and offers nine-hour bottom fishing trips for T$45 per person, game fishing trips for T$140 per person.

Palm Travel & Tours, PO Box 295, Nuku'alofa (☎ 24-920, 23-505; fax 24-914; palmtour@candw.to), does big game or bottom fishing for T$50 per hour (minimum four hours).

Golf The nine-hole golf course on the main road at Vietongo is open to visitors, with a T$5 green fee.

Organised Tours
Several companies in Nuku'alofa offer organised tours of Tongatapu. See Organised Tours at the end of the Around Tongatapu section for details.

Special Events
The Heilala Festival is Nuku'alofa's big festival of the year. A week-long celebration which features parades, workshops, fashion shows, a beauty pageant, all manner of music, arts and sports competitions, feasting and general merriment, it culminates with the King's Birthday on 4 July. If you're visiting Nuku'alofa during Heilala Week, be sure to book accommodation in advance.

Places to Stay
This section includes all accommodation in

the Nuku'alofa area. More accommodation is available at a number of pleasant resorts around Tongatapu and on the islands just offshore; they are mentioned later in this chapter. Add 7.5% tax to all prices.

Places to Stay – budget

Camping Camping is possible at the *Heilala Holiday Lodge* (T$6 per person, with tent and camping gear rental available for T$2), at the eco-tourism centre behind *Papiloa's Friendly Islander Hotel* (starting from T$5 per tent) and at the *Kulukulu Backpackers & Camping* (T$6 per tent). All are mentioned in detail later in this section.

Camping is also possible at the *Paradise Shores Resort* on Ha'atafu Beach, the *Good Samaritan Inn* on the beach at Kolovai (both on the west end of Tongatapu) and on Pangaimotu and Sun Island, two small islands just offshore from Nuku'alofa. All of these are mentioned in more detail later in this chapter.

Guesthouses & Motels Guesthouses in Nuku'alofa come and go with little warning. When you arrive, some of those mentioned here may have vanished, and new ones may have opened.

Toni's Guest House (☎ 21-049; fax 22-970; PO Box 3084) at the corner of Mateialona and Railway (or One-Way) Rds is an old backpackers' favourite. Owner Tony Matthias is an expat Brit with a laid-back nature and a penchant for discussion. Two-bed rooms with shared bath cost T$10 per person, plus tax. Children stay free. Guests can use the kitchen and are welcome to join Tony's nightly kava circle-cum-natter session, which often carries on until quite late. Tony also has bicycles for hire, offers transport around the island, and does a great island tour (T$15/20 for guests/nonguests).

Sela's Guest House (☎ 21-430; fax 22-755; PO Box 24) is just off Fatafehi Rd near the lagoon. The clean rooms and pleasant homey atmosphere make guests feel welcome. Singles/doubles are T$15/20, or T$10 per person in a six-bed dorm, all with

shared bath, kitchen and sitting areas. Doubles with private bath are T$30. One advantage of staying here is the chance to enjoy Sela's culinary prowess: breakfast/lunch/dinner are T$4/6/12, with a simple light breakfast for T$2.50.

Papiloa's Friendly Islander Hotel (see Places to Stay – middle) has a couple of shared rooms with kitchen for T$15 per person, with access to all the hotel's facilities (swimming pool, poolside restaurant/bar, etc).

The *Heilala Holiday Lodge* (☎ 29-910; fax 29-410; quick@candw.to; PO Box 1698; kalianet.candw.to/quick/home.page-html/), formerly called the Heilala Guest House, is in Tofoa, 3km south of town. Operated by German Waltraud Quick, her son Sven and Tongan host Kalolina, it's well-run, clean, quiet and friendly. Rooms with shared bath and kitchen are T$24/32 single, T$28/32 double or T$14 shared. Traditional *fales* (bungalows) are T$32/36. Prices include airport pick-up, town tour and many extras. It also has a swimming pool, email/Internet services, mountain bike and scooter rental, island tours in English or German, and is planning to open a restaurant. Buses to town pass nearby every few minutes. Visa and MasterCard are accepted.

Winnie's Guest House (☎/fax 25-215; winnies@candw.to; PO Box 3049), on Vaha'akolo Rd about 2km south of town, is a comfortable, friendly guesthouse in a spacious family home operated by Winnie Santos and her son Mark. It's clean and very pleasant. Rooms are T$25 per person, breakfast included, but only T$15 for students or long-term visitors. This is the favourite lodging for international medical students, who come to work at nearby Vaiola Hospital. It has two twin and two double rooms, a guests' kitchen, large outdoor areas, bicycles and scooters for rent, TV, access to email, and a charming atmosphere. The Vaiola bus route to town stops at the door every few minutes.

Ginette (Seneti in Tongan), the Canadian proprietor of the *Tapacraft* shop on Lavinia Rd in the centre, has one guest room with private bath for T$15/25 a single/double in the rear of the shop. There are no cooking facilities, but morning tea/coffee is provided. It isn't fancy, but it's clean, quiet and secure.

The Chinese-run *Angela Motel & Guest House* (☎ 23-930; fax 22-149; PO Box 1617) on Wellington Rd is clean, quiet and convenient. Its eight rooms, each with private bath, are T$30 for one or two people, and there's a guests kitchen. (Another branch, the Angela Motel on Taufa'ahau Rd, was closed on our last visit.)

Also Chinese-run, *Lily's Motel* (☎ 24-226; fax 24-389; PO Box 3045) on Vuna Rd, opposite Faua Jetty, has a row of simple rooms out in the garden, behind Lily's Chinese restaurant. Three rooms with shared bath are T$20; three rooms with private bath are T$30/35 a single/double.

The frequently recommended *Breeze Inn* (☎ 23-947; fax 22-970; PO Box 2739), on the waterfront west of the Royal Palace, is run by a Japanese expat, Ms Setsuko Fashimi, who will do everything she can to make your stay pleasant. It's good value at T$30/40 for clean rooms with private bath, shared kitchen and lounge.

Frangipani Accommodation (☎ 25-936; fax 24-477; PO Box 1416) has two rooms, each with its own private entrance and bath, in a large, attractive family home right beside the lagoon. It's quiet and comfortable. The single room is T$20; a large double room with its own fridge and coffee maker is T$45.

Back on the waterfront, on Vuna Rd, are a couple of older guesthouses that unfortunately have already seen better days. *Kimiko's Guest House* (☎ 22-170; fax 22-970; PO Box 1323) has nine rooms with shared bath for T$10/20 a single/double. Although the guesthouse is quite old, the Chinese restaurant here is frequently recommended. Also on Vuna Rd, the *Fasi Moe 'Afi Guest House* (☎ 22-289; fax 23-313; PO Box 1392) is another very basic old place, with singles/doubles with shared bath for T$15/30.

The *Kulukulu Backpackers & Campsite*

(☎ 22-412, ☎ /fax 24-113) on Bypass Rd in eastern Nuku'alofa, about 100m back from the sea, doesn't look very well cared for but it's cheap, with dorm beds for T$9 to T$12 in a small, simple backpackers with shared bath and kitchen.

Places to Stay – middle

The *Harbour View Motel* (☎ 25-488; fax 25-490; PO Box 83), on Vuna Rd opposite Queen Salote Wharf, is a spotless, bright and modern 12-room motel. Budget rooms with fan and shared bath are $35/50 a single/double. Standard rooms with fridge, air-con and shared bath, are T$60. Deluxe rooms with air-con, TV/video, private bath and telephone are T$75; a family room with the same amenities is T$90. The executive suite, with a private jacuzzi, is T$120 per night. All prices include continental breakfast. Cars can be rented for T$35 per day.

Papiloa's Friendly Islander Hotel (☎ 23-810; fax 24-199; papiloa@candw.to; PO Box 142) is on Vuna Rd, 2km east of Queen Salote Wharf. It has a swimming pool with a poolside pub and grill, a restaurant, an eco-tourism centre, and occasional family entertainment. Rooms face the sea or the swimming pool; all have private bath, kitchen, ceiling fan, private balcony, telephone and radio. One-bedroom units are T$50/60 a single/double; two-bedroom units are T$60/70. Or there's a shared rate of T$15 per person – backpackers are welcome here too. A separate garden section has 14 free-standing air-conditioned bungalows, each with fridge and tea/coffee facilities. One-bedroom bungalows are T$65/75 and two-bedroom bungalows are T$85/95. Papiloa is a friendly lady who does everything she can to make your stay comfortable, and though these are the official prices, she says prices can be negotiated, to suit your budget.

Hotel Nuku'alofa (☎ 24-244; fax 23-154; PO Box 32), on Taufa'ahau Rd near the basilica, is an upstairs hotel with 14 air-conditioned rooms, a restaurant and bar. Singles/doubles are T$55/70.

Places to Stay – top end

The *Pacific Royale Hotel* (☎ 23-344; fax 23-833; royale@candw.to; PO Box 74) on Taufa'ahau Rd in central Nuku'alofa is a decent business travellers hotel, with 60 air-conditioned rooms, a small swimming pool, a restaurant and bar. Economy rooms are T$70/85/95 a single/double/triple; larger 'superior' rooms are T$99/115/125. There's also a two-bedroom apartment (T$155) and a two-bedroom penthouse apartment (T$175), both with kitchen.

The big 76-room *International Dateline Hotel* (☎ 23-411; fax 23-410; PO Box 39) on Vuna Rd is considered the classiest place to stay in Nuku'alofa. It has a swimming pool, a poolside snack bar, restaurant (with traditional dancing on Wednesday and Saturday nights), a lounge bar (with live music), duty-free shopping, a booking desk and babysitting service. Nonguests can use the swimming pool for T$2 per day; the pool here is popular on Sunday. The hotel is being remodelled in 1998, and another 140 rooms are scheduled to be built before the millennium. All the rooms have air-con, telephone, refrigerator and tea/coffee facilities. The standard rooms have a great view of the sea; the 'superior' rooms are larger and newer, but lack the sea view. Standard rooms are T$81/94/105 a single/double/triple; superior rooms are T$109/120/130; suites are T$170.

The much smaller *Villa McKenzie* (☎/fax 24-998), also on Vuna Rd, is a lovely guesthouse in a renovated, gracious old villa with a wide, shady verandah facing the waterfront. Anne & Milton McKenzie of New Zealand, the friendly and helpful proprietors, have done a splendid job on the renovation. The four elegant guest rooms, each with private bath, are T$85/115 a single/double, full breakfast included. Other meals are available by arrangement. There's also a huge sitting room and a pleasant garden out the back.

The Italian-run *Kahana Lagoon Resort* (☎/fax 24-967; PO Box 3097) is on the south side of the Nuku'alofa peninsula, beside the lagoon, with a terrific lagoon view. There's a swimming pool, a poolside restaurant/bar, canoes, bicycles etc, and 11 spacious free-standing fales (bungalows), some right on the lagoon shore. Standard fales are T$65/80 a single/double, superior fales are T$80/100, and suites are T$100/120. Meal plans are available upon request; the restaurant is known for its fine Italian food. The resort was getting a facelift when we visited in 1998.

A big new hotel is being built near the airport by a Chinese investor, Dr Wong. It's been under construction for years and many people doubt that it will ever be completed. However, the tourist office says it should be finished by the year 2000. (If not, maybe by the year 3000!)

Apartments & Townhouses

All the following are fully furnished and fully self-contained apartments, with kitchen, bath, sitting rooms, etc. All can be rented either short or long term.

Haufolau Apartments (☎ 21-151) on Fatafehi Rd is a charming little place with three two-bedroom apartments set around a lovely garden with beautiful decorations made of giant clam shells. It's very well cared for, and being well back from the street, it's quiet, peaceful and safe. Each apartment costs T$18 per night, or T$300 per month.

About 1km east of the Small Industries Centre, *Leilani Apartments* (☎ 23-910; PO Box 2137) is right on the shore of the lagoon. The apartments are clean, modern and very pleasant. One/two/three-bedroom apartments are T$83/97/140 per week, T$333/385/565 per month, or you can stay by the night.

Alekina Townhouses (☎ 22-135; fax 23-548; PO Box 68) on Vuna Rd is on the waterfront at the western edge of Nuku'alofa, 15 minutes' walk west of the Royal Palace. One/two-bedroom apartments are T$50/60 per night.

Captain Cook Vacation Apartments (☎ 23-615; fax 25-600; PO Box 1959), also on Vuna Rd on the waterfront west of the Royal Palace, has six two-bedroom apartments, each with a view of the sea. Each has two bedrooms, kitchen, bathroom, sitting room and telephone. Nightly rates are T$55/65/75 a single/double/family, but discounts are always made.

Holiday Apartments (☎ 23-092; fax 24-850; PO Box 134), off Vaha'akolo Rd about 2km south of the centre, is in a quiet location and it's a bit more luxurious, with a large lawn, small swimming pool and many amenities. One/two-bedroom apartments are T$65/90 per night, or T$50/70 per night for stays of one month or more.

Long-Term Accommodation

Houses and flats for rent are listed on the bulletin board at the Tonga Visitors' Bureau and can be good value if you plan to stay for a while. Prices start around T$300 per month for a simple house; elegance will set you back upwards of T$800 per month.

The House Rental Agency (☎ 23-092; fax 24-850; PO Box 134) also keeps listings; they usually handle only long-term rentals. Its office in the Tungi Arcade is open weekdays from 9.30 am to noon.

Places to Eat

Nuku'alofa has many good places to eat. Don't forget the restaurants at the resorts around Tongatapu, and on the small islands offshore.

Restaurants *Fasi Moe 'Afi Italian Garden Restaurant*, on Vuna Rd beside the Tonga Visitors' Bureau, is one of Nuku'alofa's most popular restaurants, with tables inside under an open-air thatched roof as well as outdoors in the garden, next to the garden bar. Although you may be chewing on the tablecloths by the time your garlic bread, pizza, pasta, salad or whatever arrives, it's worth the wait. A big family-size pizza costs around T$14, and there's a wine list. Breakfast, lunch and dinner are served every day. There's live music on Friday nights, when the Garden Bar is a popular watering hole.

Little Italy Pizzeria, on the waterfront a few blocks west of the Royal Palace, is a pleasant Italian restaurant. Angelo, the Italian chef, provides not only superb food but also a comfortable atmosphere, with tables inside and out on the terrace overlooking the sea. He serves a variety of salads, 13 kinds of pasta and 25 kinds of pizza; try the giant calzone, a good deal for T$8.50. Cappuccino or espresso top off any meal.

Nuku'alofa has a growing number of Chinese restaurants. The *Fakalato Chinese Restaurant*, upstairs on Wellington Rd, is usually recommended as the best in town. It has great food, reasonable prices (most dishes cost T$5 to T$7), pleasant atmosphere, friendly service and air-conditioned comfort.

The *Emerald Chinese Restaurant* on Vuna Rd is not as popular as Fakalato, but if you're in the mood for lobster, check it out – lobster here is T$9.80, compared to T$20 or T$25 at most places in town. It has a pleasant atmosphere and friendly service. Also on Vuna Rd, *Kimiko's Chinese Restaurant*, beside Kimiko's Guest House, is a simple place with inexpensive prices, that's said to be quite good.

The *Dateline Restaurant* at the International Dateline Hotel serves all meals, every day. There's a dress code for dinner: patrons are not admitted wearing sandals (although the waiters do!), singlets or shorts, and men must wear a shirt with a collar. Nevertheless, the meals are reasonable and not too expensive. Tongan dinner buffets and floor shows are held on Wednesday and Saturday nights.

Budget Restaurants One of the most popular lunch spots in town is *Akiko's* downstairs in the basilica, with daily lunch specials for T$3. If you're not keen on the special, you can get omu rice or fried rice for T$2, or other simple fare; dinners are around T$5 to T$8.50. The teppanyaki has been recommended – ask for Steven to grill it for you at your table – and there's a variety of Chinese dishes, tempura and hamburgers.

The *Maseia Restaurant* serves authentic

Tongan dishes at good prices in a clean, pleasant atmosphere. It's upstairs on the top floor of the Maseia Building opposite the Friendly Islands Bookshop on Taufa'ahau Rd. A filling hot lunch is around T$2 to T$3.

Rudi's Pacific Cuisines on Salote Rd near Cable & Wireless is another pleasant restaurant serving traditional Tongan dishes, in addition to seafood and steaks.

At *Pot Luck Lunches* (☎ 25-091), near Queen Salote Wharf, good food and good service are provided at lunchtime by the students of the 'Ahopanilolo Technical College, which teaches catering and hospitality; this is its training restaurant. They call it 'pot luck' because one set meal is prepared, and you take your luck with it! It's open Tuesday, Wednesday and Friday from noon to 2 pm, when school is in session.

The *International Dateline Hotel* is a fancy hotel, but its poolside *Splash Cafe & Bar* is both pleasant and economical. The hot chips (French fries) are especially tasty, and it serves an array of burgers, salads, sandwiches etc. It's open every day (including Sunday) from 10 am to 2 am – a great spot for night owls and for Sunday lounging around the pool.

Fine Dining The following are Nuku'alofa's poshest restaurants. Bookings are recommended at all of them.

One of the most elegant and pricey restaurants in town is the *Seaview* (☎ 23-709), a cosy place near the British High Commission on the waterfront west of the Royal Palace. Steak and seafood are the specialities, with main courses for T$17 to T$25, starters from T$10 to T$13.

Davina's Harbourside Seafood Bar & Grill (☎ 23-385), on the waterfront opposite Queen Salote wharf, specialises in seafood. It may be a tad overpriced, but that doesn't seem to have affected its popularity. The garden bar here is very pleasant in the evening.

The *Love Boat* (☎ 23-906), beside the lagoon about 2.5km south of town, is a fine international restaurant. Marco, the affable Italian chef and host, was formerly the food and beverage manager on a Princess cruise ship, hence the restaurant's name. He has plenty of experience with international cuisines, and a flair for presentation and hospitality. English, French, Spanish and Italian are spoken. Though you can spend up if you want to, it's also possible to dine economically – at dinner an all-you-can-eat appetiser buffet is set out (T$12), and you're welcome to eat just that if you like. Main dishes are around T$16 to T$20, including the salad bar. There's a relaxed ambience and pleasant view over the lagoon. The Ambassador nightclub is next door.

Takeaways & Snacks *John's Place Takeaway & Ice Cream Corner*, on Taufa'ahau Rd right in the centre, serves a gamut of fast foods – hamburgers, hot dogs, fried chicken, fish and chips, pizza, curries, Chinese dishes etc. Another *John's Place* is in Salote Rd, opposite the police station, and there's another opposite Vaiola Hospital, about 2km south of town.

For Chinese takeaways the *Snack & Milk Bar*, downstairs from the Fakalato Chinese Restaurant on Wellington Rd, is another favourite, with Chinese dishes, curries and barbecue chicken.

Cowley's *Bread Bin* on Salote Rd makes T$1.50 lunchtime submarine sandwiches.

Freddy's Spicy Chicken on One-Way Rd serves roast or fried chicken, curries, sausages, burgers, salads, snack-pack combos etc. Free delivery is available for orders of T$10 or more (☎ 25-386).

For authentic English-style fish and chips you can't beat *Mr Chips English Style Fish & Chips* on Salote Rd, operated by a friendly British gent.

Another local favourite is *Kimiko's Snack Bar*, on Vuna Rd opposite Faua Jetty (not to be confused with the Chinese restaurant at Kimiko's Guesthouse).

In *Seilose 'O Fangaake*, the small convenience store on Taufa'ahau Rd near John's Place, a counter sells good, inexpensive ice cream.

The *Italian Ice Cream* shop, on Wellington Rd near the corner of Taufa'ahau Rd, sells Italian ice cream and other snacks. It's a popular hangout for foreigners living in Tonga.

Self-Catering *Talamahu Market* offers the best value fresh produce. Many prices are marked but if not, watch what the Tongans are paying; there are reports of foreigners being charged three times the local price.

Cowley's owns two bakeries in town, one on Taufa'ahau Rd and the other on Salote Rd, known as the *Bread Bin*. It has a variety of cakes and sweets as well as white, whole-wheat and seven-grain breads, rolls and muffins (delicious). Exceptionally sugary cakes and other baked sweets are available at the *Homestyle Bakery* on Salote Rd opposite the police station.

You can buy fresh fish at the market on Faua Jetty. The boats come in at around 6 am so get there early. Fresh fish is also sold on Vuna Wharf, usually in the afternoon. Otherwise, *'Alatini Fisheries & Meat Co* at the Small Industries Centre is great for fresh fish, and it also sells imported wines at good prices. The *Sea Star Fishing Co*, also at the Small Industries Centre, is another place to buy fresh fish.

Mince and packaged meats are sold at the *Tonga Cold Stores*; there's one on Salote Rd next to Cowley's Bread Bin and another on Vuna Rd next to the Billfish Bar/Restaurant.

Nuku'alofa has three large supermarkets. *Morris Hedstrom* is opposite Talamahu Market on Salote Rd. Ten minutes east along Salote Rd is another large supermarket in the *Kinikinilau Shopping Centre*. The *Tonga Co-Operative Federation*, on Taufa'ahau Rd opposite the Pacific Royale Hotel, has good prices.

Two shops specialise in items from the USA: the *SNAP* store, on Mateialona Rd at the corner of Vaha'akolo Rd, and the *Mini Mart USA* at the corner of One-Way and Laifone Rds. The latter accepts US dollars at the current bank value.

The *Supa-Kava Market* at the Kinikinilau

Shopping Centre also has good prices on imported wines. Another bottle shop is at the Morris Hedstrom supermarket on Salote Rd. There's a Royal beer shop at Fakafonua Centre near Queen Salote Wharf. The Royal brewery is in the Small Industries Centre; it's quite small but if you stop by you can see how the brew is made.

Tongan National Centre For something a bit different, try to eat one dinner at the *Tongan National Centre* (☎ 23-022). Their dinner programmes take place on Tuesday and Thursday evenings, beginning at 7 pm with string band entertainment, followed by a brief kava-drinking ceremony. The Tongan buffet begins at 8 pm and is followed by an hour-long programme of Tongan dancing. The evening costs T$20 (children T$10); round-trip transport is an extra T$1. Bookings must be made by 4.30 pm on the day you wish to attend.

Entertainment
Island Buffets & Traditional Dance Island-style buffets and performances of traditional Tongan music and dance are presented indoors at the Tongan National Centre on Tuesday and Thursday nights, at the International Dateline Hotel on Wednesday and Saturday nights, and outdoors by the beach at the Good Samaritan Inn in Kolovai on Friday nights. (This one has the advantage of having a great view of the sunset.) Don't miss one of these while you're on Tongatapu. They're delightful entertainment for all ages.

The Good Samaritan also has entertainment on Saturday night, with a traditional sing-along kava party, a village string band, barbecue and salad bar.

Bars Along the waterfront are three open-air garden bars which are great for socialising or for starting off the evening, before the discos and nightclubs get going. The garden bar at *Davina's Harbourside Seafood Bar & Grill* is open all day and evening. The garden bar at the *Fasi Moe 'Afi Italian Garden Restaurant* has live music on Friday nights. The *Billfish Bar/Restaurant* has live music on Wednesday and Saturday nights, and a dance floor. Food is available at all three places.

The *International Dateline Hotel* has a lounge bar with live entertainment, plus the poolside *Splash Cafe & Bar*, open every day from 10 am until 2 am. *Papiloa's Friendly Islander Hotel* also has a poolside pub and grill.

The *Octopusy* bar is 100m back from the waterfront, on the eastern fringes of town.

The males/members only *Nuku'alofa Club*, behind the palace, is a stuffy upper-crust pub and billiards hall where you can rub elbows with expats and Tongan nobles, yuppie politicians and businessmen. Technically, you must be the guest of a 'member', but well-dressed male foreigners are normally admitted.

The cheapest place to buy a beer (Royal, of course) is the *Tonga Club*, the historic pub a couple of blocks behind the International Dateline Hotel. Another option for a few drinks and a game of pool is the *Yacht Club* on Vuna Rd. The sign says 'members only' but visitors can get by for three months or so before they're expected to join. Shorts and thongs are not allowed and women must wear skirts.

Discos & Nightclubs Friday night is the big night for going out in Tonga. Discos and nightclubs get lively by around 10 pm and rock until dawn. Saturday night partying is stifled at midnight, when bars and nightclubs close with a bang to avoid revelling on Sunday. All have a cover charge of T$3/5 for women/men.

Nuku'alofa has three pleasant, attractive nightclubs: the *Blue Pacific*, the *Ambassador* and *Little Orphan Annie*.

The Blue Pacific, about 4km south-east of the centre on the eastern extension of Bypass Rd, occupies what was formerly a very fancy private estate. It has indoor and outdoor dancing and bar areas, and ample grounds sloping down to the lagoon.

The *Ambassador* nightclub, in Tofoa about 2.5km south of town, is another en-joyable spot. It hangs out over the lagoon, and has tables both inside and out on the waterside terrace, beautiful on a moonlit night. The newer Little Orphan Annie, on the eastern outskirts of Nuku'alofa, opened in 1998 and is already popular.

If you're looking for sleaze, drunken violence and obnoxious behaviour, head for *Joe's The Jungle* and *Top Club* on Salote Rd, or the *Hotel Phoenix* disco. Unaccompanied foreign women should avoid these venues.

Cinema Nuku'alofa has one movie house, *Loni's Cinema*, which shows two films nightly. The offerings range from the *Kung Fu Commandos* and *Guerrilla Grunts on Patrol* type of things to some good recent films. The sprung seats, 1940s-style sound system and cellotaped screen add to the cultural experience, and if you don't like the film you can still have an entertaining time watching the locals make out. Admission is T$3.

Other Venues *Queen Salote Memorial Hall* (☎ 25-775) at the corner of Taufa'ahau and Mateialona Rds is the venue for large-scale events. The Tonga Visitors' Bureau may have details on upcoming events.

The *'Ofa Atu Variety Entertainment Centre* at Papiloa's Friendly Islander Hotel is planning to start variety and family entertainment, which might include cultural programmes, ballroom dancing, and non-alcohol nights for young people.

'Atenisi Institute has a foundation for the performing arts, which gives performances four times a year.

Spectator Sports Tonga's favourite sport, rugby, is played at *Teufaiva Outdoor Stadium* during season, roughly from March to August. It's also played just for fun all year round almost everywhere in Tonga, wherever there's a field or open lot. Cricket is played from roughly March to July on the lawn beside the Royal Palace.

'Atele Indoor Stadium is the venue for tennis (an international tournament is held

there during Heilala Week festivities in early July), as well as volleyball, badminton, table tennis, basketball, netball and boxing. Soccer matches are held on the lawn beside the Royal Palace.

Things to Buy

Nuku'alofa offers a very good selection of handicrafts. Since quality and prices vary, it's a good idea to shop around before buying anything.

A variety of arts and crafts, including whalebone and other bone carving, tapa and woodcarving can be found upstairs at the Talamahu Market. Take your time and browse around the upstairs area – there's a lot to choose from. The Treasure Island Tongan Art Gallery here specialises in fine quality products.

The Langafonua handicrafts shop and art gallery, on Taufa'ahau Rd diagonally opposite the post office, was founded by Queen Salote in 1953 to promote women's development and continuing interest in indigenous arts. The Friendly Islands Marketing Co-Operative (FIMCO), which is on Taufa'ahau Rd opposite the Friendly Islands Bookshop, is another handicrafts shop with an even wider selection. Kalia Handicrafts is also here.

Still more traditional handicrafts are sold at the handicrafts shop at the Tongan National Centre, about 2km south of town.

There's a woodcarver in residence at a booth on the grounds of the Tonga Visitors' Bureau, on Vuna Rd. Further east on Vuna Rd, Cookie's Shell Shop offers many kinds of seashells. You can't miss it – look for the wavy white giant clam shells displayed in rows outside the shop.

Tapacraft on Lavinia Rd has handicrafts you won't find in other shops. Most everything is small, inexpensive and portable, made with travellers in mind. There are dolls and other items made of tapa, but most amazing are the original engravings from Captain Cook's voyages, printed in England in 1777 and 1784. These are true collectors' items, coming with a history telling how and when they were made and published.

The cost of T$45 to T$150 apiece is very reasonable, considering how priceless they are.

Stamp collectors should check out the Philatelic Bureau upstairs at the post office. Niuafo'ou stamps are also available here. Coin and bill collectors should visit the Federal Reserve Bank of Tonga, on Salote Rd.

Clay Works of Tonga, operated by Miriam the Canadian potter, offers handmade pottery, gifts and souvenirs in Tongan and western designs, with many small pieces travellers can easily carry. She also offers classes and made-to-order items. The studio is on Bypass Rd, one door east of the corner of Taufa'ahau Rd.

The Blue Banana shop in the Kinikinilau Shopping Centre sells distinctive handpainted T-shirts and other clothing. It also has another shop downtown. Various small shops along Taufa'ahau Road are also good for printed T-shirts and other clothing souvenirs of Tonga.

Secondhand and inexpensive clothing is available at the flea market on Vuna Rd on Saturday mornings, and upstairs at Talamahu Market.

Getting There & Away

See the Getting There & Away chapter earlier in this book for information on transport between Tongatapu and other countries. The Getting Around chapter provides information on transport between Tongatapu and other parts of Tonga.

Getting Around

To/From the Airport Taxis are on hand to meet all incoming domestic and international flights. Taxis usually charge T$10 for up to four passengers between the airport and Nuku'alofa, though the government allows fares of up to T$12. Teta Tours (☎ 21-688) and Paea Tours (☎ 21-103) send buses to meet arriving and departing international flights; the cost is T$5 per person with Paea, T$6 with Teta, between Nuku'alofa and the airport. Palm Travel & Tours (☎ 24-920, after hours 23-505) offers airport transfers for T$8 per person. Some hotels and guesthouses offer airport transport for guests.

Bus Nuku'alofa has a convenient city bus system for getting around town and 'long-distance' buses for getting around the island. 'Long-distance' buses depart from two terminals on Vuna Rd. The eastern terminal serves destinations to the east of Nuku'alofa; the western terminal serves destinations to the west. Fares range from 20 seniti to T$1.

Don't set off for anywhere after about noon unless you're planning to stay the night or are willing to take your chances hitching back. The bus service starts early, around 6 or 7 am. The last buses usually run at about 4.30 or 4.45 pm. There's no bus service on Sunday.

In urban areas of Tongatapu, bus stops are marked with a small sign reading 'Pasi'. Elsewhere, flag down a bus by waving your outstretched arm as the bus approaches. Passengers normally pay as they get off the bus but on some buses, the driver will require that you pay as you board.

Car & Van Car rental companies in Nuku'alofa include:

Avis
 (☎ 23-344) – cars, T$60 to T$91 per day
Budget Rent-A-Car
 (☎ 23-510) – cars, T$55 to T$65 per day
EM Jones Rental Cars
 (☎ 23-422, 23-423) – cars, T$50 per day, T$25 per half-day
Five Star Enterprise
 (☎ 23-429, 24-396) – cars and vans, T$55 per day
Makalita Rental Cars
 (☎ 24-823) – cars, T$45 to T$85 per day
Palm Travel & Tours
 (☎ 24-920, 23-505) – cars, T$65 per day plus T$10 insurance; also rents mini-buses, and can provide drivers

All rates include unlimited kilometres. Special rates are usually available for weekends, or for long-term rental. The Harbour View Motel rents vehicles out to its guests for T$35 per day.

Taxi Within Nuku'alofa, taxis charge a standard T$1 fare for up to four passengers. Fares to the outskirts of town are about T$2 to T$3. You can identify taxis by the presence of a 'T' on the license plate, before the numbers.

Bicycle Tongatapu is pancake-flat and perfect for cycling. Hiring a bike allows you to explore the island at leisure, stopping wherever and for as long as you like, as well as being convenient for getting around town.

Niko's Bicycle Rental, a bicycle stand on the waterfront roughly opposite the Fasi Moe 'Afi Guest House, rents out bicycles for T$8/30 per day/week, with special rates on weekends. It's open Monday to Saturday from 8 am to 5 pm. Some guesthouses also rent out bicycles.

Boat The four offshore island resorts all provide boat transport. Boat trips can also be arranged with Hakula Charters (☎ 11-236; fax 23-759), Palm Travel & Tours (☎ 24-920, 23-505; fax 24-914), Atiu Charters (☎ 22-489, 26-019; fax 24-365; or contact the Billfish Bar), or the Royal Sunset Island Resort (☎/fax 21-254).

Around Tongatapu

Travellers will invariably want to have a look around Tonga's main island. Although Tongatapu is undeniably flat, it does harbour a variety of notable natural features – beaches, caves, blowholes, a natural limestone archway and coral reefs – as well as some of the most extensive and well excavated archaeological sites in the Pacific. The entire east coast, from the southern tip of the island right up to Niutoua, is fringed with lovely white-sand beaches, and fine beaches are dotted along the south and west coasts as well.

Most of Tongatapu's interior is composed of agricultural land and rural villages. In the south are a few vanilla plantations. Most of the food crops produced here are consumed by the families that grow them.

Getting around without a car won't be a problem if you're prepared to walk or hitch several kilometres to points of interest from public bus stops. Alternatively, you can hire a bicycle and cover the island's major sites in three or four days. Guided tours, taxi tours and rental cars are good ways to see the island quickly

EASTERN TONGATAPU
Captain Cook's Landing Site
A memorial near Holonga village marks the site where Captain Cook landed on Tongatapu on his final Pacific voyage in 1777 and took a nap under a banyan tree before moving on to Mu'a to visit his friend Pau, the reigning Tu'i Tonga. The plaque reads:

Here stood formerly the great banyan *Malumalu-o-Fulilangi*, under the branches of which the celebrated navigator came ashore on his way to visit Pau, the Tu'i Tonga on the occasion of the Inasi in the year 1777.

British and Commonwealth citizens should also read the other side.

Kauvai Royal Estate
The secluded bit of royal real estate known as Kauvai is practically surrounded by the Fanga Kakau Lagoon. The palace sits on the shore at the end of a long, quiet road through neatly ordered royal plantations and rows of coconut trees. It's an odd landscape for Tonga, with a picturesque lagoon, some bizarre banyan trees and relatively lush vegetation. During the daytime, the access road is open to the public.

To get there without a vehicle, take a bus to Vaini or Folaha. From those villages, it's a 4km or 5km walk each way to Kauvai.

Mu'a & the Lapaha Archaeological Site
Sometime around the year 1200, the 11th Tu'i Tonga, Tu'itatui, moved the royal capital from Heketa (near present-day Niutoua) to Lapaha, now known as Mu'a. The Mu'a area contains the richest concentration of archaeological remnants in Tonga.

The langi, or pyramidal stone tombs, constructed in ancient Tonga were traditionally used for the burial of royalty. Commoners were buried in much simpler heaps of sand lined with volcanic stones, much as they are today. Around the vicinity of Mu'a there are 28 royal stone tombs, 15 of which are monumental. Most of the others are little more than conical mounds of stone. In addition, 17 other ancient royal tombs are scattered around the country.

Just outside the archaeological site, near the southern edge of Mu'a, the road crosses a shallow but prominent ditch. This is actually the moat which once surrounded the *kolo*, or royal capital.

Paepae 'o Tele'a Tonga's most imposing ancient burial site is the Paepae 'o Tele'a ('platform of Tele'a'), a monumental pyramid-like stone structure about 400m north of the moat. It was long thought to have housed the remains of Tele'a, or 'Ulukimata I, a Tu'i Tonga who reigned during the 16th century. Actually, his body may not be inside the 'tomb' at all, since legend has it that he was drowned and his body lost. Traditional burial sites were topped by a vault (*fonualoto*), which was dug into the sand on top of the platform and lined with stones in preparation for the body. This platform, however, contains no such vault, which supports the theory that the Paepae 'o Tele'a is not a tomb at all but, in fact, merely a memorial.

With the exception of the vault, this structure contains the best and most massive examples of all the early Tongan burial tomb construction styles. The stones used in building it are enormous. The corner stones of the bottom tier on the eastern side of the monument are L-shaped. The upper surfaces of all the stones are bevelled; their bases are firmly embedded in the earth, stabilised by the use of stone protrusions jutting out under the surface. On the south side is a stairway leading to the top.

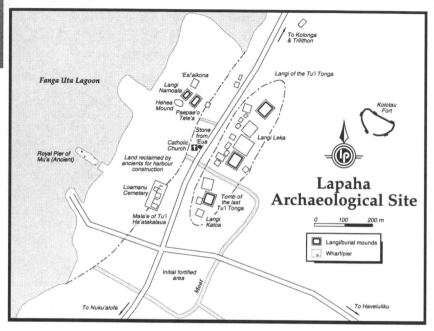

Lapaha Archaeological Site

Map labels:
- Fanga Uta Lagoon
- To Kolonga & Trilithon
- 'Esi'aikona
- Langi Namoala
- Hehea Mound
- Paepae'o Tele'a
- Stone from 'Eua
- Catholic Church
- Langi of the Tu'i Tonga
- Kolotau Fort
- Langi Leka
- Royal Pier of Mu'a (Ancient)
- Land reclaimed by ancients for harbour construction
- Loamanu Cemetery
- Mala'e of Tu'i Ha'atakalaua
- Tomb of the last Tu'i Tonga
- Langi Katoa
- Initial fortified area
- Moat
- To Nuku'alofa
- To Haveluliku
- 0   100   200 m
- Langi/burial mounds
- Wharf/pier

These and all the Lapaha construction stones are made of quarried limestone taken from dead coral reefs probably on Tongatapu and nearby Motutapu and Pangaimotu. They were transported using cradles slung between two seafaring canoes called *kalia*. (Some maintain that the stones were carried from the Ha'apai Group, or from Futuna or 'Uvea island in the now French territory of Wallis & Futuna, far to the north-west.) Oral history preserves tales of the wooden rollers, sennit ropes and incredible leverage (and of course slave labour) required in moving the enormous blocks to the construction sites once they'd been landed. The fitting together of the massive blocks was done after they were in place.

These days, the Paepae 'o Tele'a is suffering from age and weathering, but it remains obvious that it was built in memory of an individual who carried a lot of weight in the society that created it.

Langi Namoala & Langi Leka While the fonualoto is missing from the Paepae 'o Tele'a, the Langi Namoala tomb, also at the Lapaha site, has a fine example of a fonualoto – but it is empty. Typical of such structures, it was covered with a stone slab first and then with *kilikili* (pumice-like volcanic gravel) collected from Kao and Tofua in the Ha'apai Group. Kilikili is still valuable as grave decoration in Tonga.

If the Namoala tomb is typical, it would have once had a shelter of tapa, coconut fronds and fine mats on top of it. This would have housed the matapule (talking chief), who would live on the langi and from there would attend to the extensive funeral arrangements and ceremonies that followed a burial.

The Namoala langi is thought to have been the burial site of a female chief, but tradition supplies no further details. The stones used in this construction are much narrower than those in the adjacent pyramids. On the north side a stairway leads to the top.

To the north-east of the principal mounds rises the 'Esi'aikona, an elevated platform used as a rest area by the chief and his family, a sort of way-station for travelling VIPs. Near the Namoala tomb is the Hehea mound, which was originally believed to be a rubbish tip created during the construction of the langi. More recently, however, it was cleared of vegetation to reveal two fonualoto amid haphazardly placed earth and rock. Unlike the other structures the Hehea was built on artificial landfill, but it's not known who engineered this incredible reclamation project or when it was done.

The large langi which now bears a cross on top, across the road from the others in the modern cemetery, is the grave of Laufilitonga, the last Tu'i Tonga, who was deposed by King George Tupou I.

Mu'a All the guided island tours stop briefly at Mu'a's principal archaeological sites. If you like archaeology, you can make a very enjoyable day trip to Mu'a on your own, coming from town on the Mu'a bus. Not only are there the big, impressive, excavated pyramid tombs, but also a host of smaller pyramids scattered through the village and bush across the road in Langi Leka. It's interesting to see the present-day villagers living among these ancient pyramids.

Another enjoyable activity in Mu'a is to climb up the tower of the large old stone Catholic church, which affords a magnificent view. Although the church was built only around a century ago, the tropical weather and rains have aged it to look like it's been here for centuries. The church has an impressive traditional Polynesian podium and lovely stained glass work, though sadly, several years ago much of the glass was damaged in a fire.

Beside the main road outside the gate of the church there's a rather ordinary 50cm-high boulder. Tradition has it that this *makatolo* stone was hurled by the demigod

Maui from the island of 'Eua at a noisy rooster that had been keeping him awake at night. Visitors to Tonga will be particularly sympathetic to his reaction to such a situation.

If you're looking for a 'cultural experience', an old hut near Mu'a is a cinema which operates occasionally. It seems that for most locals, cinema attendance is first and foremost a social experience, and the film is relegated to second priority. People chat through the picture, catching only bits of the English dialogue, and break off conversation only during particularly exciting moments such as chase scenes and shootouts. There's no regular film schedule, but Mu'a people can tell you when something will be playing. Bring a mat to sit on, as there are no seats, and don't forget some munchies.

Getting There & Away Mu'a is easily accessible by bus. A Mu'a bus leaves from the eastern terminal in Nuku'alofa every few minutes. Head back to Nuku'alofa by 4 or 5 pm at the latest, or you could be stuck.

The Fishing Pigs of Talafo'ou
The village of Talafo'ou is known for its smart pigs. At low tide, when the coast along here becomes a tidal flat, the pigs of Talafo'ou go out on the tidal flat looking for shellfish!

Ha'amonga 'a Maui Trilithon
Near Niutoua, at the eastern end of Tongatapu, is one of ancient Polynesia's most intriguing monuments. Its name means 'Maui's burden' and according to legend it was carried by Maui from distant 'Uvea on a carrying yoke. But archaeologists and oral history credit its construction to the 11th Tu'i Tonga, Tu'itatui, who reigned at the turn of the 13th century.

The structure consists of three large coralline stones, each weighing about 40 tonnes, arranged into a trilithic gate. The uprights are about 5m high and just over 4m wide at their bases. The lintel, which rests in notched grooves in the uprights, is nearly

6m long, 1.5m wide and just over 0.5m thick.

It seems that Tu'itatui was more than a little paranoid. His name means 'leader who hits the knees', indicating that he employed the knee-striking method of warding off potential assassins. Seaward of the trilithon is a large stone, 'Esi Makafakinanga, which was supposedly used by Tu'itatui as a backrest during the construction in order to shield his back from surprise attack while directing the work.

Some suggest that the uprights were to represent the Tu'i's two sons, whom he feared would be at odds over the succession of the title upon his death. Another theory is that the uprights formed the entrance to the royal compound when Heketa, as this area was known, served as the second royal capital of Tonga.

Nowadays, it is becoming more or less accepted that the structure functioned as a sort of Stonehenge, which it slightly resembles. In the mid-1960s, King Taufa'ahau Tupou IV theorised that an odd design on the lintel may have had something to do with determining seasons. Swathes were cleared from the trilithon to the sea nearby in line with the arms of the double-V design. On 21 June 1967, the winter solstice, the sun was observed to rise and set in perfect alignment with the clearings. It was also noted that it rose and set along the other two arms on the longest day of the year.

For the ancient Tongans, the significance of the summer solstice probably related to the beginning of the *kahokaho* (yam) harvest, which was kicked off by the biggest annual festival held in ancient Tonga, the Katoanga 'Inasi. During this celebration, the year's finest yams were donated to the royal storehouses of the Tu'i Tonga.

The Ha'amonga Trilithon is now preserved in a 23-hectare National Historic Reserve. From the entrance, a walking track winds northward past several langi (known as the Langi Heketa) and 'esi (resting mounds), where interpretative signs make

sense of the remaining mounds of stones. The track then enters the forest and continues for several hundred metres to the shore. This is a lovely walk and, at the end, you're treated to a view of the bizarre limestone bluffs protruding over clear green water. Return to the road by continuing east along the coastline along the same track. It eventually meets up with one of the solstice swathes, which may be followed back to the trilithon.

A number of handicrafts tables are set up beside the trilithon. The handicrafts sold here are good quality, and are cheaper than in town.

Getting There & Away To reach the trilithon from Nuku'alofa, take the Niutoua bus and get off about 1km short of Niutoua (the driver can indicate the spot). There are only a few buses a day so try to start as early as possible and return, at the latest, in the early afternoon, or you may have problems returning to Nuku'alofa the same day.

Muihopohoponga Reserve
Near Niutoua is a 2km stretch of white-sand beach at the easternmost extreme of Tongatapu. It has been set aside as a nature reserve to protect several species of native trees and some of the natural bushland that once covered the entire island. It is accessible by walking 2km along a track leading east from Niutoua.

'Anahulu Cave & Haveluliku
Along a dirt track south of Niutoua you'll reach the village of Haveluliku, where you'll find more of Maui's stone projectiles. Turn left at the road and continue through the village to the shore to reach Tongatapu's most famous cave. The cave is replete with stalactites and stalagmites, but its natural decorations haven't been well cared for and decades of handling and vandalising have taken their toll. Still, it's a delightful other-worldly place.

Upon entering the cave, you can sometimes notice a slight musty smell caused by deposits from cave swallows, or *pekepeka*, which nest in the rock walls. Their screeching combines with the constant dripping of water to create an eerie atmosphere.

As you approach the rear wall of the cave, descend the stairway on your left to the freshwater pool. Local children use it as a swimming hole, and the more intrepid of them climb the surrounding stalagmites and dive into the cold water. Visitors are welcome to join them.

In order to walk through the cave, you must bring a torch (flashlight). For even further exploration, hire night diving lights from Beluga Diving in Nuku'alofa. Bring sensible walking shoes, too.

The village is best accessed by walking 3km from the village of Mu'a, the site of the Lapaha tombs.

'Oholei Beach
On the shore about 4km south of Haveluliku is 'Oholei Beach, where the coastline is riddled with limestone caves and the lovely, deserted, white sand goes forever. Hina Cave, along the beach, is beautiful, with soft light filtering through the open roof.

Hufangalupe
Five kilometres south of the village of Vaini is Hufangalupe ('the pigeon's gate'). This large natural archway in the coralline limestone is flanked to the south by 30m cliffs and to the north by plantation lands. The sea pounds through the opening and tears at the walls of the bridge and adjacent pit.

By public transport, you'll have to hurry to see Hufangalupe in one day, since you'll have to walk nearly 10km. Take a bus to Vaini – buses go there many times daily – and walk south for almost 5km until you reach the coast. When you reach the cliffs you'll be standing on top of the bridge. Turn around and go back until you see a very faint track leading away to the east. If you follow it for a few metres, you'll soon see the archway. It's possible to climb all the way down to the sea in the gully but it's very steep and the coral rocks are razor sharp.

A good view into the pit can be had from the span itself. A special treat is the possibility of seeing white-tailed tropic birds swooping with their long, graceful tail feathers. These dramatic white birds make their nests in the cliffs and even sometimes in the arch itself.

Following the road eastward from the span, you'll see numerous dramatic 30m cliffs and the turbulent sea below – quite a contrast to Tongatapu's calm, lazy north shore.

WESTERN TONGATAPU
Vanilla Plantations
On the south coast of Tongatapu, west of Hufangalupe, are the vanilla plantations that produce what was once Tonga's primary export crop (over the past several years, vanilla has been surpassed – and left in the dust – by the great pumpkin). Although Tonga's main vanilla-producing area is on the island of Vava'u in the Vava'u Group, this is the primary area of production on Tongatapu.

Tongan Wildlife Centre Bird Park
If you've had no luck spotting a red shining parrot (also known as 'Eua parrot) or a Niuafo'ou megapode, here's your chance to see these rare birds. The Tongan Wildlife Centre Bird Park (π/fax 23-561) was established in 1990 to promote conservation awareness, collect data, carry out captive breeding, establish reserves and translocate rare and endangered indigenous bird species.

The stars of the show are currently the highly endangered Niuafo'ou megapodes (*malau*), some of which are being transferred from their volcanic home on Niuafo'ou to the similarly volcanic (and uninhabited) island of Late in the Vava'u Group. Other endangered species on display include the magnificent red shining parrot (*koki*), the blue-crowned lorikeet (*henga*) and the friendly ground dove (*tu*). In addition to the birds, there's also the banded iguana (*fokai*), which lives throughout Tonga but is extremely difficult to spot in the bush.

The park also has a well laid tropical garden containing examples of many medicinal and food crops grown in Tonga.

Allow about 1½ hours to see the park, more if you want to spend time just strolling. It's open every day from 9 am to 5 pm, Sunday included. Admission is T$3 (children free).

Getting There & Away To get there on public transport, take the Vaini or Mu'a bus to Veitongo village and get off at the Bird Park sign. From there, continue south for just over 2km to Liku Rd. The Bird Park entrance is just south of this intersection. If you continue south along the deteriorating track for 250m, you'll reach the south coast of the island.

Keleti Beach
The clean and lovely Keleti Beach is actually a series of beaches divided by rocky outcrops. They slope gently into clear pools excellent for swimming at high tide. The outer reef consists of a line of terraces and blowholes that shoot like Yellowstone geysers when the waves hit them at high tide. At low tide the blowholes turn into calm elevated tubs which are perfect for lazing in and observing the variety of life trapped there. Just above the beach area is the Keleti Beach Resort. Taxis from town cost T$7 each way for up to four people.

Places to Stay & Eat *Keleti Beach Resort* (☎/fax 24-654; PO Box 3116, Nuku'alofa), on the cliff overlooking Keleti Beach, has eight cinder-block bungalows, each with private bath. Singles/doubles are T$30/40; larger bungalows sleeping four are T$60. The restaurant here is quite good.

Mapu'a 'a Vaca Blowholes
The Mapu'a 'a Vaca blowholes ('chief's whistles') stretch for 5km along the south shore of Tongatapu, near the village of Houma. They are best viewed on a windy day at high tide, when the maximum amount of water is forced up through natural vents in the coralline limestone

forming geyser-like fountains of seawater up to 30m high. On an especially good day, hundreds of them will be active at once (but if the surf is too high, it will wash up over the terraces containing the vents and 'extinguish' the fountains). Adjacent to the magnificent Taga Blowholes on the island of Savai'i (Samoa), they are the most impressive in the South Pacific.

For a look at the blowholes from another perspective, turn west just south of the church and school in Houma. Where this road hits the shore, there's a wonderful snorkelling beach and interesting sea level views of the blowholes.

To get there by public transport, take a bus from Nuku'alofa's western bus terminal to Houma and walk 1km south to the parking area above the blowholes.

Liahona
In the village of Liahona in central Tongatapu is a large complex constructed by the Mormon church. Tongatapu's Mormon temple is here, crowned by a large golden angel and surrounded by beautiful gardens. Only Mormons may enter the temple. Other buildings in the Mormon compound include a large Mormon high school. (Beulah College, which is the Seventh Day Adventist counterpart to Liahona, is near the village of Vaini.)

Immediately west of Liahona, on the north side of the road, is what is reputed to be Tonga's only double-headed coconut tree. Now it has actually grown into a triple-headed tree! It's a very unusual sight.

'Umu Tangata
At the intersection of three roads, just south of the planned community of Fo'ui, is the 'Umu Tangata ('man oven'). There's no oven to see here today, but there is a legend. Long ago a cannibal chef was preparing a feast here, when he became distracted by an invasion of outsiders. He left the meal unattended for so long that a tree grew out of each person in the underground oven. It's believed that descendants of these original trees remain to this day.

Kolovai & the Kolovai Flying Fox Sanctuary

The flying fox sanctuary in the village of Kolovai is an impressive sight, with hundreds of flying foxes – immense bats with wingspans of up to 1m – hanging upside-down from the casuarina trees. Although these nocturnal bats are found all over the South Pacific, Tonga is the one place where they are considered *tapu*, or sacred. While they're eaten unsparingly by gourmet islanders elsewhere, they remain protected in Tonga and only members of the royal family are permitted to hunt them for sport.

To get there from Nuku'alofa, take either the Kolovai or Hihifo buses all the way to Kolovai, or take the Fahefa bus and either walk or hitch a ride northward to Kolovai.

Places to Stay & Eat One of Tongatapu's most popular out-of-town hotels is the seaside *Good Samaritan Inn* (☎ 41-022; fax 41-095; PO Box 214, Nuku'alofa), on the coast at Kolovai. Although the beach here isn't the island's best, it's a pleasant option for a couple of quiet days away from Nuku'alofa.

Basic bungalows with shared bath are T$20/30 a single/double, great for the price. Bungalows with private bath are T$40/60. Self-contained, family-size bungalows with private bath, kitchen and living area are T$50/70. All prices include breakfast. There's also shared accommodation for T$10 per night; backpackers are welcome here. Camping is T$8 per night.

The restaurant/bar here is known as one of the island's best. Overlooking the sea, its large patio dining area offers a spectacular view of the sunset. It's open every day, 7 am to 10 pm.

Entertainment is featured several times a week. The highlight of the week is the Friday night all-you-can-eat Tongan buffet accompanied by a string band and a rousing performance of Tongan and Polynesian dance and song, all for T$18. This is one of Tongatapu's favourite Friday night activities. Ring for reservations and transport.

Saturday night there's a traditional singa-long kava party, with a string band, barbecue and salad bar, all for T$12. On Sunday there's an all-you-can-eat family-style 'umu (traditional Tongan underground oven feast) for T$15. Thursday is lobster night, for T$25.

Taxis from Nuku'alofa cost around T$10 to T$12. By bus, you'll only get as far as Kolovai, from where you'll have a good 2km walk to the hotel. (It's an easy hitch – anyone going that way will give you a lift.) Guests get free pick-up, and daily shuttles into town.

Ha'atafu Beach Reserve

Just 3km up the coast from Kolovai, the Ha'atafu Beach Reserve encompasses 8.4 hectares of shallow reef and an area of deep water just outside the breakers. The area inside the barrier reef provides excellent snorkelling at high tide, but when the water is low, most of the reef lies just below the surface. Thanks to its location at the juncture of both reef and deep sea habitats, more than 100 species of fish can be observed here.

Ha'atafu Beach is clean and white. Swimming is safe in the shallow areas, but beyond the barrier reef, strong currents, extensive coral beds and breaking surf make the prospect dangerous. The best surfing on Tongatapu is found here but only experienced surfers should attempt it, as there is a risk of being flung headfirst onto a shallow reef.

The Hihifo bus comes from Nuku'alofa right to the beach and to the door of both resorts; cost is 70 seniti. A taxi costs T$10 to T$12.

Places to Stay & Eat Two enjoyable, low-key resorts stand side by side on the same clean, quiet beach. The restaurant at Paradise Shores is open to guests and nonguests alike; the one at Ha'atafu Beach Resort is for guests only.

New in 1997, the *Paradise Shores Resort* (☎ 41-158; fax 41-158 or 24-868; paradise_shores@candw.to; kalianet.candw.to/parashor/resort.html; PO Box 976,

Nuku'alofa), is a relaxing place operated by American expat Dave Bergeron. The pleasant restaurant/bar, *George's Pub & Grill*, is open every day. The big charcoal-grilled ground sirloin hamburgers, served with chips and salad for T$7.50, are particularly famous. Traditional thatched fales (bungalows) with shared bath are T$35 for one or two people. Camping costs T$10 per person in big luxury tents (T$15 with breakfast), or T$10 per site with your own tent. Cooking facilities are available. The resort has kayaks, snorkelling gear, satellite TV, and an outdoor jacuzzi which is lovely for watching the stars at night. Free transport is provided from town or the airport if you phone ahead. Visa and MasterCard are accepted.

Next door, the *Ha'atafu Beach Resort* (☎ 41-088; fax 22-970; PO Box 490, Nuku'alofa) specialises in all-inclusive surfing holidays. Steve Burling, the Aussie surfie proprietor, has been living and surfing in Tonga for over 20 years, and his knowledge of local breaks and conditions means you can find the best surf around. Accommodation is in beachfront fales with a clean central toilet and shower block. Singles/doubles are T$90/130 per night, or T$70 per person in twin or triple share rooms, with breakfast and buffet dinner included, and discounts by the week. (These are agent prices; ask about walk-in rates, which are much cheaper.) With a maximum of just 12 guests at a time, it's a peaceful place. Surfing safaris (T$150 per person, per day, all-inclusive), boat trips and deep sea fishing trips (T$30 per hour) can all be arranged. Airport transfers cost T$30.

Christianity & Abel Tasman Landing Sites

At the extreme north-west 'horn' of Tongatapu are monuments marking the landing sites where it's believed that Abel Tasman, and much later the first Christian missionaries, first set foot on Tongatapu.

The Christianity landing site is the one you reach first. The monument is enclosed in a private yard so if there's someone around and you wish to take a photo, you may want to ask permission. About 1km back along the road toward Nuku'alofa is a plaque commemorating Tonga's first holy communion.

At the end of the road leading out to the point, you come to a gate, with a dirt road continuing through the bush on the other side. You're welcome to enter. Walk straight ahead for about five minutes to the monument marking the site where Dutch explorer Abel Tasman landed on 21 January 1643, almost at the tip of the point. There's some controversy as to whether this is the real landing site – some historians think it's a bit further back along the coast, nearer the Christianity landing site. In any case, the monument is here, and it's a very pleasant bush walk to reach it. You can explore around the tip of the island and actually this is a very pleasant spot whether Abel Tasman actually landed here or not.

The Kolovai bus travels right out to the end of the road.

Organised Tours

Island Tours An island tour is a good way to get acquainted with Tongatapu's most beautiful spots in a short time. Check with several operators, and find out the duration of their tours and exactly what is included – prices differ widely, because tours differ widely in length and the number of places visited.

All-day taxi tours of Tongatapu, including all the traditional 'tourist' sites, cost around T$60 to T$80 for up to four people. This can be a more economical option if you have several people together.

Toni's Guest House Tours
PO Box 3084, Nuku'alofa (☎ 21-049; fax 22-970). Tony Matthias offers excellent full-day, whole-island tours for T$15/20 per person for guests/nonguests (minimum five people, or share the cost of T$75 among the passengers if there are fewer than five). These tours, which are probably the best value for money in all Tonga, wind up at the Good Samaritan Inn, watching the sunset while you have dinner or a drink. Tony also offers special trips for set prices to anywhere around Tongatapu. All of

his trips and tours operate every day (including Sunday).

Tongan National Centre
PO Box 37, Nuku'alofa (☎ 23-022; fax 22-129). Tours of eastern and western Tongatapu, including lunch and a cultural tour at the centre, are T$30 per person. Whole-island tours, including lunch and the cultural tour, are T$45. The whole-island tour with lunch, the cultural tour, and the Tongan buffet dinner feast followed by entertainment at the centre is T$65. All of the tours are in a comfortable air-conditioned van. Reservations must be made no later than 10 am on the day of tour; the tours start at 10.15 am, weekdays.

Quick Tours
PO Box 1698, Nuku'alofa (☎ 29-910; fax 29-410). Operated by Waltraud (Maria) Quick and her son Sven. All-day tours of eastern or western Tongatapu, or 'Quick Tours' of the whole island, are T$35 per person; they also offer mini-bus charters and individual tours. German and English are spoken; air-con is available.

Paea Tours
PO Box 1301, Nuku'alofa (☎ 21-103). Full-day tours of the whole island are T$30 per person Monday to Saturday, including lunch. Its Sunday tours include a visit to the Wesleyan church (or you can join the tour after church), followed by a round-the-island tour and a traditional Tongan Sunday lunch, all for T$35.

Palm Travel & Tours
PO Box 295, Nuku'alofa (☎ 24-920, 23-505; fax 24-914; palmtour@candw.to). Bus tours of eastern or western Tongatapu are T$20 per person, or T$33 per person for the whole island. Mini-buses charter for T$140 per day, including driver, petrol and unlimited kilometres. The company also does customised tours, fishing trips, transfers to offshore islands etc.

Paradisland
PO Box 211, Nuku'alofa (☎ 24-939; fax 24-977; paradisland@candw.to). Specialises in tours in Italian, but can also arrange tours in English, German or Russian. Customised full-day tours of eastern or western Tongatapu are T$35 per person; full-day tours of the whole island are T$50 per person. A holiday marketing service, it also organises holiday bookings from Italy, Germany and England.

Pleasant Tongan Holidays
PO Box 1460, Nuku'alofa (☎/fax 23-716). Tours of eastern or western Tongatapu are T$12 per person for either side (T$32 with lunch). Whole-island tours are T$24 (T$44

with lunch). It also offers eight other tours including visits to the Tongan National Centre, Friday night at the Good Samaritan Inn, fishing, outer islands etc.

Teta Tours
PO Box 215, corner Railway & Wellington Rds, Nuku'alofa (☎ 21-688, 23-690; fax 23-238). Two to three-hour tours of the major sights of Nuku'alofa, eastern or western Tongatapu are T$15 per person, but they only take in a few sights. Whole-island tours are T$30. A scenic tour followed by a cultural tour and lunch at the Tongan National Centre is T$28 per person.

Kingdom Tours
PO Box 4, Nuku'alofa (☎ 25-200; fax 23-447). Offers several island tours around Tongatapu, ranging from T$17 to T$53 per person.

Boat Tours Hakula Charters (☎ 11-236; fax 23-759), based at Nuku'alofa's Faua Jetty, offers a variety of boat tours on the 40-foot (12m) motor catamaran *Hakula*. Island tours and day or overnight fun trips, harbour tours, snorkelling, sunset and champagne cruises, fishing trips etc can all be arranged. The Royal Sunset Island Resort (see the following Offshore Islands & Reefs section) also offers boat charters. Palm Travel & Tours (see Island Tours, above) organises outer island boat trips including snorkelling, etc for T$12 to T$35 per person.

Offshore Islands & Reefs

The north side of Tongatapu is a maze of islands, reefs and shoals brimming with all sorts of colourful marine life, coral and white beaches. Four of the islands, Pangaimotu, Makaha'a, Fafá, and 'Atata, contain resorts, and several of the other islands are inhabited as well.

Diving is excellent in the shallows north of Tongatapu. The water temperature reaches a comfortable 29°C in November and doesn't fall below 21°C in mid-winter. Underwater visibility near the main island averages 15m, increasing as one moves toward the barrier reefs where it averages 30 to 50m. Just about anything that would interest a diver is available – wrecks, coral, walls, caves, chasms and sand.

Avid snorkellers may want to bring their own gear or purchase inexpensive gear in Nuku'alofa. Makaha'a Reef, with its very large coralheads serving as a breeding ground and nursery for an explosion of colourful fish, is said to be one of the best easy-access snorkelling spots in Tonga.

In 1979, under the National Parks & Reserves Act of 1976, the government of Tonga established five marine reserves, four of which include reefs immediately north of Tongatapu. Entry to the reserves is free but visitors are asked not to capture, collect, or destroy any form of marine life or natural aspect of the areas. They are: Hakaumama'o Reef Reserve, Monu'afe Island Park, the Pangaimotu Reef Reserve and the Malinoa Island Park, which in addition to supporting octopuses, groupers, damselfish, clownfish and various species of shellfish, contains the graves of six assassins who attempted to kill prime minister Shirley Baker, and a non-functioning lighthouse. All of the island resorts described in the following section run day trips and picnic excursions to Malinoa island.

RESORTS

Four resorts are on the islands north of Tongatapu. Two of them – Fafá Island Resort and Royal Sunset Island Resort – are lovely but a bit expensive for the average budget traveller; they can be more economically visited on day trips. The other two – Pangaimotu Island Resort and Sun Island Resort – cater specifically to budget and middle-range travellers and locals.

Pangaimotu

Ten minutes away by launch from Faua Jetty, the *Tongan Beachcomber Resort* (☎/fax 23-759, PO Box 740, Nuku'alofa) on Pangaimotu is the closest island resort to Nuku'alofa and also the most popular. Inexpensive food and drinks are served in a pleasant open-air beach-

front restaurant/bar. On Sunday, while Tongatapu slumbers, Pangaimotu is a popular getaway for both locals and tourists. On other days it's quiet and peaceful.

Pangaimotu can be circumavigated in about 20 minutes. The shore facing Tongatapu is a marine reserve. Near the landing site, the wreck of *My Lady Lata II* serves not only as a diving site but also as a diving board – after a few beers, the locals and the more intrepid tourists get pretty daring. Snorkelling gear can be rented for T$4 per day, and the resort offers game fishing trips.

Accommodation, in the form of thatched beach fales with private facilities, including hot showers, costs T$55/65 a single/double. A dormitory fale, sleeping eight, costs T$20 per person. Or you can camp here for T$10 per person – there's plenty of space on the island for tents.

Getting There & Away Sunday trips to Pangaimotu leave from Faua Jetty at 10 and 11 am, noon and 1 pm, with return boats at 4 and 5 pm. All other days, the boat leaves Faua Jetty at 10 and 11 am, and returns from the island at 5 pm. The cost is T$10 return. Additional trips can be made by arrangement. The boat ride takes just 10 minutes.

Sun Island Resort

The Tongan-run *Sun Island Resort* (☎ 23-335, 23-283; fax 22-915; Private Bag 44, Nuku'alofa) is on tiny Makaha'a island, fringed by an idyllic beach and surrounded by some of the finest reefs in Tonga. In addition to enjoying cold drinks at the bar, you can hire snorkelling gear (T$10 per day), paddleboards or pedal boats. The resort offers a snorkelling excursion to the fabulous Makaha'a Reef for T$5 per person. Not many people come here, even on Sunday, so it's relaxed and quiet.

Accommodation is available in three Tongan-style fales, each with private bath (T$45 or T$60 per night, depending on size and proximity to the beach), or you can camp for T$10 per person. The restaurant serves all meals. It offers a day trip lunch special every day.

Unfortunately, on our last visit to Tonga, the resort on Sun Island had become very run down. We heard a rumour that it was coming under new management, so perhaps the situation will improve.

Getting There & Away The Sun Island boat leaves Faua Jetty at 10 am Monday to Saturday, and at 10 am, 11 am and noon on Sunday. It returns at around 4 or 4.30 pm. The trip takes 10 minutes and costs T$10 return, or T$15 return with lunch. Special transfers can be arranged at other times.

Fafá Island Resort
A bit further out is the German-run *Fafá Island Resort* (☎ 22-800; fax 23-592; fafa@candw.to; PO Box 1444, Nuku'alofa). Considerably more elegant than either Pangaimotu or Sun Island, it's situated on a magnificent beach on Fafá island, 7km from Nuku'alofa. The resort is the only development on the island.

Snorkelling, sailing, windsurfing and paddling are popular activities here. Equipment is free for guests and can be rented for a small fee by day trippers; snorkelling gear or paddle boards are T$5 per day. Snorkelling trips are run on request. An island bush walk takes about 20 minutes.

Accommodation is offered in 16 Tongan-style fales beautifully constructed of local materials, each with electricity, private bath and its own private outdoor area. Standard fales are T$60/75 a single/double; superior fales are T$145. Half-board (breakfast and dinner) costs an extra T$50 per day. Some of the fales are right on the beach, some are a bit inland. Guests can catch a boat ride to town twice a day.

Getting There & Away The resort offers day trips for T$30 per person, including lunch and the 30-minute boat transfers. Boats leave Faua Jetty every day at 11 am and return at 4.30 pm. Airport transfers cost T$6; boat transfers are complimentary for overnight guests.

If you just want to pop over for dinner on the island, transfers leave Faua Jetty at 5.30 pm and return at 9.30 pm, but they need a minimum of two people booked. A weekly island night buffet with dancing afterwards costs T$40; the price includes boat transfers both ways. You will need to book in advance.

Royal Sunset Island Resort
The Kiwi-run *Royal Sunset Island Resort* (☎/fax 21-254; royalsun@candw.to; PO Box 960, Nuku'alofa) on 'Atata island, 10km from the mainland, is the most elegant and remote of the four resorts. Although this island has the same spectacular beaches as the others, 'Atata is a much larger island and the Tongan village of 200 people on its northern end adds another dimension to a visit. The resort staff live in 'Atata village.

The resort has 26 free-standing beachfront bungalows, each with fridge, tea/coffee-making equipment, ceiling fan, hardwood floor, tapa-papered walls and private bath. Fales on the east (windward) side of the island cost T$110/120/160/185 a single/double/triple/quad. Those on the west (sheltered) side, with the sunset and sheltered lagoon, are T$116/135/180/204. Two mini-suites on the west side are T$170. There are no cooking facilities, but breakfasts and light lunches can be concocted with ingredients available at the resort shop. Meals and drinks are served at the restaurant/bar fale, which is an incredible structure supported by immense wooden beams. A meal plan, including all three meals, costs T$45 per day.

Amenities include a saltwater swimming pool, a billiards table and basic miniature golf and tennis facilities. Once a week, the resort stages a Tongan and European buffet and floor show featuring Tongan dancing by the staff, and on Sunday it grills up an elaborate all-you-can-eat buffet barbecue lunch. Included in the price of accommodation are activities including daily snorkelling trips to the reef, paddle boats, windsurfing and twice-weekly village visits

The Origin of Kava

'Eue'iki is the legendary site of the origin of kava.

The story goes that an 'inasi (agricultural show) was given for the Tu'i Tonga here. Unfortunately, the harvest had been poor that year, and there was a shortage of food for the king when he arrived. (Tongan kings have always been hearty eaters.)

The family designated to provide a feast for the Tu'i Tonga had a daughter sick with leprosy. They considered her expendable, so they killed her and baked her in an 'umu. The king ate well, but when he was told what he'd eaten, he was annoyed that the family had served up their daughter. He ordered them to bury what remained of the feast.

After a while, an odd-looking plant grew from the head of the grave. The family cared for it believing it was a gift from their daughter. Another plant later grew out of her feet.

One day a rat nibbled on the first plant. It grew tipsy and staggered around until it encountered the second plant. When it took a nibble of that one, it returned to its senses. At this point, the family realised the properties of both plants, kava and sugar cane, and knew how to use them.

Several less gruesome versions of this tale have been contrived to recount to young children and squeamish tourists. The original, it is assumed, was introduced by the Tu'i Tonga as a form of convenient political coercion when he was trying to outlaw cannibalism.

to see tapa making and basket weaving demonstrations.

Yacht charters and scuba diving or whale watching trips can be arranged on the resort's luxury sailing yacht, the *Impetuous* (see Activities earlier in this chapter).

Getting There & Away Day trips to the island are offered only on Sunday. The cost of T$30 includes a fabulous all-you-can-eat buffet barbecue lunch, a snorkelling trip out to the reef, and the boat transfers each way. It's well worth the price. The boat departs Faua Jetty at 10 am and returns at 4 pm. The boat trip to the island takes about 45 minutes.

Otherwise, return boat transfers to the island cost T$24 from Nuku'alofa or T$40 from the airport. There's no particular

schedule, but pick-ups at Faua jetty are normally made around 10 am. The resort meets international flights at the airport during daylight hours only.

'EUE'IKI

'Eue'iki ('little 'Eua') lies north-east of Tongatapu, just outside the barrier reef sheltering Tongatapu's lagoon. 'Eue'iki is known for the best surfing conditions in Tonga. According to legend, it is also the place where kava was given to Tonga.

Getting There & Away

There's no scheduled transport to 'Eue'iki. If you'd like to visit the island, ask around Faua Jetty in Nuku'alofa for someone who may be going that way. Expect to pay at least T$10 or T$15 for the return trip.

The Tongatapu Group

The Tongatapu Group is the largest of the Tongan island groups. In addition to Tongatapu island and its offshore motus, the group contains several other islands, including 'Eua, Kalau, 'Eue'iki and 'Ata. Minerva Reef, Tonga's southernmost extreme, is also discussed in this chapter.

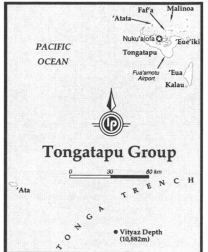

'Eua

- **area 87.44 sq km** - **population 4924**

Just a stone's throw south-east of Tongatapu is 'Eua, a beautiful island of an entirely different character to that of its larger neighbour. It is Tonga's third-largest island and one of the most mountainous, rising to 382m above the cliff-bound eastern coast. While Tongatapu is flat, well cultivated and densely populated, 'Eua is rugged and still largely wild with significant areas of natural bushland. The pace of life is slower here.

'Eua is ideal for bushwalking and the sheer limestone cliffs on 'Eua's east coast perfect for rock climbing and abseiling.

'Eua is the most naturally diverse island in Tonga, with a variety of landscapes and the last significant areas of natural bushland in Tonga south of the Niuas.

HISTORY

Abel Tasman, the first European to land on 'Eua, arrived in 1643 and named the island Middleburgh. He got on well with the Tongans he encountered and spent a few days trading. In October 1773, Captain Cook stopped for two days but recorded little of the visit. In 1796, several deserters from the US ship *Otter* went ashore at 'Eua and became the first European residents of the Tongan islands.

In September 1946, the island of Niuafo'ou erupted for the 10th time in 100 years. Although no one was killed, the government of Tonga became concerned about the potential danger of continued habitation of the island and decided to evacuate it. The residents were first transferred to Tongatapu but the lack of agricultural land there necessitated another move, this time to 'Eua. The villages of central 'Eua – 'Angaha, Futu, 'Esia, Sapa'ata, Fata'ulua, Mu'a, Mata'aho, Tongamama'o and Petani – are all named after the home villages of their inhabitants on faraway Niuafo'ou. Many people have now resettled on their home island, but a good proportion of 'Eua's population remains composed of evacuees and their descendants.

ORIENTATION

The western third of the island is a low coastal plain which merges into an area of forested hills, with north-south ridges forming the spine. The island's eastern edge consists of one and two-tier cliffs up to 100m high.

A road extends the length of 'Eua's west

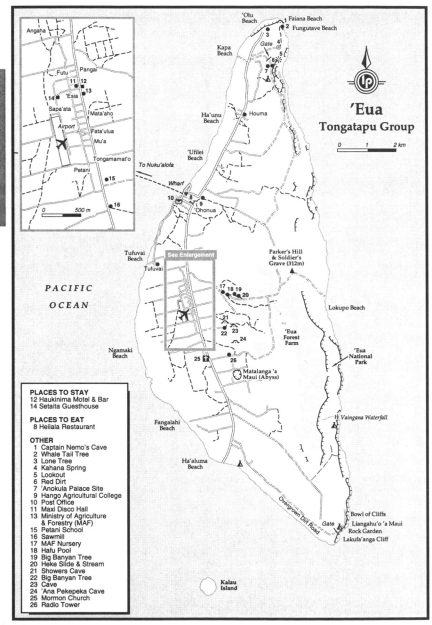

'Eua
Tongatapu Group

0   1   2 km

PACIFIC

OCEAN

PLACES TO STAY
12 Haukinima Motel & Bar
14 Setaita Guesthouse

PLACES TO EAT
8 Heilala Restaurant

OTHER
1 Captain Nemo's Cave
2 Whale Tail Tree
3 Lone Tree
4 Kahana Spring
5 Lookout
6 Red Dirt
7 'Anokula Palace Site
9 Hango Agricultural College
10 Post Office
11 Maxi Disco Hall
13 Ministry of Agriculture
   & Forestry (MAF)
15 Petani School
16 Sawmill
17 MAF Nursery
18 Hafu Pool
19 Big Banyan Tree
20 Heke Slide & Stream
21 Showers Cave
22 Big Banyan Tree
23 Cave
24 'Ana Pekepeka Cave
25 Mormon Church
26 Radio Tower

THE TONGATAPU GROUP

side. Most of the population lives between the villages of 'Ohonua in the north and Ha'atu'a in the south. This stretch is the only part of the island served by public transport. The airport is on the western edge of the island, and the ferry wharf and harbour are in 'Ohonua. Most of the island's basic services – post office, telephone office, bank, supermarket etc – are also found in 'Ohonua.

Across the hills and ridges of the interior is a network of tracks and bush roads accessible only by foot, horseback or 4WD vehicle. Only the main roads are shown on our map; a complex tangle of bush roads criss-crosses the mountains. The Ministry of Agriculture and Forestry (MAF) office has a large map of 'Eua showing all the bush track.

INFORMATION

All the basic services are in 'Ohonua, in the few blocks south of the river bridge. The post office is open weekdays from 8.30 am to 4.30 pm. The Telecom office is open 24 hours every day for domestic and international telephone and fax services.

The Bank of Tonga opens weekdays from 9 am to 12.30 pm and 1.30 to 3.30 pm. It changes major currencies in travellers cheques or cash, but is not equipped for cash advances on credit cards.

Opposite the bank is the Friendly Islands Bookshop. It doesn't have the wide selection of books that the main shop in Nuku'alofa has, but a box of paperbacks is kept under the front desk.

The MAF (☎ 50-116) is a good source of information about 'Eua Forest Farm, 'Eua National Park and other areas in the bush. There was talk of the MAF offering ecological tours of 'Eua; you might check to see if anything has been started. It's open weekdays, 8 am to 4 pm.

For Royal Tonga Airlines on 'Eua phone ☎ 50-188.

THE TONGATAPU GROUP

The Flora & Fauna of 'Eua

'Eua is known for several species of beautiful birds. Foremost among them is the large 'Eua parrot, also known as the red shining parrot, the musk or vasa parrot, or in Tongan, the *koki* or *kaka*. The beautiful little blue-crowned lorikeet is another famous native bird. Both of these parrots live in 'Eua's forest and may be difficult to spot; if you aren't able to catch a glimpse of them on 'Eua, you can always visit the Tongan Wildlife Centre Bird Park on Tongatapu to see what they look like.

Other notable 'Euan birds include the white-tailed tropic bird (*tavake*) which lives in native trees and cliffs, the white-rumped swiftlet (*pekapeka*) which lives in caves, and the Pacific black duck (*toloa*) and wild chicken (*moa kaivao*), both of which live in the bush.

The large flying fox (*peka*) or fruit bat is an impressive mammal, but the mammal you'll undoubtedly see the most of on 'Eua is the domestic pig, which seems to be everywhere.

Much of 'Eua's lower altitudes are covered in grassland, but up in the hills, 'Eua has Tonga's largest extent of natural rainforest, with dense jungle-like growth, giant tree ferns and vines, a few impressively large banyan trees and many other trees and plants.

PATRICK HORTON

'Eua's ubiquitous domestic pigs.

Why is it cooler on 'Eua?

'Eua isn't far from Tongatapu – you can see it clearly from Tongatapu's south-west shore – and yet it is much cooler. While Tongatapu is sweltering in humid heat in summer, 'Eua is perfectly pleasant. In winter, if it's chilly in Tongatapu, 'Eua can be very brisk indeed.

Why the difference? The answer lies in the combination of 'Eua's geography and the prevailing easterly trade wind.

'Eua is long north-to-south, and thin east-to-west. A mountain range stretches north-to-south along the entire east side of the island. The range rises 382m (1253 feet) above sea level at its highest point; the range as a whole is around 300m (1000 feet) high, on average.

The easterly wind hits 'Eua's east side – first the cliffs rising up out of the ocean, and then the mountain range. Blown upwards, the air is cooled. Then the cooled air blows down from the mountains, across to the west side of the island where the people live.

NORTHERN 'EUA

'Eua's northern half holds a variety of interesting destinations for day hikes as well as longer circuits. Wear good shoes, carry plenty of water and allow lots of time to explore.

Tufuvai Beach

Tufuvai Beach, near Tufuvai village, is a lovely white-sand beach. The reef here makes a natural swimming pool at high tide, though it's too shallow for swimming at low tide. There's a channel here which is suitable for swimming if you're a strong swimmer, but only at low tide – whatever you do, don't swim in this channel when the tide is going out!

Tufuvai Beach can be reached from either Pangai or 'Ohonua with a flat, easy walk of about 2km. Either head south along the coast from 'Ohonua, or turn west into Tufuvai from the main road at Pangai. A well used walking track leads between some houses and down to the beach.

The North-West Coast

North of 'Ohonua is a series of beautiful beaches. None of them is good for swimming, but you can enjoy the beauty and observe reef life. The nearest beach to 'Ohonua and the most popular for picnics and afternoon lazing is 'Ufilei, just a 20-minute walk north of the harbour.

The northern end of the island can be reached from 'Ohonua by walking along the beaches in five or six hours, but it requires quite a bit of scrambling over high rocky outcrops.

Northern End

From 'Ohonua, cross the river bridge and continue 4.5km north to the village of Houma. About 2km north of the village, the road splits into four.

The route on the far left leads down to Kapa Beach. The one leading roughly straight ahead rambles through scrubby bushland and forest and past a couple of marginal plantations. There are several minor turnings along the way but you should keep bearing north as much as possible. After about an hour of walking, you'll cross a gate and enter a broad, open pasture with magnificent views across lower tiers of rainforest and a 270° view of the sea. There is no village at this place, known as Lone Tree, but it will be obvious once you're there where the name comes from.

In the middle of the pasture, an odd copse of trees serves as an enclosure for goats. North-west of Lone Tree it's possible to bash your way down through the bush and climb down the two tiers of cliffs on the shafts of coral protruding from the surface at 80° angles. This isn't for the faint-hearted, however; use extreme caution. The Lone Tree area offers some fine campsites but steer clear of the herds of cattle – occasionally irritable bulls are among them.

Continuing east across grasslands from Lone Tree, you'll reach the cliffs of the east coast. Just below, in the side of the cliff, is the large limestone cave that Peace Corps volunteers have christened Captain Nemo's Cave. It's only one of many found in this rarely visited limestone area. Below it is Faiana Beach.

If you return to the four-way intersection and follow the second road from the right as you face north, it will lead you through heavy overgrown bush to Kahana Spring – follow the road all the way to the end, and then walk downhill to the spring. Once an open pool, the spring now feeds from its source inside a cave into a white plastic pipe funneling the water into huge, covered concrete water tanks.

From Kahana Spring, walk north a short distance on an overgrown road heading through forest and you'll come to a lookout point overlooking some dramatically high, sheer limestone cliffs, with Fungutave Beach far below. You can walk to the beach in about 45 minutes: first walk north along the overgrown road, then turn seaward onto a foot track leading towards the beach. Continue north on the foot trail until you see a tree shaped like a whale's tail, where you turn downhill towards the beach. From Kahana Spring to the Whale Tail Tree is about 20 to 25 minutes' walk; after that you go downhill towards the beach for another 20 minutes.

The road at the far right of the four-way intersection goes for 1.5km, leading you through the king's pine plantation to the Royal Estate known as 'Anokula ('red lake').

'Anokula

The ruins of 'Anokula Palace sit atop windswept 120m cliffs affording 'Eua's most spectacular vista. The rocky outcrop just to the south looks out on a view encompassing the whole of 'Eua, 'Eue'iki and even part of Tongatapu. Watch for the birds and flying foxes riding thermal currents around the cliffs.

What's left of the red lake which gave the site its name is still visible, although today it looks like a red sand trap. Just inland from

the lake is the site of 'Anokula Palace, now only a concrete foundation. Before 'Anokula Palace fell into ruin, the king used to visit to watch the full moon rising over the sea. The legend is that at full moon, if all observers remain absolutely still they can see people swimming in the incredibly turbulent water below – lost spirits on an outing.

If you continue south from 'Anokula, you'll pass through some virgin rainforest and into acacia-dotted savannas reminiscent of East Africa (minus the wildlife, of course). This area is excellent for camping, but bring your own water as no reliable supply is available and there are no coconut trees.

North-East Coast

The road heading south from 'Anokula swings to the east and drops down one tier of cliffs to a bench area below which has numerous plantations and a few scattered habitations. The cliffs above this bench are pocked with limestone caves and the more intrepid can scramble up for a better look. When in doubt, ask farmers for the best routes.

It's also possible to bushwhack your way southward along the bench to the point above Lokupo Beach where you can join the track leading down from north of the Soldier's Grave.

CENTRAL 'EUA

The central part of 'Eua east of the road is a hilly area covered with Tonga's greatest extent of natural rainforest, with dense jungle-like growth, giant tree ferns and vines and a couple of impressively large banyan trees. Much of the area is underlaid with eroded limestone, causing a Swiss-cheese landscape of caves and sinkholes. Only limited trails and routes penetrate the forest through the caves area – visitors will probably need a local guide to be assured of finding something.

From just north of Hango College you could follow the convoluted route along bush trails to the Soldier's Grave, but it's far easier to access the central part of the island by heading east along the road that runs on the south side of the MAF headquarters. Heading east from this intersection you'll go about 2km through bushland and eucalyptus groves until you reach the MAF Nursery. Opposite the building is a water tap and benches for relaxing. If you take the left fork after this point, you'll eventually come to the Soldier's Grave.

On the other hand, if you take the right fork and continue about 250m, you'll reach the small freshwater Hafu Pool. Although it appears to have been dammed by concrete culverts, Hafu Pool is actually natural. Concrete steps lead down into the pool, like some kind of 'Euan natural Roman bath.

From Hafu Pool you can continue uphill to the Heke ('slide'), where a stream courses down a long, smooth rock at about a 45° angle, creating a natural water slide. It's great fun sliding down the Heke into the muddy pool at the bottom, but be careful of a spot where there's a drop or you could bruise your bum!

To reach the Heke, follow the road uphill past Hafu Pool and then keep going uphill on a fairly well defined foot track. (How well defined it is will depend on how many people have used the track recently; on 'Eua, disused trails tend to become overgrown.) The track curves to the left, leading to a huge banyan tree growing up out of a big limestone sinkhole. You can climb down the roots into the sinkhole, or walk down on a trail to the right of the massive tree. From this banyan tree, the trail heads downhill through the forest until you come to the Heke.

While passing through the forested areas, watch and listen for Tonga's two native parrots, the blue-crowned lorikeet and the 'Eua parrot (also called the musk, vasa or red shining parrot).

Soldier's Grave
About 1km past the point where the road curves rather sharply northward, a turn-off to the right leads uphill to 'Eua's highest point. Atop the nearest hill is the Soldier's Grave, about which there is an apocryphal – or at least well embellished – tale.

It seems that in February 1943, a 24-year-old New Zealand soldier (AE Yealands) and a Tongan got themselves drunk one evening and decided to play a bizarre game of hide-and-seek. They asked a friend to hide a gun for them. It was decided that the one who first found the gun was to kill the other. Unfortunately for the soldier, the Tongan won the game. The Tongans reportedly felt so bad about the incident that they erected a monument in the soldier's honour on the island's highest point.

Unfortunately, at certain seasons the monument may be so hidden in high grass that unless you have someone to show you the way, you may not find it.

East Coast Beaches
Lokupo and Fungatave beaches lie beneath spectacular cliffs on the eastern coast. A track leads down to Lokupo Beach from just north of the Soldier's Grave, but other east coast beaches are inaccessible without technical expertise.

The area of Lokupo Beach, which is backed up by steep cliffs, offers good rock climbing but very few people – not even locals – have ever seen it. For a truly great experience, carry in your own camping equipment. Swimming in the sea here should be attempted only with extreme caution. Fresh water is sometimes available here but don't rely on it; it's wise to carry all you'll be needing.

Caves
In the lovely forested never-never south of Soldier's Grave and Hafu Pool are numerous named and even more unnamed caves and sinkholes. Dozens of constantly changing bush tracks criss-cross this region and the MAF map isn't too specific about caves. If you're wandering, it's wise to carry a compass.

Along the forestry routes marked Pine, Snowdon and Akimoni are several lovely prehistoric-looking sinkholes filled with tree ferns and lush vegetation. Farther west, on the slopes overlooking the east coast, are several interesting caves.

One of 'Eua's most easily located caves is Showers Cave, within easy striking distance north-west of the huge, prominent banyan tree on the hillside east of Petani, reputed to be the largest tree in Tonga. A steady stream of cool, clean fresh water flows through this impressive limestone cave, making it a wonderful place to visit on a hot day. For dedicated cavers, it's possible to go right through this cave and come out the other end. The passage is narrow in places, in some places it's so low that you must crawl through, and there are many places you'll have to jump up or down. Be sure to bring extra torches (flashlights).

To get to Showers Cave, head east on the dirt road immediately south of the large three-storey school on the main road in Petani. The road leads through plantations belonging to the school and then up into the hills, becoming a well defined track which leads past a cave-like rock overhang before arriving at the real cave. You'll also pass the large banyan tree on the way. When you reach a small stream, climb down the short cliff into the stream (there are footholds) and then enter the cave.

South of Showers Cave, not far from the bush road, are 'Ana Pekepeka (Swallows' Cave) and 'Ana 'Ahu, which can be found with some difficulty. Avoid the temptation to swim in the former as it's the source of part of 'Eua's water supply.

For keen spelunkers, 'Eua has scores of other caves. This area isn't for amateurs, however; anyone entering the caves will need both proper caving equipment and experience in cave exploration.

Matalanga 'a Maui

The large, dank and eerie sinkhole known as Matalanga 'a Maui is reminiscent of the massive cenotes of Mexico's Yucatán Peninsula. On a bright day it appears simply a huge hole whose walls are lined with tangled vegetation disappearing into the black void below.

The story goes that it was created when the folk hero Maui buried his planting stick in the earth and shook it back and forth. The process rocked the entire island and left an indelible hole.

To reach the Matalanga 'a Maui, walk south from the Mormon church in Ha'atu'a, take the second road on the left, the one with a red clay base, and walk inland for five to 10 minutes. At this point, it's probably best to ask directions of one of the plantation workers in the area. Unfortunately, this may be difficult because there is a bit of confusion about the place. Some maps of the island place this feature in the far south-east extreme, where the Liangahu'o 'a Maui is located, and some of the locals may not realise where you're asking to be directed to. I went there with some Tongans who had lived all their lives in Ha'atu'a, yet were unaware of the presence of the sinkhole.

If no one is able to help, head off through the plantation south of the road and look for a rather large pit planted with taro. In the north-west corner of this pit is the sinkhole, almost completely obscured by vegetation. Watch your step! You may not see the sinkhole until you are almost falling into it.

Take a torch for a good view down into the cool, moist underworld. It is possible to climb down the lianas and branches to the bottom, but it's not an easy prospect and the site is remote. Don't try it alone.

SOUTHERN 'EUA
Ve'ehula Estate

Much of the southern third of the island belongs to the large Ve'ehula Estate, in the heart of which is the Sinai prison, Tonga's largest correctional facility. Some of the best tracts of original rainforest are found here – it's obvious which parts have been planted and which remain pristine. There are many meandering bush tracks and this area has been described as 'a great place to wander around and get lost'. To keep your disorientation temporary, carry a compass.

Ha'aluma Beach

'Eua's best beach is Ha'aluma, on the south

coast, which has a lovely palm-fringed expanse of sand but is not ideal for swimming due to extensive reefs just offshore. From the beach you can plainly see the small island Kalau just 2km away.

If you're set up for camping, Ha'aluma offers the best beach camping on 'Eua. To get there, continue 4km south along the main road from Ha'atu'a, which is the south end of the bus line. Where the road makes a sharp bend to the left, a track leads off more or less straight ahead. The beach is about 1km down this track.

Southern End

An interesting bushwalk which can be completed in a long day leads around the southern end of the island to some magnificent natural features. It can also be done in a high, hardy 4WD vehicle.

As you head south from Ha'atu'a, the road grows progressively narrower and overgrown and the hills close in on the left. At some seasons the grass is much taller than a person, but you can still distinctly make out the double tracks of the dirt road. After about 10km, you'll round the southernmost tip of the island.

Shortly after a small rustic plantation, you'll arrive at a gate. After passing through, follow the track out into the pasture (be sure to close the gate) and continue along the trail into the Rock Garden. Here 'Eua's geology reads like an open book, with large slabs of eroded, grotesquely shaped coral recalling the time that this bench served as 'Eua's continental shelf. The meadow here is often full of wild horses.

The first big cliff to your right is called Lakufa'anga (`calling turtle cliff'). Women used to drop pandanus leis (garlands) from the cliff and sing to call turtles in to the shore. The turtles have been overharvested, however, and are rarely seen these days.

Although it's marked on some maps as a 'blowhole', the Liangahu'o 'a Maui is anything but. From the cliffs, keep walking northward for another 500m or so. When you see what appears to be a huge gaping

abyss through the trees on your left, turn around and make your way around the south side of it. (The trees may be so thick that you don't see the abyss; if so, just look for a very dense thicket of trees, a notable feature in this otherwise mostly grassy landscape.) About 30m into the trees, a faint trail leads over a low rise and then down to the edge of the abyss. There you'll have a spectacular view into the immense hole and through a natural archway called the Liangahu'o 'a Maui.

Maui was a folk hero of epic proportions, a sort of Paul Bunyan of Polynesia, but with a reputation for having a volatile temper. This huge abyss and the natural bridge are said to have been formed when Maui angrily threw his spear across 'Eua and it lodged in the rock wall here.

This is a lovely spot. Haunting, intermittent insect choruses begin suddenly, then crescendo and disappear. Pigeons call in the wood and the sea below roars and beats the rocks beneath the bridge. It's a cliché to say so, but no photo will ever do it justice.

Shortly beyond the Liangahu'o 'a Maui, the track continues northward to an impressive half-circle of cliffs in which the sea below churns like a flushing toilet bowl. About 2km north of this is a fine campsite with a view of the coast to the north. About 1km farther on is the lovely Vaingana Falls, where the Vaingana stream emerges from between layers of limestone and plunges more than 50m into the sea.

From the falls, the route continues northward indefinitely and in some seasons it may be possible to bash your way through nearly to 'Anokula. Allow several days for such an attempt.

Good camping is available anywhere on this open end of the island but be sure to carry enough water to last for your intended stay.

PLACES TO STAY

Plenty of suitable *campsites* are scattered through the highland areas and along the beaches. It's best to get well out of sight and avoid camping near plantations, where

Left: Flame Tree, Neiafu, Vava'u Group
Top Right: Hibiscus, 'Atata Island, Tongatapu
Middle: Frangipani, 'Atata Island, Tongatapu
Bottom: Ferns, Tofua, Ha'apai Group

NANCY KELLER

PATRICK HORTON

PATRICK HORTON

PATRICK HORTON

PATRICK HORTON

Top Left: Tongan handicrafts
Bottom Left: Decorated grave, Tongatapu
Top Right: Man carving wood mask

Middle Right: Tapa cloth, painting symbols, Tongatapu
Bottom Right: Woman weaving palm leaf mat, Tongatapu

people may be suspicious of your motives. Be sure to carry enough water for your stay, since most of 'Eua's watercourses flow through the limestone caverns underground.

Setaita Guesthouse (☎ 50-124) in 'Esia, about 500m north of the airport, is a comfortable, homey guesthouse operated by Australian Ross Archibald and his Tongan wife Setaita. It occupies a big two-storey house with three bedrooms and ample kitchen, sitting room, dining and lounge areas. The upstairs verandah provides a view of the village and of the sun setting into the sea. You can cook for yourself (T$1 per day for gas), or they'll prepare meals for you. Singles/doubles are T$25/27; since there are only three bedrooms, it's wise to reserve in advance. Camping on the big lawn is T$5 per tent. Pick-up is available from the airport (T$2) or wharf (T$3). Bicycle rental is T$10 per day, for guests and nonguests alike.

Your only other option is the scummy *Haukinima Motel* (☎ 50-088), next to the bar. It's more a hangout for boisterous alcoholics than a real lodging, so things tend to get noisy and foreign guests won't be left alone. There's no restaurant but guests may use the kitchen if they can handle the filth. For a dirty room with communal facilities, the charge is T$15/20 a single/double.

An inexpensive resort is being planned for the area near the wharf, beside the Heilala Restaurant. The plan is for the resort to include simple thatched fales, the Heilala Restaurant, ecological tours and bicycle rental.

PLACES TO EAT
You can purchase staples at the small bush stores scattered up and down the main road between Houma and Ha'atu'a, and in 'Ohonua. There's not a lot of variety so if the recipe calls for anything elaborate, bring it from Tongatapu. The Tonga Cooperative Federation (TCF) store in 'Ohonua is the island's only supermarket.

The *Heilala Restaurant* at the harbour in 'Ohonua is a friendly little place where many locals go to eat and socialise. It has

just three tables and serves typical Tongan meals – fish, chicken, chicken curry, mutton, taro etc. All meals are around T$3, beverage included. It's open Monday to Saturday from around 7 am to 10 pm.

ENTERTAINMENT
The bar at the Haukinima Motel is open from 3 to 10 pm every day except Sunday. This is the only bar on the island.

The *Maxi Disco Hall* is the red, white and blue building diagonally opposite the Haukinima Motel & Bar. It's open for dancing with a live band on Friday and Saturday nights from 8 to 11.30 pm; admission T$2. No alcohol is served.

GETTING THERE & AWAY
Many people travelling between Tongatapu and 'Eua like to go over by plane and return to Nuku'alofa by ferry. Going from Nuku'alofa to 'Eua, the ferry is heading into the swells and wind and it can be a rough trip. On the way back, the boat is going with the wind and swells and the trip is much smoother. The ferry trip takes two hours, with one hour on the open sea and one in the sheltered lagoon of Tongatapu. Flights take only 10 minutes.

See the Getting Around chapter earlier in this book for schedules, fares etc for air and sea travel between Nuku'alofa and 'Eua.

GETTING AROUND
The public bus runs between 'Ohonua and Ha'atu'a approximately every half-hour until the driver gets tired, which is normally around 2 or 3 pm.

'Eua has taxis – you can phone for one (☎ 50-039) – and there are probably others too. You can hire a taxi all day for around T$50, if you want to explore the island.

The Haukinima Motel can rustle up a car and driver for around T$30 per day. So can Setaita Guesthouse, but with them it may be more expensive. You may be able to come up with other options if you ask around – most people on 'Eua who have vehicles would probably be happy to bring in a little extra cash.

The Setaita Guesthouse rents out bicycles to guests and also nonguests for T$10 per day.

Horse hire may be organised informally for T$5 or T$10 per day. Try to make arrangements the day before. No saddles are available.

Otherwise, you shouldn't have any problems hitching rides with pick-up trucks up and down the main road between Houma and Ha'atu'a. Elsewhere, there's very little traffic so you'll probably have to walk – which is quite pleasant anyway. The normal precautions apply.

Other Islands & Reefs

'ATA

In 1683, Abel Tasman sighted this volcanic island 136km south-west of Tongatapu and named it Pylstaart. 'Ata has two volcanic peaks, but both are extinct; the higher one is 382m high. 'Ata has significant deposits of guano phosphates but they are rendered inaccessible by the lack of a harbour.

'Ata can only be accessed by private yacht. However, finding a suitable safe anchorage would be quite difficult.

MINERVA REEF

Minerva Reef, which is awash most of the time, is Tonga's southernmost extreme. It lies 350km south-west of Tongatapu and serves as little more than a rest point for yachts travelling from Tonga to New Zealand. Tonga and New Zealand are currently in dispute over ownership of the reef, but it's generally accepted as Tongan territory (although only at low tide is there any 'territory' there!). Australians Tom and Jan Ginder stopped there in their yacht *Seark* and described it this way:

Blackbirders on 'Ata

In late May 1863, the Tasmanian whaling ship *Grecian* landed at 'Ata after several rather unorthodox changes of crew under the command of Captain Thomas James McGrath. The details of what happened are hazy but, in 1929 two Tongans who were 'Ata schoolchildren at the time, reported that the ship was painted to resemble a man-of-war. The mayor of the island, Paul Vehi, went aboard and spoke with the visitors. When he returned to shore, he reported that they were interested in selling provisions and that the 'Ata people were invited to bring their wares below deck on the ship. Once their goods were accepted, they were sent into cabins, ostensibly to select items they desired in exchange. The people remaining on shore never saw them again.

John Bryan, a former crew member on the *Grecian*, reported that about 130 'Ata islanders had been taken on board. (It's also likely that the *Grecian* had been responsible for the kidnapping of 30 residents of Niuafo'ou, who had willingly left that island with the promise of lucrative jobs in Fiji.) The islanders blamed the mayor for arranging the kidnapping but it is actually unlikely that he knew anything about it beforehand.

The *Grecian* was not licensed by Peru to land with slaves at Peruvian ports, where kidnapped Pacific Islanders were normally taken. It seems that the cargo (including the Tongans) was sold to the *General Prim*, a slaver which met the *Grecian* somewhere in the Cook Islands while searching for 'recruits' to carry back to Callao (Lima). When the *General Prim* arrived in South America, its captain reported that he carried 174 slaves from the island of 'Frinately' – which was obviously a mistranscription of Friendly.

Shortly after this incident, King George Tupou I, who was concerned with the problem of blackbirding, ordered the remaining 200 residents of 'Ata to resettle on 'Eua. 'Ata remains uninhabited to this day.

After two days of fast sailing from Nuku'alofa we came to Minerva Reef and entered through a narrow pass in the circle of coral. Here in the Pacific, hundreds of miles from any terra firma, we dropped anchor and looking around saw breaking waves during high tide and two feet of intriguing brown reef at low tide. Imagine standing in the middle of a vast ocean on a few feet of exposed coral with no land in sight. While exploring for shells we found blocks of tarred pig-iron ballast, a wonderful huge anchor, and many copper nails, all that remained of some long-forgotten tragedy.

For three days and nights we lay in quiet water, although wind whipped up the seas outside our saucer. However, the combination of full moon, spring tides and foul weather could make Minerva Reef anchorage dangerous. It was just two days to full moon so, with regret, we left.

The Ha'apai Group

The solitude of Ha'apai will assault your senses. This is the South Pacific of travel posters – low coral islands, colourful lagoons and reefs, kilometres of deserted white beaches fringed with coconut palms, towering volcanoes ... All that, and tourists are so rare that each one is heartily welcomed by some of the friendliest folk in the kingdom.

The Ha'apai Group consists of 62 islands with a total land area of around 110 sq km scattered throughout approximately 10,000 sq km of sea. The islands, 17 of which are inhabited, range in size from less than one hectare up to 46.6 sq km.

The 8150 people living in 30 villages around the Ha'apai Group earn a living almost exclusively from agriculture and fishing. Many of Ha'apai's residents have opted for the faster pace of life offered by Tongatapu. Quite a few others have ventured as far afield as Australia and New Zealand, keeping the population of the island group manageably low.'

Not much has changed in Ha'apai over the last century or so. There are a few modern conveniences – telephone, radio, video, western-style clothing and houses – but life still moves at a snail's pace and one lazy day melts into the next. Youngsters play in the sea, women weave fine mats and cook meals, men throw their fishing lines out over the reef and then spend a couple of hours on their plantations. On Friday, men attend *kava* circles and teenagers watch videos or dance at the church hall. On Sunday, everyone turns out for church. That pretty much sums up life in this quiet corner of Tonga.

History

Archaeological excavations indicate that the Ha'apai Group has been settled for at least 3000 years. Lapita pottery, carbon dated at 3000 years old, has been excavated in the village of Hihifo, on the south end

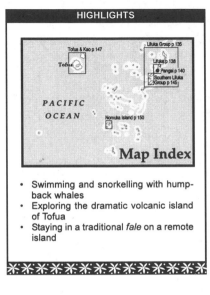

HIGHLIGHTS

Map Index

- Swimming and snorkelling with humpback whales
- Exploring the dramatic volcanic island of Tofua
- Staying in a traditional *fale* on a remote island

of Pangai. (If you want to see it, ask Virginia at the historical museum in Pangai.) Excavations indicate that settlement since those days has been continuous.

Other sites of archaeological interest on Lifuka include the Fortress of Velata, estimated to have been built in the 15th century AD, several large burial mounds, and an ancient stone quarry at Holopeka Beach.

The first European to visit the Ha'apai Group was Dutchman Abel Tasman, who stopped at Nomuka in 1643 for fresh water. Nomuka's sweet water springs were to be the focus of many visits to the group throughout the years of European Pacific exploration.

Subsequently, Ha'apai became the scene of several notable events in Tongan history. In 1777 it was here on Lifuka that Captain James Cook and his men narrowly escaped becoming the main course at a cannibalistic feast they had been invited to attend, a feast

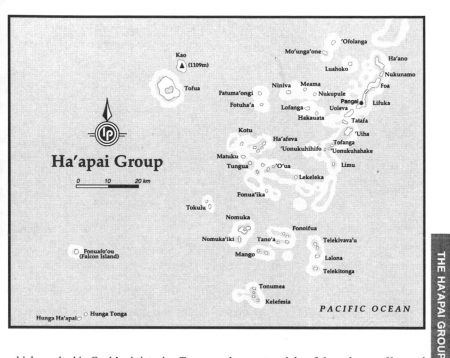

Ha'apai Group

0   10   20 km

'Ofolanga
Mo'unga'one
Kao
(1109m)
Ha'ano
Luahoko
Nukunamo
Tofua
Fatuma'ongi
Niniva   Meama
Foa
Nukupule
Pangai
Lifuka
Fotuha'a
Lofanga
Uoleva
Hakauata
Tatafa
Kotu
'Uiha
Ha'afeva
Tofanga
'Uonukuhihifo   'Uonukuhahake
Matuku
Tungua   'O'ua
Limu
Lekeleka
Fonua'ika
Tokulu
Nomuka
Fonoifua
Nomuka'iki   Tano'a
Telekivava'u
Mango
Lalona
Telekitonga
Tonumea
Kelefesia
PACIFIC OCEAN
Hunga Ha'apai   Hunga Tonga

which resulted in Cook's christening Tonga 'The Friendly Islands'. The famous mutiny on the *Bounty* occurred in Ha'apai in 1789. Still later, in 1806, the British privateer *Port-au-Prince* was ransacked off Lifuka's north coast; survivor Will Mariner's tale of his years spent in Tonga has become the classic account of pre-Christian life there; see Books in Facts for the Visitor.

Ha'apai was the first island group in the Tongan archipelago to convert to Christianity, thanks to the efforts of convert Taufa'ahau, who was baptised King George I (the first king in the House of Tupou) in 1831. He set the stage for a united Tonga and established the royal line which remains in power to this day.

Geography

Geologically, Ha'apai is right at the centre of the Tongan islands, the place to which all the other main islands are leaning thanks to the great weight of the volcanoes Kao and Tofua in the north-western extreme of the group.

The main body of the archipelago is composed of two clusters of islands and one raised barrier reef. The Nomuka Group, the cluster farthest south, takes its name from its principal island Nomuka. To the north-east is the north-east/south-west trending line of raised reefs that forms most of Ha'apai's land area; this will be referred to in this book as the Lulunga Group. It includes the islands of Ha'ano, Nukunamo, Foa, Lifuka, Uoleva, Tatafa and 'Uiha. The Ha'apai Group's principal population centre, its main wharf and airport are all on Lifuka. Volcanic outliers to the west include Hunga Tonga, Hunga Ha'apai, Tofua, Kao and Fonuafo'ou.

Ecology & Environment

The Ha'apai Conservation Area protects the

island group's lands and especially its waters, which are known for their clarity and diversity of landscape, corals and tropical fish.

Snorkelling & Diving

Experienced snorkellers and divers who see Ha'apai from the air – especially divers – tend to gaze downward and salivate. The reefs and shallows of the Ha'apai Group can compete with any in the world for their colour, diversity, clarity and diveability. Amazing underwater scenery, and canyons, walls, caves, tunnels, channels, drifts, coral gardens and volcanoes make for a great variety of dives in over 30 excellent dive spots.

The waters of the Ha'apai Group support a multitude of tropical fish, soft and hard corals, shells and other organisms. The outstanding visibility (25 to 30m in summer, up to 70m in winter) and very comfortable water temperatures (23°C to 30°C) combine to create magnificent conditions for diving.

Dolphins and sea turtles are seen from the islands throughout the year and the presence of humpback whales mating and bearing their young from June to November each year is a special bonus.

The Lifuka Group

The string of islands along the eastern barrier reef of Ha'apai is referred to as the Lifuka Group since Lifuka, with its capital town of Pangai, is the hub of activity.

LIFUKA & PANGAI

Although Pangai is the largest settlement between Tongatapu and Vava'u, it is little more than a small village and you can walk across it in a few minutes. All of Lifuka's basic services are found here (shopping, post office, bank etc), along with several inexpensive guesthouses.

Outside of Pangai, Lifuka is composed almost entirely of agricultural plantations. There's little for the visitor to do on land but explore these 'apis and wander along the empty white beaches that nearly encircle the island. The western shore offers calm blue water, excellent for swimming and snorkelling, while the eastern coast is more exposed – the prevailing easterly wind and ocean swells come from this direction. Although it's sheltered by a barrier reef, the water action on the east coast can be dra-

---

Cook's 'Friendly Islands' – Perhaps a Misnomer?

On Captain James Cook's third voyage he spent over two months (April to July 1777) in the Tongan islands. At Nomuka, his first landfall, chief Finau of Ha'apai told him of a wealthier island, Lifuka, where supplies would be available.

While visiting Lifuka, Cook and his men were treated to lavish feasting and entertainment. Needless to say, the foreigners were impressed. Cook dubbed the Ha'apai Group the 'Friendly Islands' after the apparent disposition of its inhabitants.

Thirty years later it was learned that the exhibition had been part of a conspiracy on the part of the Tongans to raid the ships *Resolution* and *Discovery* for their plainly visible wealth. The entertainment had been planned in order to gather the Englishmen into a convenient place, so that they could be quickly killed and their ships looted. There was, however, a dispute between Finau and his nobles over whether the attack would occur by day or under cover of night. Having previously agreed to follow the chief's plan to take action during the afternoon, the nobles failed to do so at the appointed time. Finau was so incensed at such a defiance of his orders that the operation was abandoned altogether and the Englishmen never learned how narrowly they had escaped.

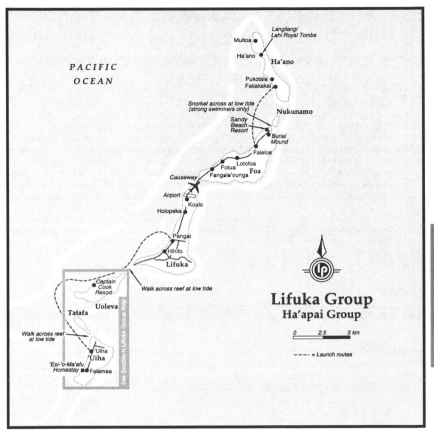

PACIFIC OCEAN

Lifuka Group
Ha'apai Group

0   2.5   5 km

---- = Launch routes

matic and the beautiful beach is wilder than its leeward counterpart.

Information

Tourist Office The Tonga Visitors' Bureau (☎/fax 60-733) is open weekdays from 8.30 am to 12.30 pm and 1.30 to 4.30 pm. It's a good source of information about Ha'apai and has the current tide table posted on the wall.

Its free brochure, *Strolling Through Lifuka*, contains a map of Pangai and historical information about Lifuka.

Money The Bank of Tonga, in Holopeka Rd, exchanges foreign currencies (cash and travellers cheques) and gives cash advances on Visa and MasterCard. It's open weekdays from 9 am to 12.30 pm and 1.30 to 3.30 pm.

Post & Communications The post office is open weekdays from 8.30 am to 3.30 pm. It's in the building opposite the Tonga Visitors' Bureau on Holopeka Rd.

Cable & Wireless/Tonga Telecom lies beneath the huge communications tower in

William Mariner

Thanks to a series of serendipitous incidents, the world has an extensive account of the customs, language, religion and government of the Tongans before the arrival of Christianity.

In February 1805, William Charles Mariner, the well-educated 15-year-old son of an English sea captain, went to sea on the privateer *Port-au-Prince*. The voyage of plunder and pillage took the ship across the Atlantic, around the Horn, up the west coast of South America, to the Sandwich (Hawaiian) Islands and finally into the Ha'apai Group of Tonga. On 29 November 1806, the crew anchored at the northern end of Lifuka and was immediately welcomed with yams and barbecued pork. Their reception seemed friendly enough, but the following day, the crew members became increasingly aware that some sort of plot was afoot and that appropriate caution should be exercised in dealing with the Tongans.

Captain Brown, the whaling master who had assumed command upon the death of the original skipper several months earlier, was convinced that the threat was imaginary and unfortunately chose to ignore it. On 1 December the attack was launched while 300 hostile Tongans were aboard the ship. The British, sorely outnumbered, chose to destroy the ship, its crew and its attackers rather than allow it to be taken. Young Mariner had gone to procure the explosives when he met with several locals, who escorted him ashore past the fallen bodies of his shipmates.

Mariner was subjected to much persecution by the Tongans until he was summoned by Finau 'Ulukalala I, still the reigning chief of Ha'apai. The king assumed that Mariner was the captain's son, or at least a young chief in his own country, and ordered that the young man's life be preserved.

the centre of Pangai. It's open 24 hours, every day, for domestic and international telephone calls. Fax service is available weekdays from 8.30 am to 4.30 pm.

Airline Offices The number for Royal Tonga Airlines in Ha'apai is ☎ 60-566.

Bookshops The Friendly Islands Bookshop has a branch on Holopeka Rd, Pangai. It doesn't have the wide selection of books that its main shop in Nuku'alofa has, but it does stock more books than is immediately apparent. A weekly delivery comes over from the Nuku'alofa store, so you can order any book you like.

Medical Services The Niu'ui Hospital is in the village of Hihifo, on the southern end of Pangai.

The water supply in Ha'apai tends to be brackish and should be used only for washing and bathing. Only drink water collected in rainwater cisterns.

Churches
On the lawn of the Methodist church is the concrete outline of a cross commemorating a 'miracle' that occurred there in 1975. Residents report that one night they saw a flame falling from the sky to land in front of the church. In the morning, they found the outline of a cross burned into the grass. The Methodists outlined the burned area with concrete and left it at that. Cynics in the village, most of them non-Methodists, attribute the whole 'miracle' to mischievous teenagers with kerosene tins and cigarette lighters.

If the Methodists had a miracle, the Catholics suffered a disaster. After Cyclone Isaac struck Lifuka in March 1982, the Catholic Church of St Teresa, at the southern end of the village, was reduced to a

Meanwhile, the *Port-au-Prince*, which hadn't been destroyed, was dragged ashore, raided and burned. The conflagration heated the cannons sufficiently to cause them to fire, creating a general panic among the Tongans. Calmly accepting his fate, Mariner pantomimed an explanation of the phenomena and thus initiated a sort of rapport with the Tongans that would carry him through the following four years.

Although a few other crew members of the *Port-au-Prince* were spared, Mariner was the only one taken so completely under the wing of Finau and he was therefore privy to most of the goings-on in Tongan politics. He learned the language well and travelled about the island groups with the chief, observing and absorbing the finer points of ceremony and protocol among the people. He was given the name Toki 'Ukamea (iron axe). In a moment of compassion, Finau appointed one of his royal wives, Mafi Hape, to be Mariner's adoptive mother, as he was sure the young man's real mother at home must have been extremely worried about him.

After the death of Finau, the king's son permitted young William to leave Tonga on a passing English vessel. Anticlimactically, back in England, Will Mariner married, fathered 12 children and became a highly unsuccessful stockbroker. Were it not for a chance meeting in a London restaurant with an amateur anthropologist, Dr John Martin, his unique Tonga experiences might forever have been lost to the world. Martin, fascinated with Mariner's tale, suggested collaboration on a book and the result, *An Account of the Natives of the Tonga islands*, is a masterpiece of Pacific literature. William Mariner drowned in a canal in southern England in 1853.

single tower and a heap of rubble. From the remaining ruined tower, it appears to have once been a very nice building. All four of the tower clocks took a licking but kept on ticking! A new Catholic church was later constructed nearby on the same property.

Royal Palace

The Ha'apai Royal Palace is the gingerbread-style building opposite the Catholic church. When the king is in residence the street is often blocked, necessitating a rather long detour around the rugby grounds.

Afa Eli Historical Museum

The Afa Eli Historical Museum is the brainchild of Virginia from Vermont, a friendly lady who has lived in Tonga for many years. It consists of a single outdoor display window always open for viewing. Probably the best display is the 3000-year-old Lapita

pottery excavated in Pangai. Exhibits change; if the pottery's not there, ask to see it at the museum's research library, in Virginia's house opposite the museum. The research library, with almost 100 interesting volumes, is open to the public.

Olovehi Tomb

Olovehi Tomb – on Loto Kolo Rd in Hihifo, the village on the south end of Pangai – was constructed in the late 1700s for Nanasipau'u, eldest sister of the reigning Tu'i Tonga. It's claimed that as part of her funeral ceremony, many people were killed and buried around the outside of this tomb to serve as her attendants in the afterlife. Latufuipeka, a daughter of Nanasipau'u, and Latufuipeka's husband, Tuita Kahomovailahi, are also buried here. The tiered retaining walls of quarried beach rock, the upright memorial stone in the tomb's southwest corner, and the casuarina trees planted

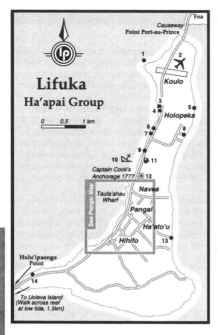

Lifuka
Ha'apai Group

0   0.5   1 km

Labels on map: Foa, Causeway, Point Port-au-Prince, Koulo, Holopeka, Captain Cook's Anchorage 1777, Taufa'ahau Wharf, Navea, Pangai, Ha'ato'u, Hihifo, Hulu'ipaongo Point, To Uoleva Island (Walk across reef at low tide, 1.5km), See Pangai Map

1 Sacking of the Port-au-Prince, 1806
2 Salote Pilolevu Arport
3 Mele Tonga Guesthouse
4 Telefoni Sunset Beach House
5 Holopeka Beach Quarry
6 Watersports Ha'apai
7 Niu'akalo Beach Hotel
8 Billy's Place
9 Melino Handicrafts
10 Shipwreck (Steam Sailing Ship, 1916)
11 Shell Petrol Tanks
12 Revd Shirley Baker's Grave & Monument & European Cemetery
13 Old Quarry & Beach
14 Hulu'ipaongo Tomb

in front of the tomb all indicate that the person inside this tomb was extremely high ranking. The modern extension to the tomb is the burial ground for people (and families of) holding the noble title of Tuita.

'Ahau Bathing Well
The highest chiefs in traditional Tongan society often owned a freshwater bathing well. On the corner of Hihifo and Loto Kolo Rds, just south of the Olovehi Tomb, the bathing well at 'Ahau belonged to the chief Laufilitonga while he and his people stayed at the Fortress of Velata during the early 1820s.

A block to the south, at the corner of Moa and Loto Kolo Rds, is the site where 3000-year-old Lapita pottery was excavated by a team of archaeologists.

Velata Mound Fortress
About 1.2km south of Pangai, a turning toward the east leads you to a large sign describing the circular Velata Mound Fortress, a ring ditch fortification of a type widely found throughout Tonga, Fiji and Samoa. It consists of a moat-like ditch – in the case of Velata, a double ditch, with one ditch 15 to 20m inside the other – whose dirt, piled on the inside, served as a platform for the construction of a 2.5 to 3m-high defensive barrier wall.

According to historical accounts, Velata was built in the 15th century. In the early 1820s it was restored and occupied by Laufilitonga, who later became the 39th and last Tu'i Tonga, as a defence against the Taufa'ahau dynasty. Laufilitonga was unsuccessful; in September 1826 he was defeated in battle by Taufa'ahau, the future King George Tupou I, who eventually unified all of Tonga under his own rule, and Velata was burned. The fortress itself is today almost indistinguishable in the forest, although a couple of vaguely artificial ridges are just visible.

Shirley Baker Monument & European Cemetery
About 800m north of Pangai lies the grave and monument of Revd Shirley Baker, Tonga's first prime minister and adviser to King George Tupou I. At one stage in his controversial political career, Baker was

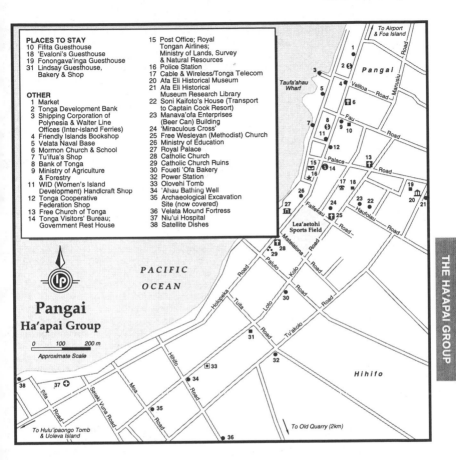

PLACES TO STAY
10 Fifita Guesthouse
18 'Evaloni's Guesthouse
19 Fonongava'inga Guesthouse
31 Lindsay Guesthouse,
   Bakery & Shop

OTHER
1 Market
2 Tonga Development Bank
3 Shipping Corporation of
  Polynesia & Walter Line
  Offices (Inter-island Ferries)
4 Friendly Islands Bookshop
5 Velata Naval Base
6 Mormon Church & School
7 Tu'ifua's Shop
8 Bank of Tonga
9 Ministry of Agriculture
  & Forestry
11 WID (Women's Island
   Development) Handicraft Shop
12 Tonga Cooperative
   Federation Shop
13 Free Church of Tonga
14 Tonga Visitors' Bureau;
   Government Rest House

15 Post Office; Royal
   Tongan Airlines;
   Ministry of Lands, Survey
   & Natural Resources
16 Police Station
17 Cable & Wireless/Tonga Telecom
20 Afa Eli Historical Museum
21 Afa Eli Historical
   Museum Research Library
22 Soni Kaifoto's House (Transport
   to Captain Cook Resort)
23 Manava'ofa Enterprises
   (Beer Can) Building
24 'Miraculous Cross'
25 Free Wesleyan (Methodist) Church
26 Ministry of Education
27 Royal Palace
28 Catholic Church
29 Catholic Church Ruins
30 Foueti 'Ofa Bakery
32 Power Station
33 Olovehi Tomb
34 'Ahau Bathing Well
35 Archaeological Excavation
   Site (now covered)
36 Velata Mound Fortress
37 Niu'ui Hospital
38 Satellite Dishes

THE HA'APAI GROUP

nearly assassinated on Tongatapu. In 1890, he was exiled from Tonga by the British 'advisers' sent to set up a protectorate and stabilise the government, which was suffering at the hands of squabbling religious factions. Baker returned to Tonga in 1898 with the permission of King George Tupou II and lived out his days in Ha'apai. He lived in Hihifo, just south of Pangai, and died there on 16 April 1903. The statue of Baker in the cemetery was commissioned by his daughters.

The monument is in the European cemetery, where you can see the graves of various 19th and early 20th century German and English traders and missionaries. The Tongan cemetery is directly opposite.

Shipwreck

The shipwreck of an old steam sailing ship, approximately 80m long, lies just off the coast in 6m of water on the west coast of Lifuka. It's about 200m offshore, opposite the petrol tanks. No one knows the ship's name, but apparently it sank in 1916.

Holopeka Beach & Old Quarries

On Lifuka's east coast, east of Holopeka village, Holopeka Beach is rarely visited. At low tide you can see the remnants of an old beach stone quarry. This and similar quarries were the source of the large stone blocks found in the retaining walls of high chiefly tombs. These types of quarries were common throughout Tonga from the 13th to 18th centuries; the site at Holopeka illustrates several different stages in block removal.

Another old quarry on the east coast, south-east of Pangai, is referred to by residents as simply the Old Quarry. There's a sandy beach here and the natural stone terraces out in the water, reminiscent of those along the south coast of Tongatapu, become tidepools at low tide, great for exploring. Several deep crevasses in the rocky shoreline, full of coral and fish, make for interesting snorkelling at low tide when the sea is calm, but only for strong swimmers and snorkellers, as the water from the open sea swells and surges inside the crevasses.

Southern Lifuka

On the south side of Pangai is the village of Hihifo, where the hospital sits on the coast beside two giant satellite dishes. From here, you can continue south along the dirt road all the way to Lifuka's southern tip, where there's a fine beach.

Along the way, note the large ancient mound on the west side of the road, the **Hulu'ipaongo Tomb**. Captain James Cook described this 'mount' when he sailed past the south end of Lifuka on 23 May 1777. The highest on Lifuka, this is the burial site of the Mata'uvave line of chiefs. The first Mata'uvave was sent to Ha'apai in the 15th century to establish political control over northern Ha'apai for Tu'i Tonga Kau'ulufonuafekai. His success resulted in his appointment as governor and Tu'i Ha'apai.

It's possible to walk between the southern tip of Lifuka and the northern tip of Uloleva, but you must use utmost care. It's a dangerous spot – a man drowned here in 1997, crossing on horseback. The crossing is about 1.5km – farther than it looks – and it takes anywhere from about 30 minutes to an hour to get across. Only cross at low tide, or an hour or two on either side of low tide. Even then, do not cross if the sea is high or the current too strong. The current is important because the pathway is often very slippery, and you could be swept away. Keep to the east of the sand dunes when crossing.

Activities

Much of the magic of Ha'apai is in the water. Roland Schwara at Watersports Ha'apai (☎/fax 60-097; medical@candw. to; VHF channel 16), PO Box 65, Pangai, based at the Niu'akalo Beach Hotel just north of Pangai, is the person to talk to about everything that can be done on or in the water. A German divemaster who has explored Ha'apai's waters and islands extensively, he offers scuba diving trips (costing T$65/95 for a one/two-tank dive using the company's equipment, T$50/80 with your own); overnight scuba diving safaris (cost T$390 per person for two days/one night including food, lodging, dives, equipment and transportation, and T$510 per person for three days/two nights) and PADI scuba diving instruction in English and German (from T$300 per person). Schwara also runs boat trips to offshore islands (three-hour trips including snorkelling gear cost T$16 per person; day trips T$25 per person); game fishing trips; guided sea kayaking trips (T$48 per person for a day trip, T$85 per person per day for a multi-day excursion); non-guided sea kayak rental (T$25 per day); guided volcano trekking trips to Tofua and Kao volcanoes; humpback whale watching trips (June to November; T$40 per person); and more.

The Sandy Beach Resort is planning to open a scuba diving operation in late 1998 or early 1999 in conjunction with the German diving company, Schöner Tauchen. It will offer PADI diving instruction in German and English, and be called Tonga Dive.

Tennis can be played at the Taufa'ahau & Pilolevu Tennis Club (contact Taufu'i, ☎ 60-179, 60-150) or the Navea Tennis Club (contact Moimoi Fakahua, ☎ 60-059). The cost is T$2 per day for nonmembers.

Horse riding can be arranged through any guesthouse.

Special Events
The four-day Ha'apai Festival takes place in early June, leading up to the Emancipation Day holiday on 4 June. Visitors are heartily welcomed.

Places to Stay
All accommodation on Lifuka can make arrangements for boat trips, bicycle and horse hire, snorkelling gear etc. Most offer free pick-up at the airport or wharf if you let them know you're coming.

Camping has recently been prohibited throughout the Ha'apai Group. The only way to legally camp here is if you are accompanied by a guide on a sea kayaking journey or something similar.

Pangai The *Fonongava'inga Guesthouse* (☎ 60-038; fax 60-200), PO Box 14, Palace Rd, Pangai, is also known as Langilangi's Guesthouse after the affable proprietor, Mrs Langilangi Vi. Standard rooms with shared bath, sitting room etc are T$10/15 a single/ double. Larger, newer rooms upstairs in the rear, with shared hot shower, are T$15/22. Guests are welcome to use the kitchen at the residence next door. Alternatively, you can opt for Langilangi's famous home cooking: breakfast or lunch T$3, dinner T$8, or T$15 for a special lobster blowout. Every Sunday, Langilangi cooks Sunday dinner in the *'umu* (underground oven); you're welcome to join in and see how it's done.

'Evaloni's Guesthouse (☎ 60-029), PO Box 56, Loto Kolo Rd, Pangai, is also pleasant, and serves some of the best meals in Pangai; ask for the home-made banana cakes for breakfast! Downstairs rooms with shared bath are T$10/15 a single/double. Upstairs, two large master bedrooms with private bath are T$25 each. Breakfast costs

T$5.50, lunch price depends on what you're having, dinner (highly recommended) costs T$12. Or you can cook for yourself (T$2 for gas).

Lindsay Guesthouse (☎/fax 60-107) is a newer establishment. It's clean, quiet, friendly and a very comfortable place to stay, with comfy shared sitting room, dining room and kitchen, and hot showers. Three single rooms and three double rooms are T$15/25 a single/double. A small grocery shop and bakery are here on the premises, and there are bicycles for rent (T$5 per day) and a boat for guests' use. You can cook for yourself or have meals prepared; breakfast or lunch are T$6, dinner T$12. The proprietors, Fatafehi (Fehi for short) and Finau, are friendly and welcoming.

Fifita Guesthouse (☎ 60-213) is in a two-storey building in Fau Rd just off the main road. Singles/doubles with shared bath and kitchen are T$15/18. Guests also have the use of the airy upstairs porch, ideal for reading and relaxing. Breakfast, lunch and dinner are available if booked in advance, or you can cook for yourself (T$2 per day for gas).

The *Government Rest House*, in the same building as the Tonga Visitors' Bureau, has three large, pleasant bedrooms with shared kitchen and bath. The cost is T$5 for Tongan civil servants, T$10 for everyone else. It's operated by the Ministry of Works (☎ 60-100).

Around Lifuka All accommodation outside Pangai is right on the beach. The east side of the island has big waves and the west is sheltered, with calm water lapping on beautiful white-sand beaches, and magnificent sunsets. All of the following places to stay are on the west coast except for Billy's Place.

Billy's Place (fax 60-200) is on the east (windward) coast of Lifuka, 1.5km north of Pangai. It's in a very private location – you have the beach all to yourself most of the time. Free-standing bungalows with private bath are T$35 and T$45 single, T$45 and T$55 double. The rates include breakfast,

THE HA'APAI GROUP

bicycles, snorkelling gear, videos, airport transfers, games, tropical fruits and town tours. Meals include pizza, burritos, seafood, pasta, sandwiches and desserts, with free delivery around the island by request. Non-guests are welcome for meals; meals must be reserved by noon, or the day before. The owners, Billy Hu'akau and his friendly American wife Sandy, have made this place a favourite with travellers in a short time (actually it might be Sandy's good cooking!).

The *Niu'akalo Beach Hotel* (☎ 60-028), PO Box 18, Pangai, is a friendly little beachfront hotel about 2km north of Pangai. Comfortable standard rooms in four-room bungalows with shared bath are T$16.50/22 a single/double. Larger 'business class' rooms with private bath in duplex bungalows are T$27.50/32. An entire bungalow, with two double rooms and a connecting lounge, is T$60. Large breakfasts cost T$6, cold lunches T$3, and elaborate family-style dinners T$12; special meals such as lobster cost T$15. Ask about their 'island nites' featuring beach barbecues and traditional Tongan dancing.

With the beach just out the door, this is a great place to stay for a few days. Plastic kayaks are rented for T$3 per day to guests and non-guests alike. For snorkelling gear, scuba diving, boat trips, sea kayaking and other water activities, talk to Roland or 'Ofa at Watersports Ha'apai, based in the bungalow on the end. The hotel offers taxi service, bicycle rental (T$10 per day), and on Sunday a trip up the coast to the beautiful beach at the north end of Foa island.

The *Telefoni Sunset Beach House* (☎ 60-270, 60-044) is a pleasant house on the beach at Koulo, 3km north of Pangai. Operated by a charming lady, Hola Telefoni Vi, it's a former family home and you'll feel right at home here. The house's three bedrooms share the bath, kitchen, sitting room, beach etc; singles/doubles are T$15/28. Bicycles are T$10 per day.

Nearby, the *Mele Tonga Guesthouse* (☎ 60-042) is small, comfy, friendly and, according to one reader, 'immaculately

clean and quiet'. Rooms in two conventional homes and one traditional *fale*, all just a breath from the beach, are T$15/20 a single/double. Breakfast or lunch are T$4, dinner T$8, or you can cook for yourself in the beachfront kitchen fale. It has a boat for guests' use, and horses and bicycles for hire (bicycles T$7 per day).

Places to Eat

There are no restaurants in Ha'apai. All places to stay make provision for their guests' meals, either by serving meals, providing a kitchen where guests can cook, or both.

You don't have to eat only at the place you are staying – all guesthouses which serve meals provide them both for guests and nonguests. *Billy's Place, 'Evaloni's Guesthouse*, the *Fonongava'inga Guesthouse, Fifita Guesthouse* and the *Niu'akalo Beach Hotel* are all good places to eat. Meals must be requested at least several hours in advance. For prices, see Places to Stay.

The upmarket *Sandy Beach Resort* serves breakfasts and dinners for guests only. But snacks are provided for nonguests.

Pangai's produce market is just north of the Tonga Development Bank, on the north end of Pangai. Pickings are often quite slim here, however.

The *Tonga Cooperative Federation* store on the main road is Ha'apai's only supermarket. Limited groceries are available from a host of small shops, some of which stay open until 9 pm.

Pangai has two bakeries: the *Matuku-etau Bakery* at the Lindsay Guesthouse, and the *Foueti 'Ofa Bakery* one block north. On Sunday the bakeries open at 5 pm, and everyone goes to get fresh bread and other staples. All other shops are closed on Sunday.

Tu'ifua's Shop on the waterfront sells fresh lobster and fish, and will prepare them for you if you ask in advance.

Entertainment

'Island nites' featuring a beach barbecue

and traditional Tongan dancing are sometimes held at the Niu'akalo Beach Hotel. The hotel also makes Sunday trips to the beautiful beach at the north end of Foa island; hotel guests and non-guests are all welcome to come along, splitting the cost of T$20 for the whole van.

On Friday nights, kava clubs meet in several halls around Pangai. Church entertainment takes place at various times; dances and other activities are sometimes held in church halls. Pangai has a couple of video rental shops.

Things to Buy
The WID (Women's Island Development) Handicraft Shop in Pangai sells women's handicrafts. So does Melino Handicrafts, in a hut on the main road just north of Pangai. Purses and fans made of tapa and pandanus, shells and shell jewellery are some of the things on offer.

Getting There & Away
Air Ha'apai's Salote Pilolevu Airport, 3km north of Pangai, is bisected by the main Lifuka-Foa road. Royal Tongan Airlines operates flights daily (except Sunday) between Ha'apai and Tongatapu, twice a week between Ha'apai and Vava'u. See the Getting Around chapter for prices etc. Reconfirm your flight out of Ha'apai at the Royal Tongan Airlines office (☎ 60-566) in Pangai 24 hours before flying.

Pacific Island Seaplanes, based in Nuku'alofa, provides transport to all islands of the Ha'apai Group, whether or not they have airstrips, and makes day trips from Tongatapu to Tofua, in the Ha'apai Group. See the Getting Around chapter for details.

Boat The MV *'Olovaha* and the MV *Tautahi* call in twice weekly at Pangai, on both their northbound and southbound runs between Tongatapu and Vava'u. The two shipping offices – the Shipping Corporation of Polynesia (☎ 60-699) and the Walter Line, both at the wharf – open only on days when the ferries arrive. See the Getting Around chapter for schedules and fares.

If you're arriving in Ha'apai by yacht, it's strongly recommended that you check in with the postmaster-cum-customs officer upon arrival, even if you've checked into the country elsewhere. There are marginally protected anchorages along the lee shores of Lifuka, Foa, Ha'ano, Uoleva, Ha'afeva, Nomuka and Nomuka'iki.

Getting Around
To/From the Airport Most of the places to stay offer free transfers to/from the airport and wharf – just let them know that you're coming and they will be there to pick you up. Taxis charge T$3 to T$5 for up to four people between the airport and Pangai. The bus that between Pangai and the airport turn-off costs 50 seniti, but it only runs twice a day.

Bus The bus service operates between Hihifo, on the south end of Pangai, and Faleloa, the northernmost village on Foa island. It goes only twice a day. The trip from Pangai to Faleloa costs T$1.

Bicycle Lifuka and neighbouring Foa, connected by a causeway and both basically flat, are ideal for exploring by bicycle. All the guesthouses either rent out bicycles, or can easily arrange rental. The Lindsay Guesthouse and Billy's Place rent out bicycles to non-guests. Rental costs around T$5 to T$10 per day. Check the brakes before accepting a bike.

Car & Horse The Tonga Visitors' Bureau can arrange car rental (T$60 per day) and horse rental (T$20 per day). Any of the guesthouses can also arrange rental of a car or horse.

Taxi Several people in Pangai operate taxis. Any guesthouse can ring a taxi for you. Try phoning Siaosi (☎ 60-072), Liano (☎ 60-155), Sione Moala (☎ 60-511) or Lemeki Lolohea (☎ 60-033). Prices are reasonable; for example, Siaosi charges T$3 from Pangai to the airport, T$6 from Pangai to the Sandy Beach Resort.

THE HA'APAI GROUP

FOA

Foa lies directly north of Lifuka; a causeway connects the two islands. Its main attractions are the wonderful beach at the extreme northern end, and the ancient burial mound beside the road about 500m south of this beach. There's a good deal of wild bushland along the middle west coast north and west of Lotofoa, where the coast is pocked with some interesting caves and sculpted rock formations.

Places to Stay

On the magnificent white-sand beach at the north end of Foa, Jürgen and Sigrid Stavenow, the German former owners of the Seaview restaurant in Nuku'alofa, have constructed the beautiful upmarket *Sandy Beach Resort* (☎/fax 60-600; sandybch@ tongatapu.net.to), PO Box 61, Pangai.

This is Ha'apai's only upmarket resort. The 12 luxurious beachfront bungalows are T$140 per night. Meals at the superb restaurant, for guests only, are T$10 for breakfast, T$35 for dinner. Prices include airport transfers, snorkelling gear (snorkelling and swimming are excellent here at all tides), kayaks, outrigger canoes, western-style canoes, bicycles, guided bush walks, Tongan culture shows, kava ceremonies, shuttles to Pangai, and the 7.5% room tax. Other, paid activities can also be arranged: scuba diving, game fishing, horse riding, tennis, day trips by boat to other islands, seaplane trips to Tofua, etc. This is the only wheelchair-accessible accommodation we found in all Tonga. Children under 12 are not accepted.

Getting There & Away

A bus goes from Hihifo, on the south end of Pangai to Faleloa, Foa's northernmost village, but it only runs twice a day. The cost is T$1 to the end of the line. The Sandy Beach Resort is 1.5km north of Faleloa, and the public beach is just north of that. You can walk up there from Faleloa in half an hour, or hitchhike, or you could come from Pangai by bicycle – the resort is 15km north

of Pangai and the terrain is quite flat. Bicycle rental is available in Pangai.

Sunday trips to the beach north of the Sandy Beach Resort are organised by the Niu'akalo Beach Hotel. Guests and non-guests are all welcome, sharing the cost of T$20 for the van to go up there and back.

NUKUNAMO

The small uninhabited island of Nukunamo, immediately north of Foa, is surrounded by a shining white beach covered with beautiful shells. The island is owned by the king. The mound here, which looks like an ancient burial mound, was in fact built as a platform, used by members of the royal family for hunting pigeons.

At low tide, Nukunamo is accessible on foot or by snorkelling from the north end of Foa, but the currents through the pass are quite powerful so only strong swimmers should attempt it. You'll also need to be in tune with the tide tables or risk being stuck on a deserted island for 12 hours longer than anticipated!

HA'ANO

The strikingly clean and well cared-for island of Ha'ano encompasses 6.6 sq km and is home to 580 people. The population is proud of its churches and four pleasant villages, which are, from north to south, Muitoa, Ha'ano, Pukotala and Fakakakai. Ha'ano also has lovely beaches.

To get to Ha'ano, take the bus to Faleloa on Foa island and catch one of the water taxis that leave for Ha'ano whenever the bus arrives in Faleloa. The fare between the islands is T$1 per person.

UOLEVA

The uninhabited island of Uoleva lies 1.5km south of Lifuka. It is composed mostly of coconut plantations and contains some of the finest, most peaceful white-sand beaches imaginable. *Pacific Islands Monthly* magazine described the strand along the north shore as 'Tonga's loveliest beach'. In the centre of the coconut planta-

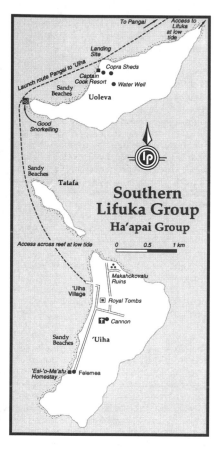

Landing Site

Copra Sheds

Captain Cook Resort ● Water Well

Sandy Beaches

Uoleva

To Pangai

Access to Lifuka at low tide

Launch route Pangai to 'Uiha

Good Snorkelling

Sandy Beaches

Tatafa

Southern Lifuka Group

Ha'apai Group

Access across reef at low tide

0   0.5   1 km

Makahōkovalu Ruins

'Uiha Village

Royal Tombs

Cannon

Sandy Beaches

'Uiha

'Esi-'o-Ma'afu Homestay   Felemea

THE HA'APAI GROUP

Pangai, is on the north-western coast of Uoleva island, on a beautiful broad, 4km white-sand beach, great for swimming, snorkelling and sunbathing (bring your own snorkelling gear). Bushwalking is good on the island, and you can walk all the way around it on the beach.

The manager and part-owner, Soni Kaifoto, offers basic single/double rooms for T$15/20 (cooking T$2 extra per day, for gas). Meals are available (breakfast T$3, dinner T$7, barbecues and 'umus T$10) but tend to be chintzy – it's better to bring your own food. No supplies are available on otherwise uninhabited Uoleva, so take all you'll be needing. Drinking water is available.

Unfortunately, Lonely Planet has received many complaints from readers in connection with this establishment. Single women in particular might want to think twice before coming here; one reader wrote begging us to warn single women about this place, and other readers have urged us to delete it from the book altogether, or to write 'not recommended'. Some travellers like the place just fine; apparently many others have had problems.

Getting There & Away

You can walk from Lifuka to Uoleva at low tide, but beware of the current between the two islands. See the Southern Lifuka section earlier on for details about this crossing.

Soni Kaifoto of the Captain Cook Resort offers transport to Uoleva for T$8/15 one-way/return; phone or contact him at home in Pangai (see the Pangai map), or check with Tu'ifua's shop (☎ 60-605) on the waterfront in Pangai, where you can arrange boat transport for the same price. Watersports Ha'apai also does boat trips for a reasonable price. The Tonga Visitors' Bureau in Pangai can arrange day trips to Uoleva for around T$40 per boatload. Another option is to hitch a ride on a 'Uiha-bound boat and ask to be dropped at Uoleva.

tions are some 16th-century burial mounds but they are difficult to find without a guide.

The reefs north of the western end of Uoleva, the broad bay at the island's south-western end, and the spot straight off the island's south-western tip, all offer fantastic snorkelling among huge coralheads. There's even a good chance of observing sea turtles.

Places to Stay

A low-key backpackers' haven, the *Captain Cook Resort* (☎ 60-014), PO Box 49,

The Margarita

On 26 January 1863, the Peruvian black-birder *Margarita* left Callao (Lima) and was never seen again. According to a preacher on 'Uiha at the time, a ship called in and lured several islanders aboard. When their families on shore realised what had happened, they banged iron pots, hoping to deceive the slavers into returning to shore to pick up more people who'd decided to go along. The ploy worked, the ship was seized, the Tongans were released and then the ship, which was probably the *Margarita*, was destroyed.

'UIHA

The clean, friendly island of 'Uiha has two villages: 'Uiha with the main wharf, and Felemea, about 1.5km south, where there's a fine place to stay.

Royal Tombs

In the centre of 'Uiha village is a large elevated burial ground which contains royal tombs. Late in 1988, the tombs of three relatively obscure members of the royal family were shifted here, two from Pangai and one from Tongatapu, accompanied by much pomp and ceremony. Ostensibly the project was to consolidate the tombs of the royal family, but there were rumours of treasure in the cemetery compound that prompted the king to look for a popular excuse to excavate the otherwise *tapu* (sacred) area. Nothing of importance was unearthed during the excavation.

Church

Walking beyond the royal tombs, you can't miss 'Uiha's odd-looking church – it resembles something out of a fairy tale. As evidence of the sinking of the *Margarita*, the 'Uihans display two cannons, one planted in the ground outside the church in 'Uiha village and the other in front of the altar inside – the latter is used as a baptismal font!

Makahokovalu Ruins

At the northern end of 'Uiha, about a 10-minute walk from the village, are the Makahokovalu ruins. The name means 'eight joined stones', but there are actually nine laid on end in an L-shape. A few similar stones are found lying about the site, reportedly scattered by a cyclone. There hasn't been much theorising as to the purpose or origin of the complex, but if you're on 'Uiha anyway, it's a pleasant walk out there.

In late 1988, while the royal tombs were being relocated, the king's daughter Princess Pilolevu took a notion to visit the site. In one day a new road was cut to the ruins and the stones were cleared of years of overgrowth. The road was cleared again for another royal visit in the early 1990s. Since then, sometimes it's cleared, and sometimes it gets overgrown.

Places to Stay

The *'Esi-'o-Ma'afu Homestay* (☎ 60-605), PO Box 36, Pangai, on the beach at Felemea village, is a wonderful place to stay. The traditional Tongan-style fales here are very well made, with coconut thatch outside, and with tapa and pandanus mats inside. When we visited they had three fales and were thinking of building two more. Singles/doubles are T$12/18. You can do your own cooking (there's a small grocery shop), or they'll prepare meals for you – breakfast or lunch are T$4, dinner T$6, lobster T$8, with a family 'umu every Sunday.

The fenced compound includes separate kitchen and bathroom fales. There's a boat for trips to other islands for picnics, swimming and snorkelling (snorkelling and fishing gear can be rented). Other activities include canoeing, horse riding, tennis and volleyball at the village sports ground, learning about village handicrafts, and joining in village activities. The homestay's friendly, hospitable owners, Hesekaia and Kaloni Aholelei, give you the perfect introduction to village life.

To get there, phone or stop by Tu'ifua's shop (☎ 60-605) on the waterfront in Pangai and it will arrange boat transport. The cost is T$10 each way, per person.

Getting There & Away
The easiest way to get to 'Uiha is by launch or fishing boat from Pangai. Arrange rides at Tu'ifua's shop (☎ 60-605) on the waterfront in Pangai. The cost is around T$10 per person for a one-way trip. The Tonga Visitors' Bureau in Pangai can arrange day trips to 'Uiha for around T$80 per boatload. Watersports Ha'apai on Lifuka will also make boat trips here if you ask.

TATAFA
Uninhabited Tatafa is a short low-tide walk across the reef from northern 'Uiha. It's surrounded by a lovely beach. There's a rainwater cistern on the island but it's still wise to carry a bit of water or ask permission (on 'Uiha or Lifuka) to drink coconuts. Don't forget to take a bush knife to open them. Tatafa has good snorkelling and a large colony of flying foxes.

Other Ha'apai Group Islands

TOFUA
Tofua, the site of the mutiny on the *Bounty*, has the most active of Tonga's volcanoes; it's constantly smoking, belching and rumbling. Some of Tonga's best and most extensive kava plantations are on Tofua.

In 1874, the king evacuated the island due to excessive volcanic activity. Later, people returned to live here again but the population seems to have drifted away – the 1976 census reported 107 residents, and the 1986 census 89, but in 1996 only five people were reported living on the island. Tofua's two small 'villages', Hokala on the

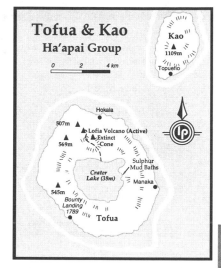

north coast and Manaka in the east, consist of only a few houses each, and people stay on the island only part time while they tend and harvest the kava crop. Tofua also produces tamanu trees for canoes and *toa* (ironwood) in small non-commercial quantities.

The island, 55 sq km in area and mostly covered in virgin tropical forest, is a circular crater, at the bottom of which is a hauntingly beautiful, crystal clear 250m-deep lake, 38m above sea level and covering 7 sq km. The active volcano, known as Lofia, smokes and spews away near the crater's 550m-high northern rim.

Mutiny on the Bounty Beach
On Tofua's south-western coast is the beach where, on 28 April 1789, Captain Bligh of the HMS *Bounty* and 18 loyals landed after the famous mutiny. Quartermaster John Norton was clubbed to death by islanders. Bligh and the rest of the men escaped and embarked on a 6500km journey to Timor in an open boat, with minimal rations and short of water, having never discovered Tofua's large freshwater lake.

Climbing Tofua & Kao

The following is an excerpt from a letter to Lonely Planet from Australian marine biologist Mick Hortle, who climbed Tofua and Kao in 1997 when working with the Ha'apai Conservation Area Project.

The climb up Kao from the landing point on the south coast is quite feasible as a day trip, provided you pick the right ridge to ascend, and weather conditions are fair. Cloud cover on the peak changes rapidly, even on a fine day. We departed base camp at 8.30 am, reached the top by midday, spent two hours absorbing the spectacular views and scenery of the peak, and returned to the tents by 5 pm. The upper slopes are covered with dense ferns, up to waist high towards the ridge at the top – there is no marked track but it is relatively easy to pick an acceptable route once above the tree line. A spectacular end to the day is a snorkel in the waters below the landing site, but it's not for the faint hearted. Coral development on the volcanic boulders is in the early stages and there are plenty of fish, but the slopes of the volcano continue underwater, disappearing into deep blue 'nothingness' 20m offshore.

The landing site at Tofua, below the old village of Hokula, is not quite as difficult as the one at Kao but still not easy, especially if a sea is running. Once ashore it's a 10-minute walk up a dry creek gully to the old village site. Fresh water is available here in a couple of concrete tanks at the old school building. To reach the rim of the old crater it's a tough one-hour climb; leave the village from a reasonably well marked track at the top of the clearing above the school. Once on the old rim the well marked track heads east and eventually descends to the kava plantations above the old village site of Manaka. Just prior to commencing the descent the track passes through a marvellous rainforest stand, with many different orchids and ferns. This track provides many spectacular views of the lake, craters and lava flows. There are a couple of small volcanic beaches with a very narrow reef system about five minutes' walk below Manaka. Allow a full day for the return journey to a campsite on the rim at the top of the track from Hokula.

The best point at which to enter the old crater is to the west of the point at which the track arrives on the rim. There is no track but it is not difficult to walk through the fern and toa skirting the many small craters until reaching a point on the rim where the ash fields commence (20-30 minutes). The point of descent into the crater is where the vegetation ceases. Scramble down the ash and walk across the open expanse and around the eastern side of the active crater to the saddle. From there it is relatively easy to reach the lake or explore the extinct cones below the active crater, the old lava flows and some of the rainforest on the northern slopes. These forests have been described by Dr Art Whistler (University of Hawai'i), the leading authority on Pacific botany, as the best in Polynesia. Large rainforest trees, with diameters up to 1m, abound; pongo ferns reach 15-20m to the forest canopy; and trees are strewn with epiphytic ferns and orchids.

Visiting the Crater

If you want to feel that you've dropped into a lost world or a Shangri-la, fly with Pacific Island Seaplanes into Tofua's hauntingly beautiful crater lake. After doing a breathtaking hop over the rim and a few tight passes around the smoking volcano, you'll come to rest on the lake and taxi to shore.

At the landing on the north shore, there's good swimming and a beach like a natural pumice foot massage. From the shore, a track leads up through a virgin forest full of birds, tree ferns, ironwood and other trees, and then up over fields of pumice and scoria to the rim of the gaping volcanic vent where you can perch at the edge of the steaming and rumbling inferno. The walk is 1¼ hours up and an easy 30 minutes back down. Follow this with a swim in the crystal clear lake and a picnic lunch.

There's plenty more scope for exploring around this barren area; you can even climb right up to the crater rim for an incredible view of neighbouring Kao.

Tofua is ideal for camping and it's legal on a guided trip, so you can stay for several days. Swimming, exploring the crater and its partially rainforested slopes and bird-watching are all possible here. Birds include honeyeaters, doves, petrels, rails, swamp harriers, barn owls, kingfishers, ducks and more.

Getting There & Away

Air Pacific Island Seaplanes offers day trips to Tofua for T$250 per person, starting from Nuku'alofa. It also provides transport for camping trips. You can go from Lifuka, too, but this costs more (T$300). See Air in the Getting Around chapter.

Boat Forest-covered red and black lava cliffs rising directly out of the surf make a sea landing on Tofua difficult, but boats do call in occasionally. If it's any consolation, Tongans believe that the passengers of any boat in the vicinity of Tofua are protected by the shark god, Tu'i Tofua. Should a boat sink, the vessel and its passengers will be carried to shore by benevolent sharks!

Watersports Ha'apai on Lifuka does guided volcano treks on the island. The cost is T$150 for transport from Lifuka by speedboat and then T$60 per person, per day, for trekking including food, equipment and guide (minimum six persons). It also offers volcanic dive safaris to Tofua and Kao.

KAO

On clear days, the immense and frighteningly beautiful volcanic cone of Kao, Tonga's highest mountain at 1109m, is visible from Lifuka and the other main islands.

Landing on uninhabited Kao is extreme-ly difficult but, once ashore, you can climb and descend the formidable-looking mountain. This of course depends on the weather; the mountain is frequently shrouded in cloud for days on end and at higher elevations the weather can get quite nasty. If you're set upon attempting this difficult climb, carry camping gear and warm, rainproof clothing.

Marlin fishing around Kao is supposed to be excellent. Contact Watersports Ha'apai on Lifuka, or the Royal Sunset Resort in the Tongatapu Group, which offers fishing charters to Ha'apai.

Getting There & Away

Getting to Kao will probably prove quite expensive. Pacific Island Seaplanes, based in Nuku'alofa, could drop you here – it makes frequent trips to nearby Tofua.

Watersports Ha'apai on Lifuka does guided volcano treks on the island. The cost is T$150 for transport from Lifuka by speedboat and then T$60 per person, per day, for trekking including food, equipment and guide (minimum six persons). The landing site is below the site called Topuefio, where there are a couple of abandoned sheds. Watersports Ha'apai also offers volcanic dive safaris to Kao and Tofua.

LUAHOKO

About 10 or 15km north-west of Pangai, Luahoko is known for the many seabirds and sea turtles which nest here. The island has official protected status to conserve the birds and turtles, but some Tongans still occasionally come here to (illegally) collect eggs.

HA'AFEVA

About 40km south-west of Lifuka, the small island of Ha'afeva has a land area of only 1.8 sq km and a population of about 300 people, making it a very crowded place. Outside the single village, all uninhabited land is occupied by plantations. Although Ha'afeva has a friendly nature, it's generally rather unkempt and lacks good beaches.

On a reef north-west of the island, the sunken fishing boat *Eki'aki* makes for good diving.

Getting There & Away
Ha'afeva is accessed most easily on the MV *'Olovaha*, which sails in here weekly on its trips between Tongatapu and Lifuka. See the Getting Around chapter for schedules. In Ha'afeva you can find small local boats going to the tiny outer islands of Matuku, Kotu and Tungua, all of which offer excellent snorkelling.

NOMUKA & NOMUKA'IKI
Only 7 sq km in area and with a population of less than 550, Nomuka was historically important because of its freshwater springs.

The first European to arrive on the island was the Dutchman Abel Tasman, who named it Rotterdam while picking up water there. Subsequent well-known visitors included Captain James Cook, Captain William Bligh and William Mariner.

Nomuka is best recognised by the large brackish lake occupying much of its hilly interior. Two smaller lakes are near the island's northern end. During drier periods of the year, one of these lakes appears reddish-orange from the air, due to algae which is concentrated as the lake dries out.

Nomuka has a reputation in Tonga for being a bit more aloof than other places. But it's an interesting little place, dominated in the centre by the lake and surrounded by raised coral formations of up to 45m high.

Nomuka's companion island, Nomuka-'iki, is used as a prison where indentured convict labourers serve their sentences on the plantations.

Getting There & Away
Access is normally by small boat coming from either Lifuka or Ha'afeva. Though it's not on their schedule, the inter-island ferries may occasionally stop here.

Pacific Island Seaplanes will stop at Nomuka, landing on the lake. See the introductory Getting Around chapter.

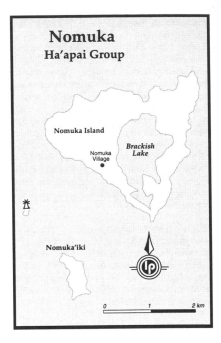

FONUAFO'OU
In 1781, the Spaniard Francisco Antonio Mourelle and in 1787, the French sailor Jean de la Pérouse both reported a shoal 30km west of Nomuka. In 1865, the passing ship HMS *Falcon* also noted it. Twelve years later smoke was seen rising from that spot by the warship *Sappho*. In 1885 a cinder, scoria and pumice island 50m high and 2km long rose from the sea, spewed up in a violent sub-marine eruption. In recognition of its birth, Tonga planted its flag on the island and claimed it for the king.

In 1894, a few years after it was first identified and named – Falcon Island by Europeans and Fonuafo'ou ('new land') by the Tongans – the island went missing. Less than two years later there appeared an island 320m high, which subsequently also disappeared. In 1927 it emerged again, however, and by 1930 it had risen in a series of fiery eruptions to 130m in height and 2.5km in length.

By 1949, there was again no trace of Fonuafo'ou, which had again been eroded by wave action into the sea. In the Vava'u Group, Late'iki island/Metis Shoal seems to be up to the same game these days.

Unless you're on a private yacht, the only way to catch a glimpse of Fonuafo'ou (assuming it's around when you're there!) is to ride one of the ferries returning to Tongatapu from Niuafo'ou, which normally pass within a few kilometres of it. Or you could charter a sailing boat on Tongatapu, or fly up with Pacific Island Seaplanes.

HUNGA TONGA & HUNGA HA'APAI

These twin volcanic islands in the far southwestern corner of the Ha'apai Group contain large guano deposits, but the lack of an anchorage makes exploitation of the resource impractical. Hunga Tonga reaches an altitude of 161m and Hunga Ha'apai 131m. Both volcanoes have been dormant since European discovery.

The Vava'u Group

Vava'u's Port of Refuge, a long, narrow channel between tussock-like limestone islands, is the best harbour between Pago Pago and New Zealand. Indeed it is one of the best harbours in the South Pacific. This, plus the fact that the Vava'u Group boasts uniquely picturesque islands, myriad jumbled channels, waterways and scores of lovely secluded anchorages, makes it one of the yachting capitals of the world.

Between August and November hundreds of cruising yachts descend on Vava'u to explore its wonders, and some sailors are so entranced that they would risk encountering a cyclone rather than leave so idyllic a setting. This was the place which Finau 'Ulukalala I warned Captain Cook not to approach because there was no good anchorage!

Vava'u is a paradise, not only for sailing, but for year-round diving and snorkelling as well. The tranquil islands have a population of about 16,000, scattered throughout the 50-odd thickly wooded islands of the group. A third of the people live in and around the capital, Neiafu.

Yachties and other world travellers like to compare Vava'u with the Bahamas, the Virgin Islands and the Rock Islands of Palau (which it closely resembles). But such comparisons do not take into account Vava'u's uniqueness. Beyond the emerald hills and islands, the white-sand beaches and the exquisite healthy, colourful coral reefs teeming with tropical fish are quiet villages, hidden caves and windswept cliffs.

Vava'u's busy tourist season is from May to November, with another flurry during the summer holidays from mid-December to late January. The place fills up with yachties from August to November, who take advantage of the easterly trade winds to reach New Zealand before the hot, rainy cyclone season, which lasts from late November to April, begins.

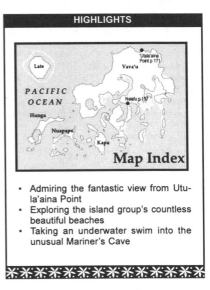

HIGHLIGHTS

Map Index

- Admiring the fantastic view from Utu-la'aina Point
- Exploring the island group's countless beautiful beaches
- Taking an underwater swim into the unusual Mariner's Cave

History

The Vava'u Group islands are believed to have been settled for around 2000 years.

The islands were discovered by Europeans, more or less accidentally, when Don Francisco Antonio Mourelle of Spain landed in 1781 while en route from the Philippines to Spanish America. Mourelle and the crew of his ship, the *Princesa*, had run short of supplies when they spotted volcanic Fonualei on the horizon. But it had no food or water, so they sailed on, naming it Amargura (bitterness).

They finally sighted the main island on 4 March 1781 and named the harbour at Neiafu Puerto de Refugio, or 'port of refuge'. Tongans knew it as Lolo 'a Halaevalu, or 'oil of the Princess Halaevalu', because of the smooth, natural, oily sheen that appears on the surface on a calm day. The sailors claimed the new-found paradise for Spain and named it Islas de Don Martin

152

Captain Cook's Fateful Turn Southward

On Captain James Cook's third voyage he spent over two months (April to July 1777) in the Tongan islands. At Nomuka he met chief Finau of Ha'apai.

When Finau announced that he was setting out to visit the Vava'u Group to the north and Cook expressed interest in accompanying him, the chief assured him that the islands contained no suitable anchorage or landing place for ships such as Cook's and that such a trip would be foolhardy. Instead of opting for adventure, the Englishman sailed southward through the convoluted reefs and shoals of the southern Ha'apai Group. Upon landing at Tongatapu, Cook learned that he had been deceived: the Vava'u Group contained the finest anchorages in the entire Tongan archipelago.

Captain James Cook

de Mayorga after the viceroy of Mexico. The islanders welcomed them and stocked their ship before it set sail again.

In 1793, Spain sent Captain Alessandro Malaspina to Vava'u to survey the new territory and formally make the Spanish claim known to the inhabitants of the Vava'u Group islands. Somewhere on the main island the captain buried a decree of Spanish sovereignty then quickly hurried on to other Pacific tasks.

William Mariner, who was adopted by the reigning chief of Ha'apai, Finau 'Ulukalala I, when his ship, *Port-au-Prince*, was sacked, also spent a great deal of time in Vava'u (in fact, he was involved in the Tongan conquest of this northern group). When the English brig the *Favourite* landed at Vava'u in early November 1810, the king of Vava'u, the son of the late Finau 'Ulukalala, permitted Mariner to return with it to Britain.

But when he saw the marvels on board the ship, the Tongan king begged to be permitted to accompany Mariner. He said he was willing to forsake his princely life in the islands for even a very low station in the land of Papalangi (the Tongans' name for Europeans, which was also used to refer to their faraway country). He wanted to learn

to read, write and operate mechanical wonders.

Captain Fisk of the *Favourite* refused young Finau's entreaties, whereupon the Tongan made Mariner swear that he would some day return to Tonga on another ship and carry the king back to England. Unfortunately, William Mariner never returned to Tonga.

Finau 'Ulukalala II's tomb can be seen today in the village of Feletoa, on the main island of Vava'u. His son was converted to Christianity by King George Tupou I of Ha'apai. When 'Ulukalala III died, George was entrusted to look after the throne of Vava'u for 'Ulukalala IV, who was just a boy. But George seized the opportunity to add Vava'u to his own realm, and eventually, in 1845, he formed a united Tonga.

Geography

Geologically, the main body of the Vava'u Group – which lies 275km north of Tongatapu – consists of a single landmass, a block of limestone tilted toward Ha'apai. The northern extreme ends in high cliffs which plunge straight into the surf, and there is very little coral offshore. The southern part of the group is a submerged zone where the summits of numerous small islands and

THE VAVA'U GROUP

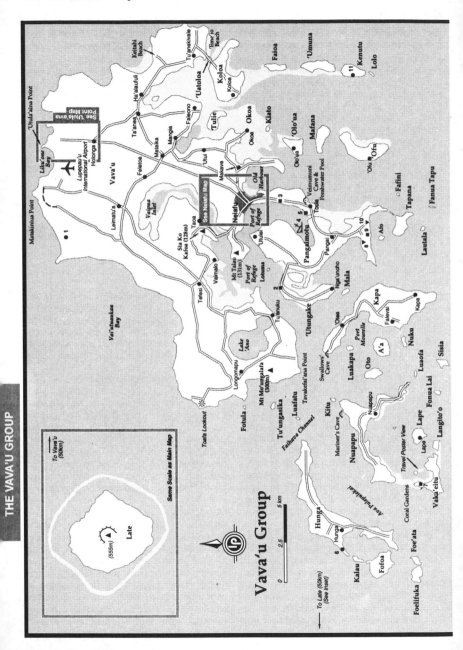

THE VAVA'U GROUP

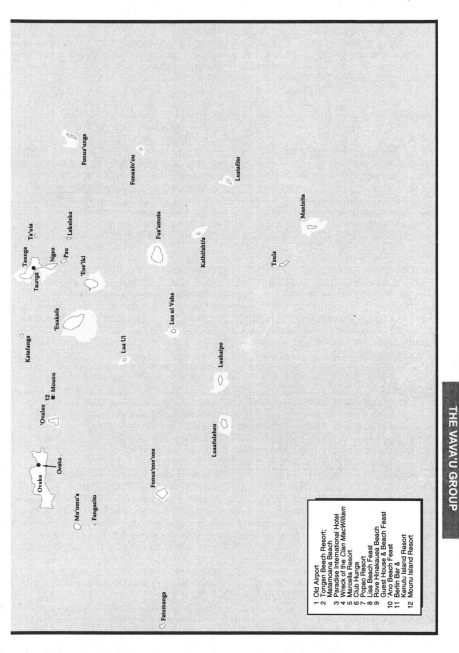

Fonua'unga

Fomuafo'ou

Luatafito

Maninita

Taunga
Ta'uta
Lekeleka
Ngau
Pau
Fua'amotu
'Eue'iki
Kulhfahifa
Taula

'Euakafa

Lua ui Vaha

Katafanga

Lua Ui

Luahaipo

'Ovalu
12 Mounu

Luaafuleheu

Ovaka
Ovaka
Mu'omu'a
Fonua'one'one
Fangasito

Fatumanga

1 Old Airport
2 Tongan Beach Resort;
   Matamoana Beach
3 Paradise International Hotel
4 Wreck of the *Clan MacWilliam*
5 Marcella Resort
6 Club Hunga
7 Popao Resort
8 Lisa Beach Feast
9 Rove Hinakauea Beach
   Guest House & Beach Feast
10 'Ano Beach Feast
11 Berlin Bar &
   Kenutu Island Resort
12 Mounu Island Resort

islets peek above the surface of the water in rounded masses not exceeding 186m high. Most of these are wholly or partially surrounded by coral reefs. Volcanic outliers of the group include Toku and Fonualei to the north and Late and Late'iki (Metis Shoal) to the west. A line of coral reefs runs southward from Vava'u.

Climate

With 2000mm of precipitation annually, the Vava'u Group has Tonga's wettest climate. Most of the rain falls from late November to April, which is also the cyclone season, but gentle warm rains and occasional downpours may occur at any time of year.

Even during the rainy season there are many fine days. Serious cyclones are rare. If you don't mind the humid heat, this can be a good time to visit Vava'u, as there aren't many tourists around.

Vava'u is warmer than Tongatapu. The average temperature at Neiafu is about 24°C, ranging from 18°C to 25°C between May and September and from 24°C to 32°C during the hot and sticky cyclone season. Easterly trade winds blow at an average of 15 knots year-round.

Neiafu

Neiafu sits smack in the centre of just about everything in Vava'u. As the administrative capital of the island group it has all the government agencies, the police headquarters, the hospital, the communications office and most of Vava'u's tourist facilities and restaurants. Over 25% of Vava'u's population lives in Neiafu and its villages.

The central area of Neiafu nestles between several low hills. To the north-west lies flat-topped Mt Talau (131m). Over the hill to the north is Vaipua (two waters) Inlet. Eastward is Neiafu Tahi (the 'Old Harbour'), and to the south is the road to Pangaimotu, where you'll find the principal yacht anchorage and the Paradise International Hotel.

History

Prior to European contact, Neiafu was considered a sacred burial ground by the indigenous people and political unrest and tribal skirmishes were forbidden. Every person entering the village was required to wear a *ta'ovala*, or waist mat, as a symbol of esteem for the chiefs entombed there.

The waterfront area around the Halaevalu Wharf is Matangimalie (pleasant winds). Formerly called Loto'alahi, it was the site of a palace built by the conqueror Finau 'Ulukalala II. In 1808, Finau built a fortification on slightly higher ground at Pou'ono. Apparently, he was ambivalent about the tapu associated with the Neiafu area in earlier times. The fort was called Vaha'akeli ('between trenches'), a reference to the moats surrounding it.

Information

Maps A detailed photocopy of the British Admiralty Chart of Vava'u showing all the anchorages (but no land-based details) is available at the Friendly Islands Bookshop for T$1.55 (black-and-white) or at The Moorings yacht office for T$12 (colour).

Tourist Office The Tonga Visitors' Bureau (☎ 70-115; fax 70-666; VHF channel 67), on Fatafehi Rd is a good source of information about Vava'u. They offer a free town map of Neiafu, a range of brochures and can answer any questions. It's open weekdays 8.30 am to 4.30 pm, Saturday 8.30 am to 12.30 pm.

Money Foreign currencies (cash or travellers' cheques) can be exchanged at any of Neiafu's three banks, all on Fatafehi Rd: the Bank of Tonga, ANZ and MBF. All are open weekdays from 9 am to 3.30 pm and on Saturday mornings. Cash advances on Visa and MasterCard are available at the Bank of Tonga and ANZ; MBF gives cash advances on MasterCard only. Currency from Samoa cannot be exchanged in Tonga.

Post & Communications The post office is on Fatafehi Rd, just above the main wharf

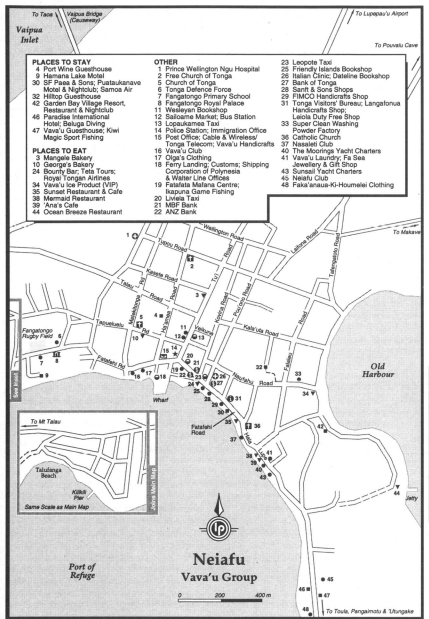

PLACES TO STAY
4 Port Wine Guesthouse
9 Hamana Lake Motel
30 SF Paea & Sons; Puataukanave Motel & Nightclub; Samoa Air
32 Hilltop Guesthouse
42 Garden Bay Village Resort, Restaurant & Nightclub
46 Paradise International Hotel; Beluga Diving
47 Vava'u Guesthouse; Kiwi Magic Sport Fishing

PLACES TO EAT
3 Mangele Bakery
10 George's Bakery
24 Bounty Bar; Teta Tours; Royal Tongan Airlines
34 Vava'u Ice Product (VIP)
35 Sunset Restaurant & Cafe
38 Mermaid Restaurant
39 'Ana's Cafe
44 Ocean Breeze Restaurant

OTHER
1 Prince Wellington Ngu Hospital
2 Free Church of Tonga
5 Church of Tonga
6 Tonga Defence Force
7 Fangatongo Primary School
8 Fangatongo Royal Palace
11 Wesleyan Bookshop
12 Sailoame Market; Bus Station
13 Lopaukamea Taxi
14 Police Station; Immigration Office
15 Post Office; Cable & Wireless/ Tonga Telecom; Vava'u Handicrafts
16 Vava'u Club
17 Olga's Clothing
18 Ferry Landing; Customs; Shipping Corporation of Polynesia & Walter Line Offices
19 Fatafata Mafana Centre; Ikapuna Game Fishing
20 Liviela Taxi
21 MBF Bank
22 ANZ Bank

23 Leopote Taxi
25 Friendly Islands Bookshop
26 Italian Clinic; Dateline Bookshop
27 Bank of Tonga
28 Sanft & Sons Shops
29 FIMCO Handicrafts Shop
31 Tonga Visitors' Bureau; Langafonua Handicrafts Shop; Leiola Duty Free Shop
33 Super Clean Washing Powder Factory
36 Catholic Church
37 Nasaleti Club
40 The Moorings Yacht Charters
41 Vava'u Laundry; Fa Sea Jewellery & Gift Shop
43 Sunsail Yacht Charters
45 Neiafu Club
48 Faka'anaua-Ki-Houmelei Clothing

THE VAVA'U GROUP

Neiafu
Vava'u Group

0   200   400 m

area. It's open weekdays from 8.30 am to 4 pm. Poste Restante mail is held for 30 days and is generally reliable.

Cable & Wireless, next door to the post office, offers domestic and international telephone services 24 hours, seven days a week. Fax services are available weekdays from 8.30 am to 4.30 pm.

The yacht-charter company The Moorings offers a fax service and may be starting an email service for travellers.

Vava'u has its own FM radio station: FM1, at around 89.3 on the FM dial.

Many businesses in Vava'u communicate by VHF radio in addition to, or in place of, telephone. A yachties' information net is on VHF channel 6 weekdays at 8.30 am.

Bookshops The Friendly Islands Bookshop, a branch of the main store in Nuku'alofa, is on Fatafehi Rd a couple of doors from the Bounty Bar. The Wesleyan Bookshop is a couple of blocks inland on Tu'i Rd.

Most places to stay have reading libraries and/or book exchanges for guests. The Moorings yacht-charter company has a book swap that anyone can use. Other travellers are also prospects for trading books.

Film & Photography Film is sold at several shops around Neiafu, including the duty-free shop beside the Visitors' Bureau. There's nowhere to purchase slide film.

Laundry Vava'u Laundry, opposite The Moorings offers wash, dry and fold, or you can do it yourself. Laundry service is also available at 'Ana's Cafe, next door to The Moorings. Most places to stay offer laundry service for guests or washing facilities.

Emergency The police station is on Tu'i Rd, in the centre of town. Emergency telephone numbers are:

Police	☎ 70-233, 70-234, 70-230
Fire	☎ 999, 70-089
Hospital	☎ 70-201, 70-202, 70-204

Medical Services For health problems see Dr Alfredo Carafa at the Italian Clinic and Pharmacy (☎ 70-607; VHF channel 68), on Pou'ono Rd behind the Bank of Tonga. Consultations cost T$25 (T$10 for Vava'u residents). The clinic is open weekdays from 9 am to 2 pm, and at other times by special appointment. There's also a clinic at the Prince Wellington Ngu Hospital (☎ 70-201) at the western end of Neiafu.

Free Wesleyan Church
Built in 1970, this church is of interest mainly for its stained-glass work, including windows which depict such diverse characters as John and Susan Wesley, Queen Salote Tupou III and Jesus Christ. It's built on the site of the old Wesleyan church which was destroyed by the devastating cyclone of 16 and 17 March 1961. All that remains of the old church is a hall, which is used as a Siu'ilikutapu College classroom by day and a kava club by night.

Hala Tafengatoto
The name means 'the road where blood flows'. Tradition has it that this sunken trail, the route to the village of Feletoa, ran with the blood of warriors killed during the conquest of Vava'u by Finau 'Ulukalala II.

This trail is one of a network of sunken clay pathways found around the main island of Vava'u. It meets the Old Harbour in Neiafu's eastern environs. The trail's ruddy clay base is still reminiscent of the source of its name. Today, Tongans collect the clay to use as a shampoo.

Pou'ono & Pou'ono Cemetery
Pou'ono means 'six posts' and refers to the traditional six posts of a meeting fale. This green was the site of the Vava'u courthouse until a new one was built in the 1990s.

Ta'emoemimi, the daughter of Tu'ipulotu'ilangi Tu'oteau, the 35th Tu'i Tonga, is buried in an ancient langi tomb in the cemetery opposite the green. The cemetery also contains the graves of two early 19th-century Wesleyan missionaries, Reverend Francis Wilson and David Cargill.

Old Harbour (Neiafu Tahi)

Neiafu's Old Harbour is much shallower than the Port of Refuge but it served as Vava'u's main landing site until the arrival of relatively large European ships, which required a deepwater port. Around 1808, Finau 'Ulukalala II, in the midst of the conquest of Vava'u, bound several resisting chiefs into decomposing canoes and left them adrift in Neiafu Tahi to drown.

Near the entrance to Hala Tafengatoto are several freshwater springs bubbling into the Neiafu Tahi. The most reliable is Matalave, which lies around the harbour to the east. Nearby is the rocky outcrop that is said to have been the primary Vava'u landing site of the *kalia*, the double-hulled canoes used in ancient times.

Hala Lupe

Hala Lupe, the 'way of doves', is the name given to the stretch of road along the waterfront between the Catholic church and The Moorings office. It is so called because the road was constructed by women prisoners convicted by the church of adultery. They often sang as they worked and listeners likened the sound to the mournful cooing of doves.

Wreck of the Clan MacWilliam

The wreck of the copra steamer *Clan MacWilliam* lies in 37m of water in the southern arm of the Port of Refuge. Built in 1918, this 127m (423-foot), 6000-ton Clan Shipping Line freighter steamed into Neiafu Harbour in late December 1927 with a smouldering fire in the No 3 copra hold. The forward holds collapsed, cracking open the steamer's plates. One legend has it that the captain and first engineer refused to abandon ship and went down with it; another relates that the captain locked the first engineer into the engine room to prevent him from abandoning the effort to save the ship! The shipwreck is now a popular dive site.

Fangatongo Rugby Field

On the road leading west to Mt Talau is the Fangatongo Rugby Field, where matches are played on Saturday from April to July. The large tree at the south end of the field reputedly provides shelter for up to 500 spectators!

Kilikili Pier

Kilikili is the name for the black volcanic slag pebbles used to decorate grave mounds throughout Tonga. Those in use today come mostly from Kao and Tofua in the Ha'apai Group. The Kilikili pier, at the far western end of Neiafu, once served as a British coaling station; it was so named because the coal loaded there by the foreigners resembled, to the Tongans, those familiar little pebbles. The area is now a popular swimming hole.

Mt Talau

Mo'unga Talau, the 131m flat-topped mountain dominating the Port of Refuge, is easily climbed in an afternoon. Continue west past the rugby field along Tapueluelu Rd and up through a residential area, until the road narrows into a bush track. When it begins to descend, a side track turns off to the right and leads steeply up over slippery rock surfaces to the summit.

The view from the three viewpoints at the top encompasses Neiafu, the Port of Refuge, the Vaipua causeway and the 128m-high Sia Ko Kafoa across Vaipua Inlet. Across the Old Harbour are Pangaimotu and 'Utungake islands. The other truncated mountain in the distance (no one knows where the top of this one wound up) is 186m-high Mo'ungalafa, rising above the freshwater Lake 'Ano at the western end of Vava'u island.

Activities

Vava'u is good for scuba diving, snorkelling, sailing, whale watching, fishing and more.

Diving Beluga Diving (☎ 70-327) operates from the Paradise International Hotel. (See Beluga Diving under Nuku'alofa in the Tongatapu chapter for price details for dives

THE VAVA'U GROUP

Mt Talau Loses its Peak

The Tongans tell an interesting tale of how Mt Talau came to lose its peak. It seems that a mischievous Samoan *tevolo*, or devil spirit, decided to filch the attractive peak and carry it away to his homeland. There is some disagreement as to what happened next; some maintain that a patriotic Tongan tevolo caught the offender and forced him to drop the peak by convincing him of the imminent arrival of daylight, the time for all devils to be back under cover. Another source claims that the mountain simply became too heavy and the thief dropped it. Whatever the case, the mountain top splash-landed in the middle of the Port of Refuge. It is now called Lotuma and is used as the Vava'u naval base of the Tongan Defence Forces.

and diving courses.) Sailboards can be rented for T$27/42 a half/full day and paragliding is planned for the near future.

Dolphin Pacific Diving (☎ /fax 70-292; VHF channel 71), PO Box 131, Neiafu, has a dive shop in Neiafu and another at the Tongan Beach Resort on 'Utungake island, Vava'u. Two-tank boat dives are T$80, snorkelling trips T$35. Diving instruction is T$500 for a PADI open water diver course, T$120 for a PADI 'discover scuba diving' course, with advanced courses also available. Information is also available at its New Zealand office, PO Box 103, Paeroa (☎ 64-7-862-7456, 862-8959, 0800-112-131; fax 64-7-862-6668; dive-adi@wave.co.nz).

Sailing The Moorings (☎ 70-016; fax 70-428; VHF channel 71), PO Box 119, Neiafu, is the world's largest yacht charter company, with five bases in the Pacific and 22 others in the Mediterranean, Caribbean etc. It offers excellent service and has a reputation for having the highest standards in the industry. Its 16 Vava'u-based yachts range from 35 feet (10.5m) to 51 feet (15m), with accommodation for two to eight passengers, and are almost exclusively built by Benetau. Prices range from US$300 to US$680 per day, depending on the size of yacht, season discounts and level of equipment; average cost is US$75 per person, per day. Bareboat charter is avail-

able as well as full or partial provisioning, skippers (T$100 per day) and cooks (T$80 per day). It is possible to make bookings locally, in the USA (☎ (800) 535-7289, (813) 535-1446; 110447.3203@compuserve.com) or in New Zealand (☎ 64-9-377-4840; 0800-500-987; fax 64-9-377-4820; sales@the moorings.co.nz).

Sunsail Neiafu (☎ 70-646; VHF channel 71) is Vava'u's second-largest yacht charter operators. It has a variety of yachts (mostly Benetau) with prices ranging from NZ$400 to NZ$800 per night in low season (January to March), NZ$510 to NZ$950 the rest of the year, with skipper, cook, provisioning etc available as extras. Bookings are made in New Zealand at Sunsail, (☎ 64-9-307-7077; fax 64-9-307-7177), PO Box 33729, Takapuna, Auckland

Sailing Safaris, (☎/fax 70-650; sailingsafaris@candw.to; VHF channel 71), PO Box 153, Neiafu, has sailing vessels ranging from 26 feet (8m) to 44 feet (13m). Bareboat charters (T$190 to T$550 per day) and crewed charters (add T$80 per day for a captain, and/or T$80 per day for a cook) are available. They also have a 36-foot (11m) catamaran, *On The Double*, sleeping eight, for T$720 per day.

Tongan Sea Adventures (☎/fax 70-209; VHF channel 16), Private Bag, Neiafu, owns the *Melinda*, a comfortable 44-foot (13m) traditional gaff ketch sleeping six guests. It offers fully-crewed charters, including full board. The company makes day trips from Neiafu for T$50 per person (minimum three people), overnight charters for T$135 per person (minimum two people), week-long charters for US$850 per person (minimum two people), and does organised surfing trips, and whale watching in season. To book in the USA, contact Tongan Sea Adventures (☎ (415) 332-8591; fax (415) 331-1182; Butterchri@aol.com).

Verne of Orion Charters Neiafu, Vava'u (VHF channel 9) teaches sailing, offers hands-on sailing trips and does day tours around the Vava'u Group on his 38-foot (11m) trimaran, the *Orion* (see Boat Tours). Contact Verne through the Paradise International Hotel in Neiafu.

Kayaking Friendly Islands Kayak Company (☎/fax 70-173; fax 22-970) Private Bag, Neiafu, operates from May to early December. It is an environmentally conscious company and runs a variety of camping and paddling expeditions around the Vava'u and Ha'apai Groups. Six-day (T$930), eight-day (T$1205) and 10-day (T$1485) packages are offered; no experience is required. All trips require a minimum of four participants (maximum 10), and include kayak and equipment rental, professional guides, meals, camping equipment and an 'umu feast on an outer island. Customised and group tours can be arranged on request. Owners Sharon and Doug Spence can be contacted in Vava'u from May to December. From January to April, contact them at: Friendly Islands Kayak Company, (☎/fax 64-3-482-1202) PO Box 142, Waitati, Otago, New Zealand.

The Paradise International Hotel rents out kayaks for T$10/20 per half/full day; pay and get paddles at the bar.

Whale Watching Whale Watch Vava'u (☎ 70-576; fax 70-493; mounu@candw.to; VHF channel 16), Private Bag, Neiafu, operates trips for T$65 per person (minimum party of six); lunch can be provided for T$10 extra. For further information and bookings in Neiafu, contact the Bounty Bar.

Dolphin Pacific Diving (☎/fax 70-292; dive-adi@wave.co.nz), PO Box 131, Neiafu, also offers whale watching trips at T$45 or T$60 per person, depending on the boat. Groups can charter a boat and discounts are given for families.

Kiwi Magic (☎/fax 70-441; kiwifish@candw.to; invited.to/kiwi.magic; VHF channel 71), PO Box 153, Neiafu, offers whale watching trips for T$55 per person.

Sailing Safaris (☎/fax 70-650; sailingsafaris@candw.to; VHF channel 71), PO Box 153, Neiafu, conducts full day whale watching trips for T$50 per person.

Tongan Sea Adventures (☎/fax 70-209; VHF channel 16), Private Bag, Neiafu, runs whale watching trips on the *Melinda*, a 44-foot (13m) traditional gaff ketch, for T$50 per person.

Fishing Kiwi Magic (☎/fax 70-441; kiwifish@candw.to; invited.to/kiwi.magic; VHF channel 71), PO Box 153, Neiafu, offers deep-sea fishing charters aboard its custom-built 34-foot (10m) sportfishing boat. Trips run from 8 am to 5 pm and concentrate on the western part of the Vava'u Group; T$150 per person, includes lunch (minimum two people).

Alternatively, Target One (☎/fax 70-647; fishtarget@candw.to) Private Bag 3, Neiafu, is a fast 27-foot (8m) gamefishing and sportfishing boat, operated by Henk & Sandra Gros. It charters for from T$150 per person (maximum three anglers), or T$450 per day for the whole boat, including all gear. Special rates can be negotiated with direct bookings.

Dora Malia (☎ 70-698, 70-416; fax 70-174), PO Box 106, Neiafu, is a 35-foot (11m) boat skippered by Paul Mead, who specialises in tuna and marlin fishing. Both light and heavy tackle are available. Charters are T$300/400 per day for two/four fishers, including gear and light lunch. Paul can be contacted at the Ikapuna Fishing Gear store in central Neiafu.

Jim McMahon at Hook-Up Vava'u ('Ofu island, Vava'u; ☎ 70-541; fax 70-184) has a 16-foot (5m) fibreglass Fisherman with a 55

HP engine, plus all fishing gear and tackle. He does one-day fishing excursions around the Vava'u Group for T$160/200 for one/two people, including petrol and the use of equipment; half-day fishing trips are T$95/130 for one/two people. He also does day tours around the Vava'u Group (see Boat Tours).

Organised Tours

Island Tours Soane's Scenic Tours (☎ 70-211) offers day tours of Vava'u island, including a barbecue lunch. It takes in sights such as Utula'aina Point, Keitahi Beach (have a swim if you like), vanilla plantations, Lake 'Ano and the Toafa Lookout. Tours last from 9.30 am to 4.30 pm and cost T$25 per person (minimum three people) or T$75 (for one or two people), lunch included. Teta Tours (☎ 70-488), beside the Bounty Bar on Fatafehi Rd offers island tours for T$25 per person (minimum four people).

Boat Tours Several Neiafu operators run day boat excursions around the main sites of interest in the Vava'u Group. They typically include Swallows' and Mariner's caves, picnicking on an uninhabited island and snorkelling at an offshore reef, but they'll also cater to individual whims. The presence of humpback whales is a special bonus from July to November.

For go-as-you-please day excursions around the Vava'u Group, try to snag *Hook-up Vava'u* (☎ 70-541; fax 70-184). Owner Jim McMahon offers day tours for up to three people or a small family; prices vary, depending on what you want to do, but are competitively priced. The advantages of exploring the islands in this way are obvious – you can go where you like, stop where you like and spend as much time as you'd like. It's all very friendly and informal; bring your own lunch. Jim provides snorkelling gear. He also does fishing trips (see Fishing). You can often find Jim at the Paradise International Hotel bar.

Verne, a popular local character, operates day trips on a 38-foot (11m) trimaran, the *Orion*. You usually sail around the islands for a couple of hours, stop on an outer island for about three hours for snorkelling and lunch and then sail back; trips last from around 10 am to 4.30 pm. The cost of T$35 per person includes snorkelling gear, lunch, coffee, tea, music and ice. Book at the front desk of the Paradise International Hotel, or see Verne at the Paradise International Hotel bar after 5 pm, or call him on VHF channel 9.

Soki's Island Tours (☎ 70-576; VHF channel 16) offers day tours for T$25 per person as long as there are four or more passengers. Book at the Bounty Bar, or through your accommodation. Niva's Tours (☎ 70-380), based at the Tongan Beach Resort, also does similar tours. Both outfits charter boats.

The on-again, off-again Lekeleka Tours, led by Vake Tapa'atoutai from 'Ofu island, offers a full day tour to several rarely visited eastern islands that most tourists never get to see, including Lekeleka (a small island near Mafana), 'Ofu and 'Umuna. Vake takes you to see small-island village life, plantations, a flying fox colony and to a cave on 'Umuna where you can swim. Bring your own lunch, or you can stop at the Berlin Bar on Kenutu island. The full day tour is T$25 per person (lunch not included). Book through the Hilltop Guesthouse.

Day tours are also offered by Sailing Safaris and Tongan Sea Adventures. See Sailing.

The Hilltop Guesthouse can usually arrange reasonably priced Tongan-style fishing trips, night snorkelling and shuttles to outer islands.

Special Events

The Vava'u Festival, the biggest festival of the year, takes place during the week leading up to 4 May, the crown prince's birthday. This week-long party includes a variety of events, from processions to weaving and dance classes to sports matches, drinking bashes and feasts.

Places to Stay

There are plenty of places to stay, both in and near Neiafu and on some of the other islands in the Vava'u Group. Check the Out of Town listing in this section and the individual offshore Islands – some of the most enjoyable places to stay are outside of town.

Places to Stay – budget

The *Hilltop Guest House* (☎/fax 70-209), Private Bag, Neiafu, atop Holopeka Hill (place of gathering bats) is one of Vava'u's most popular places to stay. It has a relaxed, friendly atmosphere and a magical setting, boasting a 180° view over the Port of Refuge, the Old Harbour, the surrounding hills, neighbouring islands and the whole of Neiafu. The view is especially fine from the swimming pool and outdoor covered patio/bar area. It's admirably run by a friendly Italian, Franco Sabatini, who can organise anything you might want to do around Vava'u.

The Hilltop offers several types of rooms. Standard rooms with garden view and shared bath are T$13/23 a single/double. Rooms with view, verandah and shared bath are T$20/27, or T$28/35 with private bath. A two-bedroom apartment with view, verandah and private bath, sleeping up to four people, is T$45/55. Mosquito nets are provided, and there's a communal kitchen, book exchange and laundry facilities and you can rent motorbikes. Pickups from the airport are available for T$7 per carload.

The *Hamana Lake Motel* (☎ 70-507; fax 70-666), Private Bag, Neiafu, on the hillside on the west side of town, also has a spectacular view – across the harbour to 'Utulei, left to Neiafu and the Port of Refuge, and right down the entrance to the Port of Refuge. The communal kitchen, dining room and comfortable sitting room all have that beautiful view. The six guest rooms are T$15/22 a single/double for the 'economy cave', T$15/30 a twin room, T$20/30 a double room, or T$25/35 a double room with view, all with shared hot bath.

The *Port Wine Guest House* (☎ 70-479), PO Box 65, Neiafu, on Ha'amea Rd in the centre of town, is a pleasant, homey place with six rooms sharing kitchen, bathroom etc. Singles/doubles are T$10/18.

Another popular place with budget travellers is Mr Mikio Filitonga's *Vava'u Guest House & Restaurant* (☎ 70-300; fax 70-441; kiwifish@candw.to), PO Box 148, Neiafu, opposite the Paradise International Hotel. It's another casual, comfortable place. In the old building, spartan but adequate rooms with shared bath are T$9/12. Four newer bungalows with private bath are T$20/25. Basic cooking facilities are available for guests, and the restaurant here is one of the best places in town to eat. Bicycles can be rented for T$10 per day. If you stay here, you can always walk across the road to the Paradise International Hotel and pay T$2 if you want to use its swimming pool.

The *Puataukanave Motel* (☎ 70-844; fax 70-080), PO Box 23, Neiafu, is downstairs from the SF Paea & Sons department store, opposite the Tonga Visitors' Bureau. Its six modern rooms each have private bath, two double beds, telephone and a balcony overlooking the harbour. Singles/doubles are T$25/35. The only drawback could be the disco downstairs, which cranks up on Thursday, Friday and Saturday nights.

The *Garden Bay Village Resort* (☎ 70-137, 70-025; fax 70-200), PO Box 102, Neiafu, on the shore of the Old Harbour, is 1.5km east of the centre and permits camping in its grounds. Standard bungalows are T$17/30; two-bedroom bungalows with private facilities are T$48. All prices include continental breakfast; other meals are also served in the restaurant. Airport transfers are free on request. The nightclub here has disco dancing on Friday and Saturday nights.

Places to Stay – middle

There are no real middle-range places to stay right in Neiafu. That gap is filled by the more expensive rooms at the Hilltop Guesthouse and the Garden Bay Village Resort, as well as the economy rooms at the Paradise International Hotel.

Places to Stay – top end
The *Paradise International Hotel* (☎ 70-211, 70-094; fax 70-184; paradise@candw.to), PO Box 11, Neiafu, is Vava'u's finest resort hotel and is among the poshest places to stay in Tonga. It's good value for money, with attractive rooms, a fine restaurant and bar, a large swimming pool and a great view overlooking the Port of Refuge. Economy rooms without hot water or air-con are T$47/52 a single/double. Standard garden view rooms with hot water and air-con are T$85/95; harbour view rooms are T$100/110. The hotel bus meets all incoming flights and provides free airport transfers for guests.

There's a pleasant restaurant and bar area beside the pool (the pool may be used by nonguests for T$2 per person). Check out the bit of aeroplane near the bar – it belongs to the hotel's owner, Carter Johnson from Kentucky, who crashed it several years ago. The other bit was donated to a children's playground in the Pou'ono area of central Neiafu. Videos are shown nightly above the reception area, except when there's dancing or other entertainment.

The main Vava'u yacht anchorage is in the Port of Refuge in front of the hotel. The hotel's wharf offers electric hookups, showers and other facilities for yachties. Beluga Diving is right alongside.

Places to Stay – out of town
On the southern tip of Vava'u island, *Marcella Resort* (☎/fax 70-687), Private Bag, Neiafu, has six bungalows, each with private bath and verandah, spaced around large grounds with a beautiful view overlooking the Port of Refuge. The resort has a tennis court, free bicycles and snorkelling gear for guests, a wharf good for swimming and a licensed restaurant/bar. It's T$40/60 for singles/doubles.

The *Tongan Beach Resort* (☎/fax 70-380; tonbeach@candw.to; www.thetongan.com; VHF channel 71), PO Box 104, Neiafu,

offers clean, secluded beach accommodation, two causeways away from Neiafu, on 'Utungake island's lovely Hikutamole beach. There are 12 beachfront bungalows, each with sea view, private bath and fridge, for T$108/120/144; luxury bungalows over the water are T$220. There's a lovely outdoor *fale* bar and a restaurant specialising in seafood and Pacific Rim cuisine; the meal plan costs T$45 per day, or T$35 per day for breakfast and dinner only. The Dolphin Pacific scuba diving company is based here.

The *Matamoana Beach Resort* (☎ 70-668; fax 70-332), next door to the Tongan Beach Resort, has four self-contained, attractive units for T$42/48 a single/double.

On the amazingly beautiful Hinakauea Beach, the *Rove Hinakauea Beach Guest House* is operated by Sione Tongia and his family, who operate one of Vava'u's best Tongan feasts. Sione has built four simple concrete bungalows along the beach, each with bedroom, sitting room and private bath. The rates of T$20/35 a single/double include snorkelling gear. Sione will supply a gas stove if you want to do your own cooking, or you can eat with the family (breakfast T$8, lunch T$10, dinner T$15). A big Tongan feast, with kava ceremony, dancing and other entertainment, is held here on Thursday evenings, and next door at 'Ano Beach on Saturday evenings. Accommodation bookings can be made on VHF channel 16, or at the Tonga Visitors' Bureau in Neiafu.

Places to Eat
For such a small town, Neiafu has several wonderful places to eat.

Restaurants The *Bounty Bar* (☎ 70-576; VHF channel 16) on Fatafehi Rd is Vava'u's answer to the inevitable hangout that springs up in every paradise, the sort of place where you'd expect to find Jimmy Buffet strumming the guitar and sipping a piña colada. Travellers, tourists and yachties alike seem to gravitate toward its airy balcony and gaze nonchalantly over the

Port of Refuge. They can spend hours drinking beer, chatting and writing letters while intermittently enjoying a variety of well prepared snacks and dishes. It's open from 8 am to 10 pm Monday to Thursday, 8 am to midnight Friday and 8 am to 2 pm Saturday.

The Italian-run *Sunset Restaurant & Cafe Bar* (☎ 70-218; VHF channel 16), on the waterfront near the Catholic church, serves pizza, pasta, seafood, steak, omelettes, snacks, salads, sandwiches, breakfast and desserts, plus yoghurt, milkshakes and the best cappuccino in Tonga, all for very economical prices. It has a very pleasant atmosphere, with good music and tables inside and out by the water. Yachties can pull right up to the jetty – they like to hang out here. It's open weekdays 9 am to 10 pm, Saturday 11 am to 10 pm.

The *Mermaid Restaurant* (☎ 70-730; VHF channel 16), on the waterfront almost next door to The Moorings, is fast becoming one of Vavau's most popular places for its great food, relaxed atmosphere and live music every night. Ron, the Canadian chef, turns out superb meals, with a varied menu which changes daily. You're welcome to come for a meal, a drink or just to hang out and enjoy the music performed by a string band composed of Ron's Tongan brothers-in-law. They welcome musicians sitting in, and this is fast becoming the musicians' hangout of Tonga. It's open every day except Sunday, 10 am to 11.30 pm during busy season (reservations recommended), 3pm to 11.30 pm during off-season.

'Ana's Cafe (☎ 70-664; VHF channel 72), on the waterfront between the Mermaid Restaurant and The Moorings, is popular with yachties. It has a good inexpensive menu, relaxed atmosphere, a good dinghy dock, and offers laundry service, informal Scrabble tournaments and a popular happy hour from 5 to 6 pm. It's open weekdays for breakfast, lunch and dinner; breakfast and lunch on Saturday.

The restaurant at the luxurious *Paradise International Hotel* (☎ 70-211) has tables, both indoors and out around the swimming pool, with a fine view over the Port of Refuge. It's open every day from 6.30 am to 11 pm; the bar is open every day from 8 am to midnight, or until 2 am on nights when there's entertainment.

The *Vava'u Guest House & Restaurant* (☎ 70-300), opposite the Paradise International Hotel, has a simple restaurant specialising in seafood, chicken, Chinese and Polynesian dishes. Breakfast is served from 7.30 to 9 am (T$3 to T$4.50), dinner from 7 to 9 pm (T$9.50 to T$12). On Sunday there's a special barbecue for T$10, a popular event in Neiafu. Book in advance for dinners, especially the Sunday barbecue.

The *Ocean Breeze Restaurant* (☎ 70-582; VHF channel 74) is on the waterfront on the Old Harbour side of Neiafu, opposite Anchorage 25. Run by a friendly British/ Tongan couple, John and Amelia Dale, it's highly regarded in Vava'u, and readers have reported being made to feel part of the family rather than paying customers. Gourmet food in large portions is the speciality here, with a varied menu including seafood, steak, chicken, lobster, vegetarian and Indian dishes (with excellent curries) and even fish and chips (perhaps a concession to John's origins). It has tables both indoors and outdoors on several terraces overlooking the Old Harbour. It's open for lunch from noon to 2 pm, dinner from 6 pm until the last guest leaves. Bookings are essential, especially from May to October. A taxi from any of the Neiafu hotels is T$1.50; it's also within easy walking distance but at night carry a torch. If you're coming by boat, you can pull right up to their jetty.

Also on the waterfront of the Old Harbour, the *Garden Bay Village Resort* (☎ 70-137) has a restaurant which serves all three meals.

The restaurant at the *Marcella Resort* (☎ 70-687) has excellent food and a fine view overlooking the Port of Refuge.

The elegant restaurant at the *Tongan Beach Resort* (☎ 70-380; VHF channel 71) on 'Utungake island specialises in seafood and Pacific Rim cuisine. It's geared mainly for resort guests, but outsiders are welcome if they book before noon on the same day. Evening meals begin at 7 pm. On Sunday they hold a beach barbecue beginning at 7 pm (T$25). Guests will especially look forward to the wonderful breakfasts, featuring freshly baked bread and a bowl of tropical fruit. If you come here for any meal (breakfast, lunch or dinner) you can use the resort's beach, kayaks etc. A taxi from town costs T$7.

Tongan Feasts If you're craving a Tongan feast, there are several to choose from in Vava'u.

Two popular ones are the weekly affairs held by Mr Matoto Lotavao at 'Ano beach (Anchorage 11) and Mr 'Aisea Sikaleti at Lisa Beach (Anchorage 10), both on Pangaimotu island. They feature welcoming kava ceremonies, weaving demonstrations, entertainment with traditional Tongan music and dance and ample buffets of Tongan specialities such as pork, lobster, clams, chicken, octopus, fruit and local vegetables. They both begin at 6 pm on Saturday (sometimes on Wednesday too) and cost T$20 per person, including transport.

A third popular feast is put on by Sione Tongia at the Rove Hinakauea Beach Guest House on Hinakauea Beach on Thursday at 6 pm also for T$20, with transport included. (Hinakauea Beach is the same lovely beach as 'Ano beach, next door.)

Bookings for all the feasts can be made through the Tonga Visitors' Bureau, The Moorings, Sunsail, Bounty Bar or your accommodation.

Self-Catering Imported grocery products are available at the *Tonga Cooperative Federation* supermarket and the more expensive *Fatafata Mafana Centre* supermarket. They're open weekdays 8.30 am to 4 pm, Saturday 8.30 am to noon.

The freshest fish can be found in the early morning at the jetty on the Old Harbour, near the Ocean Breeze restaurant, or at Neiafu's wharf. Some of the local shops also carry fresh fish.

George's Bakery is in a nondescript little white building west of the centre. Actually, on our last visit, Neiafu had four George's Bakeries! Don't miss the cinnamon rolls, they're great. On Saturday you'll have to be early buying bread, as it's normally sold out before 9 am. The bakery closes on Saturday at noon and reopens at 4 pm on Sunday. Other options are *Mangele Bakery* and *Tu'i Halamaka Bakery*.

Good European-style breads, rolls, Danish pastries, cakes etc can be ordered from Joe, the Austrian baker from Salzburg who operates the *Lighthouse Cafe* at the Popao Village Resort on Vaka'eitu island. Order them at 'Ana's Cafe beside The Moorings any day before 6 pm and you'll have them the following day – or pay a visit to Vaka'eitu.

For fresh produce, go to *Sailoame Market* just uphill from the police station on Tu'i Rd. Basic but filling meals can also be bought here, for T$3. The market may be moving elsewhere, but no one knows the venue as yet.

The German-run *Vava'u Ice Product (VIP)* factory near Garden Bay Village Resort makes delicious ice cream, ice blocks and choco-dips. It's open weekdays from 8 am to noon and 1 to 5 pm, Saturday 8 am to noon.

Entertainment
Tongan Feasts Some of Vavau's best entertainment can be found at the Tongan beach feasts (see Tongan Feasts under Places to Eat).

The *Marcella Resort* (see Places to Stay) is planning to introduce an 'island nite' which features a traditional Tongan buffet, entertainment and a floor show of Tongan dancing to be held on Saturday nights. The *Paradise International Hotel* and *Tongan Beach Resort* also hold occasional Tongan buffets with entertainment. *Club Hunga*, on Hunga island, holds 'island nites' on Friday nights during tourist season, from around May to October.

Bars, Cafes & Music The *Mermaid Restaurant* (see Places to Eat) has live music every night except Sunday. Musicians are welcome to sit in. Local aficionados call this 'the musicians' hangout of the South Pacific', and the food is great, too.

The bar at the *Paradise International Hotel* is a good place to meet tourists and expats. So are the *Bounty Bar, 'Ana's Cafe* and the *Sunset Restaurant & Cafe Bar* (see Places to Eat).

Yachties like to hang out at the *Neiafu Club*, so this is a good option if you're hoping to crew with someone. Beer and spirits are reasonably priced and it opens daily, including Sunday, from 3 pm until late. There's a full-sized pool table, darts and a few comfy chairs. Yachties also congregate at *'Ana's Cafe*, especially for the happy hour from 5 to 6 pm and for the Friday boat race.

The *Vava'u Club*, west of the centre, is a western-style saloon with a pool table.

Kava Clubs The *Nasaleti Club* offers socialising, chatting, card playing and kava drinking. Participants pay a flat fee of T$2.50 per person for all the kava they can slosh down. This is primarily a men's club; the presence of unaccompanied women would probably be misunderstood. For information about other Friday night kava clubs in Neiafu, ask any local man to steer you in the right direction.

Discos Neiafu's most popular disco, especially with many young people, is the *Puataukanave Nightclub* on the ground floor of the SF Paea & Sons building, opposite the Tonga Visitors' Bureau. It's open Thursday from 8 pm to 2 am, Friday 8 pm to 4 am (the most popular night) and Saturday from 8 to 11.45 pm. The minimum age is 18 years; admission is T$3/2 for men/women. The *Garden Bay Village Resort* also has a disco on Friday and Saturday nights, with the same admission prices (but free for guests).

Videos The Paradise International Hotel shows videos nightly at 8.30 pm, unless it's having a floor show or other entertainment. Enquire at the front desk and state your preferred videos. Admission is free for hotel guests, T$2 for everyone else.

Port of Refuge Yacht Club Friday Night Fun Races The Port of Refuge Yacht Club is based at 'Ana's Cafe. The only requirements for membership are arrival in Tonga on a yacht or launch (the *'Olovaha* doesn't count!) and payment of a registration fee of T$5, which you'll soon get back in discounts.

Each Friday at around 4 pm, a yacht race starts from 'Ana's Cafe. If you're a non-member, come down to the cafe anyway – there's a good chance someone will be looking for extra crew for the race. Every racer wins some kind of a prize. The grand prize goes not to the winner, however, but to someone among the losers whose name is pulled out of a hat! It's a fun and casual race.

Things to Buy
Neiafu has several good handicraft shops selling products made from tapa and pandanus (fans, mats, trays, wall hangings, cards), bone and shell jewellery and carvings, etc. The Langafonua Handicrafts Shop beside the Tonga Visitors' Bureau is a women's cooperative handicrafts shop. FIMCO Handicrafts is on the main road, opposite the Tonga Visitors' Bureau. DM Guttenbeil is opposite the Bank of Tonga, and Vava'u Handicrafts is beside the post office.

Fa Sea Jewellery, on the main road opposite Sunsail and The Moorings, has a large selection of carvings in bone, black coral, shells and wood, plus dolls, mats and tapa.

Leonati Fakatava carves bone, whalebone, whales' and pigs' teeth, etc. His shop is on the inland side of the main road about 250m south of the Paradise International Hotel.

Tailor-made clothing is available at Olga's (☎ 70-064) near the harbour. She can complete a suit or dress for you in just a couple of days. There's also the Faka-'anaua-Ki-Houmelei tailor shop, about 150m south of the Paradise International Hotel.

Another locally made product is the Super Clean Washing Powder made by Alexio Huni. Stop by the factory in Naufahu Rd, Neiafu and have a look! Don't forget the ice cream factory, too, Vava'u Ice Product *(VIP)*, in the same block.

For duty-free shopping, the Leiola Duty-Free Shop is beside the Tonga Visitors' Bureau.

Getting There & Away

Air Vava'u's Lupepau'u airport is on the north side of the island, about a 15-minute drive from Neiafu. Royal Tongan Airlines operates daily flights between Vava'u and Tongatapu, twice-a-week flights between Vava'u and Ha'apai, and a weekly international flight connecting Tongatapu, Vava'u and Nadi (Fiji). Samoa Air flies from Pago Pago (American Samoa) to Vava'u and return, twice a week. See Getting There & Away for information on international flights, and the Getting Around chapter for details on domestic flights.

The Royal Tongan Airlines office (☎ 70-149, 70-688) is on Fatafehi Rd, in the centre of town. The agent for Samoa Air (☎ 70-080) is the SF Paea & Sons department store, which is opposite the Tonga Visitors' Bureau.

Boat Two scheduled ferries travel each week between Tongatapu and Vava'u. See the Getting Around chapter for schedules and fares. The ferry offices are at Neiafu's main wharf.

Getting Around

To/From the Airport The Paradise International Hotel bus meets all incoming flights and provides free transport for hotel guests, T$4 per person for everyone else. Several other places to stay will provide airport transport as long as you let them know you're coming. Taxis charge T$8 between the airport and Neiafu, T$12 between the airport and the Tongan Beach Resort.

Bus Buses leave from the Sailoame Market terminal in Neiafu for most parts of Vava'u. There are buses to Pangaimotu, Tu'anekivale, Holonga and Leimatua. The buses do not run according to any strict schedule but leave when they accumulate enough passengers. These buses often come from the villages to town in the early morning and go back in the afternoon, making it difficult for travellers staying in town to use the buses for day trips to the villages.

Car & Motorcycle Five Star (☎ 70-135) in Neiafu rents cars for T$50 and T$60 a day. Liviela Taxi (☎ 70-240) in Neiafu charges T$70 per day, with discounts for longer periods. No insurance is available and there's a lot of red tape involved in case of an accident, so don't have one.

The Hilltop Guesthouse (see Places to Stay) rents motorcycles to guests and nonguests alike. A small Suzuki 50, for one person, costs T$15/20 for a half/full day. For two people, a Suzuki 100 or Yamaha 125 is T$20/25 for a half/full day.

Taxi Taxi companies in Neiafu include *Leopote* (☎ 70-136), *Liviela* (☎ 70-240), *Hamana* (☎ 70-257, 70-157), *Falepiu* (☎ 70-671) and *Lopaukamea* (☎ 70-153). Lopaukamea is open 24 hours; Liviela is open from 7 am until midnight. The maximum rate is T$1.50 for trips around Neiafu, T$7 between Neiafu and the Tongan Beach Resort, T$6 from Neiafu to 'Ano and Hinakauea beaches and T$8 between Neiafu and the airport.

Bicycle Although Vava'u is a hilly island, it's still fairly manageable by bicycle and if you're on a budget, it's an inexpensive way to tour the main island as well as Pangaimotu and 'Utungake, to which Vava'u is linked by causeways. The Vava'u Guest House rents bicycles for T$10 per day to guests and nonguests alike.

Horse Horses may be hired on a private basis; the tourist office or your accommodation can probably put you in touch with someone with a horse. Expect to pay about T$10 per day, but beginners should be warned there are no saddles available and most of the horses are barely tamed. They also seem to have minds of their own and do know what low-hanging branches are for.

Boat Several commercial charters operate in Vava'u; the Tonga Visitors' Bureau keeps a current list. See the Activities and Organised Tours sections of this chapter.

It's possible to arrange a fishing trip by talking to a boat owner. Trips to outer islands can also be arranged with yachties who might like to pick up a spare set of hands while cruising around the islands. To make connections, either post a notice on bulletin boards (try the Bounty Bar, 'Ana's Cafe, the Neiafu Club and the Paradise International Hotel) or make your presence and your wishes conspicuous around the town and the anchorage.

For straight transport to outer islands, ask around at the petrol pump on the Neiafu wharf. You'll probably be able to strike a bargain with someone who's going your way. All offshore island resorts provide boat transport, for a fee.

Kayak The Friendly Islands Kayak Company offers guided sea kayak tours around the Vava'u and Ha'apai Groups (see Kayaking). Otherwise, kayaks can be rented at the Paradise International Hotel for T$10/20 per half/full day; pay and get paddles at the bar.

Around Vava'u

Vava'u is a different world once you're outside Neiafu. Not that Neiafu is bustling, but the rest of the island is just a tranquil jumble of small villages, plantations and true bush.

In most of the villages a passing vehicle is noteworthy, and the visit of a foreigner is the event of the week. Travellers will find that the Vava'u people become warmer and more welcoming in direct proportion to their distance from the tourist centre of Neiafu. Vava'u island is full of beautiful and interesting features, most of them quite different from those of the outer islands of the Vava'u Group.

The easiest way to get around is by rental car, motorbike or guided tour but, with a bit of effort, individuals can get a fairly good idea of what there is to see on bicycle, by public transport, or on foot.

If you're travelling around the island (especially by rental car), it might prove helpful to divide your journey into two parts, east and west, because the road system lends itself to this and because a full day is required to 'do' each half.

WESTERN VAVA'U
Sia Ko Kafoa
Vaipua Inlet, which nearly bisects the island, separates the Neiafu area from western Vava'u. The inlet was used by ancient Polynesian canoes en route to the fort complex at the village of Feletoa, which means 'many brave warriors'.

The two sides of the island are connected by a causeway. On the western shore are the twin hills of Lei'ulu and Sia Ko Kafoa. Historically, this area has served as a burial ground, an 'esi or resting site, a lookout and a fortification. It can be comfortably visited from Neiafu in a morning or afternoon or as part of a road tour of the western end of the island.

From Neiafu, follow the road north past the Prince Wellington Ngu hospital, and cross over the causeway spanning Vaipua Islet. The road then turns right and climbs up to the village of Taoa (spear). The name was given by the 14th Tu'i Kanokupolu, the cruel Tuku'aho, in the late 1700s. Tuku'aho sought refuge in Taoa from a murder conspiracy plotted by Finau 'Ulukalala II. In 1799, he returned to Tongatapu, where he was executed by Vava'u assassins.

THE VAVA'U GROUP

Lei'ulu, the hill behind Taoa, is used as a burial ground. Walk downhill along the coral road behind Lei'ulu hill; when the road begins to angle right on an uphill slope, about 10 minutes from the village, you'll see the track to the summit of 128m-high Sia Ko Kafoa turning uphill to the left.

On the summit is an *'esi*, a mound used as a rest area by chiefs and nobles and a place where young virgins were presented to amorous chiefs. Originally, this particular 'esi, which measures 3m in height and 30m or so in diameter at its base, was known as Matangavaka (sight of boats).

After climbing the mound, turn left along the ridge at the base and follow the track down to the shore at the village of Vaimalo (thanks for water), before crossing back to Mata'ihoi.

Lake 'Ano

This freshwater lake at the extreme western end of the island is an eerie sort of place, accessible only by a steep, muddy climb down into its crater from the friendly village of Longomapu. If approaching it via the main road from the north, turn left at the intersection in the village and follow that road for several hundred metres. Look carefully for a track turning off to the right and leading away downhill. Under optimum conditions, the track will take you to the shore of the lake in about 10 minutes, but if there has been rain it will be more difficult. The lake is good for a refreshing swim or a bit of fishing for edible *lapila*.

Ngofe Marsh

Although Ngofe Marsh isn't a must-see, it's a beautiful expanse of reeds and wetlands in a bowl of surrounding hills. Take the main road south-east from Longomapu and turn right at the first opportunity. This rough road leads around the marsh before rejoining the circuit around Lake 'Ano. It should only be attempted in a 4WD vehicle.

Mt Mo'ungalafa

With a little effort you can climb 300m Mt Mo'ungalafa, the highest point on Vava'u

island, via a track just south of Longomapu. The spectacular view from the top takes in all of Vava'u and is well worth the effort.

Toafa Lookout

On a clear day, the Toafa Lookout cliff, north-west of Longomapu, affords a view all the way to the volcanic island of Late, providing a contrast to the more down-to-sea-level vistas on the island's south coast.

'Utula'aina Point

'Utula'aina Point provides perhaps the most spectacular view on Vava'u island and should not be missed. To get there, head north from Holonga village until you see a track cutting off sharply to the right and heading downhill. The track leads straight into the scrub; if you're in a vehicle, the parking spot is a few metres further on the right.

At this point you have three choices, but since all three can be easily accommodated in an hour or two, there's no pressure to make the right decision. The track to the right leads down into a small gully and back up the other side. After walking for less than 10 minutes, you'll see a stone burial mound on your left and an interesting tree beyond. From here, there's a fairly good view of the north coast. It's even better if you're game enough to climb the tree.

Now return to the fork in the road. If you follow the track straight ahead for 50m or so from the intersection, past the parking area, you'll notice a very faint and very steep trail cutting off to the right. Follow it downhill for about 10 minutes until it issues out onto what must be the loveliest beach on Vava'u island. More than likely, you'll have it all to yourself. A shallow shelf of coral makes it of little interest for swimming, but you can still potter around with a snorkel and the beach serves well as a sunning and picnicking spot. While you're in the water, watch your belongings closely; youths from Holonga village sometimes follow tourists to the beach and help themselves when no one is looking.

The third option is to follow the track

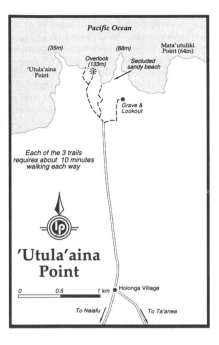

Pacific Ocean

(35m)   (68m)   Mata'utuliki
                  Point (64m)
    Overlook
    (133m)   Secluded
'Utula'aina ⚹   sandy beach
Point

    ● Grave &
    Lookout

Each of the 3 trails
requires about 10 minutes
walking each way

'Utula'aina
Point

0   0.5   1 km ● Holonga Village

To Neiafu   To Ta'anea

straight ahead from the intersection. It curves around to the left a bit and emerges into a grassy open area after 10 to 15 minutes. Bear right through the bushes, climb the short grassy knoll and you'll emerge on 'Utula'aina Point, surrounded by steep cliffs above a turbulent sea. No matter how often you visit this spot, the view and the mood will always be different. On an exceptionally clear day, you can see the volcanic outliers of Toku and Fonualei, the only land between Vava'u and the distant Niuas. Watch for whales in the surf below from July to November.

Be sure to carry water on these short walks. The sun can be intense and there's no place to buy drinks or snacks.

Feletoa

The small village of Feletoa between Neiafu and Holonga is the site of a fortification constructed in 1808 to resist the conquest of Vava'u by Finau 'Ulukalala II. At the time, Feletoa served as the government centre of the entire Vava'u Group because it was easily accessed by canoes travelling up Vaipua Inlet. The fortification is surrounded by clearly visible trenches or moats, which twice cross the main road. The mound with the large water tank is thought to have been used as a lookout.

Between Feletoa and the nearby village of Mataika, on the south side of the road, is a burial site containing the langi tomb of the ubiquitous Finau 'Ulukalala II. Finau died of what appears to have been internal haemorrhaging after an animated wrestling contest in Neiafu. This was in spite of the sacrifice of a young Neiafu child in an attempt to appease the greater powers of the day. The chief's body was carried by mourners to Feletoa for burial.

Matakiniua Point

Thanks to the high grasses and mud, the beautiful area of high cliffs north of the airport is best accessed on foot in dry weather, although under optimum conditions, it could be negotiated in a sturdy 4WD vehicle. The loop trip from Leimatu'a village to the coast, westward along the cliffs and back to Leimatu'a would require at least a half day on foot.

Old Airport

The old airport, deemed too dangerous to accommodate aircraft due to updrafts and odd air currents around the cliffs, is a beautiful spot with a fine view.

EASTERN VAVA'U
Makave

Most of your touring on the eastern half of Vava'u island will involve beach-hopping, and this beach is one of the most interesting. It's easily accessed on foot from Neiafu along the shore of the Old Harbour. Walk past the entrance to Hala Tafengatoto (see Neiafu earlier in this chapter) and follow the shore east towards Makave village, the legendary home of a mysterious dark, giant people.

After an hour's walk from Neiafu, you'll reach the beach below Makave village where you'll find an ancient canoe-mooring site beside an obtrusive rock and cave. Farther east are the springs of Matalave, which are ideal for a freshwater bathe.

The name Makave (take a stone) refers to the ancient custom of piling a stone on Kilikilitefua Wall upon the birth of a child. To visit this wall, follow the faint track leading back to the road from the end of the beach. Turn south here and continue along the peninsula until you reach a small rise. At this point the remains of the stone wall, now less than 1m high, can be seen stretching nearly 100m across the peninsula. It once reached a height of 1.5m, but bits of it were removed for use in concrete cisterns.

A second associated legend has it that the peninsula stretching south from Makave was once the island of 'Utuatea. It is believed that the village and the island were tired of being responsible for two separate tax assessments, so they decided to join forces. Under the direction of a clever chief named Tu'i'afitu, the villagers constructed a 150m-wide isthmus to connect the two areas in a single night. As yet, this story has not been confirmed by archaeologists.

Toula & Veimumuni Cave

Near the southern point of Vava'u island is Toula village. When you reach the village, turn left (east) and follow the path uphill and past a cemetery. As you begin to descend to the beach, you'll see Veimumuni Cave in the bluff. Inside is a wonderful freshwater spring and swimming hole, which is often full of local children.

Several legends are associated with this cave, all of which have as their main character a beautiful spirit maiden who appeared on the rock before the cave and teased mortal men with her beauty. But the teasing didn't stop there; she also tempted every passing soul with the contents of the mysterious cave which she guarded.

One version has her finally being outwitted by a *tea* (albino) woman, who became the first mortal to taste the water inside the cave before being tickled into submission by a pair of tevolo, or devil spirits. In reference to this story, the wells around Toula are called *vai 'ene* (tickling water). Another version of the tale has her being tricked into the clutches of an amorous young gardener. Fortunately for modern folk, both stories end in universal access to the cave's clear and refreshing waters.

From the cave, walk north along the shore to a series of further caves, which were used by Toula villagers to bury enemies from other villages. At low tide, the tidal pools hold a variety of shells. This pleasant stretch of shoreline also invites you to lie back and read a book on a hot afternoon.

Other Beaches

At the easternmost end of the island, near the village of Tu'anekivale, are a couple of pleasant beaches, better for strolling or sunbathing than for swimming or snorkelling.

The nicest is Keitahi Beach, about 2km east of the road between Ha'alaufuli and Tu'anekivale. Currents are rather dangerous at high tide, but strong snorkellers will find some interest in the large tidepools about 100m offshore. At low tide, anyone with proper footwear can wander out across the reef.

'Eme'io Beach is reached by taking the left fork from Tu'anekivale and continuing about 2km to the shore. It's a peaceful and scenic area to explore on foot but it's not good for swimming.

Farther south across the causeways to 'Uataloa and Koloa islands are a few scattered beaches, but of greater interest are the mangroves in the waterways around this swampy area.

Other Islands

PANGAIMOTU

Just across the scenic causeway from Toula village is Pangaimotu (royal island), so called because it belongs to part of the royal estate. The main village of Pangai was the home of the chief Vuna, whom Will Mariner discusses in some detail in his book. Vuna was one of the infamous 'handsome men' of Tonga, whose insatiable lust for young virgins and irresistibility to women was said to have seriously disrupted many lives.

'Ano, Hinakauea & Lisa Beaches

'Ano, Hinakauea and Lisa beaches, near the south end of Pangaimotu, are the sites of weekly Tongan feasts put on for tourists. For details, see Places to Eat.

'Ano and Hinakauea are actually two different parts of the same amazingly beautiful beach, with sheltered turquoise water, emerald vegetation, good snorkelling and a safe anchorage (No 11). Although Vava'u's best snorkelling is on the offshore islands and reefs, this is probably one of the best snorkelling spots accessible from Neiafu by land. A taxi from Neiafu costs T$6.

The *Rove Hinakauea Beach Guest House* on Hinakauea Beach is a fine place to stay; see Places to Stay – Out of Town.

From Hinakauea Beach you can cross over to Tapana island in a dinghy for T$5 per person.

Near the southern point of Pangaimotu, there was once a large, old whale-oil pot which light-hearted yachties referred to as a 'missionary cooking pot', but it seems to have disappeared.

Tavalau Beach

Tavalau Beach is a five-minute scenic walk north from the eastern end of the 'Utungake Causeway.

'Utulei

The village of 'Utulei lies across the Port of Refuge from Neiafu's Kilikili Pier. It was here that writer and long-time resident of the island Patricia Ledyard Matheson set her autobiographical accounts of island life *Friendly Isles: A Tale of Tonga* and *'Utulei, My Tongan Home*. You can kayak across the harbour from Neiafu, or park at the top of the hill and walk down to the village.

Near the turn-off to 'Utulei, a quarry has left a massive gash in the hillside. There is a beautiful view across the Port of Refuge from the top of this hill.

Getting There & Away

Public buses to Pangaimotu depart from Sailoame Market terminal in Neiafu. It's also easy to hitchhike, go by taxi or boat from Neiafu.

LOTUMA

Tongans believe that the tiny island of Lotuma, now a Tongan Defence Forces naval base, once served as the summit of truncated Mt Talau across the harbour. At some point in the dim and distant past, the summit was stolen and dumped into the water by a thieving Samoan devil. When you've seen the island, the connection will be obvious. Note that Lotuma is off-limits to non-military personnel.

'UTUNGAKE & MALA

'Utungake island is long and thin and connected by causeway to Pangaimotu. Its main attraction is the Tongan Beach Resort (see Places to Stay – out of town), on a lovely beach with a pleasant beachside restaurant and bar. Another pleasant beach is near the southern tip of 'Utungake.

The small island of Mala, just south of 'Utungake, has a good swimming and snorkelling beach but a strong current flows between these two islands and Kapa further south. Beware also of a legendary cannibal god who reputedly lives on Mala and is said to capture and devour passing boaters.

SOUTHERN VAVA'U ISLANDS
Hunga

The major westernmost island of the Vava'u Group offers excellent snorkelling. The large, placid lagoon, formed by Hunga and the neighbouring islands of Kalau and Fofoa looks like a big volcanic crater lake, with three openings that have let the sea in. This lagoon is a superb anchorage for cruising yachts (Anchorage No 13), although the entrance is rather tricky.

Club Hunga (☎/fax 70-611; VHF channel 16), Private Bag, Neiafu, is on the shore of the beautiful sheltered lagoon, at Anchorage 13. Affable owners Pete, a Kiwi yachtie, and his friendly Tongan wife Hapi (Tongavua), granddaughter of the village chief, will show you a good time while you're here. Hapi takes guests for a walk into the village, introducing you to Tongan customs, natural medicine and herbs, etc. They also do fishing trips, provide free snorkelling gear (excellent snorkelling spots are nearby), and take care of visiting yachts. The restaurant/bar features 'island nite' buffets with Tongan-style food, dancing and entertainment on Friday nights in season (May to November). Three rooms with shared bath are T$50/70 a single/double, rooms with private bath are T$95, and a two-bedroom house with kitchen, bath, sitting room etc is T$120/150/180 for two/four/six people. A meal package at the restaurant is available for T$35 per person per day.

Hunga also has a quiet, friendly village. Up on the cliffs just a five-minute walk behind the resort is a lookout point where you can often see humpback whales, in season (July to November).

There's also a peaceful village and some nice cliffs on Fofoa, immediately southwest of the main island.

Foe'ata & Foelifuka

The island of Foe'ata, immediately south of Hunga, offers glorious white beaches and good snorkelling in a secluded atmosphere. Anchorage No 14 is on the north side of Foelifuka, beside Foe'ata.

Nuapapu

Mariner's Cave Nuapapu is best known for the hidden cave at its northern end. It is now named Mariner's Cave after Will Mariner, who was apparently the first European to see it. It's interesting, however, that in his book he mistakenly placed the cave on Hunga island. This cave is one of Vava'u's most renowned tourist attractions and virtually every boat tour of the island includes it. On windy days, access will be difficult, thanks to boiling surf that can beat swimmers senseless as it pounds against the rock.

Inside the cave you'll experience a strange atmospheric phenomenon. Pacific swells surging through the entrance compress trapped air and when the sea recedes every few seconds, the moisture condenses into a heavy fog, the result of water vapour cooling as it expands. As soon as another wave enters the opening, the fog instantly vanishes.

Coral Gardens Between the southern end of Nuapapu and the adjoining island of Vaka'eitu are the Coral Gardens, which once offered some of the best snorkelling in the Vava'u Group. In 1990 they were badly damaged by Cyclone Kina, but they are now being visited again. At low tide you can walk between the two islands.

Kitu

Odd little Kitu is what's commonly known as a 'flowerpot island'. It's covered with a healthy crop of vegetation, but this raised island overhangs the sea on all sides, making a sea landing impossible.

Vaka'eitu

Vaka'eitu was once owned by the Wolfgramm family, some of Vava'u's earliest German settlers. More recently, the land has been divided into individual *'apis* (plantations). There's no village on Vaka'eitu, but the *Popao Village Resort* (☎/fax 70-308; popao@candw.to, popao@hotmail.com) hugs the jungle-clad hillside above Anchorage 16, on the otherwise uninhabited island. This backpackers' resort emphasises ecotourism, local style. The place is very rustic, with coconut-leaf fales and no electricity. Accommodation is in budget fales (T$15/25 a single/double), standard fales (T$30), standard view fales (T$40) or a view fale with private bath (T$50). No cooking facilities are available for guests, but meals are served in the restaurant (breakfast T$6, dinner T$14 or T$17) or in the Lighthouse

****

Mariner's Cave

Will Mariner writes that he was first taken to this hidden cave on Nuapapu island by Finau 'Ulukalala II.

Mariner was puzzled when he saw several chiefs dive into the water but fail to return to the surface. He was then instructed to follow their example and was guided into a 3m-long channel just a metre or so below the surface.

He emerged in a dim cathedral-like cavern, and, after returning to the canoe for a torch, he observed that it was about 14m high and 14m wide, with narrow channels branching off into darkness all around.

As they drank kava on a rock platform inside, one of the chiefs related this story:

A tyrannical governor of Vava'u learned of a conspiracy against him and ordered the primary conspirator drowned and all his family killed. The conspirator's beautiful daughter, who was betrothed to a young chief, was rescued by another chief, who also had amorous intentions. To prevent her imminent demise, he spirited her away into a secret cavern and visited her daily, bringing gifts of food, clothing, coconuts and oils for her skin. His ministrations were so sincere that, eventually, he won her heart as well as her gratitude.

Realising that he couldn't just bring her out of the cavern, he formulated an elaborate plan, which involved a secret voyage to Fiji with some underling chiefs and their wives. When they inquired why he would attempt such a trip without a Tongan wife, he replied that he would probably find one along the way. True to his word, he stopped the canoes before the bare rock above the cave entrance, dived into the water and emerged a few minutes later with the girl, whom his companions surmised to be a goddess until they recognised her as the daughter of the condemned conspirator. They all went off to Fiji, only returning to Vava'u two years later after hearing of the death of the tyrant governor.

And they all lived happily ever after.

****

Cafe run by Joe the Austrian baker from Salzburg. Round-trip transfers from Neiafu cost T$56 per person for stays of less than a week, T$34 per person for stays of more than a week; the boat trip takes 40 minutes. Activities on the island include snorkelling and bushwalking and other activities can be arranged. Accommodation and meals must be booked in advance. The Friendly Islands Kayak Company has a camp on the island.

If you're wondering where that photo which appears on all the Vava'u travel posters and brochures was taken, glance south-west toward the bight of Vaka'eitu.

Kapa

Swallows' Cave The main attraction of Kapa island is beautiful Swallows' Cave ('Anapekepeka), which perforates a cliff on the west side of its northern end. The cave is in fact inhabited not by swallows but by hundreds of swiftlets *(Collocalia spodiopygia)* that flit about in the dim light and nest in the darkness of the cave's upper reaches. Since the floor of the cave is up to 80m below the surface of the water, you'll need access to a dinghy, kayak or small boat to get inside. Small-boat island tours often stop here.

Despite the cave's depth, visibility is an incredible 50m. Snorkellers will be amazed at the colour and clarity of the water and swimming may well give you the sensation of weightlessness. If you're on a tour, stipulate in advance that you wish to snorkel in the cave during the tour or you'll just get a quick trip through. The best time to snorkel here is in late afternoon when the slanting sunlight lights up the water.

Upon entering the cave, you'll see Bell

THE VAVA'U GROUP

Swiftlets in Swallows' Cave

The birds nesting in the cave are actually not swallows, but white-rumped swiftlets, a bird common to the region and to the islands of Tonga (see D Watling's *Birds of Fiji, Tonga & Samoa*). The Tongan name for these birds is *pekepeka* and they are closely related to the swiftlets that build nests which are harvested in Southeast Asia and used in 'birds nest soup' (the white-nest and black-nest swiftlets, *Aerodramus fuciphagus* and *Aerodramus maximus)*. Luckily, the fibre content of white-rumped swiftlet nests is much higher than that of their south-east Asian relatives and therefore the nests found in Swallow's Cave are not in culinary demand.

During two trips to Swallow's Cave and other small caves in the Vava'u Group, I estimated 3000 to 4000 nests were present on the ceiling of the grotto.

David G Roseneau, USA

Rock hanging down on your left. When it is struck with a solid object, the rock emits melodic vibrations. Deeper in the cave, you'll see a shaft of light shining through a hole in the ceiling; from there, you can follow a rocky trail into the adjoining dry cave. At the rear of Swallows' Cave is a solid deposit of bird guano, which has decomposed into solid soil.

Port Mourelle Port Mourelle, on the protected western bay of Kapa island, was the original landing site of the Spaniard Don Francisco Antonio Mourelle, the first European to visit Vava'u. It was here that he took on water from the springs of the swamp near Falevai (house of water). A track from Port Mourelle leads north and south along the spine of the island. If you'd like to camp, ask permission in any of the island's three villages, Kapa, 'Otea and Falevai.

Nuku

Thanks to its lovely white beach, the tiny uninhabited island of Nuku, off Kapa, once served as the standard lunch stop on nearly all the boat tours of Vava'u – as well as being a favoured spot for numerous official functions, celebrations and private parties. There's excellent snorkelling on the south and east sides of the island – the currents are negligible, so marginal swimmers

shouldn't have problems.

Nuku's popularity is waning, however, due to the habit of locals who paddle over from Kapa to collect T$1 from anyone who stops there. This is the only beach in Tonga where anyone will ask you for money to use it. It isn't much to pay to enjoy such a beautiful place but if it bothers you, they don't collect on Sunday!

Taunga, Ngau & Pau

To enjoy an idyllic beach on a sporadically inhabited island, try the inviting islands of Ngau and Taunga, just south of Kapa.

These islands, owned by the Minister of Police, offer fine snorkelling, idyllic beaches and four good anchorages. At low tide, Ngau and Ta'unga are connected by a fine sandy beach. Ngau is in turn connected to the uninhabited island of Pau by a slender ribbon of sand which is exposed except at the turn of high tide. There's a superb anchorage (No 24) in the bight of Ngau on the eastern shore.

Ta'uta & Lekeleka

Off the east coast of Ta'unga, the scarred red island of Ta'uta appears to be a mini environmental disaster in the making. Although it has a small beach on the southern end, it couldn't be less inviting.

Ta'uta's tiny neighbour to the south, Lekeleka, is marginally better, with a lovely

---

'The Fo'ui Did It'

Back in the mists of time, a Tongan chief called Tele'a came to live on 'Euakafa because he considered Vava'u the most beautiful part of the kingdom. He took a lovely girl, Talafaiva, as his third wife and also accepted her dowry, which consisted of 100 other attractive girls. The whole family set up housekeeping on the plateau of little 'Euakafa.

Outside the royal residence grew a *fo'ui* tree, which Talafaiva wanted chopped down. However, Tele'a refused to do so. One day, while Tele'a was out fishing, Lepuha, one of Tonga's irresistible 'handsome men', arrived to 'conquer' the king's bride. By climbing the fo'ui tree, he was able to avoid the royal guard and enter the castle in order to seduce the queen. All would have been well had he not tattooed his signature mark on the queen's belly.

When Tele'a saw the mark he was outraged, but all the queen could do was blame the tree that she'd wanted to destroy in the first place. 'The fo'ui did it,' she said, and the fo'ui has served as a Tongan scapegoat ever since.

Tele'a ordered his wife beaten for her indiscretion, but in doing so his servant inadvertently killed her. The chief built her a tomb on the summit of 'Euakafa, which can still be visited, although a body has never been found. Some claim that it was stolen by Lepuha. The fo'ui, by the way, has gone as well.

---

sandy beach on the western side. The rest of the island is an elevated coconut plantation. There's lots of shallow coral around the landing site so approach carefully.

'Eue'iki

The uninhabited raised island of 'Eue'iki has easy boat access to the beach, several good camping sites and no coral near the shore, making it ideal for swimming but not so great for snorkelling. The beach surrounding 'Eue'iki has the finest and brightest white sand in Tonga – with the feel and texture of confectioners' sugar!

'Euakafa

On its plateau, the relatively small island of 'Euakafa reaches an altitude of nearly 100m and offers hiking, swimming and snorkelling.

Mounu, 'Ovalau & 'Ovaka

Just a short distance south-east of Vaka'eitu are the islands of Mounu and 'Ovalau, two more of those idyllic sunning, snorkelling, swimming and lazing-on-the-beach sort of places that travellers dream of finding.

Remarkably, Allan and Lyn Bowe, who operate the Bounty Bar in Neiafu and Whale Watch Vava'u, were able to do it. Mounu Island is now the home of the beautiful *Mounu Island Resort* (☎/fax 70-747; Private Bag, Neiafu; mounu@candw.to; VHF channel 77). The beachfront fales, each with private bath, are T$125 per night; a meal plan at the restaurant is T$60 per day. There's a minimum stay of three nights unless agreed beforehand; children under 12 are not accepted.

You can walk completely around Mounu in a few minutes and there's good snorkelling. Nearby, the larger island 'Ovaka is also pleasant, but it doesn't hold a candle to its neighbours.

Fonua'unga

On the south-eastern side of the Vava'u Group, Fonua'unga is a small, barren island peeking above the sea. Landing is thwarted by the high surf which pounds the surrounding reef. But there's little shade (the island has only three trees) and you probably wouldn't want to land, anyway!

Maninita

The tiny wooded island of Maninita in the

extreme south of the Vava'u Group is about as secluded as it's possible to get. The terraced coral reef on the approach forms lovely tidepools which trap marine life at low tide. The forests in the island's centre are pristine and peaceful, home to many birds all year round, and snorkelling is optimum. The anchorage (No 31) is on the west side of the island.

EASTERN VAVA'U ISLANDS
Transport to the eastern islands is much shorter and easier if you start from Neiafu's Old Harbour. If you start from the Port of Refuge you have to go all the way around Pangaimotu, 'Utungake and Tapana islands, and it's a long trip. Vake Tapa'atoutai, who lives on 'Ofu and sporadically operates Lekeleka Tours, sometimes takes tours to 'Ofu and the other eastern islands (see Boat Tours).

'Ofu
This friendly island south-east of the main island offers good shell hunting and is the primary habitat of the prized *'ofu* shell. Sellers will maintain that these shells are found on no other island but, in fact, they exist in limited quantities throughout the Vava'u Group. People ask about T$5 for a shell in good condition but for environmental reasons, please help squash the market for these endangered animals by resisting the temptation to buy.

The school at 'Ofu has a visitors' register and the hospitality of the people is legendary. They are all too prepared to pass out food and shell necklaces to visitors, so be prepared with some simple reciprocal gifts or you'll wind up feeling like a heel! It's a pleasant walk from the settlement around to the southern end of the island and there's a good dive site on the reef wall, about 200m south of the beach.

Kenutu, Lolo & 'Umuna
The small island of Kenutu, just east of 'Ofu, has superb beaches and the coral patches south of the island offer magnificent snorkelling and diving. The land itself is heavily wooded but there's a well defined trail across it to steep cliffs on the eastern coast. Kenutu has no village but it does have the *Kenutu Island Resort* at the Berlin Bar, Anchorage 30. This has 'dollhouses' (small fales) for T$50 and a treehouse with private bath for T$75, on a beautiful white-sand beach. It's operated by a German, Joanna, and her Tongan husband Mosese; the restaurant is known for its good, fresh seafood and curries. Contact them on VHF channel 16, through the Tonga Visitors' Bureau or the Bounty Bar. Transfers cost T$20, from Neiafu's Old Harbour.

The reef between Kenutu and Lolo island, immediately south, is very dramatic and shouldn't be missed. On the eastern side the waves crash and boil, while the crystalline waters on the western shore are calm.

In the centre of 'Umuna, the uninhabited island just north of Kenutu, is a large cave containing a freshwater pool. Both Lolo and 'Umuna are accessible from Kenutu by crossing the reef on foot at low tide.

OUTLYING VOLCANIC ISLANDS
Late
Late consists of a volcanic crater 555m high which has been dormant since 1854. On clear days, its distinctive silhouette is visible from the mainland. Its wooded 15 sq km are now uninhabited. Late was evacuated by King George I when he realised that some of the outer areas of his kingdom were being ravaged by blackbirders (South American slave traders). The people of this island were resettled in Hunga beside the lagoon.

In the 1990s, Late became the site of another resettlement project, but this time in the opposite direction. The Tongan Wildlife Centre Bird Park on Tongatapu is attempting to transfer breeding pairs of the endangered Niuafo'ou megapode to Late from its native Niuafo'ou, where habitat loss and human predation have pushed it to the verge of extinction. It is hoped that the warm volcanic soil, similar to that on the birds' home island, will prove compatible with their unusual incubation methods. For further information on this species, see the Niuas chapter.

Late'iki

Late'iki first emerged in 1858 but was gone by 1898, breaking the surface between Late and the immense cone of Kao (Ha'apai). The island was next seen on 12 December 1967, when it made a 'pulsing glow on the horizon' during a particularly violent eruption. Within a week it had reached an altitude of 18m, but subsequently went down again. In May 1979, the island Tongans nicknamed Metis Shoal began spewing and erupting.

On 7 July 1979, the king decided to take action. He sailed to the site and looked on as his son planted the Tongan flag on the new land and christened it Late'iki, which means 'little Late'. Who knows how long it will stick around this time!

Fonualei

Fonualei, 64km north-west of the main island of Vava'u, can be seen from the northern cliffs of that island on a clear day. In 1846 the island erupted, covering parts of the main island with volcanic ash. This is the island Mourelle named Amargura ('bitterness') when he discovered it was barren and wouldn't provide him and his crew with much-needed and long-awaited supplies.

The best way to have a look at Fonualei is to sail between Neiafu and the Niuas. The ferries pass within a couple of kilometres of its eastern coast.

Toku

The old, worn volcanic island of Toku, near Fonualei, was evacuated during the black-birding scare of the 1860s. Its inhabitants resettled in 'Utulei village on Pangaimotu, across the Port of Refuge from Neiafu. Toku remains uninhabited.

THE VAVA'U GROUP

The Niuas

The remote Niuas (meaning 'rich in coconuts') consist of three small volcanic
islands in the extreme northern reaches of
Tonga, occupying a total land area of only
about 70 sq km.

Tongan tradition remains very much
alive in the Niuas. Many of the inhabitants
still live in traditional thatched Tongan
fales, and Niuatoputapu and Niuafo'ou are
where the highest quality white mats in
Tonga are made.

As in the Ha'apai Group, the solitude of
their environment has given the people a
decidedly mellow attitude towards their
world and visitors. It's highly unlikely that
anyone who goes to the trouble of visiting
the Niuas will feel that the effort went un-
rewarded.

NIUATOPUTAPU
• *area 18 sq km* • *population 1160*

The island of Niuatoputapu ('very sacred
coconut'), 240km north of Vava'u, is
shaped like a shoe with the toe pointed
north-east. Topographically, it resembles a
squashed sombrero, with a steep, narrow
130m-high ridge in the centre surrounded
by a coastal plain, most of which is plantation land.

The north coast is bound by a series of
reefs, but there is a passage through to
Falehau Wharf. Yachts anchor just north-
west of the wharf.

Niuatoputapu is ideal for walking. Most
of its interesting sights can be covered in
just two days. All three villages – Falehau,
Vaipoa and the administrative capital,
Hihifo – lie in a 5.5km line along the northern coast. They are all sleepy little places,
and the presence of visitors creates an excitement that can scarcely be contained,
especially during the months when there are
no yachts at anchor. Wherever you wander
on this island, you'll be greeted with a
smile. Every child you encounter will
demand to know your name, exhausting the

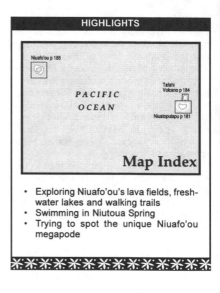

HIGHLIGHTS

Niuafo'ou p 185

PACIFIC
OCEAN

Tafahi
Volcano p 184

Niuatoputapu p 181

Map Index

• Exploring Niuafo'ou's lava fields, freshwater lakes and walking trails
• Swimming in Niutoua Spring
• Trying to spot the unique Niuafo'ou
megapode

sum total of his or her English vocabulary
(however charming, this does get a bit
tedious after a while).

Niuatoputapu has 14 churches. The two
major denominations are Wesleyan and
Catholic. Dress is conservative here – no
one should wear 'short shorts', although
long baggy ones are probably OK. Women
would do best to wear skirts below the knee.

There's good diving outside the reef, and
plenty of lobster, but no diving equipment
is available on the island.

To learn more about Niuatoputapu, especially its history and archaeology, look for
the book *Niuatoputapu: The Prehistory of a
Polynesian Chiefdom* by Patrick Kirch. The
island has many archaeological sites, but
most are overgrown and hard to find.

Information

The 'capital' of the Niuas, the sleepy village
of Hihifo on the north-west corner of Niuatoputapu boasts the police station, the post

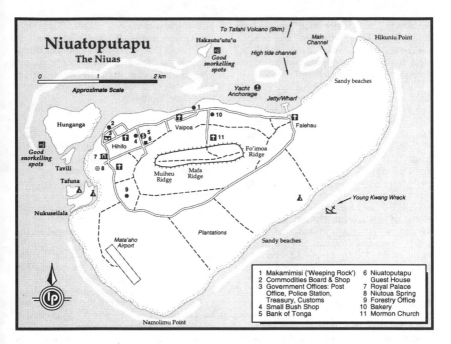

Niuatoputapu
The Niuas

To Tafahi Volcano (9km)
Hakautu'utu'u
Good snorkelling spots
High tide channel
Main Channel
Hikuniu Point

0   1   2 km
Approximate Scale

Sandy beaches

Yacht Anchorage
Jetty/Wharf

Hunganga

1
10
Vaipoa
Falehau

2
3
5
6
4
Hihifo
11
Fo'imoa Ridge

Good snorkelling spots

7
8
Muiheu Ridge
Mafa Ridge

Tavili

Tafuna

9

Young Kwang Wreck

Nukuseilala

Plantations
Sandy beaches

Mata'aho Airport

1 Makamimisi ('Weeping Rock')
2 Commodities Board & Shop
3 Government Offices: Post
   Office, Police Station,
   Treasury, Customs
4 Small Bush Shop
5 Bank of Tonga
6 Niuatoputapu
   Guest House
7 Royal Palace
8 Niutoua Spring
9 Forestry Office
10 Bakery
11 Mormon Church

Namolimu Point

office and a small cooperative store. Money can be changed at the Treasury. Telephone service commenced in 1998.

Niutoua Spring

The cool, sparkling pool of Niutoua Spring flows through a crack in the rock just west of Hihifo. It's full of friendly fish. A swim here will take the bite out of a typical sticky day in the Niuas.

The legend of the spring is equally charming, whichever version you hear – and there are at least four! One relates that the son of a former chief, Ma'atu, married a princess from Tongatapu but shortly thereafter, their marriage fell on the rocks and the princess began having outside dalliances. Polite society of the day, however, did not permit such indiscretions and the girl was sentenced to execution. Defiant to the end, as she was being carried away she spat on the ground, thereby forming the

spring. Apparently worried that the water would be cursed, chief Ma'atu placed a ban on fishing in the spring.

If you intend to bathe at Niutoua (which isn't banned), bear in mind that the spectacle of *palangis* swimming will quickly draw an audience. This show must be pretty good value for Tongans: kids will ditch school and adults will abandon their work in order to attend the free entertainment. If you don't want to upset the entire island, swim with a minimum of exposed skin – wear at least a T-shirt and long, baggy shorts.

Beaches

Niuatoputapu is surrounded by magnificent white beaches displaying a remarkable diversity. You could walk around the island on the 11km stretch of beach in about seven to eight hours.

The most beautiful beaches are on the north-west side of the main island and on

Hunganga, the offshore islet, especially in the channel between the two. The beaches north-east of the wharf are tranquil and ideal for cool early-morning walks before the sun begins to beat down.

Along the 'sole' of the island you can walk for hours on sandy, deserted beaches. The reef is close in, making swimming difficult, and the shallows are full of marine life, including thousands of sea cucumbers. Makamimisi (weeping rock), right on the coast, is the outlet to the sea for a spring that's a little way inland; when it's dry, you can pound on this rock with another rock and it will bring up fresh water.

Near the eastern end of the island is the wreck of the Korean fishing boat *Young Kwang*, which ran aground in the mid-1980s. There isn't much left of it, only metal scraps. Oddly enough, a ship of the same name sits on the reef on Aunu'u Island in American Samoa!

Western Waterways

Near Hihifo, a maze of shallow waterways wind between the intermittent islets of Nukuseilala, Tafuna, Tavili and Hunganga. At low tide, they form vast expanses of sand and leaning palms, and you can walk anywhere in the area by wading through a few centimetres of water. At high tide, the passages (especially between Niuatoputapu and Hunganga) are excellent for swimming. In the early morning you can watch locals net fishing near Hunganga; notice the line of sticks marking fish traps between Hunganga and the main island.

Ridge Walk

The central ridge, which comprises three smaller ridges, affords a grand view of the coastal plain and the multicoloured reefs of the lagoon. Reaching it will take a bit of effort. It's not a difficult climb, just heavily vegetated and, in places, nearly vertical.

The best way to go, it seems, is from the village of Vaipoa. Pass the bakery and the Mormon church and continue upwards through the maze of trails until you reach a very steep taro plantation. Scramble up as

best you can. Once you're about 20m above the highest taro plant, you're on the ridge.

You can follow the ridge in either direction; this will require some bushwalking. The eastern route entails a near-vertical rock climb of about 10m but it's easy to do, with clear footholds.

Hakautu'utu'u

The tiny islet of Hakautu'utu'u ('reef sticking above the water') is a pleasant spot for a picnic. Two good snorkelling spots are offshore from the islet's east side.

Places to Stay & Eat

If you're set up for camping, you'll find lots of excellent *campsites* around the convoluted waterways near Hihifo and on the beach along the south coast. If you want to camp on Hunganga island – you can walk to it at low tide – you must get permission from Sione, the guesthouse caretaker. As appealing as it may seem, any enthusiasm you may have for camping on the ridge will be considerably dampened by excessive wildlife of the buzzing variety.

For formal accommodation the choice is easy because there's only one, the friendly, clean and homey *Niuatoputapu Guest House* (☎ 85-021) at the south end of Hihifo, operated by Kalo & Sione Vea. There's no sign, but everyone knows where it is. Single/double rooms are T$18/22. You can also have meals there but you must book them in advance. Breakfast/lunch/dinner are T$4/5/10; coffee and a snack costs around T$3.

It's a good idea to bring your own food with you when you come to the island – remember you are going to a remote place where little food is available. Limited groceries may be purchased at several small shops. Bread is available at the bakeries in Hihifo and Vaipoa after about noon every day (including Sunday).

Getting There & Away

Air See the Getting Around chapter for information on flights to/from Niuatoputapu. Mata'aho airport is 2km south of Hihifo.

During the summer holiday season, roughly from early December to late January, lots of Tongans are travelling and the flights can be fully booked up. At other times of year, don't believe it if the Royal Tongan Airlines office clerks in Tongatapu or Vava'u tell you the planes going to Niuatoputapu are full. If that happens, your best bet is to ask to be put on the wait list, ascertain the departure time of the next flight and work to purchase your ticket at the airport just prior to departure. The obvious drawback to this system will be the return leg of the trip – it's important to book your return flight (or at least get on the wait list) *before* you fly up there. If the return flight you want appears to be booked up, there's still a chance of getting a seat by going to the airport at the time of the flight, but it's best to get a confirmed seat. Any trip to the Niuas should be handled with flexibility.

Boat Getting to Niuatoputapu by boat can be tricky but it's not impossible. A passenger freighter calls in from Vava'u about every two or three months, having come from Tongatapu via Ha'apai. The boat comes to both Niuatoputapu and Niuafo'ou, spending a day at each island (about eight hours, enough to load and unload cargo). The boat takes about 24 hours to get from Vava'u to Niuatoputapu, and it's about another 12 to 15 hours between Niuatoputapu and Niuafo'ou (either island may be visited first, depending on weather conditions). The trip to or from Nuku'alofa takes up to 2½ days.

Passenger freighters are scheduled to come to the Niuas eight to 10 times a year. Since sailings to the Niuas are unscheduled, you'll have to enquire at the Nuku'alofa shipping offices for information regarding sailings. The MV *'Olovaha* makes a point of calling in once at the end of the school term (early December) and again at the beginning of the new school term (mid-to-late January or early February). These are two difficult times to get on flights, due to the high volume of Tongans travelling at this time – but read the boxed text in the Getting

Around chapter before deciding to hop on a boat as an alternative.

Most visitors to Niuatoputapu arrive on private yachts – typically about three or four yachts arrive each week during cruising season, from around June to September. Since Niuatoputapu is a port of entry, many yachts stop over here en route from the Samoas to the Vava'u Group. During this season it shouldn't be too difficult to crew on for Niuatoputapu from 'Apia (Samoa) or Pago Pago (American Samoa). Around September and October there may be even more chances, as hurricane season begins on 1 November and the yachts are clearing out of the tropical cyclone belt, heading for calmer seas further south. The yachts head from Samoa to Niuatoputapu, then on to Vava'u, and then further south.

TAFAHI
• *area 3.42 sq km* • *population 150*
From the north coast of Niuatoputapu, the perfect cone of Tafahi dominates the view. If there were ever a search for an island fitting the description of the mythical Bali Hai, Tafahi would be a contender. One can't help gazing out across the water and wondering what it's like over there.

Tafahi, 9km north of Niuatoputapu, is an extinct volcanic cone 656m high, with a base area of 3.42 sq km. Vanilla and kava are grown in small quantities and the island supports a permanent population of 150 people. Some of Tonga's best kava comes from this island.

If you get a very early start, you can climb to the crater and down in a day. An intermittent trail connecting the two landing sites, on the west and south sides of the island, leads up the relatively gradual northern slope to within striking distance of the summit. At the crater on a clear day you can see the peak of Savaii's Mt Silisili (Samoa), which is 1850m high and over 200km distant. Carry food and plenty of water.

Getting There & Away
The northern landing is the one that is used, but it's difficult – you can only come in on

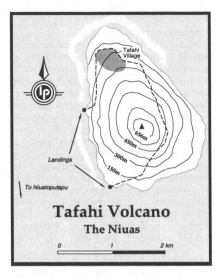

Tafahi Volcano
The Niuas

a wave, and only at high tide; same for leaving. If the tide is with you, you can go over from Niuatoputapu in the morning and go back in the afternoon. The boat ride from Niuatoputapu's Falehau wharf takes about an hour.

When Deanna was working on the first edition of this book in 1988, travellers could catch an informal lift between Falehau and Tafahi for around T$5; now people are asking as much as T$50 to T$80. A fair price is probably closer to T$30 or T$40, due to the high prices for diesel here. Be sure to arrange return transport in advance, especially if your conveyance away from Niuatoputapu is departing anytime in the near future!

Tafahi has a primary but not a secondary school, so some families bring students from Tafahi over to Niuatoputapu on Monday and back to Tafahi again on Friday. You might catch a ride cheaper if you can arrange to go with one of these boats.

NIUAFO'OU
• *area 50.27 sq km* • *population 735*
Niuafo'ou, also known as Tin Can Island, is

the most remote island in Tonga, lying 640km north and slightly west of Tongatapu. The name Tin Can Island was coined by a pre-WWII palangi resident, CS Ramsey, in honour of the island's unusual postal service. Since there was no anchorage or landing site on the island, mail and supplies for its residents were sealed up in a biscuit tin and tossed overboard from a passing supply ship. Strong swimmers would retrieve the parcels. Outbound mail was tied to the end of metre-long sticks, and swimmers would carry it, balanced overhead, to the waiting ship.

To most Tongans, Niuafo'ou is an enigma. Most of them have a vague idea where it is but psychologically it is unimaginably far, like a Timbuktu or a Shangri-la, and most Tongans are more familiar with such distant countries as Britain and Canada than they are with this remote corner of their home country. Perhaps for this reason, Niuafo'ou's inhabitants are credited with fortitude and often regarded with reverence by other Tongans. In 1852 Walter Lawry, an early missionary, wrote of them:

... they prefer a land vitrified and comparatively sterile, without water and having no harbour or landing-place and where the sea is generally very turbulent, because, they say, their fathers lived there before them and there they are buried.

Although the situation isn't as bleak as all that these days, a full third of the island consists of barren and impassable lava flows. Most of the water supply is contained in its large crater lakes and in a sulphur spring.

Very little English is spoken on Niuafo'ou, but the government workers can speak it, and a couple of US Peace Corps volunteers are stationed here. Niuafo'ou is the only island in Tonga that has a distinctly different dialect from the rest of the country, a dialect closer to the Samoan language.

History
During the past 150 years, Niuafo'ou has

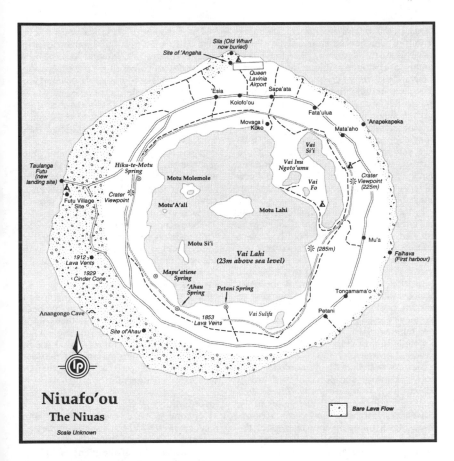

Niuafo'ou

The Niuas

Scale Unknown

Bare Lava Flow

experienced 10 major volcanic eruptions, causing the destruction of three villages. In the eruption of 1853, the village of 'Ahau on the south-west corner of the island was flattened by a lava flow, leaving this area the most wild and desolate part of the island. In the devastating eruption of 1929, the village of Futu on the western end of the island was buried beneath sea-bound lava. This area has now been re-colonised by a few hardy souls and serves as a very marginal landing site. In 1943, a particularly violent eruption destroyed plantations and decimated natural vegetation, causing a general famine.

The most significant eruption, however, certainly wasn't the worst. In September 1946, earthquakes and lava flows on the northern slope buried the erstwhile wharf and capital village of 'Angaha. Although there were no injuries due to the quick evacuation of the area, and although eight other villages escaped unscathed, the village of 'Angaha was destroyed and officials' homes were levelled or damaged.

The government then debated whether

THE NIUAS

'Angaha, the seat of government, should be rebuilt or whether the entire island should be abandoned. Assuming that the island could not continue without local government and that future eruptions could render the place uninhabitable anyway, Queen Salote decided that evacuation was the answer. Beginning in late October, the reluctant islanders were shuttled by boat to Tongatapu and thence resettled on 'Eua. The few recalcitrant inhabitants, 22 in number, who refused to leave during the general evacuation were forcefully collected in October 1947, and the island was left uninhabited.

In the same year, 608 Niuafo'ou people had already petitioned the government to be allowed to return home but they were refused. By 1950, a few copra workers had made their way back but they remained only a year before returning to Tongatapu.

In 1958, eight years and many more petitions later, the government decided to relent and allow resettlement of Niuafo'ou, but they refused government aid to anyone who returned. Two years later the island had a population of 345, which has grown steadily to reach over 700.

Visitors will find the Niuafo'ou people fiercely patriotic and proud of their lonely island. In the words of one who was taken to 'Eua against his will and returned 14 years later: 'Here we intend to stay. If Niuafo'ou blows up again, however great the fire and danger, I shall never leave the island. I prefer to stay here and die.'

Geography
Geologically, the doughnut-shaped island is a collapsed volcanic cone. The island's land area consists of a caldera 5km in diameter encircled by new lava flows. The crater is occupied almost completely by Vai Lahi (big lake, an appropriate name), a freshwater lake which contains four major islands: Motu Lahi (big island), Motu Si'i (small island) and Motu Molemole (smooth island), which has its own crater lake; the fourth island, Motu 'A'ali, appears above the surface when the water level is low.

Three smaller lakes, Vai Si'i ('small lake', also known as Vai Mata'aho after the nearby village), Vai Inu and Vai Fo, lie in the north-east corner of the crater separated from the big lake by casuarina-covered sand hills. One other significant lake, Vai Sulifa, also called Vai Kona ('poison water'), is a bubbling sulphur spring, found at the southern extreme. There are no significant water sources outside the crater.

It is thought that the volcano once reached an altitude of 1300m, but these days the highest point is only about 285m above sea level. Although there's been no obvious volcanic activity since 1946, the volcano is still classified as active.

The island is surrounded by open ocean – there is no coral reef around it, and no sandy beaches. People do not swim in the sea here, but rather in the lake, if at all.

Flora & Fauna
Niuafo'ou's most unusual inhabitant is the Niuafo'ou megapode. Apart from the beautiful barn owl (*lulu*), the only other wildlife of note is the lapila fish (in English, the telapia fish) of the crater lakes. Like the megapode, these are a staple of the local diet, but as yet, there's no sign that the species is endangered.

Information
Telephone service to Niuafo'ou commenced in 1998. Mail usually comes via aeroplane – a plane stops in once every three weeks – but if the plane is full, the mail will be left behind. Money can be changed at the Treasury.

Things to See & Do
Anyone fortunate enough to reach Niuafo'ou will undoubtedly just want to explore. There's a track leading right around the doughnut, which may be walked in about six hours at a leisurely pace. Even so, Niuafo'ou is worth more time. It's the sort of place you'd like to settle into for a month or two (if you miss the boat or plane, you may have to!) and try to grasp its remote appeal.

The Niuafo'ou Megapode

A line in a popular song written by a lamenting Niuafo'ou exile goes: 'Megapodes, speak your mind while you're near to your burrows, else turn away without looking back ...', referring to the Niuafo'ou megapode (*Megapodius pritchardii*), locally known as *malau*, which is native only to this island.

This fascinating brown and grey bird subsists on seeds, insects, worms, fruit and even small geckos. Although it spends the days on the forest floor, at night, it roosts in the tree-tops.

Pairs of megapodes usually inhabit a territory of about two hectares somewhere along the shores of Niuafo'ou's crater lakes, keeping track of each other with a sort of mating duet. When it's time to lay an egg, a megapode hen digs a burrow one to 2m deep in the unconsolidated volcanic soil near active steam vents (usually in the same place where she herself hatched). In the burrow, she deposits a disproportionately large egg and covers it with earth, leaving it to incubate unattended in the naturally heated volcanic environment. A hen may lay up to 10 eggs, normally at intervals of about two weeks.

After around four weeks, the chicks hatch, and are then forced to make their own way to the surface. This gruelling job can take a couple of days. On the way to daylight, they are at risk from the long-legged ants, which prey on newly hatched chicks by first going for their eyes. When they finally emerge, they already bear a full coat of feathers and are able to fly and fend for themselves.

Owls and domestic cats also prey on adult megapodes, but as in so many cases, the greatest threat is from humans. People and their animals not only destroy the megapode's habitat, but due to the bird's superior flavour, megapode eggs and flesh are preferred by the islanders to domestic chickens. Naturally, this has had dramatic effects on the island's megapode population and, sadly, this incredible bird is currently threatened with extinction. At present, the Tongan Wildlife Centre Bird Park on Tongatapu is experimenting with transplanting chicks to the safely uninhabited volcanic island of Late in the Vava'u Group, hoping they will breed and prosper in the protected environment.

If you're interested in protecting the megapode and its habitat or would like further information, contact the Tongan Wildlife Centre Fund for International Bird Conservation, Private Bag 52, Nuku'alofa, Kingdom of Tonga (☎/fax 23-561).

One Niuafo'ou sight which must be seen is the splendid lake, Vai Lahi, which nearly fills the island's large and mysterious crater.

Along the southern and western shores is a vast, barren moonscape of lava flows. In the late 19th and early 20th centuries they oozed over the villages of 'Ahau and Futu, burying them completely.

Near the airport on the north shore, there's a variety of interesting features – mounds of volcanic slag, lava tubes, vents and craters – readily accessible from the main road. Beneath this flow is the village of 'Angaha, a sort of Tongan Pompeii.

Between Mu'a and Mata'aho, a trail leads up to a magnificent view of Vai Si'i, Vai Lahi and the islands. Between Futu and 'Esia, another trail affords a view of the entire expanse of Vai Lahi. From Mu'a, a rough road crosses the sandy isthmus between the two major lakes and leads down to the shore of Vai Lahi.

All around the crater, small trails lead to interesting sites, including a sulphur spring and lava vents. The bubbling sulphur lake, Vai Sulifa (also called Vai Kona), is best reached from Petani village.

Places to Stay & Eat

There are numerous excellent *campsites* on

THE NIUAS

Landing at Niuafo'ou

Niuafo'ou has no anchorage and no wharf, and the entire island is exposed to the full wrath of the sea. Ships stop about 150m offshore and the crew drops two lines into the water, which are retrieved by swimmers and carried to the cement platform that serves as the landing site. Passengers, luggage and cargo are literally dropped or thrown into a wooden dory at an opportune moment and ferried ashore, where hulking Tongans wait to pluck them out of the rolling and pitching craft and deposit them on a platform.

Returning craft are filled nearly to the gunwales with copra. Oil drums and pens of squealing pigs are thrown (again, literally) on top of the sacks, then stalks of taro, yams, bananas and other agricultural produce are tucked in wherever there's a bit of space. Finally, passengers are heaped and balanced on top of all this paraphernalia! When there are only a few centimetres of freeboard remaining, water is pouring into the boat and the centre of gravity of the whole mess hovers at least 1m above the gunwales, the boats are shoved off through the surf. Passengers are constantly forced to lean in one direction or another to prevent what would appear to be the imminent capsize of the vessel. Upon arrival at the ship, passengers, cargo, pigs, etc are rolled, herded and pitched aboard.

---

the crater, especially on the lake shores, where drinking water is available, though you must boil the lake water to make it safe to drink. In other areas, locals are normally happy to let you fill your water bottles from their rainwater tanks. Bear in mind, though, that camping is not the ordinary custom here and it will draw a lot of attention and curiosity, including onlookers you may not have wanted, and people coming to check on you.

A new guesthouse is scheduled to open in 1998. Operated by Paea Sisi (☎ 80-052), it will be opposite the government rep's house, in 'Esia village. It shouldn't be too difficult to arrange a stay with locals if you'll be on the island for a while.

Several small shops are scattered through the villages, but they rarely have anything of interest, or anything at all, unless the boat has recently come in. Ordinarily, only local food is available, and there's not much variety. It's wise to bring all your food with you, if you can.

Getting There & Away

Due to its volcanic nature, Niuafo'ou lacks a decent anchorage or landing site, leaving access reliant on the mercy of the wind and waves.

Air The Queen Lavinia airport was opened near the site of 'Angaha in 1980. Although Friendly Island Airways (the forerunner of Royal Tongan Airlines) attempted a brief period of scheduled service in the mid-1980s, for over a decade the airport was used almost exclusively for royal charters. Prior to the re-introduction of scheduled air service in the early 1990s, Niuafo'ou was one of the least accessible inhabited islands in the world.

Access is now much easier than in the past. Every third week, a flight comes from Tongatapu, via Vava'u. See the Getting Around chapter for fares and flying times.

As with Niuatoputapu flights, the ticket agents in Nuku'alofa don't seem to want to sell tickets to the Niuas. If an agent tells you that Niuafo'ou flights are full for the next two years, don't despair. In reality, the flights are rarely full and you'll almost certainly get a seat, except if you're trying to get there during the busy December-January school holiday season. You can buy your ticket at the airport at the time of departure, once seat availability has been confirmed.

The biggest problem with flying to Niuafo'ou is simply that the flights come here only once every three weeks, meaning that if you want to visit the island at all, three weeks is the minimum amount of time you can stay here, if you're depending on air transport.

Boat Getting to Niuafo'ou by boat is a fraught business – not only because of the gruelling boat ride up here, but also the landing (see boxed text). See the Niuatoputapu section – these are the same boats that come to Niuafo'ou – and the Getting Around chapter for more information. If the weather isn't at its best, the boat must turn around and leave without stopping.

Glossary

'alo – son or daughter
'api – plantation of 3.4 hectares

fa'e – mother
faikakai – breadfruit pudding
faka Tonga – the 'Tongan way'
fakaleiti – a custom where a male dresses and behaves as a female.
fakapale – a custom associated with Tongan dancing. The word means literally 'to award a prize'.
feke – octopus
fale – a traditional thatched house
falekai – restaurant
feta'aki – single piece of tapa cloth
fingota – shellfish

haka – movements in ma'ulu'ulu dance
hiapo – mulberry tree *(Broussonetia papyrifera)*, which grows primarily on the islands of 'Eua and Tongatapu

'ika – fish
'ike – ironwood mallet
'inasi – an agricultural fair derived from a traditional festival

kailao – war dance
kalia – large seafaring canoes
kava – an intoxicating drink made from the root of the pepper shrub
kiekie – a decorative waist band with dangling strips of pandanus, strands of seeds, bits of cloth or fibre cords
koloa – wealth
kumala – sweet potato
kupesi – relief of tapa pattern

lafo – Tongan game played with pieces called *pa'anga*
lakalaka – a traditional dance
langanga – strips of tapa
langi – burial tomb
lu pulu – a dish of corned beef and boiled taro in coconut cream

mali – spouse
malau – local name for the Niuafo'ou megapode *(Megapodius pritchardii)*
matapule – 'talking chief' involved in ceremonies and burial rituals of the nobility
ma'ulu'ulu – dance performed at feasts
motu – coral islet

ngatu – the name of the finished tapa product made from the paper mulberry tree

palangi – foreigner
papa – base of a kupesi
pekepeka – cave swallows, or white-rumped swiftlets
popao – outrigger canoe
punake – dance choreographer

sipi – mutton

tamai – father
ta'ovala – waist mat worn at formal occasions
tapa – mulberry bark cloth
tau'olunga – a graceful traditional dance performed by a solo woman at ceremonies
toa – ironwood
tokoua – brother or sister, often used broadly to include cousins
tutua – anvil
tui'aniu – design made with coconut fronds
tupenu – a wraparound skirt which extends below the knees
tutu – the underbark of the mulberry tree
tapu – sacred
tiki – wooden statue representing old Polynesian god
tevolo – devil spirit
Tu'i Tonga – royal title

'umu – a traditional underground oven

vahenga – high-ranking dancer
vala – gifts presented to university graduates

Language

Tongan belongs to the Austronesian family of languages which includes other Polynesian languages such as Samoan, Hawaiian, Maori and Tahitian, as well as Malay, Malagasy and Melanesian languages. This connection forms the most solid basis for the accepted theory that the Polynesian peoples originated in South-East Asia.

The same Tongan language is spoken on all the islands in Tonga, with one exception: on Niuafo'ou, the most north-westerly island, a dialect which is closer to Samoan language is spoken.

Both Tongan and English languages are used in the schools throughout Tonga, so you won't have any problem using English to communicate. On major islands (Tongatapu, Vava'u), almost everyone can speak English as a second language. On smaller, more remote islands people may speak less English, but communication can always somehow be achieved.

Pronunciation

The Tongan alphabet has only 16 letters, with five vowels and 11 consonants.

It's worth listening to the way native speakers pronounce vowels because vowel length can affect the meaning of some words. You may see vowels written with a superscribed bar or *toloi* (a 'macron' in English) which indicates that they are long. The long sound is simply an extended and accented (stressed) version of the short vowel. Stress is placed on the next to last syllable in most Tongan words, unless there's a long vowel, in which case that syllable receives the stress.

Another important element of Tongan language is the glottal stop, represented by an apostrophe ('). It signals a momentary halt in the flow of air through the vocal chords, similar to the non-voice between the syllables of 'oh-oh'.

Diphthongs, or combinations of vowels, are pronounced by enunciating each of the component sounds individually. When a glottal stop is inserted between two vowels, a stop must be made in the pronunciation. This, too, is a significant element of Tongan language that changes not only the pronunciation but also the meaning of words: for example, *tae* means 'cough', but *ta'e* means 'fæces'! *Hau* means 'earring', but *ha'u* means 'come here'.

Even if you do mistake the pronunciation of glottal stops, and long and short vowels, Tongan people are usually helpful about it and they'll still try to understand what you're saying.

The letters used in the Tongan alphabet are pronounced more or less as follows:

Vowels

a	as in 'far' or as in 'ball'
e	as in 'end'
i	as in 'Fifi'
o	as in 'go'
u	as in 'tune'

Consonants

f	as in 'far'
h	as in 'here'
k	as the 'c' in 'curd'
l	as in 'love', with a slap of the tongue
m	as in 'me'
n	as in 'no'
ng	as in 'singer', not as in 'finger'
p	midway between the 'p' in 'park' and the 'b' in 'bark'
s	as in 'sand'
t	midway between the 't' in 'tip' and the 'd' in 'dip'
v	as in 'very'

Some Basic Vocabulary

Since their language is spoken only in Tonga, the Tongans are both pleased and surprised when foreigners make an attempt to use it at all. The following useful words and phrases will get you started.

Pronouns

I/mine	*koau/'a'aku*
you/yours	*ko koe/'a'au*
he, she, it	*ia*
we/ours	*'oku mau/mautolou*
you/yours (pl)	*ko moutolu/ko moua*
they	*'oku nau/nautolu*

Greetings & Civilities

Hello.	*Malo e lelei.*
Good-bye.	*'Alu a.* (to someone leaving)
	Nofo a. (response to someone staying)
Good morning.	*Malo e lelei ki he pongipongini.*
Good evening.	*Malo e lelei ki he efiafini.*
Welcome.	*Talitali fiefia.*
Please/Excuse me.	*Faka molemole/ Kataki.*
I'm sorry. (forgive me)	*Faka molemole 'iau.*
Thank you. (very much).	*Malo ('aupito).*
You're welcome.	*'Io malo.*
Yes/No.	*'Io/ 'Ikai.*
Maybe.	*Mahalo pe.*
How are you?	*Fefe hake?*
Fine, thank you.	*Sai pe, malo.*

Essentials

I understand.
  'Oku mahino kiate 'au.
I don't understand.
  'Oku ikai ke mahino kiate 'au.
Do you speak English?
  'Oku ke lava 'o lea faka palangi?
Does anyone speak English?
  'Oku 'iai ha taha 'oku lea faka palangi?
I don't speak ...
  'Oku 'ikai te u lea ...

Where are you from?
  Ko ho'o ha'u mei fe fonua?
I'm from ...
  Ko 'eku ha'u mei ...
Age?/How old are you?
  Ta'u?/Koe ha ho ta'u motua?

I'm ... years old.
  'Oku 'ou ta'u ... ta'u motua.
I love you.
  'Oku ou 'ofa 'iate koe.
Help!
  Tokoni!
Go away!
  'Alu mama'o!
Call a doctor/the police!
  Ui ha toketa/polisi!

Small Talk

What's your name?	*Ko hai ho hingoa?*
My name is ...	*Ko hoku hingoa ko ...*
I'm a tourist/ student.	*Ko 'eku ha'u eve'eva/ taha ako.*
Are you married?	*Kuo ke'osi mali?*
Do you like ...?	*'Oku ke sai'ia 'ihe ...?*
I like it very much.	*'Oku 'ou sai'ia 'aupito.*
I don't like ...	*'Oku ikai teu sai'ia ...*
Just a minute.	*Tali si'i.*
May I?	*Faka molemole kau?*
It's all right/ no problem.	*'Io 'oku sai/sai pe ia.*
How do you say ...?	*Koe ha ho lea ...?*
What is this called?	*Ko 'e ha hono hingoa 'o 'e me'a ko 'eni?*
How much?	*'Oku fiha?*
How many?	*Ko e me'a 'e fiha?*
When do you open/ close?	*Temou ava/tapuni he fiha?*
cheap/expensive	*ma'ama'a/mamafa*
good/bad	*lelei/kovi*
pretty	*faka 'ofa 'ofa*
European	*palangi* (originally *papalangi*)
Japanese	*siapani*
Miss/Mrs/Mr	*ta'ahine/fine'eiki/ tangata'eiki*
man/woman	*tangata/fefine*
boy/girl	*tamasi'i/ta'ahine*

Getting Around

I want to go to ...
  'Oku ou fie 'alu ki ...
I want to book a seat for ...
  'Oku 'ou fiemau hoku nofo anga ki he ...

How long does the trip take?
Koe ha 'ae loloa o e folau?
Where is the ... to (Vava'u?
Ko fe'ia ... ki (Vava'u)?
What time does the ... leave/arrive?
Koe ha taime'oe ... 'e 'alu ai/foki mai?
Where does the ... leave from?
Ko fe feitu'u ... 'oku 'alu mei ai?

aeroplane	*vakapuna*
bus	*koe pasi*
boat	*vaka*
canoe	*koe papao*
ferry	*vaka foko tu'u*

one-way (ticket)	*'alu pe (tikite)*
	or *ha'u pe (tikite)*
return (ticket)	*'alu moe ha'u (tikite)*
ticket	*tikite*
ticket office	*loki faka tau tikite*
timetable	*taimi tepile*

I'd like to hire a ... *'Oku o'u fiema'u*
ho'o ...

bicycle	*pasikala*
motrcycle	*paiki*
car	*ka*
guide	*faka 'eve'eva'i*
horse	*hoosi*

Directions
Where is ...?
Ko fe'ia a'e ...?
How do I get to ...?
Teu 'alu fefe ki ...?
Is it near/far?
'Oku 'ofi/mama'o?
Where can I find a place to stay?
Ko e fe ha feitu'u lava 'o nofo ai?
Where is the toilet?
Ko fe 'a e fale malolo?
Where can I buy ...?
Teu fakatau mei fe ha ...?
How far is it to ...?
Ko 'e ha hono mama'o 'o ... mei heni?
Stop/Go.
Tu'u/'alu.
(Go) straight ahead.
(`Alu) hangatonu ai pe.
(Turn) left/right.
(Afe) to'ohema/to'omata'u ...

at the next/second/third corner
... 'i he hoko/fika ua/fika tolu tafa'aki

behind	*'i mui*
opposite	*fehangahangai*
up/down	*'olunga/lalo*

here/there	*heni/he*
everywhere	*fetu'u kotoa pe*
east/west	*hahake/hihifo*
north/south	*tokelau/tonga*

street/road	*hala*
suburb	*lotokolo*
village	*kolo si'i si'i*

Useful Signs
Entrance	*Teu hu i fe (Hu'anga)*
Exit	*Hu'anga ki tu'a*
Guesthouse	*Fale nofo totongi*
Hotel	*Hotele*
Information	*Fakamatala*
Open/	*'Oku ava*
Closed	*'Oku tapuni*
Police	*Polisi*
Police Station	*Fale Polisi*
Prohibited/Keep	
Out	*Tapu*
Toilets	*Fale malolo*
Men's toilet	*Fale malolo tangata*
Women's toilet	*Fale malolo fefine*

Around Town
I want to make a telephone call.
'Oku 'ou fie ma'u keu telefoni.
I'd like to change some ...
'Oku 'ou fiema'u kefetongi 'eku ...
money/travellers' cheques
silini/sieke

bank	*pangike*
currency exchange	*'ofisi vete pa'anga*
beach	*matatahi*
bridge	*hala kavakava*
church	*fale lotu*
city centre	*i loto kolo*
embassy	*'api 'oe 'amipasitoa*
hospital	*fale mahaki*
market	*maketi*
palace	*palasi*

post office	*positi 'ofisi*
restaurant	*fale kai*
telephone office	*fale telefoni*
tourist office	*'ofisi taki mamata*

island	*motu*
lake	*ano vai*
ruins	*maumau*
sea/deep ocean	*tahi/moana*
sun/wind/rain	*la'a/matangi/'uha*
tower	*taua*

Accommodation

I'm looking for ...
   Ko 'eku kumi ...
Do you have a ... available?
   'Oku 'iai ha'o ... 'ata'ata'a?

bed	*mohe'anga*
cheap room	*loki ma'ama'a*
single room	*mohenga toko taha*
double room	*mohenga toko ua*

for one night/two nights
   po e taha/po e ua
How much is it per night/person?
   'Oku fiha 'ae (po e taha/
    ki he toko taha)?
Is breakfast included?
   'Oku kau ai e kai pongopongi?
Can I see the room?
   Teu lava'o sio?
Do you have hot water?
   'Oku 'iai ha'o vai mafana?
Do you have a clean sheet?
   'Oku 'iai ha'o kafu ma'a?
I'm/We're leaving now.
   Teu/Te mau 'alu he taimi ni.

shower	*saoa*

Shopping

How much does it cost?
   Fiha hono totongi?
I'd like to buy it.
   'Oku ou fie fakatau ia.
It's too expensive for me.
   Fu'u mamafa kiate au.
Can I look at it?
   Teu sio ki ai?
I'm just looking.
   'Oku ou siosio pe.

I'm looking for ... *Ko 'eku kumi ...*
  the chemist *fale talatalavai*
  clothing *vala*
  souvenirs *mea'ofa*

Do you take travellers cheques?
   'Oku ke tali 'ae sieki?
Do you have another colour/size?
   'Oku i'ai hao toe lanu/fika?

big/bigger	*lahi/lahi ange*
small/smaller	*si'i si'i/si'i si'i ange*
more/less	*lahi/si'i*
cheaper	*ma'a ma'a ange*

Food

I'm hungry/thirsty.	*'Oku o'u fiekaia/*
	fieinua.
breakfast	*kai pongipongi*
lunch	*kai ho'ata*
dinner	*kai efiafi*
set menu	*koe ha ho'o mou u*
	me'a kai

food stall	*kai tepile*
grocery store	*fale koloa*
supermarket	*supamaketi*
market	*maketi*
restaurant	*falekai*

bread	*ma*
chicken	*moa*
eggs	*fo'ai moa*
fish	*ika*
food	*me'akai*
fruit	*fo'i 'akau*
meat	*kakano'i manu*
pepper	*polo*
pork	*puaka*
salt	*masima*
soup	*supo*
sugar	*suka*
vegetables	*vesitapolo*

beer	*pia*
coffee	*kofi*
milk	*hu'akau*
mineral water	*hina vai (sota)*
tea	*ti*
wine	*uaine*

hot/cold	*vela/momoko*	5	*nima*
with	*teu 'aimoe*	6	*ono*
without	*he'ikai teu 'ai*	7	*fitu*
		8	*valu*
Times & Dates		9	*hiva*
When? (past)	*'Anefe?*	10	*hongofulu*
When? (future)	*'Afe?*	11	*taha taha*
today	*'ahoni*		(or *hongofulu ma taha*)
tonight	*'apo*	12	*taha ua*
tomorrow	*'apongipongi*		(or *hongofulu ma ua*)
day after tomorrow	*'aho 'osi 'apongi-pongi*	13	*taha tolu*
			(or *hongofulu ma tolu*)
yesterday	*'ane'afi*	14	*taha fa*
all day	*'aho kotoa*		(or *hongofulu ma fa*)
everyday	*'aho kotoape*	15	*taha nima*
			(or *hongofulu ma nima*)
What time is it?	*Koe ha e taimi ko 'eni?*	16	*taha ono*
It's ... o'clock.	*Koe hoko e ...*		(or *hongofulu ma ono*)
1.15	*taha tahanima*	17	*taha fitu*
1.30	*taha tolu noa*		(or *hongofuluma fitu*)
1.45	*taha fa nima*	18	*taha valu*
in the morning	*taimi pongipongi*		(or *hongofulu ma valu*)
in the evening	*taimi 'efi'afi*	19	*taha hiva*
			(or *hongofulu ma hiva*)
Monday	*Monite*	20	*uanoa* (or *uafulu*)
Tuesday	*Tusite*	21	*uanoa taha*
Wednesday	*Pulelulu*		(or *uafulu ma taha*)
Thursday	*Tuapulelulu*	30	*tolunoa* (or *tolungofulu*)
Friday	*Falaite*	31	*tolu taha*
Saturday	*Tokanaki*		(or *tolungofulu ma taha*)
Sunday	*Sapate*	40	*fanoa* (or *fangofulu*)
		50	*nima noa* (or *nimangofulu*)
January	*Sanuali*	60	*ononoa* (or *'onongofulu*)
February	*Fepueli*	70	*fitunoa* (or *fitungofulu*)
March	*Ma'asi*	80	*valunoa* (or *valungofulu*)
April	*'Epeleli*	90	*hivanoa* (or *hivangofulu*)
May	*Me*	100	*teau*
June	*Sune*	101	*teau taha*
July	*Siulai*	110	*teau hongofulu*
August	*'Akosi*	200	*uangeau*
September	*Sepitema*	300	*tolungeau*
October	*'Okatopa*	1000	*tahaafe*
November	*Novema*	1001	*tahaafe taha*
December	*Tisema*	10,000	*tahamano*
		11,000	*tahamano tahaafe*
Numbers		12,000	*tahamano uaafe*
1	*taha*	20,000	*uamano*
2	*ua*	100,000	*tahakilu*
3	*tolu*	200,000	*uakilu*
4	*fa*	one million	*tahamiliona*

Health

I'm diabetic/epileptic/asthmatic.
  Koau 'oku o'u suka/
    mahaki moa/mahaki hela.
Don't give me penicillin/antibiotics.
  'Oua e 'omai ae penisilini/
    antibiotics kia au.

antiseptic	*faito'o tamate siemu*
aspirin	*'asipilini*
condoms	*konitomu*
contraceptive	*mea ta 'ofi fanau*
diarrhoea	*fakalele*
medicine	*foi akau*
nausea	*tokakovi*
sunblock cream	*kilimi la'a*
tampons	*hafe*

Index

LONELY PLANET PHRASEBOOKS

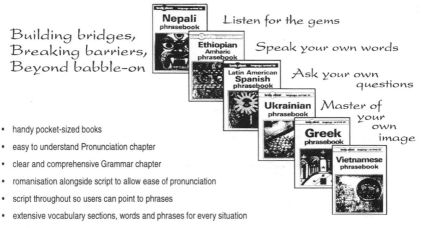

Building bridges,
Breaking barriers,
Beyond babble-on

Listen for the gems

Speak your own words

Ask your own
questions

Master of
your
own
image

- handy pocket-sized books
- easy to understand Pronunciation chapter
- clear and comprehensive Grammar chapter
- romanisation alongside script to allow ease of pronunciation
- script throughout so users can point to phrases
- extensive vocabulary sections, words and phrases for every situation
- full of cultural information and tips for the traveller

'...vital for a real DIY spirit and attitude in language learning' – **Backpacker**

'the phrasebooks have good cultural backgrounders and offer solid advice for challenging situations in remote locations' – **San Francisco Examiner**

'...they are unbeatable for their coverage of the world's more obscure languages' – **The Geographical Magazine**

Arabic (Egyptian)
Arabic (Moroccan)
Australia
   *Australian English, Aboriginal and
   Torres Strait languages*
Baltic States
   Estonian, Latvian, Lithuanian
Bengali
Brazilian
Burmese
Cantonese
Central Asia
Central Europe
   *Czech, French, German, Hungarian,
   Italian and Slovak*
Eastern Europe
   *Bulgarian, Czech, Hungarian, Polish,
   Romanian and Slovak*
Ethiopian (Amharic)
Fijian
French
German
Greek

Hindi/Urdu
Indonesian
Italian
Japanese
Korean
Lao
Latin American Spanish
Malay
Mandarin
Mediterranean Europe
   *Albanian, Croatian, Greek,
   Italian, Macedonian, Maltese,
   Serbian and Slovene*
Mongolian
Nepali
Papua New Guinea
Pilipino (Tagalog)
Quechua
Russian
Scandinavian Europe
   *Danish, Finnish, Icelandic, Norwegian
   and Swedish*

South-East Asia
   *Burmese, Indonesian, Khmer, Lao,
   Malay, Tagalog (Pilipino), Thai and
   Vietnamese*
Spanish (Castilian)
   Basque, Catalan and Galician
Sri Lanka
Swahili
Thai
Thai Hill Tribes
Tibetan
Turkish
Ukrainian
USA
   *US English, Vernacular,
   Native American languages and
   Hawaiian*
Vietnamese
Western Europe
   *Basque, Catalan, Dutch, French,
   German, Irish, Italian, Portuguese,
   Scottish Gaelic, Spanish (Castilian)
   and Welsh*

LONELY PLANET JOURNEYS

JOURNEYS is a unique collection of travel writing – published by the company that understands travel better than anyone else. It is a series for anyone who has ever experienced – or dreamed of – the magical moment when they encountered a strange culture or saw a place for the first time. They are tales to read while you're planning a trip, while you're on the road or while you're in an armchair, in front of a fire.

JOURNEYS books catch the spirit of a place, illuminate a culture, recount a crazy adventure, or introduce a fascinating way of life. They always entertain, and always enrich the experience of travel.

ISLANDS IN THE CLOUDS
Travels in the Highlands of New Guinea
Isabella Tree

Isabella Tree's remarkable journey takes us to the heart of the remote and beautiful Highlands of Papua New Guinea and Irian Jaya – one of the most extraordinary and dangerous regions on earth. Funny and tragic by turns, *Islands in the Clouds* is her moving story of the Highland people and the changes transforming their world.

Isabella Tree, who lives in England, has worked as a freelance journalist on a variety of newspapers and magazines, including a stint as senior travel correspondent for the *Evening Standard.* A fellow of the Royal Geographical Society, she has also written a biography of the Victorian ornithologist John Gould.

'One of the most accomplished travel writers to appear on the horizon for many years . . . the dialogue is brilliant' – Eric Newby

---

SEAN & DAVID'S LONG DRIVE
Sean Condon

Sean Condon is young, urban and a connoisseur of hair wax. He can't drive, and he doesn't really travel well. So when Sean and his friend David set out to explore Australia in a 1966 Ford Falcon, the result is a decidedly offbeat look at life on the road. Over 14,000 death-defying kilometres, our heroes check out the re-runs on tv, get fabulously drunk, listen to Neil Young cassettes and wonder why they ever left home.

Sean Condon lives in Melbourne. He played drums in several mediocre bands until he found his way into advertising and an above-average band called Boilersuit. *Sean & David's Long Drive* is his first book.

'Funny, pithy, kitsch and surreal . . . This book will do for Australia what Chernobyl did for Kiev, but hey you'll laugh as the stereotypes go boom'
– Time Out

LONELY PLANET TRAVEL ATLASES

Lonely Planet has long been famous for the number and quality of its guidebook maps. Now we've gone one step further and produced a handy companion series: Lonely Planet travel atlases – maps of a country produced in book form.

Unlike other maps, which look good but lead travellers astray, our travel atlases have been researched on the road by Lonely Planet's experienced team of writers. All details are carefully checked to ensure the atlas corresponds with the equivalent Lonely Planet guidebook.

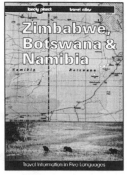

The handy atlas format means no holes, wrinkles, torn sections or constant folding and unfolding. These atlases can survive long periods on the road, unlike cumbersome fold-out maps. The comprehensive index ensures easy reference.

- full-colour throughout
- maps researched and checked by Lonely Planet authors
- place names correspond with Lonely Planet guidebooks
  – no confusing spelling differences
- legend and travelling information in English, French, German, Japanese and Spanish
- size: 230 x 160 mm

Available now:
Chile & Easter Island • Egypt • India & Bangladesh • Israel & the Palestinian Territories •Jordan, Syria & Lebanon • Kenya • Laos • Portugal • South Africa, Lesotho & Swaziland • Thailand • Turkey • Vietnam • Zimbabwe, Botswana & Namibia

---

LONELY PLANET TV SERIES & VIDEOS

Lonely Planet travel guides have been brought to life on television screens around the world. Like our guides, the programmes are based on the joy of independent travel, and look honestly at some of the most exciting, picturesque and frustrating places in the world. Each show is presented by one of three travellers from Australia, England or the USA and combines an innovative mixture of video, Super-8 film, atmospheric soundscapes and original music.

Videos of each episode – containing additional footage not shown on television – are available from good book and video shops, but the availability of individual videos varies with regional screening schedules.

Video destinations include: Alaska • American Rockies • Australia – The South-East • Baja California & the Copper Canyon • Brazil • Central Asia • Chile & Easter Island • Corsica, Sicily & Sardinia – The Mediterranean Islands • East Africa (Tanzania & Zanzibar) • Ecuador & the Galapagos Islands • Greenland & Iceland • Indonesia • Israel & the Sinai Desert • Jamaica • Japan • La Ruta Maya • Morocco • New York • North India • Pacific Islands (Fiji, Solomon Islands & Vanuatu) • South India • South West China • Turkey • Vietnam • West Africa • Zimbabwe, Botswana & Namibia

The Lonely Planet TV series is produced by:
Pilot Productions
The Old Studio
18 Middle Row
London W10 5AT UK

For video availability and ordering information contact your nearest Lonely Planet office.

Music from the TV series is available on CD & cassette.

PLANET TALK

Lonely Planet's FREE quarterly newsletter

We love hearing from you and think you'd like to hear from us.

When...is the right time to see reindeer in Finland?
Where...can you hear the best palm-wine music in Ghana?
How...do you get from Asunción to Areguá by steam train?
What...is the best way to see India?

For the answer to these and many other questions read PLANET TALK.

Every issue is packed with up-to-date travel news and advice including:

* a letter from Lonely Planet co-founders Tony and Maureen Wheeler
* go behind the scenes on the road with a Lonely Planet author
* feature article on an important and topical travel issue
* a selection of recent letters from travellers
* details on forthcoming Lonely Planet promotions
* complete list of Lonely Planet products

To join our mailing list contact any Lonely Planet office.

Also available: Lonely Planet T-shirts. 100% heavyweight cotton.

LONELY PLANET ONLINE

Get the latest travel information before you leave or while you're on the road

Whether you've just begun planning your next trip, or you're chasing down specific info on currency regulations or visa requirements, check out Lonely Planet Online for up-to-the minute travel information.

As well as travel profiles of your favourite destinations (including maps and photos), you'll find current reports from our researchers and other travellers, updates on health and visas, travel advisories, and discussion of the ecological and political issues you need to be aware of as you travel.

There's also an online travellers' forum where you can share your experience of life on the road, meet travel companions and ask other travellers for their recommendations and advice. We also have plenty of links to other online sites useful to independent travellers.

And of course we have a complete and up-to-date list of all Lonely Planet travel products including guides, phrasebooks, atlases, Journeys and videos and a simple online ordering facility if you can't find the book you want elsewhere.

www.lonelyplanet.com
or
AOL keyword: lp

LONELY PLANET PRODUCTS

Lonely Planet is known worldwide for publishing practical, reliable and no-nonsense travel information in our guides and on our web site. The Lonely Planet list covers just about every accessible part of the world. Currently there are nine series: *travel guides, shoestring guides, walking guides, city guides, phrasebooks, audio packs, travel atlases, Journeys – a unique collection of travel writing and Pisces Books - diving and snorkeling guides.*

EUROPE

Amsterdam • Austria • Baltic States phrasebook • Berlin • Britain • Canary Islands• Central Europe on a shoestring • Central Europe phrasebook • Czech & Slovak Republics • Denmark • Dublin • Eastern Europe on a shoestring • Eastern Europe phrasebook • Estonia, Latvia & Lithuania • Finland • France • French phrasebook • Germany • German phrasebook • Greece • Greek phrasebook • Hungary • Iceland, Greenland & the Faroe Islands • Ireland • Italian phrasebook • Italy • Lisbon • London • Mediterranean Europe on a shoestring • Mediterranean Europe phrasebook • Paris • Poland • Portugal • Portugal travel atlas • Prague • Romania & Moldova • Russia, Ukraine & Belarus • Russian phrasebook • Scandinavian & Baltic Europe on a shoestring • Scandinavian Europe phrasebook • Slovenia • Spain • Spanish phrasebook • St Petersburg • Switzerland •Trekking in Spain • Ukrainian phrasebook • Vienna • Walking in Britain • Walking in Italy • Walking in Switzerland • Western Europe on a shoestring • Western Europe phrasebook

Travel Literature: The Olive Grove: Travels in Greece

NORTH AMERICA

Alaska • Backpacking in Alaska • Baja California • California & Nevada • Canada • Chicago • Deep South• Florida • Hawaii • Honolulu • Los Angeles • Mexico • Mexico City • Miami • New England • New Orleans • New York City • New York, New Jersey & Pennsylvania • Pacific Northwest USA • Rocky Mountain States • San Francisco • Southwest USA • USA phrasebook • Washington, DC & the Capital Region

Travel Literature: Drive thru America

CENTRAL AMERICA & THE CARIBBEAN

•Bahamas and Turks & Caicos •Bermuda •Central America on a shoestring • Costa Rica • Cuba •Eastern Caribbean •Guatemala, Belize & Yucatán: La Ruta Maya • Jamaica

SOUTH AMERICA

Argentina, Uruguay & Paraguay • Bolivia • Brazil • Brazilian phrasebook • Buenos Aires • Chile & Easter Island • Chile & Easter Island travel atlas • Colombia Ecuador & the Galápagos Islands • Latin American Spanish phrasebook • Peru • Quechua phrasebook • Rio de Janeiro • South America on a shoestring • Trekking in the Patagonian Andes • Venezuela

Travel Literature: Full Circle: A South American Journey

ISLANDS OF THE INDIAN OCEAN

Madagascar & Comoros • Maldives• Mauritius, Réunion & Seychelles

AFRICA

Africa - the South • Africa on a shoestring • Arabic (Moroccan) phrasebook • Cairo • Cape Town • Central Africa • East Africa • Egypt • Egypt travel atlas• Ethiopian (Amharic) phrasebook • Kenya • Kenya travel atlas • Malawi, Mozambique & Zambia • Morocco • North Africa • South Africa, Lesotho & Swaziland • South Africa, Lesotho & Swaziland travel atlas • Swahili phrasebook • Tunisia • Trekking in East Africa • West Africa • Zimbabwe, Botswana & Namibia • Zimbabwe, Botswana & Namibia travel atlas

Travel Literature: The Rainbird: A Central African Journey • Songs to an African Sunset: A Zimbabwean Story

MAIL ORDER

Lonely Planet products are distributed worldwide.They are also available by mail order from Lonely Planet, so if you have difficulty finding a title please write to us. North American and South American residents should write to 150 Linden St, Oakland CA 94607, USA; European and African residents should write to 10a Spring Place, London NW5 3BH; and residents of other countries to PO Box 617, Hawthorn, Victoria 3122, Australia.

NORTH-EAST ASIA

Beijing • Cantonese phrasebook • China • Hong Kong • Hong Kong, Macau & Guangzhou • Japan • Japanese phrasebook • Japanese audio pack • Korea • Korean phrasebook • Mandarin phrasebook • Mongolia • Mongolian phrasebook • North-East Asia on a shoestring • Seoul • Taiwan • Tibet • Tibet phrasebook • Tokyo

Travel Literature: Lost Japan

MIDDLE EAST & CENTRAL ASIA

Arab Gulf States • Arabic (Egyptian) phrasebook • Central Asia • Central Asia phrasebook • Iran • Israel & the Palestinian Territories • Israel & the Palestinian Territories travel atlas • Istanbul • Jerusalem • Jordan & Syria • Jordan, Syria & Lebanon travel atlas • Lebanon • Middle East • Turkey • Turkish phrasebook • Turkey travel atlas • Yemen

Travel Literature: The Gates of Damascus • Kingdom of the Film Stars: Journey into Jordan

ALSO AVAILABLE:

Brief Encounters • Travel with Children • Traveller's Tales

INDIAN SUBCONTINENT

Bangladesh • Bengali phrasebook • Delhi • Goa • Hindi/Urdu phrasebook • India • India & Bangladesh travel atlas • Indian Himalaya • Karakoram Highway • Nepal • Nepali phrasebook • Pakistan • Rajasthan • Sri Lanka • Sri Lanka phrasebook • Trekking in the Indian Himalaya • Trekking in the Karakoram & Hindukush • Trekking in the Nepal Himalaya

Travel Literature: In Rajasthan • Shopping for Buddhas

SOUTH-EAST ASIA

Bali & Lombok • Bangkok • Burmese phrasebook • Cambodia • Ho Chi Minh City • Indonesia • Indonesian phrasebook • Indonesian audio pack • Jakarta • Java • Laos • Lao phrasebook • Laos travel atlas • Malay phrasebook • Malaysia, Singapore & Brunei • Myanmar (Burma) • Philippines • Pilipino phrasebook • Singapore • South-East Asia on a shoestring • South-East Asia phrasebook • Thailand • Thailand's Islands & Beaches • Thailand travel atlas • Thai phrasebook • Thai audio pack • Thai Hill Tribes phrasebook • Vietnam • Vietnamese phrasebook • Vietnam travel atlas

AUSTRALIA & THE PACIFIC

Australia • Australian phrasebook • Bushwalking in Australia • Bushwalking in Papua New Guinea • Fiji • Fijian phrasebook • Islands of Australia's Great Barrier Reef • Melbourne • Micronesia • New Caledonia • New South Wales • New Zealand • Northern Territory • Outback Australia • Papua New Guinea • Papua New Guinea phrasebook • Queensland • Rarotonga & the Cook Islands • Samoa • Solomon Islands • South Australia • Sydney • Tahiti & French Polynesia • Tasmania • Tonga • Tramping in New Zealand • Vanuatu • Victoria • Western Australia

Travel Literature: Islands in the Clouds • Sean & David's Long Drive

ANTARCTICA

Antarctica

THE LONELY PLANET STORY

Lonely Planet published its first book in 1973 in response to the numerous 'How did you do it?' questions Maureen and Tony Wheeler were asked after driving, bussing, hitching, sailing and railing their way from England to Australia.

Written at a kitchen table and hand collated, trimmed and stapled, *Across Asia on the Cheap* became an instant local bestseller, inspiring thoughts of another book.

Eighteen months in South-East Asia resulted in their second guide, *South-East Asia on a shoestring*, which they put together in a backstreet Chinese hotel in Singapore in 1975. The 'yellow bible', as it quickly became known to backpackers around the world, soon became *the* guide to the region. It has sold well over half a million copies and is now in its 9th edition, still retaining its familiar yellow cover.

Today there are over 350 titles, including travel guides, walking guides, language kits & phrasebooks, travel atlases and travel literature. The company is the largest independent travel publisher in the world. Although Lonely Planet initially specialised in guides to Asia, today there are few corners of the globe that have not been covered.

The emphasis continues to be on travel for independent travellers. Tony and Maureen still travel for several months of each year and play an active part in the writing, updating and quality control of Lonely Planet's guides.

They have been joined by over 80 authors and 200 staff at our offices in Melbourne (Australia), Oakland (USA), London (UK) and Paris (France). Travellers themselves also make a valuable contribution to the guides through the feedback we receive in thousands of letters each year and on our web site.

The people at Lonely Planet strongly believe that travellers can make a positive contribution to the countries they visit, both through their appreciation of the countries' culture, wildlife and natural features, and through the money they spend. In addition, the company makes a direct contribution to the countries and regions it covers. Since 1986 a percentage of the income from each book has been donated to ventures such as famine relief in Africa; aid projects in India; agricultural projects in Central America; Greenpeace's efforts to halt French nuclear testing in the Pacific; and Amnesty International.

'I hope we send people out with the right attitude about travel. You realise when you travel that there are so many different perspectives about the world, so we hope these books will make people more interested in what they see. Guidebooks can't really guide people. All you can do is point them in the right direction.'

– Tony Wheeler

LONELY PLANET PUBLICATIONS

Australia
PO Box 617, Hawthorn 3122, Victoria
tel: (03) 9819 1877 fax: (03) 9819 6459
e-mail: talk2us@lonelyplanet.com.au

USA
150 Linden St
Oakland, CA 94607
tel: (510) 893 8555 TOLL FREE: 800 275-8555
fax: (510) 893 8572
e-mail: info@lonelyplanet.com

UK
10a Spring Place,
London NW5 3BH
tel: (0171) 428 4800 fax: (0171) 428 4828
e-mail: go@lonelyplanet.co.uk

France:
71 bis rue du Cardinal Lemoine, 75005 Paris
tel: 01 44 32 06 20 fax: 01 46 34 72 55
e-mail: bip@lonelyplanet.fr

World Wide Web: http://www.lonelyplanet.com
or *AOL keyword: lp*